Comprehension and Composition

wee
third ol
en years old. On
ay, I stood on the
essed vaguely from
rying to and fro i
l was about to hap
waited on the step
the mass of honeys
and fell on my uptu
most unconsciously
s which had just c
n spring. I did n
rvel or suprise fo
d upon me conti
ceeded t

Comprehension and Composition

AN INTRODUCTION TO THE ESSAY

Ann B. Dobie
Andrew J. Hirt

University of Southwestern Louisiana
Lafayette

Macmillan Publishing Co., Inc.
NEW YORK

Collier Macmillan Publishers
LONDON

MACMILLAN PUBLISHING CO., INC.
866 THIRD AVENUE, NEW YORK, NEW YORK 10022

COLLIER MACMILLAN CANADA, LTD.

Library of Congress Cataloging in Publication Data

Main entry under title:
Comprehension and composition.

  Includes index.
  1. College readers.   2. English language—Rhetoric.
I. Dobie, Ann B.   II. Hirt, Andrew J.
PE1417.C638   808'.0427   78-26598
ISBN 0-02-329920-7

Printing: 1 2 3 4 5 6 7 8   Year: 0 1 2 3 4 5 6

For Rosemary Hirt Rost and Lila K. Brewster

PREFACE

Comprehension and Composition: An Introduction to the Essay is based on the premise that reading and writing are uniquely interwoven. Though some might say such a premise is an old and battered one, none can deny that it is an old and tested one, for reading traditionally provides much of the information used to make comparisons, formulate opinions, and understand experience. Reading, moreover, supplies models writers can imitate when they are ready to record their thinking. In short, the person who has read widely and well has the tools with which to become a competent writer. *Comprehension and Composition,* by integrating the two related activities, offers the writing student and his or her teacher a text comprising a generous selection of brief essays that are well-conceived and executed, concerned with a wide variety of subjects, and graded by reading level. They have been selected because they provoke analysis, invite imitation, and generate originality.

More specifically, *Comprehension and Composition* is made up of 128 short essays arranged under the four major forms of discourse: narration, description, exposition, and argumentation—a rather artificial grouping, but one that produces categories to give a sense of direction to the untutored but searching mind. Each of the four categories consists of thirty-six essays ordered by four levels of difficulty that allow a student to start where he is most at ease—where he can develop a feeling for how sentences are formed and how they build ideas into paragraphs, where he can sense the elements of good writing and try to imitate them, where he can think about techniques and strategies.

Section One of the text provides basic information that will help the student not only to understand what he is reading but also to see how the parts of essays are arranged and made effective. It is also concerned with student writing, its meaning, organization, and style. Students are encouraged both to compose essays of analysis and to originate essays in a number of different forms.

One essay on each level of difficulty has been analyzed to provide specific examples of the information presented theoretically in Section One. The analyses, in addition to explaining the major elements of the essays, furnish models for the student to follow as he writes his own critiques. After each of the other essays the "One Point for Analysis" draws attention to a particular critical element. The suggested writing topics provide subjects and types of organization similar to those in the essays they follow. It should be understood that when a writing topic mentions library research, the student is not expected to do the traditional research paper with footnotes and bibliography. Whatever information is needed can be quickly found in any standard encyclopedia.

The Handbook section of the text is called a "Practical" Handbook. Designed to serve as a ready source of information concerning mechanical and stylistic problems, it is not intended to be an exhaustive treatment of any of the subjects it covers. It will not, for example, discuss every possible use of the comma or every method of correcting a sentence fragment; it will, however, provide students with quick answers and remedies to problems most frequently encountered.

No single text can solve all the reading and writing problems that students face. Intelligent reading and good writing are the results of years of diligent study and practice. *Comprehension and Composition,* however, should provide an effective starting point.

Many people have graciously helped us with this book. Although they are too numerous to name, some deserve special notice. We are particularly grateful to Albert Fields, Paul Nolan, Mary Dichmann, Herb Fackler, Jack Ferstel, Carl Wooton, Joseph Riehl, Bolivar Lee Hait, J. C. Broussard, Tom Gannett, Walter Dobie, Paul Rost, Angelo Russo, and Terry Girouard. Members of the Freshman Committee have encouraged our efforts. Katie B. Davis has been an inspiration, and Sydney Lasseigne a companion, constantly working on manuscript. Barbara Lyman's expertise and Ben Lyman's suggestions have added immeasurably to the quality of our work. Our good editor Tony English has offered invaluable assistance and support. We thank them all.

ANN B. DOBIE
ANDREW J. HIRT

CONTENTS

3 The Descriptive Essay   117

5 The Persuasive Essay   287

CONTENTS

7 Appendix   431

xiv

Comprehension and Composition

1

THE ESSAY

WHAT IS AN ESSAY?

Some people call everything they read "a story." They make no distinction between a newspaper editorial and "Casey at the Bat." If they were aware of the differences between journalism and narrative poetry, they would probably increase their enjoyment of both.

Because you will be reading essays in this book, we must begin by discussing the differences between essays and other forms of writing. What is the difference between an essay and a story? How do essays differ from poems, plays, novels, short stories, and newspaper articles?

One of the main differences between an essay and other types of writing is that an essay gives the reader factual information. It seldom uses imaginary situations or fictional people as the main props for making its point. Instead, it discusses a subject by presenting history, current news, and even personal experience.

Despite these differences, the essay does have some similarities to other kinds of writing. Like drama, it can appeal to the emotions of the reader. Like fiction, it can use people and their experiences as examples of some general situation. Sometimes it makes pictures with words in the same way that poetry does.

Purpose

With so many similarities, you may be wondering how a writer decides whether he should present his ideas, his experiences, and his feelings in a poem or a play or an essay. After all, many poets, playwrights, and novelists write essays too. Most of the time the writer's purpose will help him to choose among written forms. When will his purpose lead him to the essay? If he wants to present facts to explain what something is or how it operates, he will probably choose to write an essay. If he wants to per-

2

suade his reader to accept his opinions about some problem or to adopt a course of action, he may write an essay. Perhaps the writer wants to describe a particular place or tell about something that once happened to him. Again, the essay will probably be his choice.

Sometimes these purposes, to explain, persuade, describe, and recount experience, are combined. For example, a writer cannot get very far with an argument unless he can explain his position, and to explain his position he may have to describe the problem and solutions. When he describes a situation, he may find himself writing a short narrative. In other words, the four major purposes for which essays are written work together to present factual information about a particular subject.

The essays you will read in this book have been divided into four groups, according to their main purpose. The narrative essays, the first group, have been written by authors who want to tell you about an experience they or someone else has had. The second group is made up of descriptive essays. They should make you see and hear and feel and perhaps even smell a particular place and time, even if you have never been there. The expository essays explain something. They are directed to helping you understand what something is, how it operates, or of what it is composed. The final group, the persuasive essays, will argue about controversial subjects. The authors of these essays will try to make you agree with their ideas.

As you are reading the essays you will notice that one type of discourse (one type of written language) helps another. In the expository section, for instance, you will discover elements of description, persuasion, and narration. Rarely will you find an essay that uses only exposition or description or persuasion or narration. It would probably be very dull if you did. Nevertheless, a good essayist will know his major purpose before he begins to write. He will then choose as his main type of discourse the one that will best serve his purpose: to tell of an experience, to describe, to explain, or to persuade.

Diction

The use of facts is only one of the differences between essays and other types of writing. Another is that an essay does not use words as the others do. For example, in a short story the writer has the characters talk to each other. Through their dialogue the plot may go forward, ideas can be examined, judgments may be made. In a play the dramatist must rely completely on what the characters say and do to develop his ideas. Poems, in contrast to essays, may make a single word carry the meaning of several more. The essayist uses as many words as he needs to make sure that his meaning is clearly and precisely expressed, but the poet may suggest what he means and leave the reader to think about the possibilities of his words. His poem may even be a puzzle that the reader must solve.

Essays are ordinarily written in Standard English, that form of our language used by more speakers than any other form. Standard English can be understood by educated people from all parts of the country because it does not include regional sayings, local slang, or ethnic expressions. It is the language found in most newspapers, magazines, and textbooks.

Of course, an essay can be effectively written in a specialized form of English. For example, a medical doctor may write an article using professional terms understood by other doctors but incomprehensible to a general audience. An essay written in Black English can be enjoyed by those who understand Black English, but, again, most readers will have difficulty following it. Both the medical essay and the one written in Black English can suit the particular audience for which they are written, but they will not appeal to the largest possible audience. Because most essayists hope to reach as many readers as they can, they write in Standard English.

Organization

One final point needs to be made if we are to determine what an essay is. An essay is generally organized by a form that can be divided into three parts: the introduction, the body, and the conclusion. The introduction serves to announce the subject, maybe even to state the central idea of the essay. It should also set the feeling of the essay. That is, after the introduction the reader normally should know two things: (1) what the essay is about; (2) whether what follows will be funny, serious, sad, exciting, and so on. The longest of the three parts, because it is the most important, is the body. In this section the main idea of the essay is discussed. The shortest section is usually the conclusion. Sometimes only two or three sentences are enough to let the reader know that the discussion is ended.

The essay is an old form of written discussion. Readers and writers have for several centuries enjoyed sharing ideas and experiences in essays. Through this book you will join them as you read and react to what other people have written, and as you set down your own ideas in new essays.

4

HERE IS AN ESSAY

DIALECTS AND STANDARD ENGLISH

Everyone speaks a dialect. Some people speak more than one. By the time a child reaches elementary school, he senses that he should not speak to his teacher in the same way that he talks to his friends on the playground. Teenagers use the slang of their group, sometimes to confuse parents and outsiders. Adults shift from the way they talk to customers or the boss at work to a different kind of language when they go to a bar on the way home from their job. The loudmouthed football fan complaining about a referee's call against his team is hardly recognizable as the same person when he is called upon to say a few words at a friend's retirement party.

Most people make these language shifts without thinking. They seem to occur naturally. Occasionally, however, a person finds himself in a situation where he is not sure how to speak. He does not know what is correct. Consider the following situation.

A college freshman from a small town in a remote part of the state wins a scholarship to a school several hundred miles away. Because of the distance, he is unable to return to his family for a visit until the Christmas holidays. His return is eagerly awaited not only by his large family but also by many people in the town who have known him since he was a child. On the first morning after his return, friends, aunts, uncles, and cousins drop by to visit with him. As they sit around the kitchen table drinking coffee, the college student suddenly becomes aware that he as acquired many expressions from his new friends at the university, expressions his family and old friends do not know. Even worse, he finds that the townspeople "sound funny" to him. How, he wonders, should he talk to them? Should he talk in their "funny" way, as he did as a child? Or should he use the speech patterns he has grown accustomed to at college?

The student has several choices. First of all, he can choose to speak as he does at college. After all, he has been told that he should use "correct grammar." He notices quickly, however, that his old friends are offended by the way he seems to sound "superior" to them, as if he is too good to be one of them any longer.

On the other hand, he could forget all he has learned at college, and slip back into the old patterns he grew up with as a child. But to choose this course of action would involve some pretense, some dishonesty about himself. After all, he has left his hometown to pursue a college education. He is no longer just a member of the town's culture; he is that and more.

How can he remain honest to his new pursuits without sounding like a snob? In this instance he can have the best of two worlds. On the one hand, his pronunciation can be dialectal, that is, in the "old" manner; on the other hand, his choice of words can conform to the practices of Standard English. Standard English does not demand that the speaker use a single pronunciation. It does require that one choose words and constructions that are understood by educated people from all regions and cultures. A Texan can drawl through "Ah'm afraid Cuba is no longa' conformin' to internashnul law." Crisply, the Bostonian will say: "I'm afraid Cuber is no longer conforming to international lar." If both were to write what they have spoken, neither would have any difficulty in understanding the sentence, for in both cases it would be written: "I am afraid Cuba is no longer conforming to international law."

For an educated person to communicate effectively in writing, he must use Standard English, the language most people understand. But even in Standard English the writer has various ways of stating the same fact. One could write: "I'm worried about Cuba's attitude toward international law." Or "Cuba's respect for the international situation shows serious deterioration." Dozens of sentences could be written in Standard English to state the same point. How does a writer decide which standard words and sentence patterns to use? The person who wants to write effective Standard English must be concerned with whether his language is appropriate to his audience, himself, his subject, and the occasion.

The intended audience determines what level of language difficulty is appropriate for an essay. For example, if a person is writing a newspaper article on the latest Superbowl, he realizes that his audience is composed of a cross-section of the reading public. His language, therefore, will be general. On the other hand, if he is writing an analysis of the defensive plays of the first half for a group of football coaches, his language will be far more technical, more specialized. Both articles will be in Standard English; their degree of difficulty will be determined by the audience.

6

Written language that honestly reflects the writer requires that he know how he wants to present himself in a particular instance. When writing a letter to a friend, a person can relax and talk informally about matters that concern him. Because he knows his audience, he can afford to reveal himself in a rather personal way. When, however, he is writing a letter of application for a job, he wants to present the professional, serious side of himself; thus he will choose words and sentences that are more formal and less personal.

The subject of an essay has much to do with how a person writes about it. Every professional field has its own jargon, its own vocabulary. For example, to discuss music knowledgeably, a person should know the difference between *retardando* and *a tempo*. Even when the subject does not require special terms, the person concerned with using language effectively will recognize that he does not use the same words with every subject. He does not discuss how to assemble a motor in the same way he discusses how to organize a political campaign. The subjects themselves cause the writer to use different types of language.

Occasions, like subjects, affect the type of language an essayist uses. If an employee describes an office party for the company newspaper, doubtless he will omit the fact that the boss was drunk and obscene. On another occasion, this same employee might, for the Sunday paper, write an essay on the subject of office parties in general. Here he indeed may describe drunken bosses and their unusual behavior at office parties. The occasions are different; the writing is different.

To write Standard English is not hard. It requires only that the writer follow certain accepted practices. To write appropriate and effective Standard English demands more. It requires that one choose the words, fashion the sentences, and build the paragraphs that will precisely state one's ideas and, at the same time, effectively communicate them to the reader. Can a written dialect accomplish these ends? Ordinarily not. A dialect is indeed useful in spoken situations where the audience is familiar with it. But a dialect is most of the time not appropriate for writing an effective essay. A reading audience goes beyond cultural and regional boundaries. It demands suitable Standard English.

WHAT IS AN ANALYSIS?

If you were asked to explain how a clock works, how would you go about finding out? Possibly you would sit down with a clock and carefully take it apart, note how the major parts work together, then reassemble it so that it could continue to keep time. In short, you would have analyzed a clock.

The analysis of any subject, whether a clock, a bicycle, or a poem, involves the same process. The subject must be divided into its important components so that they can be observed individually and as parts of the whole. Then these parts must be reassembled so that the entire item can function once again. The analysis of an essay follows this pattern.

An essay can be divided into three major parts for analysis: meaning, organization, and style. Each of these three can be broken down into smaller units, depending on how detailed the writer wants the analysis to be. Sometimes an analysis will be so detailed that only one of the elements will be examined. For example, if you are particularly interested in a writer's ideas, you may want to do a thorough study of the meaning of one of his essays. However, because meaning, organization, and style all work together to create the essay, an analysis will usually mention each one.

Meaning

When you have finished reading a well-written essay, you should be able to summarize what it has said in one sentence. You will not be able to mention all the interesting details or each of the supporting points, nor under any circumstances should you simply tell the "story," but you can state the central idea the writer was narrating, explaining, describing, or arguing in a single sentence. That single sentence is called the thesis statement. For example, in the preceding essay, "Dialects and Standard English," the thesis is that whereas dialects are useful in spoken and informal communication an essay requires the use of Standard English. Before the writer sat down to write his essay, he had to be quite clear in his own mind about his thesis statement. As the analyst of his essay, you too must clearly understand his main idea.

The thesis statement may or may not appear in the essay. When it does appear, it is frequently stated toward the end of the introduction or at the beginning of the conclusion. (See final paragraph of the preceding essay, "Dialects and Standard English.") On the other hand, a writer may simply discuss his major points and leave it to the reader to pull them together into a single general statement. In any case, the thesis statement is the core idea to which everything else in the essay contributes.

How do you find the thesis statement if the author has chosen to place it in the essay? Often you can look for a clear, concise statement that will comment on the title of the essay. If, for example, the essay is called "Getting Out of Vietnam," look for a statement that explains how or why Americans were evacuated in the final days of the war. Such a sentence should be the thesis of the essay.

How do you find the thesis statement if the author has chosen not to place it in the essay? You should recognize his major points and analyze how they fit together. From this analysis you then devise a sentence that is a general statement of those major points.

Whether the thesis is stated or implied, an analysis of the meaning of an essay notes the major points that explain, support, or develop the thesis. Sometimes they are easy to find because they have been listed in the introduction as being the main topics to be discussed. Examples are often used to make them clear.

The final step in analyzing the meaning of an essay is evaluation. That is, do you agree with what the writer has said? Do you think he has stated accurate information? Has he told the whole story or only the parts that help him to argue his opinion? The reader is never required to agree with what the writer says, but any reader who does not must be able to explain why he disagrees.

Organization

Like a clock, an essay must be put together in an orderly way if it is to work. There is no single pattern to be followed in detail, but some general principles that apply to almost all essays furnish basic guidelines for analyzing organization. Organization is sometimes called *structure*.

First of all, an essay should have a *beginning,* a *middle,* and an *end.* The beginning is the introduction. Its purpose is to announce the subject to be discussed, to interest the reader in the essay, and to establish the kind of writing that will follow. Sometimes the thesis sentence will be stated in the introduction.

The middle part of an essay is called the body or the development section. It is the longest of the three parts. In it the major points that develop the central idea are taken up one by one. Each point is given at least one paragraph, and in a long essay a single point may be given several pages of discussion. The divisions between the major points are usually marked by a word, phrase, or sentence that signals that the writer has finished one section of his discussion and is moving on to another. Some of those signals, which are called transitions, are *however, therefore, in the second place, on the other hand, another point, in contrast,* and *this leads to another consideration.* (See *Transitions,* Handbook.)

The major points in the development section can be arranged in many different ways. The writer will use the order that helps him to develop his thesis. For one thesis he may choose to arrange the points as they usually take place. For example, if he is explaining how to drive a car, he may begin with a discussion of starting the car, then go on to talk about acceleration and braking, steering, parking, and finally turning off the ignition. He will follow the steps a driver would normally go through. Another common way to arrange points is to put them in the order of their importance, starting with the least important and moving up to the most important. Other organizations for the body of an essay include comparison and contrast of two items, dividing a general subject into its parts, and showing the cause and effect of the subject. The reader-analyst should be aware of how the writer has arranged major points.

The final section of an essay, the conclusion, is sometimes the most important. If the writer has been building up to his major point, his thesis statement, throughout the essay, the final section will be the climax of his discussion. (This form is used in "Dialects and Standard English.") If, however, he has stated his thesis in the beginning and tied each major point into that thesis, his conclusion may be only a brief restatement of what the reader already knows. In either case, the conclusion should give the reader a sense of completion and wholeness. It should prevent any feeling of ending abruptly, just as saying good-bye does at the end of a telephone conversation.

In sum, when you analyze the organization of an essay, you should notice whether each of the major points is sufficiently developed. For example, if the writer has spent several pages discussing one point but has given only a single paragraph to another equally important point, the thesis will not be thoroughly developed. You should also question whether the points are clearly discussed. Are enough examples cited to make them easily understood? In what order are they arranged? Does that arrangement help you to understand the thesis? And, finally, do the introduction and conclusion help you to follow and remember the major points?

Note that the major points are developed in individual paragraphs. Just as an essay is designed to explore one main idea, a paragraph is designed to develop a single point; that is, each sentence of a paragraph must be concerned with the same topic. In fact, the opening sentence is often a topic sentence. The purpose of a topic sentence is similar to that of the thesis statement of an essay: to announce the subject to be considered. The remaining sentences of the paragraph explore the subject in more specific terms. There should be enough developmental sentences to discuss the topic thoroughly, each growing out of the sentence that precedes it and leading naturally to the one that follows it. Such a sequence will create unity and coherence. A paragraph has unity if all the sentences are about the same topic; it has coherence if they follow each other in an orderly fashion. Transitions between paragraphs move you from one major point to the next. (See *Paragraphs* and *Transitions,* Handbook.)

Style

The third step in the analysis of an essay is to look at the style it is written in. The word *style* has many meanings when applied to writing, just as it does when it is used to discuss clothes or home decoration. Most generally, however, it refers to the words, sentences, and tone of an essay.

The words of an essay should be precise and clear. Mark Twain once said that the difference between using the right word and the almost right word is like the difference between lightning and a lightning bug. No two words ever mean exactly the same thing. Finding the right one, the one that will say exactly what the writer wants to say, is one of the most difficult aspects of composition. The right word is not necessarily a long or unusual word. In fact, unless a long or uncommon word adds something to the meaning that no other word can provide, the writer is probably better off using more ordinary, concrete language.

The words of an essay, its diction, should be appropriate to the audience, the subject, the occasion, and the writer. As discussed in "Dialects and Standard English," there are always several ways of saying anything. The careful writer uses the way that will be most appropriate and thus most effective.

Sentences also come in many varieties. Some are long, tying themselves in knots, doubling back over themselves, winding through several points before coming to a stop. Some are short. Some state single facts; some show relationships between points. Thus an important consideration in analyzing the sentences of an essay is whether they are varied enough to keep you interested in the discussion. The repetitious rhythm set up by using the same sentence pattern over and over, or by writing too many long or too many short sentences, is wearisome. The monotony of the sentences undermines their strength of meaning. How do you feel when you read this? "The pitcher threw the ball. The batter was ready. He took a swing at the ball. It was a home run." For some, even a home run is unexciting when described in such a style.

The tone of an essay, the third element of style, is sometimes hard to determine because it is never stated. Just as you must sense the feelings

11

of a friend by his tone of voice in a telephone conversation, so you must sense the tone of an essay, the attitude of the writer toward his material. You can easily discover his attitude by asking yourself whether or not he is being serious. If you decide he is serious, question what kind of serious feeling he has. Is he angry? Is he sad? Critical?

The thesis, the arrangement of points, and the words and sentences all contribute to developing the tone of the essay. Thus the tone should be the same throughout. To shift from a serious tone to a silly one, or vice versa, will only be confusing.

Analyzing the style of a piece of writing can be a long and complicated process, but it can also be a pleasure to see the subtle ways in which a single word or sentence can change the sound of a discussion. Precise wording, varied sentences, and a consistent tone create an effective writing style.

The final step in any analysis, after examining the ideas, the organization, and the style, is to put the parts back together. Just as a clock that has been taken apart will not run again until all the wheels and springs are returned to their proper places, so an analysis of a subject will not be useful until you can see how the meaning, structure, and style all work together to form the whole. How do they point to the thesis? How do they reinforce each other? The good analysis breaks its subject into parts, looks at each one carefully, and then reassembles those parts into a whole that is more meaningful because it is understood better than before. Now you are ready to write.

READING CHECKLIST

Do you . . .
  1. understand the thesis of the essay?
  2. feel the author has sufficiently developed his thesis?
  3. recognize the major divisions of the essay?
  4. sense the author's feelings?
  5. think you can relate the essay to your own experiences?

TURNING AN ANALYSIS INTO AN ESSAY

As you read an essay, you make an informal analysis of the ideas, the organization, and the style of the work. You concentrate on understanding its meaning. You may even mark the major points to help you remember them. You notice whether the language is clear and the sentences are varied. After making some judgments about each of the three elements of the essay (meaning, organization, and style), you are ready to record your analysis in an essay of your own.

Thesis Statement

One of your first steps in writing an essay of analysis will be to write a thesis statement summing up your judgment of the essay you are analyzing. You may decide to use your thesis statement at the beginning or the end of your essay. Perhaps, like some other essayists, you will not directly state your thesis; instead, you will imply it throughout your analysis. If you choose to place your thesis statement at the beginning of your essay, you must adhere to it and the attitudes it announces. It will control everything that follows it. At the same time you will disclose something of your stance, which in the case of exposition may be helpful. If, however, your position is contrary to that of your reader, announcing your thesis early in the paper may make persuasion more difficult. Not announcing your thesis at all will allow you to create a sense of objectivity long enough to get the reader "hooked" before starting to mold impressions or influence opinions. Regardless of how or whether it appears, the thesis statement of your analysis must be completely clear to you before you begin to write.

In some instances, your thesis statement will be as simple as, "John Doe's essay 'The Nature of War' argues that man needs combat to satisfy his aggressive drive." Notice: there is no "I" in this thesis statement, nor should there be. Your analysis will be concerned with the essay and not with you.

Supporting Points

The second step in planning your essay is to select at least three points that will explain, support, or exemplify your thesis statement. You must make sure that each of them is either a generally accepted fact or a statement that can be logically supported. To argue an opinion on the basis of unproved assumptions, called *begging the question* (see *Fallacies*, Handbook), is objectionable. For instance, to say that an author's conclusions are stupid and therefore should be ignored is an example of begging the question. You must first logically establish that his conclusion are actually stupid. In other words, you are responsible for proving the validity of every general statement you make.

13

Examples

One of the best ways of demonstrating the worth of your points is by giving examples. Examples not only support the points but also help to make them clear. A reader can follow a discussion much more easily if he has examples that help him to see a situation.

The supporting points should be arranged in a logical order. Common means of organization include ordering by time (chronology), comparison and contrast, division into parts, and others. Regardless of which type of organization is used, examples are helpful for support and clarity.

Transitions

Transitions (see *Transitions*, Handbook) assist in giving the points an appearance of order. Their function is to link the supporting parts of the discussion to each other and to the thesis. They provide bridges between ideas. Without them readers may lose track of the discussion.

Introduction

The introduction to an essay is one of the hardest parts to write. It has important functions to fulfill, but it is not the main part of the discussion. Some people find it helpful to write the introduction after composing the rest of the essay. After all, it is difficult to introduce something that does not yet exist.

Introductions can follow several different patterns. You can catch a reader's attention by stating a startling statistic. For example, "Ten thousand people died last month from smoking." You can also begin with some general remarks about the subject, gradually narrowing down to a statement of the thesis. (See "Away with Big-Time Athletics.") Another method of writing an introduction is to begin with an example, a short incident that illustrates the central idea of the essay. (See "Dialects and Standard English.")

Conclusion

The conclusion can move in either of two directions. It can either summarize what has already been said or broaden the discussion so that it touches on related subjects. The former looks inward to what has been discussed (see "Dialects and Standard English"); the latter looks outward to the future (see "Raising Children in the Year 2000"). In either case, the conclusion should serve to bring the essay to a comfortable close. At no time should it become a "sermonette," telling the reader what he ought or ought not to do.

Diction

The diction of your essay of analysis should generally be formal. That is, it should be written in formal Standard English. Reserve slang, regional sayings, and ethnic expressions for informal essays. Remember that if you want your reader to understand your ideas and respond to them, you must use those words and only those words that communicate clearly and concretely what you want to say. Sometimes using too many words can cause just as much confusion in a reader's mind as using the wrong words. (See *Deadwood*, Handbook.)

Sentences

Your sentences should give your reader variety. They should not all begin with the same words, nor should they be the same length or follow the same pattern. What you want to say will help you to decide whether a sentence should be simple or complicated. Of course, the most complicated sentence can be better understood by the reader if it is punctuated correctly. The simplest structure can be confusing if it is not. (See *Punctuation*, Handbook.)

In contrast to your sentences, which should offer a variety of forms, the tone should be consistent. If you begin with a serious attitude, you should continue with it throughout the essay. If you begin jokingly, you cannot suddenly say, "But seriously now . . .". The reader will probably not make the shift with you. (See *Tone*, Handbook.)

In short, then, when you write an essay of analysis, or any essay, you should pay close attention to the same elements you notice when you are reading and analyzing an established author's writing. Remember, your reader will be trying to understand your ideas, looking for the organization of the major points of development, and noticing the words, sentences, and tone of your writing. By carefully reading and analyzing the essays in this book, you can find procedures and techniques of writing that you too can use. They should provide you with models that you can follow as you develop your own writing skills.

PREWRITING CHECKLIST

Have you, in your mind or on note cards . . .
1. expressed your thesis in one sentence?
2. selected at least three major points to support your thesis?
3. chosen examples to illustrate your points?
4. decided how you will introduce the subject and how you will conclude it?
5. determined how to attract and maintain your reader's attention?

WRITING CHECKLIST

Meaning
Have you . . .
1. refrained from saying, "In this essay I am going to discuss . . ."?
2. stated or strongly implied your thesis in your essay?
3. developed at least three major points to support your thesis?
4. proved or illustrated each of your major points?

Organization
Have you . . .
1. aroused the interest of your reader in the introduction?
2. enumerated the major points of the essay in your introduction?
3. devoted at least one paragraph to each major point?
4. given each paragraph a topic sentence and several developmental sentences?
5. written a conclusion that, by summary or by projection into the future, gives your reader a sense of completion?
6. avoided giving a "sermonette" in the conclusion?

Style
Have you . . .
1. used Standard English?
2. avoided contractions, abbreviations, slang, regional and ethnic expressions, and clichés in formal Standard English?
3. specifically avoided the following words and expressions: *very, in conclusion, truly, a lot, in this modern world of today, as Webster's Dictionary states, as everyone knows?*
4. left out all unnecessary words?
5. checked for undue repetition of words?
6. made sure that every *this* is followed by a noun?
7. varied the opening words of your sentences?
8. made certain that your sentences are of different lengths?
9. tied your sentences and paragraphs together with transitions?
10. kept the same tone throughout the essay?
11. put a title on your paper?
12. restated the title in your introduction?
13. used the Handbook to help you with some of the preceding points?

Mechanics

Have you . . .

1. written complete sentences?
2. avoided comma splices and fused sentences?
3. avoided unnecessary shifts of person, subject, and tense?
4. punctuated properly?
5. checked *Word Usage* in the Handbook about questionable words?
6. made sure every pronoun has a clear antecedent?
7. given every singular subject a singular verb and every plural subject a plural verb?
8. checked your dictionary about the meaning and spelling of questionable words?
9. used the Handbook to help you with some of the preceding points?

2

THE NARRATIVE ESSAY

INTRODUCTION TO NARRATION

From the time we are small children until we grow old and wise, we enjoy hearing and telling tales. We move, as we mature, from hearing "Little Red Riding Hood" to reading Aesop's *Fables* and Edith Hamilton's *Mythology*. We enjoy exchanging stories with our friends, eagerly listening to what happened to someone else, and just as eagerly sharing our own experiences. Few people are exempt from the basic pleasure human beings take in storytelling. Scheherazade, it is said, even avoided her own death by inventing stories that kept her husband so interested that he postponed her execution for a thousand and one nights.

Two types of storytelling, or narration, exist: imaginative and factual. Imaginative narration springs from the mind of the author, not solely from his experiences. He creates the characters and events, bringing into being people and occurrences that have never happened. Factual narration, in contrast, tells a story that has happened. Because essays deal with facts, we will be concerned only with stories that have actually occurred. Many of the most interesting stories come from life itself.

Like imaginative stories, factual ones must be based on action that covers a period of time. They arise from a series of events dealing with a problem. When the problem is solved, or at least over, the story comes to an end. The problem may be between people, within a person, or between an individual and his world. Whatever form the conflict (problem) takes, its beginning marks the start of the story, and its resolution marks the end of the story. Even if the writer chooses to describe the events out of the order in which they actually happened, their original order (chronology) furnishes the basic shape of the story.

Writers of narrative essays are ordinarily not content merely to set down the events that happened. Most of the time they also want to discover and state the importance of the experience they are telling. They

20

want to find its meaning. The thesis statement of a narrative essay (either present or implied) will deal with the meaning of the story.

Narrative essays depend heavily on the other types of prose writing we have discussed: description, exposition, and argumentation/persuasion. Because even a factual story has to be set in a particular place and time, descriptive passages help us to see where and when the events occur. Some explanation of causes or meanings of experiences may take the form of exposition. Or the writer may use his story to argue for or against certain practices.

Consider, as you read the following narrative essays, what experiences of your life hold importance for you. What events could be set down as illustrative of something you generally believe to be true or something you think should be changed? Therein will lie your own subjects for narrative essays. Therein will lie the factual stories that you can retell.

38 WHO SAW MURDER DIDN'T CALL THE POLICE

MARTIN GANSBERG

Originally published in The New York Times, *this essay tells of an actual occurrence that horrified and baffled many people. It raises questions about the actions of "good" people.*

For more than half an hour 38 respectable, law-abiding citizens in Queens watched a killer stalk and stab a woman in three separate attacks in Kew Gardens.

Twice their chatter and the sudden glow of their bedrooms lights interrupted him and frightened him off. Each time he returned, sought her out, and stabbed her again. Not one person telephoned the police during the assault; one witness called after the woman was dead.

That was two weeks ago today.

Still shocked is Assistant Chief Inspector Frederick M. Lussen, in charge of the borough's detectives and a veteran of 25 years of homicide investigations. He can give a matter-of-fact recitation of many murders. But the Kew Gardens slaying baffles him—not because it is a murder, but because the "good people" failed to call the police.

"As we have reconstructed the crime," he said, "the assailant had three chances to kill this woman during a 35-minute period. He returned twice to complete the job. If we had been called when he first attacked, the woman might not be dead now."

This is what the police say happened beginning at 3:20 A.M. in the staid, middle-class, tree-lined Austin Street area:

Twenty-eight-year-old Catherine Genovese, who was called Kitty by almost everyone in the neighborhood, was returning home from her job as manager of a bar in Hollis. She parked her red Fiat in a lot adjacent to the Kew Gardens Long Island Rail Road Station, facing Mowbray Place. Like many residents of the neighborhood, she had parked there day after day since her arrival from Connecticut a year ago, although the railroad frowns on the practice.

She turned off the lights of her car, locked the door, and started to walk the 100 feet to the entrance of her apartment at 82-70 Austin Street, which is in a Tudor building, with stores in the first floor and apartments on the second.

The entrance to the apartment is in the rear of the building because the front is rented to retail stores. At night the quiet neighborhood is shrouded in the slumbering darkness that marks most residential areas.

Miss Genovese noticed a man at the far end of the lot, near a seven-story apartment house at 82-40 Austin Street. She halted. Then, nervously, she headed up Austin Street toward Lefferts Boulevard, where there is a call box to the 102nd Police Precinct in nearby Richmond Hill.

She got as far as a street light in front of a bookstore before the man grabbed her. She screamed. Lights went on in the 10-story apartment house at 82-67 Austin Street, which faces the bookstore. Windows slid open and voices punctuated the early-morning stillness.

Miss Genovese screamed: "Oh my God, he stabbed me! Please help me! Please help me!"

From one of the upper windows in the apartment house, a man called down: "Let that girl alone!"

The assailant looked up at him, shrugged, and walked down Austin Street toward a white sedan parked a short distance away. Miss Genovese struggled to her feet.

Lights went out. The killer returned to Miss Genovese, now try-ing to make her way around the side of the building by the parking lot to get to her apartment. The assailant stabbed her again.

"I'm dying!" she shrieked. "I'm dying!"

Windows were opened again, and lights went on in many apart-ments. The assailant got into his car and drove away. Miss Geno-vese staggered to her feet. A city bus, 0-10, the Lefferts Boulevard line to Kennedy International Airport, passed. It was 3:35 A.M.

The assailant returned. By then, Miss Genovese had crawled to the back of the building, where the freshly painted brown doors to the apartment house held out hope for safety. The killer tried the first door; she wasn't there. At the second door, 82-62 Austin Street, he saw her slumped on the floor at the foot of the stairs. He stabbed her a third time—fatally.

It was 3:50 by the time police received their first call, from a man who was a neighbor of Miss Genovese. In two minutes they were at the scene. The neighbor, a 70-year-old woman, and another woman were the only persons on the street. Nobody else came forward.

The man explained that he had called the police after much delib-eration. He had phoned a friend in Nassau County for advice and then he had crossed the roof of the building to the apartment of the elderly woman to get her to make the call.

"I didn't want to get involved," he sheepishly told the police.

Six days later, the police arrested Winston Moseley, a 29-year-old business-machine operator, and charged him with homicide. Mose-ley had no previous record. He is married, has two children and owns a home at 133-19 Sutter Avenue, South Ozone Park, Queens. On Wednesday, a court committed him to Kings County Hospital for psychiatric observation.

When questioned by the police, Moseley also said that he had slain Mrs. Annie May Johnson, 24, of 146-12 133d Avenue, Jamaica, on Feb. 29 and Barbara Kralik, 15, of 174-17 140th Avenue, Spring-field Gardens, last July. In the Kralik case, the police are holding Alvin L. Mitchell, who is said to have confessed that slaying.

The police stressed how simple it would have been to have gotten in touch with them. "A phone call," said one of the detectives, "would have done it." The police may be reached by dialing "O" for operator or SPring 7-3100.

Today witnesses from the neighborhood, which is made up of

one-family homes in the $35,000 to $60,000 range with the exception of the two apartment houses near the railroad station, find it difficult to explain why they didn't call the police.

A housewife, knowingly if quite casual, said, "We thought it was a lover's quarrel." A husband and wife both said, "Frankly, we were afraid." They seemed aware of the fact that events might have been different. A distraught woman, wiping her hands in her apron, said, "I didn't want my husband to get involved."

One couple, now willing to talk about that night, said they heard the first screams. The husband looked thoughtfully at the bookstore where the killer first grabbed Miss Genovese.

"We went to the window to see what was happening," he said, "but the light from our bedroom made it difficult to see the street." The wife, still apprehensive, added: "I put out the light and we were able to see better."

Asked why they hadn't called the police, she shrugged and replied: "I don't know."

A man peered out from a slight opening in the doorway to his apartment and rattled off an account of the killer's second attack. Why hadn't he called the police at that time? "I was tired," he said without emotion. "I went back to bed."

It was 4:25 A.M. when the ambulance arrived to take the body of Miss Genovese. It drove off. "Then," a solemn police detective said, "the people came out."

AN ANALYSIS OF "38 WHO SAW MURDER DIDN'T CALL THE POLICE"

Martin Gansberg's article "38 Who Saw Murder Didn't Call the Police" was written for a newspaper, the *New York Times*. Some newspaper articles try not only to inform their readers but also to make them think. In telling the story of the murder of Catherine Genovese, Mr. Gansberg has done both.

Anyone who starts to read about the horrifying experience of Miss Genovese will probably read to the end. The opening sentence entices the reader to go on because it states a shocking fact that nobody wants to believe. Also, it sets a scene of mystery and violence that would make any reader curious.

After the completion of the introduction, indicated by the white space following the sixth paragraph, the article is told as a story that has characters and a setting. The events are arranged in chronological order. Dialogue is used to present the reactions and thoughts of the characters.

After the facts surrounding the murder have been objectively presented, Mr. Gansberg tells the story again, from a different point of view. A transitional paragraph (beginning "It was 3:50 by the time the police received their first call . . .") moves the reader from the factual account of the murder to the various accounts given by witnesses to the crime. Gansberg quotes what these witnesses saw and thought and felt. The reader begins to wonder which story is more horrifying, the unprovoked murder of an innocent victim or the reluctance of people to help her. The last paragraph pulls both versions of the story together. It states: "It was 4:25 A.M. when the ambulance arrived to take the body of Miss Genovese. It drove off. 'Then,' a solemn police detective said, 'the people came out.'"

This essay follows journalistic style. For example, the paragraphs are brief, mostly one and two sentences. One reason short paragraphs are used by newspapers is that they are printed in narrow columns, making only a few sentences appear to be a long paragraph. Another requirement of journalistic style is that the article immediately tell the reader five points of informatuon: who, where, what, when, and how. By the end of the fifth sentence of the essay, the reader has this information concerning Catherine Genovese's murder.

Gansberg uses a device of punctuation to imply meaning where he does not actually make a statement. In the fourth paragraph he places quotation marks around the words "good people," even though he is not writing dialogue. He does so to point out his intention to use the words in a special sense. In this case he finds it hard to call these people "good," although they would usually fall into that category. The quotation marks allow him to suggest his opinion of them without actually stating it.

The narrative form of this essay gives it more appeal than it would have as an expository report. The quotations from the Inspector and from Miss Genovese herself make the event seem real. Knowing that the murder indeed was real causes the reader to think about who was responsible for Miss Genovese's death and about why "good" people failed to help her. The essay has informed its readers and also made them think.

25

A STRANGE LOVE AFFAIR

JAN MYRDAL

This selection is a vignette from a book that is composed of a series of such essays arranged without regard to time. Each piece gives some significant insight into the complex, intellectual, and human man who is writing about himself.

In the fall of 1947 I was in love with B. She was good-looking, intelligent and we said we thought that we had much in common. We were going steady for some time, but she did not allow me to sleep with her. In December that year I left for Belgrade. When I came back to Sweden I married another girl. In February 1949 I came to Stockholm by train from Herrljunga. Met B. Having met again we both realized that we actually were very much in love with each other. I followed her to her room and now she wanted "to give herself to me," as she expressed it.

Suddenly I remembered that I had not washed my feet for several days. There were reasons for this. I had hitch-hiked up through Sweden, had spent the night at the county jail of Herrljunga, and had been put on the train to Stockholm. It was in the middle of winter and it was cold.

But as I was afraid that my feet stank—which would not correspond to the image I wanted B to have of me—I tried to find a way to escape from the situation. Unfortunately the fact that my feet (probably) stank did not strike me until B had started to undress. I could not find anything more convincing to say than that I seemed to love the girl I was married to. B was very understanding and we sat for a long time talking about self, soul and love.

And all this because I had forgotten to wash my feet. Or was it?

One Point for Analysis: The question at the end of the last paragraph projects the essay into a number of other possible meanings.
Writing Topics:
   1. Narrate an experience in which some large enterprise is prevented because of a seemingly insignificant detail.
   2. Tell the story of your significant loves.

3. Write a narrative essay, ending with a question that introduces the possibility of multiple interpretations of the story's meaning.

NOT REALLY SAVED

LANGSTON HUGHES

Langston Hughes was a leader of the Black Literary Renaissance, a movement of black writers active in the 1920's. He was one of the first to gain attention for writing about the experiences of Negroes in America.

I was saved from sin when I was going on thirteen. But not really saved. It happened like this. There was a big revival at my Auntie Reed's church. Every night for weeks there had been much preaching, singing, praying and shouting, and some very hardened sinners had been brought to Christ, and the membership of the church had grown by leaps and bounds. Then just before the revival ended, they held a special meeting for children, "to bring the young lambs to the fold." My aunt spoke of it for days ahead. That night I was escorted to the front row and placed on the mourners' bench with the other young sinners, who had not yet been brought to Jesus.

My aunt told me that when you were saved you saw a light, and something happened to you inside! And Jesus came into your life! And God was with you from then on! She said you could see and hear and feel Jesus in your soul. I believed her. I had heard a great many old people say the same thing and it seemed to me they ought to know. So I sat there calmly in the hot crowded church, waiting for Jesus to come to me.

The preacher preached a wonderful rhythmical sermon, all moans and shouts and lonely cries and dire pictures of hell, and then he sang a song about the ninety and nine safe in the fold, but one little lamb was left out in the cold. Then he said: "Won't you come? Won't you come to Jesus? Young lambs, won't you come?" And he held out his arms to all us young sinners there on the mourners'

27

bench. And the little girls cried. And some of them jumped and went to Jesus right away. But most of us just sat there.

A great many old people came and knelt around us and prayed, old women with jet-black faces and braided hair, old men with work-gnarled hands. And the church sang a song about the lower lights are burning, some poor sinners to be saved. And the whole building rocked with prayer and song.

Still I kept waiting to *see* Jesus.

Finally all the young people had gone to the altar and were saved, but one boy and me. He was a rounder's son named Westley. Westley and I were surrounded by sisters and deacons praying. It was very hot in the church, and getting late now. Finally Westley said to me in a whisper: "God damn! I'm tired o' sitting here. Let's get up and be saved." So he got up and was saved.

Then I was left all alone on the mourners' bench. My aunt came and knelt at my knees and cried, while prayers and songs swirled all around me in the little church. The whole congregation prayed for me alone, in a mighty wail of moans and voices. And I kept waiting serenely for Jesus, waiting, waiting—but he didn't come. I wanted to see him, but nothing happened to me. Nothing! I wanted something to happen to me, but nothing happened.

I heard the songs and the minister saying: "Why don't you come? My dear child, why don't you come to Jesus? Jesus is waiting for you. He wants you. Why don't you come? Sister Reed, what is this child's name?"

"Langston," my aunt sobbed.

"Langston, why don't you come? Why don't you come and be saved? Oh, Lamb of God! Why don't you come?"

Now it was really getting late. I began to be ashamed of myself, holding everything up so long. I began to wonder what God thought about Westley, who certainly hadn't seen Jesus either, but who was now sitting proudly on the platform, swinging his knickerbockered legs and grinning down at me, surrounded by deacons and old women on their knees praying. God had not struck Westley dead for taking his name in vain or for lying in the temple. So I decided that maybe to save further trouble, I'd better lie, too, and say that Jesus had come, and get up and be saved.

So I got up.

Suddenly the whole room broke into a sea of shouting, as they saw me rise. Waves of rejoicing swept the place. Women leaped in the air. My aunt threw her arms around me. The minister took me by the hand and led me to the platform.

When things quieted down, in a hushed silence, punctuated by a few ecstatic "Amens," all the new young lambs were blessed in the name of God. Then joyous singing filled the room.

That night, for the last time in my life but one—for I was a big boy twelve years old—I cried. I cried, in bed alone, and couldn't stop. I buried my head under the quilts, but my aunt heard me. She woke up and told my uncle I was crying because the Holy Ghost had come into my life, and because I had seen Jesus. But I was really crying because I couldn't bear to tell her that I had lied, that I had deceived everybody in the church, and I hadn't seen Jesus, and that now I didn't believe there was a Jesus any more, since he didn't come to help me.

One Point for Analysis: The first two sentences of the essay summarize the tale that follows.

Writing Topics:

1. In the third paragraph Hughes describes the emotional setting in which the revival took place. Recount a story set in a similarly emotional setting that caused you to react in an unplanned and surprising manner.
2. Tell the story of the events that once caused you to cry.
3. Like Hughes, tell the story of a personal experience that makes a comment about an important social institution, such as the church, family, or school.

A FIRST EXPERIENCE WITH WORDS

HELEN KELLER

A remarkable woman, Helen Keller conquered serious physical handicaps to become a leading personality of her day. This essay recounts her first experience with words.

The most important day I remember in all my life is the one on which my teacher, Anne Mansfield Sullivan, came to me. I am filled with wonder when I consider the immeasurable contrast between

From *The Story of My Life* by Helen Keller. New York: Doubleday & Company, Inc., 1954.

the two lives which it connects. It was the third of March, 1887, three months before I was seven years old.

On the afternoon of that eventful day, I stood on the porch, dumb, expectant. I guessed vaguely from my mother's signs and from the hurrying to and fro in the house that something unusual was about to happen, so I went to the door and waited on the steps. The afternoon sun penetrated the mass of honeysuckle that covered the porch, and fell on my upturned face. My fingers lingered almost unconsciously on the familiar leaves and blossoms which had just come forth to greet the sweet southern spring. I did not know what the future held of marvel or surprise for me. Anger and bitterness had preyed upon me continually for weeks and a deep languor had succeeded this passionate struggle.

Have you ever been at sea in a dense fog, when it seemed as if a tangible white darkness shut you in, and the great ship, tense and anxious, groped her way toward the shore with plummet and sounding-line, and you waited with beating heart for something to happen? I was like that ship before my education began, only I was without compass or sounding-line, and had no way of knowing how near the harbour was. "Light! give me light!" was the wordless cry of my soul, and the light of love shone on me in that very hour.

I felt approaching footsteps. I stretched out my hand as I supposed to my mother. Some one took it, and I was caught up and held close in the arms of her who had come to reveal all things to me, and, more than all things else, to love me.

The morning after my teacher came she led me into her room and gave me a doll. The little blind children at the Perkins Institution had sent it and Laura Bridgman had dressed it; but I did not know this until afterward. When I had played with it a little while, Miss Sullivan slowly spelled into my hand the word "d-o-l-l." I was at once interested in this finger play and tried to imitate it. When I finally succeeded in making the letters correctly I was flushed with childish pleasure and pride. Running downstairs to my mother I held up my hand and made the letters for doll. I did not know that I was spelling a word or even that words existed; I was simply making my fingers go in monkey-like imitation. In the days that followed I learned to spell in this uncomprehending way a great many words, among them *pin, hat, cup* and a few verbs like *sit, stand* and *walk.* But my teacher had been with me several weeks before I understood that everything has a name.

One day, while I was playing with my new doll, Miss Sullivan put my big rag doll into my lap also, spelled "d-o-l-l" and tried to make me understand that "d-o-l-l" applied to both. Earlier in the day we had had a tussle over the words "m-u-g" and "w-a-t-e-r." Miss Sullivan had tried to impress it upon me that "m-u-g" is *mug* and that "w-a-t-e-r" is *water,* but I persisted in confounding the two. In despair she had dropped the subject for the time, only to renew it at the first opportunity. I became impatient at her repeated attempts and, seizing the new doll, I dashed it upon the floor. I was keenly delighted when I felt the fragments of the broken doll at my feet. Neither sorrow nor regret followed my passionate outburst. I had not loved the doll. In the still, dark world in which I lived there was no strong sentiment or tenderness. I felt my teacher sweep the fragments to one side of the hearth, and I had a sense of satisfaction that the cause of my discomfort was removed. She brought me my hat, and I knew I was going out into the warm sunshine. This thought, if a wordless sensation may be called a thought, made me hop and skip with pleasure.

We walked down the path to the well-house, attracted by the fragrance of the honeysuckle with which it was covered. Some one was drawing water and my teacher placed my hand under the spout. As the cool stream gushed over one hand she spelled into the other the word *water,* first slowly, then rapidly. I stood still, my whole attention fixed upon the motions of her fingers. Suddenly I felt a misty consciousness as of something forgotten—a thrill of returning thought; and somehow the mystery of language was revealed to me. I knew then that "w-a-t-e-r" meant the wonderful cool something that was flowing over my hand. That living word awakened my soul, gave it light, hope, joy, set it free! There were barriers still, it is true, but barriers that could in time be swept away.

I left the well-house eager to learn. Everything had a name, and each name gave birth to a new thought. As we returned to the house every object which I touched seemed to quiver with life. That was because I saw everything with the strange, new sight that had come to me. On entering the door I remembered the doll I had broken. I felt my way to the hearth and picked up the pieces. I tried vainly to put them together. Then my eyes filled with tears; for I realized what I had done, and for the first time I felt repentance and sorrow.

I learned a great many new words that day. I do not remember what they all were; but I do know that *mother, father, sister, teacher* were among them—words that were to make the world blossom for me, "like Aaron's rod, with flowers." It would have been difficult to find a happier child than I was as I lay in my crib at the close of that eventful day and lived over the joys it had brought me, and for the first time longed for a new day to come.

One Point for Analysis: The third paragraph is a dramatic metaphor that serves as a transition between Keller's awaiting the arrival of her new teacher and the actual presence of Miss Sullivan.
Writing Topics:
1. Tell the story of someone you know who, like Miss Keller, has overcome great handicaps because of a strength of will and a fierce spirit.
2. Recount an event in your life when you suddenly "saw" the importance of something you had taken for granted.
3. Write a narrative in which you are awaiting the arrival of a special person or event, and bridge this anticipation and the actual presence of the person or event with an emotional metaphor. (See the third paragraph.)

WEIRD THINGS OCCUR IN THE BLACK HOLE
JACQUELINE HARRIS

This essay explores a strange phenomenon in the immensity of space. It is a subject that has fascinated science fiction writers as well as scientists.

The Jove-39X mission to Galaxy 7 was in trouble. For some unknown reason their gravitational monitors were spinning off the wall. Through the ports, growing larger and larger, could be seen a single star that seemed to have a small black disk superimposed

Special permission granted by *Current Science,* published by Xerox Education Publications, © Xerox Corp., 1971.

32

over it. Some mysterious force was pulling the Jove-39X craft toward the strange star.

Their speed increased. Continuous retro-rocket firings failed to stop their headlong pace. Soon the spacecraft was sucked into the black disk. Down it went into a black hole, spinning faster than the speed of light. The ship was torn to pieces by the tremendous forces in the hole—the pieces ripped into fragments.

The very atoms of which the craft was made were stripped of their electrons—the nuclei broken apart. Within seconds there was not a trace of the craft. Its atomic fragments had joined the spinning radiation in the black hole.

The tragic fate of the Jove-39X is fictitious. But it could happen, should a spacecraft venture near a collapsed star that scientists call a black hole.

Nearly 40 years ago, scientists studying the physics of space and stars predicted that such black holes might exist in outer space. Now Dr. A. G. W. Cameron of Yeshiva University in New York City believes he has detected one. It is in the two-star system Epsilon Aurigae. One star is a bright celestial body; the other is a dark body called the "dark companion."

The two bodies are kept together by gravity—much as the earth and moon are. Periodically the dark companion passes in front of the bright star and is seen as a kind of dark disk.

Dr. Cameron thinks the dark companion is a collapsed star, or black hole. The star grew old and collapsed because of its own tremendous gravitational forces squeezing it together. Only radiation spinning faster than the speed of light was left.

Such black holes have gravitational attractions so strong that any kind of matter or energy entering the hole could never escape.

The idea of the black hole is still a theory that scientists are investigating. Anyone like to fly by Epsilon Aurigae and find out for sure?

One Point for Analysis: A fictitious narrative introduces this essay.
Writing Topics:
1. Invent a suspenseful yet possible story that leads you into a discussion of devil worship or some other occult practice.
2. Narrate an interesting story about the effect of gravity on you or one of your friends.
3. When the Olympics are held in cities that are substantially

higher than sea level (for example, Mexico City), some foreign participants have difficulty in adjusting their breathing, etc., to this new height. Explain, by means of a story, how one athlete failed to achieve his potential in the games because of this height differential.

AN ELEPHANT HUNT
LOUIS COTLOW

Explorer, writer, lecturer, Louis Cotlow has led many expeditions to the upper Amazon, Africa, and New Guinea. Interested in primitive peoples, he has written a number of books about their habits and customs.

When the Pygmy hunters have located their elephants, they study the terrain carefully, compare the elephants, and select the one they are after. They prefer the elephant with the largest tusks, but they must choose one that is on the edge of the group, not in the middle. The elephants are not aware of the Pygmies at this time, for the hunters keep out of the wind, and they have also smeared themselves with elephant dung, found in plentiful supply along the trail.

The Pygmies move back into the forest a few hundred yards and smoke hemp, or marijuana, to bolster their courage. They obtain this from the villagers, who have found it one of the most binding ties between the forest folk and their Negro "masters."

With the most experienced hunter in the lead, the Pygmies return to the elephants, which may be asleep in the noonday heat or quietly munching whatever greens are within reach. To anyone except a Pygmy, the project appears completely ludicrous at this stage. Here are six, eight, or ten elephants, the largest land animals in the world, about to be attacked by three, four, or five of the tiniest humans in the world. But Pygmy spears are razor sharp, and Pygmy strength is greater than their size indicates. Their biggest asset, however, is courage, of which they have plenty even without the aid of marijuana.

If the designated elephant lifts its trunk and turns its head as if it has heard or smelled something, the approaching Pygmies freeze into immobility. The elephant sniffs only what smells like another elephant, sees nothing move—its eyesight is not very good—lowers its head, and goes on eating or dozing.

When the hunters decide upon hamstringing, one of the two common methods of hunting elephants, two of them step cautiously from the rear until they stand beside the huge hind legs. The others place themselves to rout the other animals and then take up pursuit of the hunted one.

At a silent signal, the two leading Pygmies reach out with their sharp spears and slash at the tendons behind the elephant's knees. They dart away at once as the wounded elephant whirls to grab them with its trunk. The other Pygmies shout and jump for all they are worth to frighten the other elephants into a stampede. Usually the beasts are so startled that they rush away. The wounded one tries to follow, but it can barely drag itself along, since its hind legs are useless.

The wounded elephant bellows angrily, pulls itself painfully along the ground with its hind legs dragging. It reaches out and grabs a tree with its trunk and, unless the tree is huge, rips it up by the roots. With the other elephants out of the way, the Pygmy hunters dart in close to thrust their spears into the elephant's belly. The animal lashes out at them with its trunk, but the hunters attack first from one side and then the other. Sometimes the elephant manages to move some distance, with the Pygmies following and harassing it, until the belly wounds bring it to earth.

Sometimes, of course, the plan does not work out. Perhaps the tendons are not completely severed, and the elephant snatches up one of the hunters and tramples or gores him to death. Perhaps the other elephants refuse to stampede and attack the hunters instead. Bill Spees told me of one Pygmy hunter who was separated from his companions while trailing an elephant that had been wounded but not incapacitated. The elephant circled around to foil his pursuer and attacked him from the rear, goring him in the side. The hunter dropped to the ground and, although bleeding badly, retained consciousness and his quick wit. He lay motionless. The elephant approached, poked the hunter with his trunk several times, and seemed to conclude that the Pygmy was dead. Then, like most good elephants, it had to bury its victim. The elephant dug a hole with its tusks, pushed the hunter into it with its trunk, then tried to

35

cover the man with dirt, brush, and leaves. The Pygmy said later that this was his most difficult time—trying to keep his nose free to breathe without moving enough to show the elephant that he was still alive.

The elephant did not make things any easier for the Pygmy by going away at once, but stayed nearby awhile to make sure there was no movement from the man. (Buffalo may do the same thing after they have killed a man.) At last the elephant went on his way and the wounded hunter pushed himself up into the air. Within a few minutes, the other Pygmies came and found him. Fortunately they carried him to the mission rather than the village witch doctor. Penicillin, cleanliness and rest healed the Pygmy's wounds, and during the time he spent at the mission he became converted to Christianity. Spees thought that in view of this momentous change in his outlook on things, the Pygmy might give up elephant hunting. But the young man shook his head and said, "No, once an elephant hunter always an elephant hunter."

One Point for Analysis: Several images in this story (see the eighth paragraph) are disturbing because they suggest extreme suffering: first of animals, then of men.

Writing Topics:

1. Narrate a story that demonstrates that hemp, marijuana, or LSD does not bolster a person's courage.
2. Tell the "big" tale in which you hunted and finally killed a large animal. Perhaps the tale may be about the huge fish that "got away."
3. After surviving burial by the elephant, the young Pygmy was intent on resuming the hunt: "once an elephant hunter always an elephant hunter." Using this type of "heroism" as a theme, recount the story of someone who continues a pursuit that has almost cost him his life.

JIM THORPE

STEVE GELMAN

Jim Thorpe is still remembered as one of America's greatest athletes. In the 1912 Olympics he won both the pentathlon and the decathlon. In spite of his success, he died an unhappy, disillusioned man. Steve Gelman, who writes about him here, was a reporter for Sport *magazine.*

The railroad station was jammed. Students from Lafayette College were crowding onto the train platform eagerly awaiting the arrival of the Carlisle Indian School's track and field squad. No one would have believed it a few months earlier. A school that nobody had heard of was suddenly beating big, famous colleges in track meets. Surely these Carlisle athletes would come charging off the train, one after the other, like a Marine battalion.

The train finally arrived and two young men—one big and broad, the other small and slight—stepped onto the platform.

"Where's the track team?" a Lafayette student asked.

"This is the team," replied the big fellow.

"Just the two of you?"

"Nope, just me," said the big fellow. "This little guy is the manager."

The Lafayette students shook their heads in wonder. Somebody must be playing a joke on them. If this big fellow was the whole Carlisle track team, he would be competing against an entire Lafayette squad.

He did. He ran sprints, he ran hurdles, he ran distance races. He high-jumped, he broad-jumped. He threw the javelin and the shot. Finishing first in eight events, the big fellow beat the whole Lafayette team.

The big fellow was Jim Thorpe, the greatest American athlete of modern times. He was born on May 28, 1888, in a two-room farmhouse near Prague, Oklahoma. His parents were members of the Sac and Fox Indian tribe and he was a direct descendant of the famous warrior chief, Black Hawk.

As a Sac and Fox, Jim had the colorful Indian name Wa-Tho-

Huck, which, translated, means Bright Path. But being born an Indian, his path was not so bright. Although he had the opportunity to hunt and fish with great Indian outdoorsmen, he was denied opportunity in other ways. The United States government controlled the lives of American Indians and, unlike other people, Indians did not automatically become citizens. It was almost impossible for an Indian to gain even a fair education and extremely difficult, as a result, for an Indian to rise high in life.

Young Bright Path seemed destined to spend his life in the Oklahoma farmland. But when he was in his teens, the government gave him the chance to attend the Carlisle Indian School in Pennsylvania. Soon Carlisle was racing along its own bright path to athletic prominence. In whatever sport Jim Thorpe played, he excelled. He was a star in baseball, track and field, wrestling, lacrosse, basketball and football. He was so good in football, in fact, that most other small schools refused to play Carlisle. The Indian school's football schedule soon listed such major powers of the early twentieth century as Pittsburgh, Harvard, Pennsylvania, Penn State and Army.

Thorpe was a halfback. He was six-feet, one-inch tall, weighed 185 pounds and had incredible speed and power. He built upon these natural gifts daily. He would watch a coach or player demonstrate a difficult maneuver, then he would try it himself. Inevitably, he would master the maneuver within minutes.

Thorpe was not only a fine runner, he was also a crunching blocker and tackler. And he could pass, punt and place-kick. In 1908, he kicked three field goals to help beat powerful Penn State, 12–5. In 1911 he scored 17 points in 17 minutes against Dickinson, then led Carlisle to upset victories over Pittsburgh, Pennsylvania and Lafayette. Finally, he kicked four field goals as Carlisle beat the nation's top-ranked team, Harvard.

During every game, opponents piled on Thorpe, trampled him, kicked him and punched him, trying to put him out of action. They were never successful. Years later someone asked him if he had ever been hurt on the field. "Hurt?" Thorpe said. "How could anyone get hurt playing football?"

But Jim never played his best when he felt he would have no fun playing. "What's the fun of playing in the rain?" he once said. And his Carlisle coach, Pop Warner, once said, "There's no doubt that Jim had more talent than anybody who ever played football, but you could never tell when he felt like giving his best."

38

Despite occasional lapses, he usually gave his best. In 1912, he scored 198 points, including 25 touchdowns. Against heavily favored Army he carried three opponents across the goal line to score Carlisle's first touchdown, passed for the second touchdown, ran back a punt 90 yards for the third touchdown and ran back another punt 95 yards for the fourth. The little school of Indians won, 27–6.

Football, though, did not provide Thorpe with his finest hour. He was selected for the United States Olympic track team in 1912, and went to Sweden with the team for the Games. On the ship, while the other athletes limbered up, Thorpe slept in his bunk. In Sweden, while other athletes trained, Thorpe relaxed in a hammock. He never strained when he didn't feel it necessary.

Thorpe came out of his hammock when the Games began, to take part in the two most demanding Olympic events. He entered the pentathlon competition, a test of skill in five events: 200-meter run, 1500-meter run, broad jump, discus and javelin; and the decathlon competition, a series of ten events: 100-meter run, 400-meter run, 1500-meter run, high hurdles, broad jump, high jump, pole vault, discus, javelin and shot put. Though most athletes were utterly exhausted by the decathlon alone, Thorpe breezed through both events, his dark hair flopping, his smile flashing, his muscled body gliding along the track. He finished first in both the pentathlon and decathlon, one of the great feats in Olympic history.

"You sir," King Gustav V of Sweden told Thorpe as he presented him with two gold medals, "are the greatest athlete in the world." And William Howard Taft, the President of the United States, said, "Jim Thorpe is the highest type of citizen."

King Gustav V was correct, but President Taft was not. Though Jim Thorpe had brought great glory to his nation, though thousands of people cheered him upon his return to the United States and attended banquets and a New York parade in his honor, he was not a citizen. He did not become one until 1916. Even then, it took a special government ruling because he was an Indian.

Jim Thorpe was a hero after the Olympics and a sad, bewildered man not too much later. Someone discovered that two years before the Olympics he had been paid a few dollars to play semiprofessional baseball. Though many amateur athletes had played for pay under false names, Thorpe had used his own name. As a result, he was not technically an amateur when he competed at Stockholm

39

as all Olympic athletes must be. His Olympic medals and trophies were taken away from him and given to the runners-up.

After this heartbreaking experience, Thorpe turned to professional sports. He played major league baseball for six years and did fairly well. Then he played professional football for six years with spectacular success. His last pro football season was in 1926. After that, his youthful indifference to studies and his unwillingness to think of a nonsports career caught up with him. He had trouble finding a job, and his friends deserted him. He periodically asked for, but never was given back, his Olympic prizes. From 1926 until his death in 1953, he lived a poor, lonely, unhappy life.

But in 1950 the Associated Press held a poll to determine the outstanding athlete of the half-century. Despite his loss of the Olympic gold medals and a sad decline in fortune during his later years, Thorpe was almost unanimously chosen the greatest athlete of modern times.

One Point for Analysis: The verbs (and sentence units) in the eighth paragraph are short, thus imitating the swiftness of a track star.

Writing Topics:

1. Thorpe's coach said, "You could never tell when he felt like giving his best." In a narrative essay, demonstrate how "instability" can end in disaster.
2. Write a narrative essay in which a minority-group athlete rises to great fame.
3. Thorpe ended his life as a sad man. Write a narrative in which you discuss "the wheel of fortune": dizzying heights of fame, the top of the wheel, can end in utter dejection through one half-turn.

WEDDING ON THE BAYOU

HARNETT KANE

Harnett Kane has written often about the history and legends of Louisiana. One of his best-known works is Bayous of Louisiana, *from which this essay is taken.*

Monsieur Charles Durand was "an original," in the words of his granddaughter, Mrs. Stella Madère, who rocked in her rocker and told me about it that day. He had his own notions, and not all the Madame Grundys of the bayou could dissuade him from the smallest of them. He came from France, shortly before 1820, already wealthy; and his first actions on arrival were broad ones. He established one of the most extensive plantations for many miles about. He bought scores of slaves. He wanted many trees about him, and he decided to have a long avenue, three miles in extent. Once they began to grow, the alternate pines and oaks became show-things of the upper Teche.

Along with the trees, the Durand family waxed. An addition came almost every year, until the children numbered twelve. He, his wife, and the smaller Durands led a spacious life and a mirthful one, for Monsieur Durand believed that wealth was to be enjoyed. Some were certain that, as he sat before his massive desk, he tried to devise ways of spending his riches that no others had ever conceived. He came close to success, his neighbors thought.

He acquired a set of carriages with ornaments of gold, including the harness. The countryside stopped to watch them, glittering in the sun, as Monsieur Durand and all the Durands bowed right and left. He gave orders that the family was to be waked in the morning with sprays of perfume. More and more pleased by this fancy, he installed large supplies and bathed in waters well strewn with crystals which gave off those fine aromas. He suggested that the other Durands follow his example. They did, and they liked it, and insisted that their guests do the same thing. Papa had such gay ideas!

Then the first Madame Durand died, and Papa was as extravagant in sorrow as in everything else. Never would he see the face of another woman without thinking of his poor lost wife; never would

41

he marry again. He swore it for the world to hear and be guided thereby. Daily he went to the cemetery across the Teche and knelt before the tomb. He made his trip in good weather and in bad; when it rained, he wore a covering against the elements. To perpetuate the memory of his grief, he ordered an artist to create an iron statue of him, on his knees, hands crossed, clad in his raincoat; the statue, too, was protected. At the base was an inscription telling of his oath never to be false to the dear one.

Within less than a year, Charles Durand met a girl whom he liked and was married again. The town tittered. Boys of the area, doing what their elders did not dare do, crept into the cemetery and tossed stones at the statue until the head dropped. Someone scrawled over the graven words at the base: "Do Not Tell Such Lies!"

But Monsieur Durand was not one to concern himself with over-meticulous consistencies. His second marriage was as undisturbed, as undilutedly jolly, as his first. Again a child came with every year or so, and again the total reached twelve. His granddaughter said that he had informed everybody: "The number must be the same as before. I cannot be unfair to either lady." There was a man with a delicate sense of the rightness of things.

A few years before the outbreak of the Civil War, two of his daughters simultaneously accepted the marriage proposals of members of native Louisiana families. Bayou Teche looked for something unusual from Monsieur Durand for the occasion. Few expected anything like the thing that they experienced.

The planter sat long at that desk, and concentrated, before he conceived his project. He chose spiders for the basis of the ornamentation. One source says that he imported a cargo of enormous creatures from Cathay. His granddaughter insists that he sent merely to the woods near Catahoula, Louisiana. In any event, they were large spiders, capable of large deeds.

Shortly before the marriage day, the spiders were set loose, while the slaves watched, big-eyed, among the trees in the long avenue. For days the spiders worked, lacing the spaces between the trees with yards of delicate webs. All wondered; would it rain between then and the wedding day, and his efforts melt away? Monsieur Durand was not one to fret over trifles. It would not rain.

It did not rain. On that morning, the planter called his slaves, gave them bellows and supplies of silver and gold dust. Over the long canopy of cobwebs, says the tradition, they spread this gos-samer covering. ("It must have been superb," said Mrs. Madère, softly. "So many times have they told of it. . . .") Others worked beneath the canopy, laying a series of carpets to cover most of the three-mile passage under the trees. At one end of the avenue they placed an open-air altar; between the trees, at the sides, were tables covered with food, to be served by as many of the slaves, domestic and field, as could be fitted with aprons and drilled for the oc-casion. Bands played from strategic points. The wedding was open to all—French and Americans—up and down the Teche.

Thousands attended and watched. Toasts, dancing, songs, and the giving of gifts continued until dusk. Then up the bayou came a steamboat, to take the two couples on their honeymoon to New Orleans. The crowd accompanied them to the landing, shot off fire-works, and bade the young people good-by; and the four stood at the rail and waved until they were out of sight.

One Point for Analysis: In the beginning of the fifth paragraph there is an abrupt and humorous transition. The short sentence that follows it calls attention to its humor.

Writing Topics:

1. Tell the story of some particularly elaborate ceremonial event in which you participated.
2. Write the story of someone you know who, like M. Durand, is "an original."
3. Like Kane, tell a story from the past that has taken on the aura of legend.

THE EYE OF A DEER

SHIRLEY DOLPH

This emotional narrative recounts an experience that took the author one step toward maturity.

Red caps and heavy black leather boots, soggy and muddy, were strewn about the entry shed. I gingerly picked my way through them and glanced apprehensively around for signs of blood. Several

Shirley L. Dolph, "The Eye of a Deer," reprinted by permission of the author.

43

rifles leaned against the back wall, and a handful of shells lay scattered on top of the woodbox. In the fading light the puddles forming around the boots on the old wooden floor were dark and murky. I felt small and lonely, with an inexplicable sense of losing something. I stared at the puddles for a moment and, realizing I was shivering, I quickly slipped out of my white snow boots and went into the house.

The family was sitting around the big kitchen table waiting for dinner. The pleasant conversation and the warmth of the kitchen combined with the smell of bread baking soon salved my wounded mood.

In excited tones my older brothers were recounting their day's adventure in the woods. They had tracked a big white-tailed buck and had come upon him suddenly, unexpectedly. Stan, the youngest, was the only one in a firing position. An older brother swore, "Damn kid, froze on the trigger! Let a ten-pointer get clean away! That's what happens when you let a boy try to do a man's job." A small sigh of relief escaped me, unnoticed by the others. I searched Stan's eyes for a message, but he fixed them on the floor in an intent stare.

I exulted silently. "He couldn't do it—I knew he wouldn't!" Stan, at twelve, was two years older than I, and, when he wasn't teasing me to the point of tears, he was my best friend. When our father died, Stan and I had become especially close. He shared my reverence for all living things, especially animals. Together we had raised, loved, and played with a variety of pets, mostly cats, dogs, and rabbits. We delighted in hanging over the rails to watch the squealing baby pigs. We'd climb trees in the woods and watch squirrels and chipmunks and imitate birds. Stan was marvelous at splinting broken wings and coaxing abandoned baby animals to eat from an eye dropper. If one of his tiny patients succumbed, we would hold a sad funeral, always with a stone-ringed grave, a small stick cross, and tenderly planted wild flowers.

Stan and I both hated the sight of blood and never watched the slaughtering of the pigs or cows on the farm. We avoided the chicken coop when we knew one of those unfortunate fowl was about to lose its head to an ax. It would run wildly about, headless, for several seconds like an unearthly creature, screaming noiselessly.

The men were eating ravenously now and talking about their

plans for the next day's hunting. Stan was quiet and still avoiding my eyes. I picked at my dinner, and my thoughts went back to three months earlier. Stan and I were in a tree at the far edge of the cow pasture when Stan grabbed my arm and motioned for me to be quiet. There, cautiously edging towards a salt lick block, was the most magnificent animal I had ever seen. It was a male white-tailed deer. It stood regally, its fuzzy brown antlers resembling a velvet crown. I looked at Stan. His eyes were wide with awe and admiration, and he was holding his breath. The buck raised his head, and we could see his huge dark eyes. He sensed our presence then, and in two graceful leaps he was back in the woods. Stan let out his breath in a low whistle, "Whooeeee, wasn't he something!" I nodded eagerly, and Stan took my hand to help me down the tree.

My mother's concerned voice brought me back to the dinner table. I assured her that I was feeling fine and started to help clear the dishes.

The next day, while my brothers hunted, I tried to read and keep busy but could not keep my attention focused on anything. When I heard the old Ford coming up the road earlier than expected, I knew. Hesitantly I looked out of my window at the once proud and graceful buck, now draped ignominiously over the fender of the car, its eyes staring sightlessly and its antlers still threatening. My tears were tears of pity—for the killed deer and for my brother, Stan, who had been forced to watch it be killed.

The men came in triumphantly. This had been a clever one, they said. But they had finally tracked him down. Several of them had a bead on him, but it was Stan's bullet that brought him down. Stan's bullet! I couldn't believe it. The men were slapping Stan on the back and saying something about his growing up. Stan looked flushed and pleased. Then he saw the confusion and questioning in my eyes and said harshly, "You're just a kid. A girl. A man's gotta put food on the table—can't you understand that?"

I saw my dark, heavy sadness mirrored in the great staring eyes of the deer. I had lost my best friend.

AN ANALYSIS OF "THE EYE OF A DEER"

By means of a simple and moving narrative, Shirley Dolph in her essay "The Eye of a Deer" demonstrates the rite of passage from innocence to

45

experience in the lives of two people. Stan, the young man who reveres animals, kills a deer because "A man's gotta put food on the table"; Stan's younger sister reacts to this slaughter because she knew that, through it, Stan had changed and she had lost a best friend. In reality, both had changed; both had moved out of the Garden of Eden into the world of experience.

The introduction to this personal essay establishes a tone of anxiety. The young sister apprehensively looks for "signs of blood." Instead she sees those things that remind her of slaughter: "red caps," "heavy black leather boots, soggy and muddy," "several rifles," "a handful of shells." This symbolic diction expands the statement she makes that foreshadows things to come: "I felt small and lonely, with an inexplicable sense of losing something."

After the stylistically excellent introduction, the narrative is organized around two hunting trips, symbols of the changes that one must confront in his life. In the first, Stan was not ready to enter the world of an adult. He had a chance to kill the big white-tailed buck that he knew, but "Damn kid, froze on the trigger!" Nor was his sister ready to enter that world, because she exulted in Stan's innocence: "He couldn't do it—I knew he wouldn't."

The second trip was a different matter. This time the buck was killed and "it was Stan's bullet that brought him down." He had grown up. Now he was a man, "flushed and pleased."

But his sister was not pleased. She too, however, had grown, but not in the same way. Her growth was an experience in deepening and different emotion: "My tears," she says, "were tears of pity—for the killed deer and for my brother. . . ."

The essay is successful, not so much for what it says, but rather for what it implies: At different periods in one's life, people and events occasion change. The change is not always pleasant.

A CONCENTRATION CAMP EXPERIENCE

VIKTOR E. FRANKL

A distinguished psychotherapist, Frankl has taught at Harvard, Southern Methodist University, and Stanford. Man's Search for Meaning, *from which this essay is taken, has been translated into many languages and has, in this country, sold more than a million and a half copies.*

I spent some time in a hut for typhus patients who ran very high temperatures and were often delirious, many of them moribund. After one of them had just died, I watched without any emotional upset the scene that followed, which was repeated over and over again with each death. One by one the prisoners approached the still warm body. One grabbed the remains of a messy meal of potatoes; another decided that the corpse's wooden shoes were an improvement on his own, and exchanged them. A third man did the same with the dead man's coat, and another was glad to be able to secure some—just imagine—genuine string.

All this I watched with unconcern. Eventually I asked the "nurse" to remove the body. When he decided to do so, he took the corpse by its legs, allowing it to drop into the small corridor between the two rows of boards which were the beds for the fifty typhus patients, and dragged it across the bumpy earthen floor toward the door. The two steps which led up into the open air always constituted a problem for us, since we were exhausted from a chronic lack of food. After a few months' stay in the camp we could not walk up those steps, which were each about six inches high, without putting our hands on the door jambs to pull ourselves up.

The man with the corpse approached the steps. Wearily he dragged himslf up. Then the body: first the feet, then the trunk, and finally—with an uncanny rattling noise—the head of the corpse bumped up the two steps.

My place was on the opposite side of the hut, next to the small, sole window, which was built near the floor. While my cold hands clasped a bowl of hot soup from which I sipped greedily, I happened to look out the window. The corpse which had just been removed stared in at me with glazed eyes. Two hours before I had spoken to that man. Now I continued sipping my soup.

If my lack of emotion had not surprised me from the standpoint of professional interest, I would not remember this incident now, because there was so little feeling involved in it.

One Point for Analysis: The tone of this narrative essay is flat and unemotional, matching the feeling of the narrator at the time the incident took place.

Writing Topics:
1. Write an account of an incident to which you reacted in a way that surprised you at the time and as you look back on it. Try to understand, like Frankl, why you felt as you did.
2. Recount an incident you have witnessed of "man's inhumanity to man."
3. Tell a story in the first person, using a tone that will make the reader feel the same emotions you did when the experience occurred.

A SLAVE TO LUST

ST. AUGUSTINE OF HIPPO

A Father of the Church, St. Augustine wrote his confessions in A.D. 399. This selection shows the human side of one of the great thinkers of Western Civilization.

Meanwhile my sins were being multiplied. The woman with whom I was in the habit of sleeping was torn from my side on the grounds of being an impediment to my marriage, and my heart, which clung to her, was broken and wounded and dropping blood. She had returned to Africa after having made a vow to you [God] that she would never go to bed with another man, and she had left with me the natural son I had had by her. But I, in my misery, could not follow the example of a woman. I had two years to wait until I could have the girl to whom I was engaged, and I could not bear the delay. So, since I was not so much a lover of marriage as a

From *The Confessions of St. Augustine,* translated by Rex Warner. Copyright © 1963 by Rex Warner. Reprinted by arrangement with The New American Library, Inc., New York, N.Y.

slave to lust, I found another woman for myself—not, of course, as a wife. In this way my soul's disease was fed and kept alive so that it might reach the domination of matrimony just as strong as before, or stronger, and still the slave of an unbreakable habit. Nor was the wound healed which had been made by the cutting off of my previous mistress. It burned, it hurt intensely, and then it festered, and if the pain became duller, it became more desperate.

One Point for Analysis: The emotional intensity of the last sentence gives the reader a sense of Augustine's desperation.

Writing Topics:

1. Like St. Augustine, recall a painful experience from the past in which you suffered because you knew you were at fault.
2. St. Augustine says that he was not so much a lover of marriage as he was a slave to lust. Write the story of someone who was not so much a philanthropist as he was an individual who loved the acclaim paid to a generous benefactor.
3. Write a story which rises to its climax at the end, summing up the experience in an intensely emotional final statement.

KICKING DRUGS: A VERY PERSONAL STORY

WILLIAM S. BURROUGHS

William Burroughs, at one time himself a heroin addict, was in the 1950's loosely identified with the Beat Movement. His best-known works include The Naked Lunch *and* Nova Express.

Addiction is an illness of exposure. By and large those who have access to junk become addicts. In Iran, when opium was sold openly in shops there were three million addicts. But there is no pre-addict personality any more than there is a pre-malarial personality, all the hogwash of psychiatry to the contrary. (Parenthetically it is my opinion that nine out of ten psychiatrists should be broken down to veterinarians and their books called in for pulping). To say it country-simple, most folks enjoy junk. Having once experienced this pleasure the human organism will tend to repeat it and repeat it and repeat it. The addict's illness *is* junk.

Knock on any door. Whatever answers, give it four half-grain shots of God's Own Medicine every day for six months and the so-called "addict personality" is there . . . an old junky selling Christmas seals on North Clark Street—the "Priest" they called him, seedy and with furtive, cold fish eyes that seem to be looking at something other folks can't see. That something he is looking at is junk. The whole addict personality can be summed up in one sentence: *The addict needs junk.* He will do a lot to get junk just as you would do a lot for water if you were thirsty enough.

You see junk *is* a personality—a seedy gray man; a rooming house; a shabby street; a room on the top floor; stairs; cough; the "Priest" pulling himself up along the banister; bathroom with yellow wood panels, dripping toilet, works stashed under the wash basin; back in his room now cooking up. A gray shadow on a distant wall—that used to be me, mister.

I was on junk for almost fifteen years. In that time I took ten cures. I have been to Lexington and have taken the reduction treatment. I have taken abrupt withdrawal treatments and prolonged withdrawal treatments; cortisone, tranquilizers, antihistamines and the prolonged sleep cure. In every case I relapsed at the first opportunity.

Why do addicts voluntarily take a cure and then relapse? I think on a deep biological level most addicts want to be cured. Junk *is* death and your body knows it. I relapsed because I was never physiologically cured until 1957. Then I took the apomorphine treatment under the care of a British physician, the late Dr. John Yerbury Dent. Apomorphine is the only agent I know that evicts the "addict personality," an old friend who used to inhabit my body. I called him Opium Jones. We were mighty close in Tangier in 1957, shooting 15 grains of methadone every hour which equals 30 grains of morphine and that's a lot of junk. I never changed my clothes. Jones likes his clothes to season in stale rooming-house flesh until you can tell by a hat on the table, a coat hung over a chair, that Jones lives there. I never took a bath. Old Jones don't like the feel of water on his skin. I spent whole days looking at the end of my shoe just communing with Jones.

Then one day I saw that Jones was not a real friend, that our interests were in fact divergent. So I took a plane to London and found Dr. Dent, with a charcoal fire in the grate, Scottish terrier, cup of tea. He told me about the treatment and I entered the nursing home the following day. It was one of those four-story buildings on Cromwell Road; my room with rose wallpaper was on the third floor. I had a day nurse and a night nurse and received an injection of apomorphine—one twentieth grain—every two hours.

Now every addict has his special symptom, the one that hits him hardest when his junk is cut off. Listen to the old-timers in Lexington talking:

"Now with me it's puking is the worst."

"I never puke. It's this cold burn on my skin drives me up the wall."

"My trouble is sneezing."

With me it's feeling the slow painful death of Mr. Jones. I feel myself encased in his old gray corpse. Not another person in this world I want to see. Not a thing I want to do except revive Mr. Jones.

The third day with my cup of tea at dawn the calm miracle of apomorphine began. I was learning to live without Jones, reading newspapers, writing letters (usually I can't write a letter for a month), and looking forward to a talk with Dr. Dent who isn't Jones at all.

Apomorphine had taken care of my special symptom. After ten days I left the hospital. During the entire cure I had received only two grains of morphine, that is, less than I had been using in one shot. I went back to Tangier, where junk was readily available at that time. I didn't have to use will power, whatever that is. I just didn't want any junk. The apomorphine treatment had given me a long calm look at all the gray junk yesterdays, a long calm look at Mr. Jones standing there in his shabby black suit and gray felt hat with his stale rooming-house flesh and cold undersea eyes.

One Point for Analysis: Burroughs personifies his addict self as "Mr. Jones."

Writing Topics:

1. Write a narrative essay in which you tell how addiction to cigarettes is "an illness of exposure," not a personality defect.
2. Recount the struggles of someone who has given up smoking.

3. Personify a side of yourself that you conceive to be a "Mr. Jones," and recount a conflict that has taken place between him and your better self.

I KNOW WHY THE CAGED BIRD SINGS

MAYA ANGELOU

A prolific author, Maya Angelou has been successful in a number of artistic endeavors. She is not only an essayist but also a playwright, poet, professional stage and screen actress, and singer.

> *"What you looking at me for?*
> *I didn't come to stay . . ."*

I hadn't so much forgot as I couldn't bring myself to remember. Other things were more important.

> *"What you looking at me for?*
> *I didn't come to stay . . ."*

Whether I could remember the rest of the poem or not was immaterial. The truth of the statement was like a wadded-up handkerchief, sopping wet in my fists, and the sooner they accepted it the quicker I could let my hands open and the air would cool my palms.

> *"What you looking at me for . . . ?"*

The children's section of the Colored Methodist Episcopal Church of Stamps, Arkansas, was wiggling and giggling over my well-known forgetfulness.

The dress I wore was lavender taffeta, and each time I breathed it rustled, and now that I was sucking in air to breathe out shame it sounded like crepe paper on the back of hearses.

As I'd watched Momma put ruffles on the hem and cute little tucks around the waist, I knew that once I put it on I'd look like a movie star. (It was silk and that made up for the awful color.) I was going to look like one of the sweet little white girls who were everybody's dream of what was right with the world. Hanging softly over the black Singer sewing machine, it looked like magic, and when people saw me wearing it they were going to run up to me and say, "Marguerite [sometimes it was 'dear Marguerite'], forgive us, please, we didn't know who you were," and I would answer generously, "No, you couldn't have known. Of course I forgive you."

Just thinking about it made me go around with angel's dust sprinkled over my face for days. But Easter's early morning sun had shown the dress to be a plain ugly cut-down from a white woman's once-was-purple throw-away. It was old-lady-long too, but it didn't hide my skinny legs, which had been greased with Blue Seal Vaseline and powdered with the Arkansas red clay. The age-faded color made my skin look dirty like mud, and everyone in church was looking at my skinny legs.

Wouldn't they be surprised when one day I woke out of my black ugly dream, and my real hair, which was long and blonde, would take the place of the kinky mass that Momma wouldn't let me straighten? My light-blue eyes were going to hypnotize them, after all the things they said about "my daddy must of been a Chinaman" (I thought they meant made out of china, like a cup) because my eyes were so small and squinty. Then they would understand why I had never picked up a Southern accent, or spoken the common slang, and why I had to be forced to eat pigs' tails and snouts. Because I was really white and because a cruel fairy stepmother, who was understandably jealous of my beauty, had turned me into a too-big Negro girl, with nappy black hair, broad feet, and a space between her teeth that would hold a number-two pencil.

"What you looking . . ." The minister's wife leaned toward me, her long yellow face full of sorry. She whispered, "I just come to tell you, it's Easter Day." I repeated, jamming the words together, "Ijustcometotellyouit's-EasterDay," as low as possible. The giggles hung in the air like melting clouds that were waiting to rain on me. I held up two fingers, close to my chest, which meant that I had to go to the toilet, and tiptoed toward the rear of the church. Dimly, somewhere over my head, I heard ladies saying, "Lord bless the child," and, "Praise God." My head was up and my eyes were open, but I didn't see anything. Halfway down the aisle, the church exploded with, "Were you there when they crucified my Lord?" and I tripped over a foot stuck out from the children's pew. I stumbled and started to say something, or maybe to scream, but a green persimmon, or it could have been a lemon, caught me between the legs and squeezed. I tasted the sour on my tongue and felt it in the back of my mouth. Then before I reached the door, the sting was burning down my legs and into my Sunday socks. I tried to hold, to squeeze it back, to keep it from speeding, but when I reached the church porch I knew I'd have to let it go, or it would probably run right back up to my head and my poor head would burst like a dropped watermelon, and all the brains and spit and tongue and eyes would roll all over the place. So I ran down into the yard and let it go. I ran, peeing and crying, not toward the toilet out back but to our house. I'd get a whipping for it, to be sure, and the nasty children would have something new to tease me about. I laughed anyway, partially for the sweet release; still, the greater joy came not from being liberated from the silly church but from the knowledge that I wouldn't die from a busted head.

If growing up is painful for the Southern Black girl, being aware of her displacement is the rust on the razor that threatens the throat. It is an unnecessary insult.

One Point for Analysis: The use of dialect in this essay lends authenticity to the setting.

Writing Topics:

1. Recount an embarrassing experience of your childhood that helped you form your idea of who you are.
2. Recount a favorite childhood fantasy that pictured you as you secretly wanted to be.
3. Write a narrative essay that uses dialect to establish a sense of place and characters.

MEMORIES OF DASHIELL HAMMETT

LILLIAN HELLMAN

A legend in her own time, Lillian Hellman has had notable successes with her autobiographical remembrances such as Pentimento *and* An Unfinished Woman.

We met when I was twenty-four years old and he was thirty-six in a restaurant in Hollywood. The five-day drunk had left the wonderful face looking rumpled, and the very tall thin figure was tired and sagged. We talked of T. S. Eliot, although I no longer remember what we said, and then went and sat in his car and talked at each other and over each other until it was daylight. We were to meet again a few weeks later and, after that, on and sometimes off again for the rest of his life and thirty years of mine.

Thirty years is a long time, I guess, and yet as I come now to write about them the memories skip about and make no pattern and I know only certain of them are to be trusted. I know about that first meeting and the next, and there are many other pictures and sounds, but they are out of order and out of time, and I don't seem to want to put them into place. (I could have done a research job, I have on other people, but I didn't want to do one on Hammett, or to be a bookkeeper of my own life.) I don't want modesty for either of us, but I ask myself now if it can mean much to anybody but me that my second sharpest memory is of a day when we were living on a small island off the coast of Connecticut. It was six years after we had first met: six full, happy, unhappy years during which I had, with help from Hammett, written *The Children's Hour*, which was a success, and *Days to Come*, which was not. I was returning from the mainland in a catboat filled with marketing and Hammett had come down to the dock to tie me up. He had been sick that summer—the first of the sicknesses—and he was even thinner than usual. The white hair, the white pants, the white shirt made a straight, flat surface in the late sun. I thought: Maybe that's the handsomest sight I ever saw, that line of a man, the knife for a nose, and the sheet went out of my hand and the wind went out of the sail. Hammett laughed as I struggled to get back the sail. I don't know why, but I yelled angrily, "So you're a Dostoevsky sinner-saint. So you are." The laughter stopped, and when I finally came in to the dock we didn't speak as we carried up the packages and didn't speak through dinner.

Later that night, he said, "What did you say that for? What does it mean?"

I said I didn't know why I had said it and I didn't know what it meant.

Years later, when his life had changed, I did know what I had meant that day: I had seen the sinner—whatever is a sinner—and sensed the change before it came. When I told him that, Hammett said he didn't know what I was talking about, it was all too religious for him. But he did know what I was talking about and he was pleased.

But the fat, loose, wild years were over by the time we talked that way. When I first met Dash he had written four of the five novels and was the hottest thing in Hollywood and New York. It is not remarkable to be the hottest thing in either city—the hottest kid changes for each winter season—but in his case it was of extra interest to those who collect people that the ex-detective who had bad cuts on his legs and an indentation in his head from being scrappy with criminals was gentle in manner, well educated, elegant to look at, born of early settlers, was eccentric, witty, and spent so much money on women that they would have liked him even if he had been none of the good things. But as the years passed from 1930 to 1948, he wrote only one novel and a few short stories. By 1945, the drinking was no longer gay, the drinking bouts were longer and the moods darker. I was there off and on for most of those years, but in 1948 I didn't want to see the drinking anymore. I hadn't seen or spoken to Hammett for two months until the day when his devoted cleaning lady called to say she thought I had better come down to his apartment. I said I wouldn't, and then I did. She and I dressed a man who could barely lift an arm or a leg and brought him to my house, and that night I watched delirium tremens, although I didn't know what I was watching until the doctor told me the next day at the hospital. The doctor was an old friend. He said, "I'm going to tell Hammett that if he goes on drinking he'll be dead in a few months. It's my duty to say it, but it won't do any good." In a few minutes he came out of Dash's room and said, "I told him. Dash said O.K., he'd go on the wagon forever, but he can't and he won't."

But he could and he did. Five or six years later, I told Hammett that the doctor had said he wouldn't stay on the wagon.

Dash looked puzzled. "But I gave my word that day."

I said, "Have you always kept your word?"

"Most of the time," he said, "maybe because I've so seldom given it."

He had made up honor early in his life and stuck with his rules, fierce in the protection of them. In 1951 he went to jail because he and two other trustees of the bail bond fund of the Civil Rights Congress refused to reveal the names of the contributors to the fund. The truth was that Hammett had never been in the office of the Congress, did not know the name of a single contributor.

The night before he was to appear in court, I said, "Why don't you say that you don't know the names?"

"No," he said, "I can't say that."

"Why?"

"I don't know why. I guess it has something to do with keeping my word, but I don't want to talk about that. Nothing much will happen, although I think we'll go to jail for a while, but you're not to worry because"—and then suddenly I couldn't understand him because the voice had dropped and the words were coming in a most untypical nervous rush. I said I couldn't hear him, and he raised his voice and dropped his head. "I hate this damn kind of talk, but maybe I better tell you that if it were more than jail, if it were my life, I would give it for what I think democracy is, and I don't let cops or judges tell me what I think democracy is." Then he went home to bed, and the next day he went to jail.

One Point for Analysis: The conversational tone of the essay makes the reminiscence more personal.

Writing Topics: .

1. By focusing on one incident from the life of a person, imply, as Hellman does, that person's entire lifestyle.
2. After library research, write a narrative sketch of the life of Lillian Hellman.
3. Write a narrative essay that uses the title of Hellman's book from which this essay is taken, *An Unfinished Woman*. In your essay imply why you are an unfinished person.

57

MY FIRST LOVE

THOMAS MERTON

Thomas Merton, a Trappist monk, wrote a number of meditative and religious works. His autobiography, The Seven Storey Mountain, *is his best-known book.*

In three months, the summer of 1931, I suddenly matured like a weed.

I cannot tell which is the more humiliating: the memory of the half-baked adolescent I was in June or the glib and hard-boiled specimen I was in October when I came back to Oakham full of a thorough and deep-rooted sophistication of which I was both conscious and proud.

The beginning was like this: Pop wrote to me to come to America. I got a brand-new suit made. I said to myself, "On the boat I am going to meet a beautiful girl, and I am going to fall in love."

So I got on the boat. The first day I sat in a deck chair and read the correspondence of Goethe and Schiller which had been imposed on me as a duty, in preparation for the scholarship examinations at the university. What is worse, I not only tolerated this imposition but actually convinced myself that it was interesting.

The second day I had more or less found out who was on the boat. The third day I was no longer interested in the Goethe and Schiller. The fourth day I was up to my neck in the trouble that I was looking for.

It was a ten-day boat.

I would rather spend two years in a hospital than go through that anguish again! That devouring, emotional, passionate love of adolescence that sinks its claws into you and consumes you day and night and eats into the vitals of your soul! All the self-tortures of doubt and anxiety and imagination and hope and despair that you go through when you are a child, trying to break out of your shell, only to find yourself in the middle of a legion of full-armed emotions against which you have no defense! It is like being flayed alive. No one can go through it twice. This kind of a love affair can really happen only once in a man's life. After that he is calloused. He is no longer capable of so many torments. He can suffer, but not from so many matters of no account. After one such crisis he has experience and the possibility of a second time no longer exists, because the secret of the anguish was his own utter guilelessness. He is no longer capable of such complete and absurd surprises. No matter how simple a man may be, the obvious cannot go on astonishing him for ever.

I was introduced to this particular girl by a Catholic priest who came from Cleveland and played shuffleboard in his shirt sleeves without a Roman collar on. He knew everybody on the boat in the first day, and as for me, two days had gone by before I even realized that she was on board. She was traveling with a couple of aunts and the three of them did not mix in with the other passengers very much. They kept to themselves in their three deck chairs and had nothing to do with the gentlemen in tweed caps and glasses who went breezing around and around the promenade deck.

When I first met her I got the impression that she was no older than I was. As a matter of fact she was about twice my age: but you could be twice sixteen without being old, as I now realize, sixteen years after the event. She was small and delicate and looked as if she were made out of porcelain. But she had big wide-open California eyes and was not afraid to talk in a voice that was at once ingenuous and independent and had some suggestion of weariness about it as if she habitually stayed up too late at night.

To my dazzled eyes she immediately became the heroine of every novel and I all but flung myself face down on the deck at her feet. She could have put a collar on my neck and led me around from that time forth on the end of a chain. Instead of that I spent my time telling her and her aunts all about my ideals and my ambitions and she in her turn attempted to teach me how to play bridge. And that is the surest proof of her conquest, for I never allowed anyone else to try such a thing as that on me, never! But even she could not succeed in such an enterprise.

We talked. The insatiable wound inside me bled and grew, and I was doing everything I could to make it bleed more. Her perfume and the peculiar smell of the denicotinized cigarettes she smoked followed me everywhere and tortured me in my cabin.

I made a declaration of my undying love. I would not, could not,

59

ever love anyone else but her. It was impossible, unthinkable. If she went to the ends of the earth, destiny would bring us together again. The stars in their courses from the beginning of the world had plotted this meeting which was the central fact in the whole history of the universe. Love like this was immortal. It conquered time and outlasted the futility of human history. And so forth.

She talked to me, in her turn, gently and sweetly. What it sounded like was: "You do not know what you are saying. This can never be. We shall never meet again." What it meant was: "You are a nice kid. But for heaven's sake grow up before someone makes a fool of you." I went to my cabin and sobbed over my diary for a while and then, against all the laws of romance, went peacefully to sleep.

However, I could not sleep for long. At five o'clock I was up again, and walking restlessly around the deck. It was hot. A grey mist lay on the Narrows. But when it became light, other anchored ships began to appear as shapes in the mist. One of them was a Red Star liner on which, as I learned from the papers when I got on shore, a passenger was at that precise moment engaged in hanging himself.

At the last minute before landing I took a snapshot of her which, to my intense sorrow, came out blurred. I was so avid for a picture of her that I got too close with the camera and it was out of focus. It was a piece of poetic justice that filled me with woe for months.

Of course the whole family was there on the dock. But the change was devastating. With my heart ready to explode with immature emotions I suddenly found myself surrounded by all the cheerful and peaceful and comfortable solicitudes of home. Everybody wanted to talk. Their voices were full of questions and information. They took me for a drive on Long Island and showed me where Mrs. Hearst lived and everything. But I only hung my head out of the window of the car and watched the green trees go swirling by, and wished that I were dead.

One Point for Analysis: The diction of this essay is extravagant, but appropriately so as it recounts the emotions of a sixteen-year-old boy in love.

Writing Topics:
1. Recall and narrate an experience of your childhood or youth, using diction appropriate to the age at which the experience occurred.
2. Recount the story of some situation in which a person prolonged his suffering because he was enjoying it.
3. Write a narrative essay in which the introduction, like Merton's, is a series of brief paragraphs that give an overview of the detailed story that follows.

SAGA OF THE BAREFOOT BAG ON CAMPUS

JOHN RILEY

Originally written for Life *magazine, this essay recounts an unusual situation that led a group of college students to reexamine their own identities.*

At the beginning of the academic term at Oregon State University this year, the students in a ten-week speech course entitled "Persuasion" noticed right away that one among them was different. He wore a black cotton cloth bag that covered him entirely and he sat, Oriental-style, in the back of the room, well away from his more conventional fellows. When his turn came to introduce himself and explain what he expected from the course, he begged off, saying only "I prefer not to."

Professor Charles Goetzinger assured the suspicious class that "The Bag" was indeed a bona fide, full-fledged student who had simply asked to attend the course in that outfit. "I'm enough of a nut," the professor explained, "to try anything once."

For the first several weeks The Bag was seldom mentioned in the class, which met three times a week. Then one day a student delivered a required three-minute oration to demonstrate the powers of persuasion that he was supposed to be learning. His theme: The Bag doesn't bother me at all, no siree, not one bit. No, it doesn't bother *me*, he kept saying.

In commenting on his speech, the other students agreed that they had been persuaded: The Bag didn't bother him. But then it came out: The Bag bothered the hell out of *them*. One freshman followed The Bag as he walked from the classroom and tried to paste a "Kick Me" label on him. In a later session, The Bag sat opposite the offending freshman and stared at him intently through the black cloth. In horror, the freshman screamed: "Get away from me!"—and probed at The Bag with an umbrella.

Word that a black bag was attending the course spread rapidly through the university and various attempts were made to find out who was inside. (The speech department guarded the class roster like a state secret.) The OSU newspaper, the *Daily Barometer*, defended The Bag's right to be a bag. Gawkers began to cluster about the building before and after class. One day two class members followed The Bag on foot across the campus after class. The Bag was alone, and he felt trapped. But he kept his head and slowly walked four blocks to the Chemistry-Physics Building. He entered; went upstairs; they followed. The Bag picked an office at random, hoping it would be unoccupied at the lunch hour. It was. The Bag calmly closed the door after him, and the sleuths, suspecting that The Bag might be a physics professor, gave up and went to lunch.

As the weeks went by, department heads, deans and graduate students began dropping in on the speech class. Some professors sniped at Goetzinger in their own classes. One social scientist chided him for not introducing proper "sociological controls" in the "experiment," if indeed it was an experiment, but admitted that he would never allow such an exercise in his own classes, with or without controls.

Signs appeared that opinion toward having The Bag in the class was beginning to change. People sounded nicer when they talked to him, and he began to respond. He took to sitting in chairs like the other students. He spoke more. That was a mistake: a silent mystery was all right, but a talking bag required some getting used to. And furthermore, The Bag talked with a New England accent.

The class began almost to feel a certain nostalgia for the silent and presumably "safe" bag who had delivered his first three-and-a-half-minute "speech" merely by standing before them without uttering a word.

Near the end of the term, reporters and television crews descended upon Speech 113. One day the class found itself in a shooting match with no less than three TV crews. The students felt that the invasion was endangering the delicate understanding that had flowered between them and The Bag. Most of them stalked out and reassembled in Goetzinger's office. There a wonderful thing happened to the class—and to The Bag. Later, The Bag explained it to me:

"Everybody seemed suddenly to unite in fear of a common thing. It was beautiful. We were just all talking, and I forgot I was inside the bag. It was the first time I forgot. I just shot my mouth off. And after I stopped I said to myself, 'Hey, wait a minute, I'm still in the bag.' And I felt that the rest of the class for a moment had forgotten it too. I can't really see people's facial reactions through the cloth. Maybe it was mental telepathy."

At the next class session Goetzinger, The Bag and the rest of the class hashed over the meaning of it all. The students found themselves admitting that their hostility had turned to respect and protectiveness. As for The Bag, he felt humble: "I'm not Jesus Christ or anything. I'm just one of you in a bag."

This moved one student to make a confession. In the course of trying to persuade his fraternity brothers that The Bag was no joke, he himself had secretly doubted The Bag's motives.

"For some reason he seemed to be in *two bags,*" the student explained, as though that explained anything.

At this, Professor Goetzinger scooted across the class, shoved his face in front of the student and shouted, "Do you feel any empathy for what this poor man felt six weeks ago?"

"If my *mother* tried to take that bag off him," the student replied, "I'd beat the hell out of her."

The discussion then turned to whether they really wanted to know who was inside. With a show of hands, all indicated that they did not need to know his identity. The Bag had persuaded them to accept him on his own terms. When the bell rang, they rose and without a word between them formed a phalanx to escort him through a crowd of students who had been hooting at him through a window.

Having silently convinced his classmates to accept him, The Bag seemed assured of a passing mark in "Persuasion."

"Everybody's in some kind of a bag," he explains. "I just wear mine on the outside."

One Point for Analysis: The essayist uses dialogue to develop the narrative.

Writing Topics:

1. Write a narrative essay about someone you know who has, like The Bag, persuaded others to accept him on his own unusual terms.
2. Tell the story of a person whom others feel it necessary to protect.
3. Write an account of a bizarre situation, using dialogue to develop the narrative.

HOLDING MY LIFE IN MY MIND

RICHARD WRIGHT

Not having much formal education, Richard Wright turned to books as a means of self-education. His autobiography Black Boy, *is now a classic.*

I knew of no Negroes who read the books I liked and I wondered if any Negroes ever thought of them. I knew that there were Negro doctors, lawyers, newspapermen, but I never saw any of them. When I read a Negro newspaper I never caught the faintest echo of my preoccupation in its pages. I felt trapped and occasionally, for a few days, I would stop reading. But a vague hunger would come over me for books, books that opened up new avenues of feeling and seeing, and again I would forge another note to the white librarian. Again I would read and wonder as only the naïve and unlettered can read and wonder, feeling that I carried a secret, criminal burden about with me each day.

That winter my mother and brother came and we set up housekeeping, buying furniture on the installment plan, being cheated and yet knowing no way to avoid it. I began to eat warm food and to my surprise found that regular meals enabled me to read faster. I may have lived through many illnesses and survived them, never suspecting that I was ill. My brother obtained a job and we began to save toward the trip north, plotting our time, setting tentative

From pp. 220–222 (under the title "Discovering Books") in *Black Boy* by Richard Wright. Copyright 1937, 1942, 1944, 1945 by Richard Wright. Reprinted by permission of Harper & Row Publishers, Inc.

dates for departure. I told none of the white men on the job that I was planning to go north; I knew that the moment they felt I was thinking of the North they would change toward me. It would have made them feel that I did not like the life I was living, and because my life was completely conditioned by what they said or did, it would have been tantamount to challenging them.

I could calculate my chances for life in the South as a Negro fairly clearly now.

I could fight the southern whites by organizing with other Negroes, as my grandfather had done. But I knew that I could never win that way; there were many whites and there were but few blacks. They were strong and we were weak. Outright black rebellion could never win. If I fought openly I would die and I did not want to die. News of lynchings were frequent.

I could submit and live the life of a genial slave, but that was impossible. All of my life had shaped me to live by my own feelings and thoughts. I could make up to Bess and marry her and inherit the house. But that, too, would be the life of a slave; if I did that, I would crush to death something within me, and I would hate myself as much as I knew the whites already hated those who had submitted. Neither could I ever willingly present myself to be kicked, as Shorty had done. I would rather have died than do that.

I could drain off my restlessness by fighting with Shorty and Harrison. I had seen many Negroes solve the problem of being black by transferring their hatred of themselves to others with a black skin and fighting them. I would have to be cold to do that, and I was not cold and I could never be.

I could, of course, forget what I had read, thrust the whites out of my mind, forget them; and find release from anxiety and longing in sex and alcohol. But the memory of how my father had conducted himself made that course repugnant. If I did not want others to violate my life, how could I voluntarily violate it myself?

I had no hope whatever of being a professional man. Not only had I been so conditioned that I did not desire it, but the fulfillment of such an ambition was beyond my capabilities. Well-to-do Negroes lived in a world that was almost as alien to me as the world inhabited by whites.

What, then, was there? I held my life in my mind, in my consciousness each day, feeling at times that I would stumble and drop it, spill it forever. My reading had created a vast sense of distance

65

between me and the world in which I lived and tried to make a living, and that sense of distance was increasing each day. My days and nights were one long, quiet, continuously contained dream of terror, tension, and anxiety. I wondered how long I could bear it.

AN ANALYSIS OF "HOLDING MY LIFE IN MY MIND"

The narrative Richard Wright recounts in "Holding My Life in My Mind" is not built around action or adventure. Instead, it is a record of the boyhood speculations the writer once had about experiences that might occur in the future. Because he is not writing about events that happened, but about those that might happen, nothing actually takes place in the essay. Concerned with Wright's inner life when he was a boy, the essay's "action" takes place in his heart and mind rather than in his outward acts.

The life of the mind began for Wright, he says, with reading. The books he met made him dissatisfied with his life and desirous of finding a way out of the role into which he was cast by birth. The plans and possibilities examined created the narration of this essay.

The plans and possibilities are of three types. The first involves moving North (second paragraph). This section is not fully developed; Wright only suggests what the outcome of such an action might be.

Following the single sentence of the third paragraph, which furnishes a transition, he explores the avenues of action open to him if he stays in the South. He could rebel, organize, and probably die (fourth paragraph). He could submit to the whites or to a wife, and again some part of him would die (fifth paragraph). He could fight with other blacks (sixth paragraph) or escape through sex and alcohol (seventh paragraph). This series of short paragraphs presents several vignettes, not one of which tells a complete story within itself. When they are joined together, they form a total picture of the boy and his anxieties.

The eighth paragraph recounts, in contrast to the preceding ones, what the narrator does not feel he can hope to be: a professional man. Whereas he can imagine the pattern of his life that would result from such choices (those already mentioned, for example), he cannot conceive of being a successful well-to-do Negro. There is no story to be told in this area.

The concluding paragraph continues Wright's unusual approach to narration. It does not, as in most stories, resolve conflicts and give the reader a sense that the tale is ended. Instead, Wright uses here an "open ending," one that suggests that the characters and problems continue to exist well beyond the point at which the essay ends.

The first-person point of view, from which this essay is written, brings the reader close to the inner life of the troubled boy. The reader shares his frustrations, fears, and dreams, unconcerned that in his essay, "nothing happens."

THE DEATH OF SOCRATES

PLATO

Plato, the pupil of Socrates in the fourth century B.C., *gives us in this essay a moving account of the death of his master.*

A man of sense ought not to say, nor will I be very confident, that the description which I have given of the soul and her mansions is exactly true. But I do say that, inasmuch as the soul is shown to be immortal, he may venture to think, not improperly or unworthily, that something of the kind is true. The venture is a glorious one, and he ought to comfort himself with words like these, which is the reason why I lengthen out the tale. Wherefore, I say, let a man be of good cheer about his soul, who having cast away the pleasures and ornaments of the body as alien to him and working harm rather than good, has sought after the pleasures of knowledge; and has arrayed the soul, not in some foreign attire, but in her own proper jewels, temperance, and justice, and courage, and nobility, and truth—in these adorned she is ready to go on her journey to the world below, when her hour comes. You, Simmias and Cebes, and all other men, will depart at some time or other. Me already, as a tragic poet would say, the voice of fate calls. Soon I must drink the poison; and I think that I had better repair to the bath first, in order that the women may not have the trouble of washing my body after I am dead.

When he had done speaking, Crito said: And have you any commands for us, Socrates—anything to say about your children, or any other matter in which we can serve you?

Nothing particular, Crito, he replied: only, as I have always told you, take care of yourselves; that is a service which you may be ever rendering to me and mine and to all of us, whether you promise to do so or not. But if you have no thought for yourselves, and

67

care not to walk according to the rule which I have prescribed for you, not now for the first time, however much you may profess or promise at the moment, it will be of no avail.

We will do our best, said Crito: And in what way shall we bury you?

In any way that you like; but you must get hold of me, and take care that I do not run away from you. Then he turned to us, and added with a smile:—I cannot make Crito believe that I am the same Socrates who have been talking and conducting the argument; he fancies that I am the other Socrates whom he will soon see, a dead body—and he asks, How shall he bury me? And though I have spoken many words in the endeavour to show that when I have drunk the poison I shall leave you and go to the joys of the blessed,—these words of mine, with which I was comforting you and myself, have had, as I perceive, no effect upon Crito. And therefore I want you to be surety for me to him now, as at the trial he was surety to the judges for me: but let the promise be of another sort; for he was surety for me to the judges that I would remain, and you must be my surety to him that I shall not remain, but go away and depart; and then he will suffer less at my death, and not be grieved when he sees my body being burned or buried. I would not have him sorrow at my hard lot, or say at the burial, Thus we lay out Socrates, or, Thus we follow him to the grave or bury him; for false words are not only evil in themselves, but they inflict the soul with evil. Be of good cheer then, my dear Crito, and say that you are burying my body only, and do with that whatever is usual, and what you think best.

When he had spoken these words, he arose and went into a chamber to bathe; Crito followed him and told us to wait. So we remained behind, talking and thinking of the subject of discourse, and also of the greatness of our sorrow; he was like a father of whom we were being bereaved, and we were about to pass the rest of our lives as orphans. When he had taken the bath his children were brought to him (he had two young sons and an elder one); and the women of his family also came, and he talked to them and gave them a few directions in the presence of Crito; then he dismissed them and returned to us.

Now the hour of sunset was near, for a good deal of time had passed while he was within. When he came out, he sat down with us again after his bath, but not much was said. Soon the jailer, who

was the servant of the Eleven, entered and stood by him, saying:—
To you, Socrates, whom I know to be the noblest and gentlest and
best of all who ever came to this place, I will not impute the angry
feeling of other men, who rage and swear at me, when, in obe-
dience to the authorities, I bid them drink the poison—indeed, I am
sure that you will not be angry with me; for others, as you are
aware, and not I, are to blame. And so fare you well, and try to bear
lightly what must needs be—you know my errand. Then bursting
into tears he turned away and went out.

Socrates looked at him and said: I return your good wishes, and
will do as you bid. Then turning to us, he said, How charming the
man is: since I have been in prison he has always been coming to
see me, and at times he would talk to me, and was as good to me as
could be, and now see how generously he sorrows on my account.
We must do as he says, Crito; and therefore let the cup be brought,
if the poison is prepared: if not, let the attendant prepare some.

Yet, said Crito, the sun is still upon the hill-tops, and I know that
many a one has taken the draught late, and after the announcement
has been made to him, he has eaten and drunk, and enjoyed the society of his beloved: do not hurry—there is time enough.

Socrates said: Yes, Crito, and they of whom you speak are right
in so acting, for they think that they will be gainers by the delay;
but I am right in not following their example, for I do not think that
I should gain anything by drinking the poison a little later; I should
only be ridiculous in my own eyes for sparing and saving a life
which is already forfeit. Please then to do as I say, and not to refuse
me.

Crito made a sign to the servant, who was standing by; and he
went out, and having been absent for some time, returned with the
jailer carrying the cup of poison. Socrates said: You, my good
friend, who are experienced in these matters, shall give me directions how I am to proceed. The man answered: You have only to
walk about until your legs are heavy, and then to lie down, and the
poison will act. At the same time he handed the cup to Socrates,
who in the easiest and gentlest manner, without the least fear or
change of colour or feature, looking at the man with all his eyes,
Echecrates, as his manner was, took the cup and said: What do you
say about making a libation out of this cup to any god? May I, or
not? The man answered: We only prepare, Socrates, just so much as
we deem enough. I understand, he said: but I may and must ask

the gods to prosper my journey from this to the other world—even so—and so be it according to my prayer. Then raising the cup to his lips, quite readily and cheerfully he drank off the poison. And hitherto most of us had been able to control our sorrow; but now when we saw him drinking, and saw too that he had finished the draught, we could no longer forbear, and in spite of myself my own tears were flowing fast; so that I covered my face and wept, not for him, but at the thought of my own calamity in having to part from such a friend. Nor was I the first; for Crito, when he found himself unable to restrain his tears, had got up, and I followed; and at that moment, Apollodorus, who had been weeping all the time, broke out in a loud and passionate cry which made cowards of us all. Socrates alone retained his calmness: What is this strange outcry? he said. I sent away the women mainly in order that they might not misbehave in this way, for I have been told that a man should die in peace. Be quiet then, and have patience. When we heard his words we were ashamed, and refrained our tears; and he walked about until, as he said, his legs began to fail, and then he lay on his back, according to directions, and the man who gave him the poison now and then looked at his feet and legs; and after a while he pressed his foot hard, and asked him if he could feel; and he said, No; and then his leg, and so upwards and upwards, and showed us that he was cold and stiff. And he felt them himself, and said: When the poison reaches the heart, that will be the end. He was beginning to grow cold about the groin, when he uncovered his face, for he had covered himself up, and said—they were his last words—he said: Crito, I owe a cock to Asclepius; will you remember to pay the debt? The debt shall be paid, said Crito; is there anything else? There was no answer to this question; but in a minute or two a movement was heard, and the attendants uncovered him; his eyes were set, and Crito closed his eyes and mouth.

Such was the end, Echecrates, of our friend; concerning whom I may truly say, that of all men of his time whom I have known, he was the wisest and justest and best.

One Point for Analysis: The calm, logical attitude of Socrates gives dignity to his death.

Writing Topics:

   1. Recount an incident involving the "wisest and justest and best" person whom you have know.

2. Like Plato, narrate with intimate details an emotional crisis in the life of someone you know.
3. After library research, recount the story of why Socrates was executed.

SAMURAI'S SURRENDER

HENRY MITCHELL

The late surrender of the last combat Japanese soldier from World War II made news around the world. This essay is an ironic treatment of that surrender.

The Japanese lieutenant who required 30 years to achieve surrender and stop fighting World War II in the Philippines took one look at the lox and bagel on his plate and indicated to his honorable hostess here in suburban New York that he was not all that hungry.

In his self-appointed guerrilla years, Hiroo Onoda lived decades without a square meal, without a sound sleep, without a good bath. He almost fainted from joy when the Japanese youth who finally got to him in his island hideout gave him a can of beans.

"For the first time in 30 years," he said afterward, "I was eating something fit for human consumption."

But lox and bagel—well. There are limits.

You might assume from his 30-year war that Onoda is not the most flexible or adaptable fellow in the world. He may smile at strangers, especially if it's his duty (as author making a tour for his book sales) to do so, and he will even gaze at the Super Bowl on television, though it can hardly mean anything to him, his first day of a brief trip through America. But Onoda is a man of great caution—he lasted 30 years in enemy territory without getting shot—and not a man of snap decisions.

His book is called *No Surrender,* though he did, in fact, surrender last February. But something like "NEVER" is central to his character, and whether this quality has ever made him happy or ever will is something he does not discuss in the book.

He was terribly surprised that Japan surrendered. He had sup-

From *The Washington Post,* January 14, 1975. © 1975 *The Washington Post.*

posed the Japanese would die to the last man before that happened. When he himself surrendered, they gave him back his sword, as a nice gesture of respect for his 30 years of faithfulness to duty as he saw it. He said that when he saw that respect for what he had believed in, he felt for a second "the pride of the samurai."

The facts are plain enough, at least from Onoda's version of them, and it's hard to understand any human without beginning with the facts as he sees them.

First, he was an intelligence officer, not an infantryman. He was isolated on a small sparsely populated island of no consequence and when it was said the war was over, he had no reason to believe it. The enemy was always telling lies to demoralize you. He was left with two companions, both of them later shot by natives—hostile, because Onoda and his buddies kept stealing rice and burning barns and killing cows and occasionally killing the men, because they thought of themselves as still being at war.

That sounds reasonable enough, at the beginning of peacetime. But for 30 years?

Well, it is true that in those 30 years Onoda did think the war was going on awfully long, and he did, of course, hear rumors of peace. The Japanese government spent a fortune trying to get the message to him, dropping leaflets from planes, sending special missions to fetch him back. Twice, members of Onoda's family were sent to the island and he heard them at a distance, on their loudspeakers, begging him to return because the war was over.

But if a man doesn't want to believe something (and no samurai wishes to believe his nation has been defeated) then it is almost impossible to produce evidence he will find convincing. No matter what anybody did or said, Onoda found some reason to believe otherwise. He thought the newspapers had been censored just to entrap him, and he thought the radio broadcasts (which indicated peace had returned to Japan) were merely propaganda to make him betray his mission.

It is hard to believe that, but it helps to remember that Onoda was isolated. When you live a certain life for year after year in the forest, you do not see things the same way you do if you live in town and go to work every day. One cardinal element was always missing, Onoda says:

If the war was really over, and if he really was supposed to surrender and go home, then why had he not received any direct orders from his superiors? All they had to do was order him to surrender. But they never did, not until last February. The minute he got those orders, he followed them, he says, and surrendered and went home.

One attractive irony was that what the Japanese government failed to do in its large effort to get through to him was accomplished by a young college dropout named Suzuki, who simply took it into his head one day to go find Onoda. He did. He found out Onoda was not going to budge without orders. He went back to Japan. Explained that. The orders came promptly. What the state failed at, the dropout accomplished, that is, the end of Onoda's long war.

Just here, as the story ends (and the book ends), the real questions begin. Even if you assume Onoda interpreted events exactly as he said he did (and it is the simplest explanation, for any other explanation is even less believable), and even if you assume that thanks to his military indoctrination, due to his samurai sense of mission (and the kamikaze pilots were understandable only on the basis that they believed in their duty, just as they said they did), and even if you make allowances for a certain mental cast, if not mental disorder, from living so isolated a life, you are still left with an overwhelming question:

What happens to a man whose whole world has crumbled, whose sufferings of 30 years appear to have been useless, or ludicrous, or wasted? What happens when a faith that the nation would die, rather than surrender, proves false? What happens when you tear yourself to pieces in order to achieve the discipline that allows you to continue your guerrilla mission for 30 years—giving up home and sex and luxury and comfort—only to wonder if it was worth it, and only to see some people grin?

What does a man do who fought a mortal enemy for 30 years, only to find himself presented with lox and bagels in the very citadel of the enemy nation, in a room full of photographers and reporters looking as if they thought maybe you were some sort of rare specimen, if not a certified psychotic jackass?

And what happens to a man who after so many years goes back home to a popular hero's welcome, and then feels lost, and feels increasingly that his own people—for whom he suffered all those years—have become materialistic, grubby, cynical, a bit blind to honor, a bit indifferent to sacrifice?

73

In Onoda's case, he took one look at Japan and headed off to Brazil for a new life as a farmer and cattle raiser. His favorite brother moved to Brazil after the war, so they'll be there together. But Brazil can never be home, as Japan was.

One Point for Analysis: The loyalty of Mr. Onoda is presented as ridiculous and laughable rather than as pathetic or admirable, because it was unreasonably extravagant.

Writing Topics:
1. Write an account of a person like Mr. Onoda whose virtue, taken to extremes, leads him into a ridiculous situation.
2. A Samurai is a noble warrior. Mr. Onoda, by the time of his surrender, was hardly such a man. Write a narrative essay in which you suggest an ironic approach beginning with the title.
3. Rewrite the story of Mr. Onoda, treating him as a hero worthy of the world's respect.

DESTINY IS MADE KNOWN SILENTLY

AGNES DE MILLE

This famous dancer-choreographer has written about her art in many outstanding periodicals such as The Atlantic Monthly, Theater Arts, Esquire, Horizon, *and* Vogue.

Sometime during the beginning of the sophomore year a revue was put on in the college auditorium for the benefit of student victims of a campus fire. I volunteered and danced French *bergerettes* in the manner of Watteau and that was the first time in my life I stepped on a stage. The next day I was rushed by three sororities. I joined one which later became the Beta Xi chapter of Kappa Alpha Theta.

For four years this lovely life lasted. I continued in a happy somnambulistic state, blousy, disheveled, dropping hairpins, tennis balls, and notebooks wherever I went, drinking tea with Dr. Lily Campbell and the professors, lapping up talk of books and history, drinking tea with classmates and Elizabeth Boynton, the librarian, having dates or nearly having dates with the two *M*'s on either side of me, Macon and Morgan, having dates with Leonard Keeler, who was working out campus thefts and misdemeanors with the first lie detector, falling asleep in all afternoon lectures, late for every appointment (once when I entered English history on time the whole class burst out laughing). With the smell of iris and budding acacia coming through the windows, the sound of scholasticism filling my dreams with a reassuring hum, I sank deeper and deeper into a kind of cerebral miasma as I postponed all vital decisions. I had some vague, soothing fantasy of living in Mother's garden indefinitely and studying until I slipped gracefully into old age while I wrote exquisitely about—what? No doubt it would all become apparent in time.

Occasionally I staged dances for the student rallies, mostly to Chopin, mostly about yearning for beauty and always accompanied by sorority sisters who were not trained. Campbell shook her head. "This is not good," she said. "You simply haven't a dancer's body. I'd like you to write, but if you must go on the stage, act. I believe you're a tragic actress. Stop dancing. Look at yourself in the mirror."

In my junior year I presented a skit at the Press Club Vod based on the idea of how closely allied jazz dancing was to the jungle. I represented the jungle. Father for a wonder was in the house—he hadn't been up to this point—and was, along with the student body, markedly impressed. He told me the next day with quiet gratification that my sketch made a real dramatic point, and that he thought it good enough to incorporate into his next picture. I went to bed dizzy. I lay awake hours planning each shot, thinking of lighting, rhythm, camera angles, experiments that I have never seen to this day. I prepared to write it all down and present it to him. But the next night he came home to dinner with the announcement that he had given the idea to Kosloff and told him to get to work on it. Kosloff thought it was good, he added.

I can't remember whether I left the table or not. Probably not. I probably ate as usual. But if he had slapped me I couldn't have been more stunned. And yet I was not wholly unprepared. Father simply could not consider any member of his household as a professional with professional rights. He must have noticed something of my bitter disappointment. He was extremely uncomfortable for a

75

few hours, but he came home the next night with everything solved; he had decided not to use the dance after all.

I usually danced about Beauty and how one should be ready to die for it. I did a good number of Petrarch's sonnets at one football rally when the men got their letters. I suspect the student body must have had pretty nearly enough of me. But this last performance had one happy aspect. I dressed the girls exactly like Botticelli nymphs with draperies split to the crotch and was forthwith summoned into the director's office to explain why. Dr. Moore knew all about Botticelli; he was also acquainted with eighteen-year-old glands. I listened, with profound respect but refused to alter a stitch.

In order to get back up on my numb points, I had started exercising again. At first only for a couple of weeks before each show, but gradually, with God knows what contingency in mind, because I swear I had banished from conscious intention all thought of going back on the stage, I got to practicing every day. It could not be for very long, and it was always late at night after I had finished studying. I used to fall asleep over my books, and then toward midnight force myself awake, and shaking with fatigue perform between the bureau and the closet mirrors, *relevés* in every position, on toes that went pins and needles with the unexpected pressure. I tried not to shake the floor out of concern for the sleeping family. Once, while I prodded along the upstairs hall in a particularly stumpy *pas de bourrée,* Father stepped out of his study, pipe in one hand, book in the other, and contemplated me. I kept going. I was in my petticoat, face blanched and wet with weariness. At length he spoke, "All this education and I'm still just the father of a circus." He went back in his room and shut the door.

One Point for Analysis: After the opening brief sentence of the second paragraph, an unusually long sentence made up of parallel phrases presents a picture of "this lovely life."

Writing Topics:
  1. Write a narrative essay about a person who was told that he could not succeed in a particular endeavor, but went on to do it well.
  2. Recount an experience you have had in which someone advised you to continue or to abandon a college education.

3. Using the sixth paragraph as a model, write a narrative essay based on having to explain and perhaps defend some action or stand that you have taken.

THE EXECUTION OF MARY, QUEEN OF SCOTS

JAMES ANTHONY FROUDE

James Anthony Froude was a noted British historian. As Paul T. Nolan says, he "read history as the account of actions of great men. Character description thus plays a larger part in his histories than in most."

"Allons donc," she then said—"Let us go," and passing out attended by the Earls, and leaning on the arm of an officer of the guard, she descended the great staircase to the hall. The news had spread far through the country. Thousands of people were collected outside the walls. About three hundred knights and gentlemen of the county had been admitted to witness the execution. The tables and forms had been removed, and a great wood fire was blazing in the chimney. At the upper end of the hall, above the fireplace, but near it, stood the scaffold, twelve feet square and two feet and a half high. It was covered with black cloth; a low rail ran round it covered with black cloth also, and the Sheriff's guard of halberdiers were ranged on the floor below on the four sides to keep off the crowd. On the scaffold was the block, black like the rest; a square black cushion was placed behind it, and behind the cushion a black chair; on the right were two other chairs for the Earls. The axe leant against the rail, and two masked figures stood like mutes on either side at the back. The Queen of Scots as she swept in seemed as if coming to take a part in some solemn pageant. Not a muscle of her face could be seen to quiver; she ascended the scaffold with absolute composure, looking round her smiling, and sate down. Shrewsbury and Kent followed and took their places, the Sheriff stood at her left hand, and Beale then mounted a platform and read the warrant aloud.

In all the assembly Mary Stuart appeared the person least interested in the words which were consigning her to death.

77

"Madam," said Lord Shrewsbury to her, when the reading was ended, "you hear what we are commanded to do."

"You will do your duty," she answered, and rose as if to kneel and pray.

The Dean of Peterborough, Dr. Fletcher, approached the rail. "Madam," he began with a low obeisance, "the Queen's most excellent Majesty"; "Madam, the Queen's most excellent Majesty"— thrice he commenced his sentence, wanting words to pursue it. When he repeated the words a fourth time, she cut him short.

"Mr. Dean," she said, "I am a Catholic, and must die a Catholic. It is useless to attempt to move me, and your prayers will avail me but little."

"Change your opinion, Madam," he cried, his tongue being loosed at last; "repent of your sins, settle your faith in Christ, by him to be saved."

"Trouble not yourself further, Mr. Dean," she answered; "I am settled in my own faith, for which I mean to shed my blood."

"I am sorry, Madam," said Shrewsbury, "to see you so addicted to Popery."

"That image of Christ you hold there," said Kent, "will not profit you if he be not engraved in your heart."

She did not reply, and turning her back on Fletcher, knelt for her own devotions.

He had been evidently instructed to impair the Catholic complexion of the scene, and the Queen of Scots was determined that he should not succeed. When she knelt he commenced an extempore prayer in which the assembly joined. As his voice sounded out in the hall she raised her own, reciting with powerful deep-chested tones the penitential Psalms in Latin, introducing English sentences at intervals, that the audience might know what she was saying, and praying with especial distinctness for her Holy Father the Pope.

From time to time, with conspicuous vehemence, she struck the crucifix against her bosom, and then, as the Dean gave up the struggle, leaving her Latin, she prayed in English wholly, still clear and loud. She prayed for the Church which she had been ready to betray, for her son, whom she had disinherited, for the Queen whom she had endeavoured to murder. She prayed God to avert his wrath from England, that England which she had sent a last message to Philip to beseech him to invade. She forgave her enemies, whom she had invited Philip not to forget, and then, praying to the saints to intercede for her with Christ, and kissing the crucifix and crossing her own breast, "Even as thy arms, O Jesus," she cried, "were spread upon the cross, so receive me into thy mercy and forgive my sins."

With these words she rose; the black mutes stepped forward, and in the usual form begged her forgiveness.

"I forgive you," she said, "for now I hope you shall end all my troubles." They offered their help in arranging her dress. "Truly, my lords," she said with a smile to the Earls, "I never had such grooms waiting on me before." Her ladies were allowed to come up upon the scaffold to assist her; for the work to be done was considerable, and had been prepared with no common thought.

She laid her crucifix on her chair. The chief executioner took it as a perquisite, but was ordered instantly to lay it down. The lawn veil was lifted carefully off, not to disturb the hair, and was hung upon the rail. The black robe was next removed. Below it was a petticoat of crimson velvet. The black jacket followed, and under the jacket was a body of crimson satin. One of her ladies handed her a pair of crimson sleeves, with which she hastily covered her arms; and thus she stood on the black scaffold with the black figures all around her, blood-red from head to foot.

Her reasons for adopting so extraordinary a costume must be left to conjecture. It is only certain that it must have been carefully studied, and that the pictorial effect must have been appalling.

The women, whose firmness had hitherto borne the trial, began now to give way, spasmodic sobs bursting from them which they could not check. "Ne criez vous," she said, "j'ay promis pour vous." Struggling bravely, they crossed their breasts again and again, she crossing them in turn and bidding them pray for her. Then she knelt on the cushion. Barbara Mowbray bound her eyes with a handkerchief. "Adieu," she said, smiling for the last time and waving her hand to them, "Adieu, au revoir." They stepped back from off the scaffold and left her alone. On her knees she repeated the Psalm, In te, Domine, confido, "In thee, O Lord, have I put my trust." Her shoulders being exposed, two scars became visible, one on either side, and the Earls being now a little behind her, Kent pointed to them with his white wand and looked inquiringly at his companion. Shrewsbury whispered that they were the remains of two abscesses from which she had suffered while living with him at Sheffield.

79

When the psalm was finished she felt for the block, and laying down her head muttered: "In manus, Domine tuas, commendo animam meam." The hard wood seemed to hurt her, for she placed her hands under her neck. The executioner gently removed them, lest they should deaden the blow, and then one of them holding her slightly, the other raised the axe and struck. The scene had been too trying even for the practised headsman of the Tower. His arm wandered. The blow fell on the knot of the handkerchief, and scarcely broke the skin. She neither spoke nor moved. He struck again, this time effectively. The head hung by a shred of skin, which he divided without withdrawing the axe; and at once a metamorphosis was witnessed, strange as was ever wrought by wand of fabled enchanter. The coif fell off and the false plaits. The laboured illusion vanished. The lady who had knelt before the block was in the maturity of grace and loveliness. The executioner, when he raised the head, as usual, to shew it to the crowd, exposed the withered features of a grizzled, wrinkled old woman.

One Point for Analysis: In the first paragraph, the repeated use of the word *black* suggests the somberness that is impending.

Writing Topics:

1. Tell the story of someone you know who is willing to die for a principle.
2. In the seventeenth paragraph, Froude's "voice" momentarily interrupts the essay. Following Froude, write a narrative in which you, at times, interrupt your story by inserting a personal comment.
3. Recount the execution of another famous person (Sir Thomas More, for example).

KNEE DEEP IN SCORPIONS

GERALD DURRELL

Brother of writer Lawrence Durrell, the author of this essay recounts a boyhood exploit that involved the two. (See "Towards an Eastern Landfall.") Gerald Durrell's lifelong interest in animals is reflected in this incident from his childhood.

Then one day I found a fat female scorpion in the wall, wearing what at first glance appeared to be a pale fawn fur coat. Closer inspection proved that this strange garment was made up of a mass of tiny babies clinging to the mother's back. I was enraptured by this family, and I made up my mind to smuggle them into the house and up to my bedroom so that I might keep them and watch them grow up. With infinite care I manoeuvred the mother and family into a match-box, and then hurried to the villa. It was rather unfortunate that just as I entered the door lunch should be served; however, I placed the match-box carefully on the mantelpiece in the drawing room, so that the scorpions should get plenty of air, and made my way to the dining room and joined the family for the meal. Dawdling over my food, feeding Roger surreptitiously under the table, and listening to the family arguing, I completely forgot about my exciting new captures. At last Larry, having finished, fetched the cigarettes from the drawing room, and lying back in his chair he put one in his mouth and picked up the match-box he had brought. Oblivious of my impending doom I watched him interestedly as, still talking glibly, he opened the match-box.

Now I maintain to this day that the female scorpion meant no harm. She was agitated and a trifle annoyed at being shut up in a match-box for so long, and so she seized the first opportunity to escape. She hoisted herself out of the box with great rapidity, her babies clinging on desperately, and scuttled onto the back of Larry's hand. There, not quite certain what to do next, she paused, her sting curved up at the ready. Larry, feeling the movement of her claws, glanced down to see what it was, and from that moment things got increasingly confused.

He uttered a roar of fright that made Lugaretzia [the maid] drop a

81

plate and brought Roger out from beneath the table, barking wildly. With a flick of his hand he sent the unfortunate scorpion flying down the table, and she landed midway between Margo and Leslie [the two other children], scattering babies like confetti as she thumped onto the cloth. Thoroughly enraged at this treatment, the creature sped towards Leslie, her sting quivering with emotion. Leslie leaped to his feet, overturning his chair, and flicked out desperately with his napkin, sending the scorpion rolling across the cloth towards Margo, who promptly let out a scream that any railway engine would have been proud to produce. Mother, completely bewildered by this sudden and rapid change from peace to chaos, put on her glasses and peered down the table to see what was causing the pandemonium, and at that moment Margo, in a vain attempt to stop the scorpion's advance, hurled a glass of water at it. The shower missed the animal completely, but successfully drenched Mother, who, not being able to stand cold water, promptly lost her breath and sat gasping at the end of the table, unable even to protest. The scorpion had now gone to ground under Leslie's plate, while her babies swarmed wildly all over the table. Roger, mystified by the panic, but determined to do his share, ran round and round the room, barking hysterically.

"It's that bloody boy again . . ." bellowed Larry.

"Look out! Look out! They're coming!" screamed Margo.

"All we need is a book," roared Leslie; "don't panic, hit 'em with a book."

"What on earth's the *matter* with you all?" Mother kept imploring, mopping her glasses.

"It's that bloody boy . . . he'll kill the lot of us. . . . Look at the table . . . knee-deep in scorpions. . . ."

"Quick . . . quick . . . do something. . . . Look out, look out!"

"Stop screeching and get a book, for God's sake. . . . You're worse than the dog. . . . Shut *up*, Roger. . . ."

"By the grace of God I wasn't bitten. . . ."

"Look out . . . there's another one. . . . Quick . . . quick. . . ."

"Oh, shut up and get me a book or something. . . ."

"But *how* did the scorpions get on the table, dear?"

"That bloody boy. . . . Every match-box in the house is a death-trap. . . ."

"Look out, it's coming towards me. . . . Quick, quick, do something. . . ."

"Hit it with your knife . . . *your knife*. . . . Go on, hit it. . . ."

Since no one had bothered to explain things to him, Roger was under the mistaken impression that the family were being attacked, and that it was his duty to defend them. As Lugaretzia was the only stranger in the room, he came to the logical conclusion that she must be the responsible party, so he bit her in the ankle. This did not help matters very much.

By the time a certain amount of order had been restored, all the baby scorpions had hidden themselves under various plates and bits of cutlery. Eventually, after impassioned pleas on my part, backed up by Mother, Leslie's suggestion that the whole lot be slaughtered was quashed. While the family, still simmering with rage and fright, retired to the drawing-room, I spent half an hour rounding up the babies, picking them up in a teaspoon, and returning them to their mother's back. Then I carried them outside on a saucer and, with the utmost reluctance, released them on the garden wall.

One Point for Analysis: After the escape of the scorpions, the actions and reactions of everyone (including the dog) are an example of slapstick.

Writing Topics:
1. Recount something you did that resulted in pandemonium.
2. Rewrite this essay from the mother's point of view.
3. Write a narrative essay about someone you know who is remarkably kind to animals.

LE PIRATE

RICHARD ATCHESON

Interested in human behavior, Richard Atcheson has published articles in a number of popular magazines and newspapers. This essay reflects his fascination with people and their involvements.

There is a crazy restaurant in the south of France where you are expected to eat well and copiously, to drink to excess, to listen to music and perhaps to spin to it—and also to break up the joint before you leave. The name of the place is Le Pirate. It sits on an otherwise empty stretch of rocky beach at Cap Martin and commands an unobstructed view across a bay to the lights of Menton. Relatively few people can avail themselves of the prospect, however, because Le Pirate, in addition to being wild, is wildly expensive.

The night I was there I was a guest in a party of 10 and so I never did discover what our bill was. Cost was never mentioned during the evening, and no prices are displayed, but I learned later that the *addition* at Le Pirate depends to a great extent on how much you break. Two American millionaires who departed one night without settling up must have done considerable damage because next morning they sent a messenger around with a leather pouch containing 2,000 gold pieces said to be worth about $1,000 altogether. For ordinary citizens, I am told, the equivalent of $50 a person would be on the lower end of the scale.

Frenchmen who know Le Pirate say it is very "American," a reference perhaps to the fact that what is of paramount importance is not the food but the total experience. The secret of the restaurant's success, put simply, is excess—loud, raw, tasteless, outrageous waste and profligacy. And for that one must play plenty.

My introduction to the place came when a French friend of mine called me up in Monte Carlo. "Tonight," he said, "we make a big party at Le Pirate. Americans like it very much. Frank Sinatra likes it very much. We shall break up the place. You come and you will see."

We drove along the coast to a rocky beach and parked in front of a high barricade with a gate in it. Some roughneck was leaning against the gate, picking his teeth with a knife. He could have been just another Côte d'Azur hippie, for he was stripped to the waist, had a scarf tied around his head and wore one gold earring, but in fact he was Le Pirate's only road sign, a sort of Elsa Maxwell version of a proper pirate.

My companions and I passed through the barricade and found ourselves in an open-air court with a few tables and chairs scattered around, and big rocky outcrops with open fires blazing away furiously in them. There were torches set on poles to provide flickering illumination as the twilight deepened.

Several bare-chested "pirates" were rushing around with trays of drinks, and popping flat round loaves of bread into and out of the fires. There was much yelling, swaggering, wrestling and showing off of high spirits. I took a martini from a nearby pirate and tried to get into this thing.

The people I was with were standing around making witty conversation, but I noticed that their eyes were rolling like crazy trying to take everything in, and when Le Pirate himself showed up—a tall, sallow, Satanic-looking guy with jangling gold coin necklaces and a toothy smile—our party gazed at him with undisguised amazement. His name is really Robert Viale, and he is as much entertainer as restaurateur; when he's doing his number (which is apparently all the time) he is given to grand and sweeping gestures, grandiloquent overstatement ("Eeeuuu are all my darrling fraahnds") and a sort of balletic direction of his staff. While he talks to you, hands out his business card and caresses the gold coins around his neck, he is simultaneously twitching, ogling and going "pssst" at his youthful employes, who are alert to his merest shrug, leaping six feet through the air to light the cigarettes of women who've only just started to fumble with their packs, bounding back to produce chairs for portly gentlemen who've only just begun to glance around for one. Le Pirate and his crew do nothing without flourish; you begin to realize that you are not just at a restaurant for dinner but are an integral part of a carefully choreographed event.

The drinks keep coming (this is *not* French) and the sunset is, perhaps therefore all the more remarkable. The yelping youths and Le Pirate himself begin to jolly and cajole you toward the door of the restaurant proper, then down a set of stairs into a low-ceilinged, wood-paneled room where colored-glass balls hang in fishnets from the pillars, the tables are covered with red-and-white checkered cloths and candles sputter everywhere. On one wall is a signed photograph of Frank Sinatra; lesser celebrities flank him.

As you sit down, more drinks are produced; then pirates rush forward with bowls and crocks and soon a steaming pile of *moules marinière* is before you, and other pirates are pouring white wine. Though you attempt to converse with your neighbors, there is such an urgency about these young men serving you and such an intrusive concern on the part of Le Pirate, who is swaggering from table to table, that it's hard to maintain a line of thought. Particularly when the mussels taste so good, and when Le Pirate suddenly claps his hands imperiously and shrieks for gypsies. Immediately the room is full of beautiful girls in bare-midriff dresses with polka-dot flounces, all going "yi-yi-yi" and "yip-yip-yip" and whirling and clapping their hands and stomping furiously on the floor right by your chair. Guitars are whanging, people are dancing and screaming, and you are so busy looking that you can hardly find your mouth with your fork.

The pace never slackens. On comes the soup, on comes the steak and the lobster (all very non-French this, but fine eats), and you scarcely notice because of the high jinks, not to mention the wine— bottle after bottle. And it's amazing how witty you've become after so much wine; whenever you can make yourself heard above the din your flushed companions positively roar with laughter at every- thing they think you're saying.

Le Pirate is keeping up a steady monologue in French; it's all about his life, about love and joy and unutterable sadness, and sometimes he's speaking and at other times singing. Soon the two become interchangeable, and at a certain point, he embarks on this long, melancholy song about how he's growing older and how his beloved son (there stands the lout, tall and blond and blushing a bit, accompanying his father on the guitar) wants to go his own way, to leave him (sob). But the song concludes that this is Right, this is Good, this is Joy. So out come the gypsies, screaming and stamping even louder; it's dessert time, champagne time, and while you're breaking a meringue with your spoon, the bubbly is surging forth from 10 bottles at a time, and Le Pirate is sampling each and the ones he doesn't like, he hurls full force into the fire.

So the corks are popping, the bottles are smashing, and you're still dining in a frenzy of drunken excitement when suddenly you find serpentine streamers by your plate and then the air is full of uncoiling colored paper and everybody is pelting everybody else. Now the music is augmented by horns and trumpets. There is screaming in the background and you turn to see that a braying donkey, garlanded with flowers, has been introduced into your midst; he is plodding up to your table and lowering his great gray muzzle into your plate; he is eating up your meringue and grazing your chin with his soft ears. At this point a lot of people are starting to fling their champagne glasses at the fireplace, so of course you do, too.

There is no shortage of champagne glasses—there are always more champagne glasses—and you keep drinking and throwing and find you have stepped directly Through The Looking Glass.

Because the plates now start to go SMASH! CRASH! Shards of glass and crockery are flying around the room. People seize the vases, flowers and all: ZOOM BOOM! The salts and the peppers, the tablecloths, the silverware are all in the air. Madness! Your companions are lifting up the table itself; tables rise on shoulders all over the room. There's a big parade of tables and drunks and gypsies and horn players out of the room, into the courtyard. The big fires in the stone outcrops are still burning, and the tables are flung into the flames, with everybody cheering and hollering and applauding. And as the heat rushes forward to your cheeks in the night air, as the warmth flares around you, people look at one another with wild eyes and wicked, heedless grins, and there is laughter from some deep-down, dangerous, untapped place.

And is the evening over now, in the light of these hungry flames? Hardly, because the son of Le Pirate happens to have a discotheque just across the road, and we can all skip and dance over there by the light of the moon, the moon, and rush in and dance off our energies in a final paroxysm of sweat, laughter, drinks and fragmented conversation.

The trouble for members of the bourgeoisie like me is that it's hard for us to take stuff like this in our stride. The rich don't have any problems with things like breaking up a joint; that's one of the ways in which they are different from us. They break something, they buy something else. The bourgeoisie survive Le Pirate, though, but their hearts may go boom-boom the whole night afterward.

Only the other Sunday there was a mention, in a story I read about Americans who like to live on the Riviera, of some "affluent American" who particularly prizes his Côte d'Azur villa because Le Pirate, his favorite restaurant, is only 20 minutes away. Never in a million years could I describe Le Pirate as my favorite—and I guess that marks one obvious difference between the rich (him) and the bourgeois (me). For all that I wouldn't have missed it for anything.

One Point for Analysis: This narrative essay is heavily laced with description.
Writing Topics:
  1. Write an account of an extraordinary evening you have had "on the town."

2. Recount an experience you, like Atcheson, enjoyed once but would not choose to repat.
3. Write a narrative essay in which you rely heavily on description.

A WELL IN INDIA

PEGGY AND PIERRE STREIT

The rigid caste system of India is vividly portrayed in this essay.

The hot dry season in India. . . . A corrosive wind drives rivulets of sand across the land; torpid animals stand at the edge of dried-up water holes. The earth is cracked and in the rivers the sluggish, falling waters have exposed the sludge of the mud flats. Throughout the land the thoughts of men turn to water. And in the village of Rampura these thoughts are focused on the village well.

It is a simple concrete affair, built upon the hard earth worn by the feet of five hundred villagers. It is surmounted by a wooden structure over which ropes, tied to buckets, are lowered to the black, placid depths twenty feet below. Fanning out from the well are the huts of the villagers—their walls white from sun, their thatched roofs thick with dust blown in from the fields.

At the edge of the well is a semi-circle of earthen pots and, crouched at some distance behind them, a woman. She is an untouchable—a sweeper in Indian parlance—a scavenger of the village. She cleans latrines, disposes of dead animals and washes drains. She also delivers village babies, for this—like all her work—is considered unclean by most of village India.

Her work—indeed, her very presence—is considered polluting, and since there is no well for untouchables in Rampura, her water jars must be filled by upper-caste villagers.

There are dark shadows under her eyes and the flesh has fallen away from her neck, for she, like her fellow outcastes, is at the end of a bitter struggle. And if, in her narrow world, shackled by tradition and hemmed in by poverty, she had been unaware of the power of the water of the well at whose edge she waits—she knows it now.

Shanti, 30 years old, has been deserted by her husband, and supports her three children. Like her ancestors almost as far back as history records, she has cleaned the refuse from village huts and lanes. Hers is a life of inherited duties as well as inherited rights. She serves, and her work calls for payment of one chapatty—a thin wafer of unleavened bread—a day from each of the thirty families she cares for.

But this is the haitus between harvests; the oppressive lull before the burst of monsoon rains; the season of flies and dust, heat and disease, querulous voices and frayed tempers—and the season of want. There is little food in Rampura for anyone, and though Shanti's chores have continued as before, she has received only six chapatties a day for her family—starvation wages.

Ten days ago she revolted. Driven by desperation, she defied an elemental law of village India. She refused to make her sweeper's rounds—refused to do the work tradition and religion had assigned her. Shocked at her audacity, but united in desperation, the village's six other sweeper families joined in her protest.

Word of her action spread quickly across the invisible line that separates the untouchables' huts from the rest of the village. As the day wore on and the men returned from the fields, they gathered at the well—the heart of the village—and their voices rose, shrill with outrage: a *sweeper* defying them all! Shanti, a sweeper *and* a woman challenging a system that had prevailed unquestioned for centuries! Their indignation spilled over. It was true, perhaps, that the sweepers had not had their due. But that was no fault of the upper caste. No fault of theirs that sun and earth and water had failed to produce the food by which they could fulfill their obligations. So, to bring the insurgents to heel, they employed their ultimate weapon; the earthern water jars of the village untouchables would remain empty until they returned to work. For the sweepers of Tampura the well had run dry.

No water: thirst, in the heat, went unslaked. The embers of the hearth were dead, for there was no water for cooking. The crumbling walls of outcaste huts went untended, for there was no water for repairs. There was no fuel, for the fires of the village were fed with dung mixed with water and dried. The dust and sweat and the filth of their lives congealed on their skins and there it stayed, while life in the rest of the village—within sight of the sweepers—flowed on.

89

The day began and ended at the well. The men, their dhotis wrapped about their loins, congregated at the water's edge in the hushed post-dawn, their small brass water jugs in hand, their voices mingling in quiet conversation as they rinsed their bodies and brushed their teeth. The buffaloes were watered, their soft muzzles lingering in the buckets before they were driven off to the fields. Then came the women, their brass pots atop their heads, to begin the ritual of water drawing: the careful lowering of the bucket in the well, lest it come loose from the rope; the gratifying splash as it touched the water; the maneuvering to make it sink; the squeal of rope against the wooden pulley as it ascended. The sun rose higher. Clothes were beaten clean on the rocks surrounding the well as the women gossiped. A traveler from a near-by road quenched his thirst from a villager's urn. Two little boys, hot and bored, dropped pebbles into the water and waited for their hollow splash, far below.

As the afternoon wore on and the sun turned orange through the dust, the men came back from the fields. They doused the parched, cracked hides of their water buffaloes and murmured contentedly, themselves, as the water coursed over their own shoulders and arms. And finally, as twilight closed in, came the evening procession of women, stately, graceful, their bare feet moving smoothly over the earth, their full skirts swinging about their ankles, the heavy brass pots once again balanced on their heads.

The day was ended and life was as it always was—almost. Only the fetid odor of accumulated refuse and the assertive buzz of flies attested to strife in the village. For, while tradition and religion decreed that sweepers must clean, it also ordained that the socially blessed must not. Refuse lay where it fell and rotted.

The strain of the water boycott was beginning to tell on the untouchables. For two days they had held their own. But on the third their thin reserve of flesh had fallen away. Movements were slower; voices softer; minds dull. More and more the desultory conversation turned to the ordinary; the delicious memory of sliding from the back of a wallowing buffalo into a pond; the feel of bare feet in wet mud; the touch of fresh water on parched lips; the anticipation of monsoon rains.

One by one the few tools they owned were sold for food. A week passed, and on the ninth day two sweeper children were down with fever. On the tenth day Shanti crossed the path that separated

90

outcaste from upper caste and walked through familiar, winding alleyways to one of the huts she served.

"Your time is near," she told the young, expectant mother. "Tell your man to leave his sickle home when he goes to the fields. I've had to sell mine." (It is the field sickle that cuts the cord of newborn babies in much of village India.) Shanti, the instigator of the insurrection, had resumed her ancestral duties; the strike was broken. Next morning, as ever, she waited at the well. Silently, the procession of upper-caste women approached. They filled their jars to the brim and without a word they filled hers.

She lifted the urns to her head, steadied them, and started back to her quarters—back to a life ruled by the powers that still rule most of the world: not the power of atoms or electricity, nor the power of alliances or power blocs, but the elemental powers of hunger, of disease, of tradition—and of water.

One Point for Analysis: The movement from the last sentence of the third paragraph to the first sentence of the fourth paragraph is the type of transition that gives remarkable clarity to this essay.

Writing Topics:

1. Tell the story of someone in your neighborhood who serves an important function yet is looked down on by those who live there.

2. In the style of Peggy and Pierre Streit, recount the story of some controversy in which the weaker of two parties must submit because of his weakness.

3. Write a narrative about the importance of one of many things we take for granted.

THE BULLFIGHT

KATHERINE ANNE PORTER

This Pulitzer Prize-winning author has pleased both critics and the public. Her popular novel is Ship of Fools.

I took to the bullfights with my Mexican and Indian friends. I sat with them in the cafés where the bullfighters appeared; more than once went at two o'clock in the morning with a crowd to see the bulls brought into the city; I visited the corral back of the ring where they could be seen before the corrida. Always, of course, I was in the company of impassioned adorers of the sport, with their special vocabulary and mannerisms and contempt for all others who did not belong to their charmed and chosen cult. Quite literally there were those among them I never heard speak of anything else; and I heard then all that can be said—the topic is limited, after all, like any other—in love and praise of bullfighting. But it can be tiresome, too. And I did not really live in that world, so narrow and so trivial, so cruel and so unconscious; I was a mere visitor. There was something deeply, irreparably wrong with my being there at all, something against the grain of my life; except for this (and here was the falseness I had finally to uncover): I loved the spectacle of the bullfights, I was drunk on it, I was in a strange, wild dream from which I did not want to be awakened. I was now drawn irresistibly to the bullring as before I had been drawn to the race tracks and the polo fields at home. But this had death in it, and it was the death in it that I loved. . . . And I was bitterly ashamed of this evil in me, and believed it to be in me only—no one had fallen so far into cruelty as this! These bullfight buffs I truly believed did not know what they were doing—but I did, and I knew better because I had once known better; so that spiritual pride got in and did its deadly work, too. How could I face the cold fact that at heart I was just a killer, like any other, that some deep corner of my soul consented not just willingly but with rapture? I still clung obstinately to my flattering view of myself as a unique case, as a humane, blood-avoiding civilized being, somehow a fallen angel, perhaps? Just the same, what was I doing there? And why was I beginning secretly to abhor Shelley as if he had done me a great injury, when in fact he had done me the terrible and dangerous favor of helping me to find myself out?

In the meantime I was reading St. Augustine; and if Shelley had helped me find myself out, St. Augustine helped me find myself again. I read for the first time then his story of a friend of his, a young man from the provinces who came to Rome and was taken up by the gang of clever, wellborn young hoodlums Augustine then ran with; and this young man, also wellborn but severely brought up, refused to go with the crowd to the gladiatorial combat; he was opposed to them on the simple grounds that they were cruel and criminal. His friends naturally ridiculed such dowdy sentiments; they nagged him slyly, bedeviled him openly, and, of course, finally some part of him consented—but only to a degree. He would go with them, he said, but he would not watch the games. And he did not, until the time for the first slaughter, when the howling of the crowd brought him to his feet, staring: and afterward he was more bloodthirsty than any.

Why, of course: oh, it might be a commonplace of human nature, it might be it could happen to anyone! I longed to be free of my uniqueness, to be a fellow-sinner at least with someone: I could not bear my guilt alone—and here was this student, this boy at Rome in the fourth century, somebody I felt I knew well on sight, who had been weak enough to be led into adventure but strong enough to turn it into experience. For no matter how we both attempted to deceive ourselves, our acts had all the earmarks of adventure: violence of motive, events taking place at top speed, at sustained intensity, under powerful stimulus and a willful seeking for pure sensation; willful, I say, because I was not kidnapped and forced, after all, nor was that young friend of St. Augustine's. We both proceeded under the power of our own weakness. When the time came to kill the splendid black and white bull, I who had pitied him when he first came into the ring stood straining on tiptoe to see everything, yet almost blinded with excitement, and crying out when the crowd roared, and kissing Shelley on the cheekbone when he shook my elbow and shouted in the voice of one justified: "Didn't I tell you? Didn't I?"

AN ANALYSIS OF "THE BULLFIGHT"

"The Bullfight" by Katherine Anne Porter is more than the simple narrative of a lazy afternoon at a corrida. Her presence there was an act that "had all the earmarks of adventure: violence of motive, events taking place at top speed, at sustained intensity, under powerful stimulus and a willful seeking for pure sensation." In three long paragraphs, she arrives at this concluding thesis. But in those paragraphs she narrates with labored introspection the process that led to this thesis, punctuated with rapid, excited phrases moving with the alacrity of the matador in his first dangerous encounter with the bull.

The first paragraph is a good contrast between those who know and live and love the sport, and the author, who "did not really live in that world, so narrow and so trivial, so cruel and so unconscious." And the contrast deepens because surprisingly what attracts the author, who unlike the aficionados is a "humane, blood-avoiding civilized being," is the anticipation of death in the bullring.

The second paragraph of the narrative alludes to an incident in the *Confessions of St. Augustine* in which a civilized young man finally realizes that he too has lust for blood in watching the gladiatorial games. The last paragraph consolidates the first two and leads to Ms. Porter's dramatic thesis.

The allusions to Shelley and to Augustine's friend supply the springboard for the author's narrative. But they are more than a springboard; they are the rationalization of her own fascination with death. In the frenzy of the kill, Shelley is figuratively there, shouting, "Didn't I tell you? Didn't I?"

The essay ends on this feverish pitch, and the reader is left with the feeling that he too has seen the kill of the "splendid black and white bull"; that he too has seen the blood. And though St. Augustine would disapprove, his young friend and Shelley and Porter are reason enough to make it all right.

ANGELS ON A PIN

ALEXANDER CALANDRA

Alexander Calandra, a university professor, recounts in this essay an unusual story involving relationships between teachers and students.

Some time ago, I received a call from a colleague who asked if I would be the referee on the grading of an examination question. He was about to give a student a zero for his answer to a physics question, while the student claimed he should receive a perfect score and would if the system were not set up against the student. The instructor and the student agreed to submit this to an impartial arbiter, and I was selected.

I went to my colleague's office and read the examination question: "Show how it is possible to determine the height of a tall building with the aid of a barometer."

The student had answered: "Take the barometer to the top of the building, attach a long rope to it, lower the barometer to the street, and then bring it up, measuring the length of the rope. The length of the rope is the height of the building."

I pointed out that the student really had a strong case for full credit, since he had answered the question completely and correctly. On the other hand, if full credit were given, it could well contribute to a high grade for the student in his physics course. A high grade is supposed to certify competence in physics, but the answer did not confirm this. I suggested that the student have another try at answering the question. I was not surprised that my colleague agreed, but I was surprised that the student did.

I gave the student six minutes to answer the question, with the warning that his answer should show some knowledge of physics. At the end of five minutes, he had not written anything. I asked if he wished to give up, but he said no. He had many answers to this problem; he was just thinking of the best one. I excused myself for interrupting him, and asked him to please go on. In the next minute, he dashed off his answer which read:

"Take the barometer to the top of the building and lean over the

95

edge of the roof. Drop the barometer, timing its fall with a stop-watch. Then, using the formula $S = \frac{1}{2}at^2$, calculate the height of the building."

At this point, I asked my colleague if *he* would give up. He conceded, and I gave the student almost full credit.

In leaving my colleague's office, I recalled that the student had said he had other answers to the problem, so I asked him what they were. "Oh, yes," said the student. "There are many ways of getting the height of a tall building with the aid of a barometer. For example, you could take the barometer out on a sunny day and measure the height of the barometer, the length of its shadow, and the length of the shadow of the building, and by the use of a simple proportion, determine the height of the building."

"Fine," I said. "And the others?"

"Yes," said the student. "There is a very basic measurement method that you will like. In this method, you take the barometer and begin to walk up the stairs. As you climb the stairs, you mark off the length of the barometer along the wall. You then count the number of marks, and this will give you the height of the building in barometer units. A very direct method.

"Of course, if you want a more sophisticated method, you can tie the barometer to the end of a string, swing it as a pendulum, and determine the value of 'g' at the street level and at the top of the building. From the difference between the two values of 'g,' the height of the building can, in principle, be calculated."

Finally he concluded, there are many other ways of solving the problem. "Probably the best," he said, "is to take the barometer to the basement and knock on the superintendent's door. When the superintendent answers, you speak to him as follows: 'Mr. Superintendent, here I have a fine barometer. If you will tell me the height of this building, I will give you this barometer.' "

At this point, I asked the student if he really did not know the conventional answer to this question. He admitted that he did, but said that he was fed up with high school and college instructors trying to teach him how to think, to use the "scientific method," and to explore the deep inner logic of the subject in a pedantic way, as is often done in the new mathematics, rather than teaching him the structure of the subject. With this in mind, he decided to revive scholasticism as an academic lark to challenge the Sputnik-panicked classrooms of America.

One Point for Analysis: The title, suggestive of excessive hair-splitting argumentation, is an excellent metaphor for what follows.
Writing Topics:
1. Like Calandra, write a narrative in which a practical solution was far better than a theoretical one.
2. After library research, write a sketch of Aristotle, the "father" of logical reasoning.
3. Recount the story of a student who rebelled at the way he was being taught.

MY DAYS IN BASEBALL

PHILIP ROTH

In 1960 Philip Roth won the National Book Award for fiction with his novel Goodbye, Columbus. *He is perhaps best known for* Portnoy's Complaint.

In one of his essays, George Orwell writes that though he was not very good at the game, he had a long hopeless love affair with cricket until he was sixteen. My relations with baseball were similar. Between the ages of 9 and 13, I must have put in a forty-hour week during the snowless months over at the neighborhood playfield—softball, hardball, and stickball pick-up games—while simultaneously holding down a full-time job as a pupil at the local grammar school; as I remember it, news of two of the most cataclysmic public events of my childhood—the death of President Roosevelt and the bombing of Hiroshima—reached me while I was out "playing ball."

I could never make the high school team, yet I remember that in one of the two years I vainly (in both senses of the word) tried out, I did a good enough imitation of a baseball player's style to be able to fool (or amuse) the coach right down to the day he cut the last of the dreamers from the squad and gave out the uniforms.

My disappointment, keen as it was, did not necessitate a change in my plans for the future. Playing baseball was not what Jewish boys of our lower-middle class neighborhood did in later life for a vocation. Had I been cut from the high school itself, then there would have been hell to pay in my house, and much confusion and shame in me; as it was, my family took my chagrin in stride and lost no more faith in me than I actually did in myself. They probably would have been shocked if I had made the team.

Maybe I would have been, too. Surely it would have put me on a somewhat different footing with this game that I loved with all my heart, not simply for the fun of playing it (fun was secondary, really), but for the mythic and esthetic dimension that it gave to an American boy's life (particularly one whose grandparents hardly spoke English). For someone whose roots in America were strong but only inches deep, and who had no experience, such as a Catholic child might, baseball was a kind of secular church that reached into every class and region of the nation and bound us together in common concerns, loyalties, rituals, enthusiasms, and antagonisms. Baseball made me understand what patriotism was about, at its best.

Not that Hitler, and the Bataan Death March, and the battle for the Solomons, and the Normandy invasion, didn't make of me and my contemporaries what surely must have been the most patriotic generation of American schoolchildren in our history (and the most willingly and successfully propagandized). But the war that began when I was eight and had thrust the country into what seemed to a child—and not only to a child—a struggle to the death ("unconditional surrender") between Good and Evil. Fraught with perilous, unthinkable possibilities, it inevitably nourished a patriotism that fixes a bayonet to a Bible.

It seems to be that through baseball I came to understand and experience patriotism in its tender and humane aspects, lyrical rather than martial or righteous in spirit.

To sing the National Anthem in school auditorium every week, even during the worst of the war years, generally left me cold; the enthusiastic lady teacher waved her arms in the air and we obliged with the words: "See! Light! Proof! Night! There!" Nothing stirred within, strident as we might be—in the end just another school exercise. But on Sundays out at Ruppert Stadium (a green wedge of pasture miraculously walled in among the factories, warehouses and truck depots of Newark's industrial "Ironbound" section), waiting for the Newark Bears to take on the enemy from across the marshes, the hated Jersey City Giants (within our church the schisms are profound), it would have seemed to me an emotional thrill forsaken, if we had not to rise first to our feet (my father, my brother, and me—together with our inimical countrymen, Newark's Irishmen, Germans, Italians, Poles, and out in the Africa of the bleachers, Newark's Negroes) to celebrate the America that had given to this disparate collection of men and boys a game so grand and beautiful.

Just as during my high school days I first learned the names of the great institutions of higher learning, not from our "college adviser," but from trafficking in college football pools for a neighborhood bookmaker, so I came to have a stronger sense of the American landscape from following the major league clubs in their road trips, and reading about the dozens of minor league teams in the back pages of The Sporting News, than from looking at maps of pioneer trails in school.

The size of the continent got through to you finally when you had to stay up to 10:30 p.m. in New Jersey (where it was raining) to hear via radio "ticker tape," Cardinal pitcher Mort Cooper throw the first strike of the night to Brooklyn shortstop Pee Wee Reese out in steamy Sportsman's Park in St. Louis, Missouri.

Not until I got to college and was introduced to literature did I find anything with a comparable emotional atmosphere and as strong an esthetic appeal. I don't mean to suggest that it was a simple exchange, one passion for another. Between first discovering the Newark Bears and the Brooklyn Dodgers at age 7 or 8 and first looking into Conrad's *Lord Jim* at age 18, I had done some growing up. I am only saying that my discovery of literature, and fiction in particular, and the "love affair"—to some degree hopeless, but still earnest—that has ensued, derives in part from this childhood infatuation with baseball.

Baseball, as played in the big leagues, was something completely outside my own life that could nonetheless move me to ecstasy and to tears, something that could excite the imagination and hold the attention with its minutiae as with its high drama—Mel Ott's cocked leg striding into the ball, Jackie Robinson's pigeon-toed shuffle as he moved out to second base, as deeply affecting over the years as that night—"inconceivable," "inscrutable," as any night Conrad's Marlow might struggle to comprehend—the night that Dodger wild man, Rex Barney (who never lived up to "our" expectations, who should have been "our" Koufax) not only went the distance without walking in half a dozen runs but, of all things, threw a no-hitter. A thrilling mystery, marvelously enriched by the

99

fact that a drizzle had been falling in the early evening, and Barney, figuring the game was going to be postponed, had eaten a hot dog just before being told to take the mound.

This detail was passed on to us by Red Barber, the Dodger radio sportscaster of the forties, a respectful, mild Southerner with a subtle rural tanginess to his vocabulary and a soft country parson tone to his voice. For the adventures of "dem bums" of Brooklyn—a region then the very symbol of urban wackiness and tumult—to be narrated from Red Barber's highly alien but loving perspective constituted a genuine triumph of what my literature professors would later teach me to call "point of view." Henry James might himself have admired the implicit cultural ironies and the splendid possibilities for oblique moral and social commentary. And as for the detail about Rex Barney eating his hot dog, it was irresistible, joining as it did the spectacular to the mundane, and furnishing an adolescent boy with a glimpse of an unexpectedly ordinary, even humdrum, side to male heroism.

One Point for Analysis: The closing summary paragraph is effective because of the references to individuals.

Writing Topics:

1. Recount an experience in which you or someone you know was "cut" from a team or some other group.
2. Roth says, "baseball was a kind of secular church." Write a narrative essay in which you tell of a significant group to which you belong that acts as a kind of secular church.
3. Roth says that his love for literature comes in part from his love of baseball. Using this essay as a model, recount how your great love for one thing has led you into a "love affair" with another thing.

A HANGING

GEORGE ORWELL

Having spent his boyhood in India, George Orwell was well aware of the influence of Britain on the colonies of its empire. He is best known for his political satires Animal Farm *and* 1984.

It was in Burma, a sodden morning of the rains. A sickly light, like yellow tinfoil, was slanting over the high walls into the jail yard. We were waiting outside the condemned cells, a row of sheds fronted with double bars, like small animal cages. Each cell measured about ten feet by ten and was quite bare within except for a plank bed and a pot for drinking water. In some of them brown silent men were squatting at the inner bars, with their blankets draped round them. These were the condemned men, due to be hanged within the next week or two.

One prisoner had been brought out of his cell. He was a Hindu, a puny wisp of a man, with a shaven head and vague liquid eyes. He had a thick, sprouting moustache, absurdly too big for his body, rather like the moustache of a comic man on the films. Six tall Indian warders were guarding him and getting him ready for the gallows. Two of them stood by with rifles and fixed bayonets, while the others handcuffed him, passed a chain through his handcuffs and fixed it to their belts, and lashed his arms tight to his sides. They crowded very close about him, with their hands always on him in a careful, caressing grip, as though all the while feeling him to make sure he was there. It was like men handling a fish which is still alive and may jump back into the water. But he stood quite unresisting, yielding his arms limply to the ropes, as though he hardly noticed what was happening.

Eight o'clock struck and a bugle call, desolately thin in the wet air, floated from the distant barracks. The superintendent of the jail, who was standing apart from the rest of us, moodily prodding the gravel with his stick, raised his head at the sound. He was an army doctor, with a grey toothbrush moustache and a gruff voice. "For God's sake hurry up, Francis," he said irritably. "The man ought to have been dead by this time. Aren't you ready yet?"

101

Francis, the head jailer, a fat Dravidian in a white drill suit and gold spectacles, waved his black hand. "Yes sir, yes sir," he bubbled. "All iss satisfactorily prepared. The hangman iss waiting. We shall proceed."

"Well, quick march, then. The prisoners can't get their breakfast till this job's over."

We set out for the gallows. Two warders marched on either side of the prisoner, with their rifles at the slope; two others marched close against him, gripping him by arm and shoulder, as though at once pushing and supporting him. The rest of us, magistrates and the like, followed behind. Suddenly, when we had gone ten yards, the procession stopped short without any order or warning. A dreadful thing had happened—a dog, come goodness knows whence, had appeared in the yard. It came bounding among us with a loud volley of barks, and leapt round us wagging its whole body, wild with glee at finding so many human beings together. It was a large woolly dog, half Airedale, half pariah. For a moment it pranced round us, and then, before anyone could stop it, it had made a dash for the prisoner and, jumping up, tried to lick his face. Everyone stood aghast, too taken aback even to grab at the dog.

"Who let that bloody brute in here?" said the superintendent angrily. "Catch it, someone!"

A warder, detached from the escort, charged clumsily after the dog, but it danced and gambolled just out of his reach, taking everything as part of the game. A young Eurasian jailer picked up a handful of gravel and tried to stone the dog away, but it dodged the stones and came after us again. Its yaps echoed from the jail walls. The prisoner, in the grasp of the two warders, looked on incuriously, as though this was another formality of the hanging. It was several minutes before someone managed to catch the dog. Then we put my handkerchief through its collar and moved off once more, with the dog still straining and whimpering.

It was about forty yards to the gallows. I watched the bare brown back of the prisoner marching in front of me. He walked clumsily with his bound arms, but quite steadily, with that bobbing gait of the Indian who never straightens his knees. At each step his muscles slid neatly into place, the lock of hair on his scalp danced up and down, his feet printed themselves on the wet gravel. And once, in spite of the men who gripped him by each shoulder, he stepped slightly aside to avoid a puddle on the path.

102

It is curious, but till that moment I had never realized what it means to destroy a healthy, conscious man. When I saw the prisoner step aside to avoid the puddle I saw the mystery, the unspeakable wrongness, of cutting a life short when it is in full tide. This man was not dying, he was alive just as we are alive. All the organs of his body were working—bowels digesting food, skin renewing itself, nails growing, tissues forming—all toiling away in solemn foolery. His nails would still be growing when he stood on the drop, when he was falling through the air with a tenth-of-a-second to live. His eyes saw the yellow gravel and the grey walls, and his brain still remembered, foresaw, reasoned—reasoned even about puddles. He and we were a party of men walking together, seeing, hearing, feeling, understanding the same world; and in two minutes, with a sudden snap, one of us would be gone—one mind less, one world less.

The gallows stood in a small yard, separate from the main grounds of the prison, and overgrown with tall prickly weeds. It was a brick erection like three sides of a shed, with planking on top, and above that two beams and a crossbar with the rope dangling. The hangman, a grey-haired convict in the white uniform of the prison, was waiting beside his machine. He greeted us with a servile crouch as we entered. At a word from Francis the two warders, gripping the prisoner more closely than ever, half led half pushed him to the gallows and helped him clumsily up the ladder. Then the hangman climbed up and fixed the rope round the prisoner's neck.

We stood waiting, five yards away. The warders had formed in a rough circle round the gallows. And then, when the noose was fixed, the prisoner began crying out to his god. It was a high, reiterated cry of "Ram! Ram! Ram! Ram!" not urgent and fearful like a prayer or cry for help, but steady, rhythmical, almost like the tolling of a bell. The dog answered the sound with a whine. The hangman, still standing on the gallows, produced a small cotton bag like a flour bag and drew it down over the prisoner's face. But the sound, muffled by the cloth, still persisted, over and over again: "Ram! Ram! Ram! Ram! Ram!"

The hangman climbed down and stood ready, holding the lever. Minutes seemed to pass. The steady, muffled crying from the prisoner went on and on, "Ram! Ram! Ram!" never faltering for an instant. The superintendent, his head on his chest, was slowly poking

103

the ground with his stick; perhaps he was counting the cries, allow-ing the prisoner a fixed number—fifty, perhaps, or a hundred. Ev-eryone had changed color. The Indians had gone grey like bad cof-fee, and one or two of the bayonets were wavering. We looked at the lashed, hooded man on the drop, and listened to his cries—each cry another second of life; the same thought was in all our minds: oh, kill him quickly, get it over, stop that abominable noise!

Suddenly the superintendent made up his mind. Throwing up his head he made a swift motion with his stick. "Chalo!" he shouted almost fiercely.

There was a clanking noise, and then dead silence. The prisoner had vanished, and the rope was twisting on itself. I let go of the dog, and it galloped immediately to the back of the gallows; but when it got there it stopped short, barked, and then retreated into a corner of the yard, where it stood among the weeds, looking ti-morously out at us. We went round the gallows to inspect the pris-oner's body. He was dangling with his toes pointed straight down-wards, very slowly revolving, as dead as a stone.

The superintendent reached out with his stick and poked the bare brown body; it oscillated slightly. *"He's* all right," said the superin-tendent. He backed out from under the gallows, and blew out a deep breath. The moody look had gone out of his face quite sud-denly. He glanced at his wrist-watch. "Eight minutes past eight. Well, that's all for this morning, thank God."

The warders unfixed bayonets and marched away. The dog, so-bered and conscious of having misbehaved itself, slipped after them. We walked out of the gallows yard, past the condemned cells with their waiting prisoners, into the big central yard of the prison. The convicts, under the command of warders armed with lathis, were already receiving their breakfast. They squatted in long rows, each man holding a tin panikin, while two warders with buckets marched round ladling out rice; it seemed quite a homely, jolly scene, after the hanging. An enormous relief had come upon us now that the job was done. One felt an impulse to sing, to break into a run, to snigger. All at once everyone began chattering gaily.

The Eurasian boy walking beside me nodded towards the way we had come, with a knowing smile: "Do you know, sir, our friend [he meant the dead man] when he heard his appeal had been dismis-sed, he pissed on the floor of his cell. From fright. Kindly take one of my cigarettes, sir. Do you not admire my new silver case, sir?

From the boxwalah, two rupees eight annas. Classy European style."

Several people laughed—at what, nobody seemed certain.

Francis was walking by the superintendent, talking garrulously: "Well, sir, all hass passed off with the utmost satisfactoriness. It was all finished—flick! like that. It iss not always so—oah, no! I have known cases where the doctor wass obliged to go beneath the gallows and pull the prissoner's legs to ensure decease. Most disagreeable!"

"Wriggling about, eh? That's bad," said the superintendent.

"Ach, sir, it iss worse when they become refractory! One man, I recall, clung to the bars of hiss cage when we went to take him out. You will scarcely credit, sir, that it took six warders to dislodge him, three pulling at each leg. We reasoned with him. 'My dear fellow,' we said, 'think of all the pain and trouble you are causing to us!' But no, he would not listen! Ach, he wass very troublesome!"

I found that I was laughing quite loudly. Everyone was laughing. Even the superintendent grinned in a tolerant way. "You'd better all come out and have a drink," he said quite genially. "I've got a bottle of whisky in the car. We could do with it."

We went through the big double gates of the prison into the road. "Pulling at his legs!" exclaimed a Burmese magistrate suddenly, and burst into a loud chuckling. We all began laughing again. At that moment Francis' anecdote seemed extraordinarily funny. We all had a drink together, native and European alike, quite amicably. The dead man was a hundred yards away.

One Point for Analysis: In the sixth paragraph, Orwell juxtaposes the horror of men with the happiness of an "irrational" animal.

Writing Topics:

1. Like Orwell, write a concrete narrative that clarifies an abstract notion.
2. Tell the story of some horrendous event that you or a friend witnessed.
3. Write a narrative in which you demonstrate that, with time, people forget horror.

CELLINI AND THE POPE

BENVENUTO CELLINI

*Cellini, a celebrated goldsmith of sixteenth-century Italy, is re-
membered not only for his* Autobiography *but also for his
bronze sculpture of Perseus.*

Not many days had passed before, my medal being finished, I
stamped it in gold, silver, and copper. After I had shown it to Messer Pietro, he immediately introduced me to the Pope. It was on a
day in April after dinner, and the weather very fine; the Pope was
in the Belvedere. After entering the presence, I put my medals
together with the dies of steel into his hand. He took them, and
recognising at once their mastery of art, looked Messer Pietro in the
face and said: "The ancients never had such medals made for them
as these."

While he and the others were inspecting them, taking up now the
dies and now the medals in their hands, I began to speak as sub-
missively as I was able: "If a greater power had not controlled the
working of my inauspicious stars, and hindered that with which
they violently menaced me, your Holiness, without your fault or
mine, would have lost a faithful and loving servant. It must, most
blessed Father, be allowed that in those cases where men are risk-
ing all upon one throw, it is not wrong to do as certain poor and
simple men are wont to say, who tell us we must mark seven times
and cut once. Your Holiness will remember how the malicious and
lying tongue of my bitter enemy so easily aroused your anger, that
you ordered the Governor to have me taken on the spot and
hanged; but I have no doubt that when you had become aware of
the irreparable act by which you would have wronged yourself, in
cutting off from you a servant such as even now your Holiness hath
said he is, I am sure, I repeat, that, before God and the world, you
would have felt no trifling twinges of remorse. Excellent and virtu-
ous fathers, and masters of like quality, ought not to let their arm in
wrath descend upon their sons and servants with such inconsid-
erate haste, seeing that subsequent repentance will avail them nothing. But now that God has overruled the malign influences of the
stars and saved me for your Holiness, I humbly beg you another
time not to let yourself so easily be stirred to rage against me."

The Pope had stopped from looking at the medals and was now

106

listening attentively to what I said. There were many noblemen of the greatest consequence present, which made him blush a little, as it were for shame; and not knowing how else to extricate himself from this entanglement, he said that he could not remember having given such an order. I changed the conversation in order to cover his embarrassment. His Holiness then began to speak again about the medals, and asked what method I had used to stamp them so marvellously, large as they were; for he had never met with ancient pieces of that size. We talked a little on this subject; but being not quite easy that I might not begin another lecture sharper than the last, he praised my medals, and said they gave him the greatest satisfaction, but that he should like another reverse made according to a fancy of his own, if it were possible to stamp them with two different patterns. I said that it was possible to do so. Then his Holiness commissioned me to design the history of Moses when he strikes the rock and water issues from it, with this motto: *Ut bibat populus*. At last he added: "Go, Benvenuto; you will not have finished it before I have provided for your fortune." After I had taken leave, the Pope proclaimed before the whole company that he would give me enough to live on wealthily without the need of labouring for any one but him. So I devoted myself entirely to working out this reverse with the Moses on it.

One Point for Analysis: In the first paragraph, Cellini asserts a tone of self-assuredness when he refers to his medal as a "mastery of art."

Writing Topics:
1. Relate an intimate account of one aspect of a particular artist's personality.
2. In a narrative about one of your accomplishments, imitate Cellini's tone.
3. After library research, recount a famous story from the Italian Renaissance.

AN ARDENT LOVE

PETER ABELARD

Peter Abelard was a twelfth-century philosopher who fell in love with his student Héloïse. It was a love affair that was to have drastic consequences.

Now there dwelt in that same city of Paris a certain young girl named Héloïse, the niece of a canon who was called Fulbert. Her uncle's love for her was equalled only by his desire that she should have the best education which he could possibly procure for her. Of no mean beauty, she stood out above all by reason of her abundant knowledge of letters. Now this virtue is rare among women, and for that very reason it doubly graced the maiden, and made her the most worthy of renown in the entire kingdom. It was this young girl whom I, after carefully considering all those qualities which are wont to attract lovers, determined to unite with myself in the bonds of love, and indeed the thing seemed to me very easy to be done. So distinguished was my name, and I possessed such advantages of youth and comeliness, that no matter what woman I might favour with my love, I dreaded rejection of none. Then, too, I believed that I could win the maiden's consent all the more easily by reason of her knowledge of letters and her zeal therefor; so, even if we were parted, we might yet be together in thought with the aid of written messages. Perchance, too, we might be able to write more boldly than we could speak, and thus at all times could we live in joyous intimacy.

Thus, utterly aflame with my passion for this maiden, I sought to discover means whereby I might have daily and familiar speech with her, thereby the more easily to win her consent. For this purpose I persuaded the girl's uncle, with the aid of some of his friends, to take me into his household—for he dwelt hard by my school—in return for the payment of a small sum. My pretext for this was that the care of my own household was a serious handicap to my studies, and likewise burdened me with an expense far greater than I could afford. Now, he was a man keen in avarice, and likewise he was most desirous for his niece that her study of letters should ever go forward, so, for these two reasons, I easily won his consent to the fulfillment of my wish, for he was fairly agape for my money, and at the same time believed that his niece would vastly benefit by my teaching. More even than this, by his own earnest entreaties he fell in with my desires beyond anything I had dared to hope, opening the way for my love; for he entrusted her wholly to my guidance, begging me to give her instruction whensoever I might be free from the duties of my school, no matter whether by day or by night, and to punish her sternly if ever I should find her negligent of her tasks. In all this the man's simplicity was nothing short of astounding to me; I should not have been more smitten with wonder if he had entrusted a tender lamb to the care of a ravenous wolf. When he had thus given her into my charge, not alone to be taught but even to be disciplined, what had he done save to give free scope to my desires, and to offer me every opportunity, even if I had not sought it, to bend her to my will with threats and blows if I failed to do so with caresses? There were, however, two things which particularly served to allay any foul suspicion: his own love for his niece, and my former reputation for continence.

Why should I say more? We were united first in the dwelling that sheltered our love, and then in the hearts that burned with it. Under the pretext of study we spent our hours in the happiness of love, and learning held out to us the secret opportunities that our passion craved. Our speech was more of love than of the books which lay open before us; our kisses far outnumbered our reasoned words. Our hands sought less the book than each other's bosoms; love drew our eyes together far more than the lesson drew them to the pages of our text. In order that there might be no suspicion, there were, indeed, sometimes blows, but love gave them, not anger; they were the marks, not of wrath, but of a tenderness surpassing the most fragrant balm in sweetness. What followed? No degree in love's progress was left untried by our passion, and if love itself could imagine any wonder as yet unknown, we discovered it. And our inexperience of such delights made us all the more ardent in our pursuit of them, so that our thirst for one another was still unquenched.

One Point for Analysis: The first paragraph is written in the style of a fairy tale.

109

Writing Topics:

1. Abelard was an eminent scholastic philosopher. Write a brief sketch of his life.
2. Write a narrative in which trickery leads to the gratification of some passion.
3. Recount a story in which there was a serious conflict between love and studies.

A VICTIM

BRUNO BETTELHEIM

Bettelheim, himself a prisoner in a Nazi war camp, is an eminent psychiatrist.

Many students of discrimination are aware that the victim often reacts in ways as undesirable as the action of the aggressor. Less attention is paid to this because it is easier to excuse a defendant than an offender, and because they assume that once the aggression stops the victim's reactions will stop too. But I doubt if this is of real service to the persecuted. His main interest is that the persecution cease. But that is less apt to happen if he lacks a real understanding of the phenomenon of persecution, in which victim and persecutor are inseparably interlocked.

Let me illustrate with the following example: in the winter of 1938 a Polish Jew murdered the German attaché in Paris, vom Rath. The Gestapo used the event to step up anti-Semitic actions, and in the camp new hardships were inflicted on Jewish prisoners. One of these was an order barring them from the medical clinic unless the need for treatment had originated in work accident.

Nearly all prisoners suffered from frostbite which often led to gangrene and then amputation. Whether or not a Jewish prisoner was admitted to the clinic to prevent such a fate depended on the whim of an SS private. On reaching the clinic entrance, the prisoner explained the nature of his ailment to the SS man, who then decided if he should get treatment or not.

I too suffered from frostbite. At first I was discouraged from trying to get medical care by the fate of Jewish prisoners whose attempts had ended up in no treatment, only abuse. Finally things got worse and I was afraid that waiting longer would mean amputation. So I decided to make the effort.

When I got to the clinic, there were many prisoners lined up as usual, a score of them Jews suffering from severe frostbite. The main topic of discussion was one's chances of being admitted to the clinic. Most Jews had planned their procedure in detail. Some thought it best to stress their service in the German army during World War I: wounds received or decorations won. Others planned to stress the severity of their frostbite. A few decided it was best to tell some "tall story," such as that an SS officer had ordered them to report at the clinic.

Most of them seemed convinced that the SS man on duty would not see through their schemes. Eventually they asked me about my plans. Having no definite ones, I said I would go by the way the SS man dealt with other Jewish prisoners who had frostbite like me, and proceed accordingly. I doubted how wise it was to follow a preconceived plan, because it was hard to anticipate the reactions of a person you didn't know.

The prisoners reacted as they had at other times when I had voiced similar ideas on how to deal with the SS. They insisted that one SS man was like another, all equally vicious and stupid. As usual, any frustration was immediately discharged against the person who caused it, or was nearest at hand. So in abusive terms they accused me of not wanting to share my plan with them, or of intending to use one of theirs; it angered them that I was ready to meet the enemy unprepared.

No Jewish prisoner ahead of me in the line was admitted to the clinic. The more a prisoner pleaded, the more annoyed and violent the SS became. Expressions of pain amused him; stories of previous services rendered to Germany outraged him. He proudly remarked that *he* could not be taken in by Jews, that fortunately the time had passed when Jews could reach their goal by lamentations.

When my turn came he asked me in a screeching voice if I knew that work accidents were the only reason for admitting Jews to the clinic, and if I came because of such an accident. I replied that I knew the rules, but that I couldn't work unless my hands were freed of the dead flesh. Since prisoners were not allowed to have knives, I asked to have the dead flesh cut away. I tried to be matter-

111

of-fact, avoiding pleading, deference, or arrogance. He replied: "If that's all you want, I'll tear the flesh off myself." And he started to pull at the festering skin. Because it did not come off as easily as he may have expected, or for some other reason, he waved me into the clinic.

Inside, he gave me a malevolent look and pushed me into the treatment room. There he told the prisoner orderly to attend to the wound. While this was being done, the guard watched me closely for signs of pain but I was able to suppress them. As soon as the cutting was over, I started to leave. He showed surprise and asked why I didn't wait for further treatment. I said I had gotten the service I asked for, at which he told the orderly to make an exception and treat my hand. After I had left the room, he called me back and gave me a card entitling me to further treatment, and admittance to the clinic without inspection at the entrance.

Because my behavior did not correspond to what he expected of Jewish prisoners on the basis of his projection, he could not use his prepared defenses against being touched by the prisoner's plight. Since I did not act as the dangerous Jew was expected to, I did not activate the anxieties that went with his stereotype. Still he did not altogether trust me, so he continued to watch while I received treatment.

Throughout these dealings, the SS felt uneasy with me, though he did not unload on me the annoyance his uneasiness aroused. Perhaps he watched me closely because he expected that sooner or later I would slip up and behave the way his projected image of the Jew was expected to act. This would have meant that his delusional creation had become real.

One Point for Analysis: The first paragraph is a general, complex statement of a problem. The rest of the essay clarifies this statement by narrative.

Writing Topics:
1. Following Bettelheim's method, state a complex problem, then clarify it by a story.
2. Recount an incident in which preconceived ethnic notions of a person were changed by the actions of someone in that ethnic group.

3. Recall a story in which you were severely affected by the weather.

STOKOWSKI IN REHEARSAL

MICHAEL KERNAN

This narrative sketch presents a striking portrait of a man who was for many years one of the world's leading orchestral conductors.

Shuffling onstage at Kennedy Center where the National Symphony Orchestra musicians were taking their places for rehearsal, Leopold Stokowski leaned on his rubber-tipped cane. As he started into a narrow file between rows of music desks, he saw that someone else was coming toward him and stepped aside with that patient prudence the old use in the face of headlong youth. (He had been a hurdles runner and a boxer once, in his Oxford days, but that was 70 years ago.)

The famous white mane—he used to have it spotlighted at concerts—was thinner than one remembered, and ruffled. The light-gray suit and dark-blue shirt looked just a little baggy on the spare frame, somewhat shrunken from the 6 feet 2 of his prime.

But he moved to the podium with deliberation, his fine hawk nose jutting and his hair blown back as though facing into a wind. He muttered a few words to the concertmaster, then stepped up carefully, set the cane aside and clapped his hands once without force. The sound was all but lost in the rich marmalade of musical tootlings and scrapings, whining arpeggios, aimless oompahs, scales and phrases that are an orchestra tuning up.

He clapped again. The oboe sang the pure A that everyone else tuned by. At last, silence.

"In the Mozart, at Number 4," he said, his head down over the score. The famous hands went up, the music started. Four bars later he clapped, and the musicians stopped raggedly.

"Bow separately, violins," he said. "Use your judgment. Think freely. When you bow together you can hear it, it makes an accent."

From *The Washington Post*, March 12, 1972. © 1972 *The Washington Post*.

(For generations conductors have insisted on all the bows moving together; this is one of Stokowski's most celebrated departures from tradition. Another: the violins were massed at the left and wood-winds on the right, tending, some critics said, to sacrifice sharpness of definition for powerful effect. The seating arrangements changed at almost every concert. Once at Philadelphia he put a piccolo player in the concertmaster's seat.)

Playing only a few measures each time, he took the group through the trouble spots of the previous two sessions. Mostly he wanted changes in volume. Asking the woodwinds for a certain effect, he was told it was not possible.

"Not possible?" he said softly. The whole orchestra sat there with a guilty smile, rebuked.

Again he clapped, the little dry-handed clap that by now commanded instant attention. It was time to work on the slow movement of Beethoven's Seventh Symphony, one of the most beautiful dirges ever written. One could see the logic of his seating now, for the melody and its counterpoint moved visibly from one string section to the next, a stately cortege.

And suddenly Stokowski was a different man. Thirty years dropped away. His arms carved the air with great legato sweeps, his glance flashed from one section to another, his whole body radiated energy. He pulled the players together, concentrated them at their very best to produce work of tremendous power, marvelously articulated and clear, speaking a grief beyond pathos. They played the whole movement without interruption. When it was over the conductor's shoulders slumped a little, the mouth sagged into its accustomed dewlapped petulance.

It was time for a rest period, and Stokowski leaned on the tall stool and sipped orange juice while the world bustled around him.

He was an authentic prodigy, playing Mozart, Beethoven, Chopin and Debussy at 7 on violin and piano. At 10, attracted by Bach's organ music, he learned the organ at a neighborhood church in his native London. Studying in England, France and Germany, he learned all the instruments, a vital part of the conductor's art, which must make an entire orchestra into a single instrument.

When he came to America at 18, he became a church organist in New York and a few years later took over the Cincinnati symphony.

It was not until his long association with Philadelphia, however, that his flair for publicity blossomed: the angry remarks addressed to noisy audiences (once he retaliated by having some of his musicians straggle in, coughing and shuffling, after he had started), the furious radio station scuffle in 1955 over his birthdate—his entry in *Who's Who* still carries the 1887 date he insisted on in the face of birth records—the movies he made, and the constant uproar over his musical innovations, his tinkering with instruments, seating, acoustics, amplifiers and the very notes of the masters, his Bach transcriptions, his refusal to use a baton, even his time-saving insistence that orchestras use scores from his personal library, marked in his own interpretation.

The National Symphony had such scores. They turned to the Moussorgsky now, brought to life by the handclap. Halfway through, jarringly, the whole section of first violins came in one bar too soon. All of them.

It was so shocking a sound that everything stopped. All eyes turned to Stokowski. He leaned toward the second violins and murmured conspiratorially, "What shall we do to them?" Everyone laughed.

For another hour he worked steadily, sharpening, tightening, clarifying. At the end, he called for a little Scriabin piece he had orchestrated, a special favorite ever since he had heard the great pianist in Paris when a child. Toward the end the harpist added a cadenza which Stokowski had requested. It seemed a bit elaborate. He clapped his hands.

"I asked for a cadenza," he said drily, "not a recital." Laughter.

They tried the passage again and finished. The musicians started to leave. His shoulders sank. He stepped off the podium, carefully.

One Point for Analysis: The parenthetical seventh paragraph allows the author to insert information that without parentheses would not be coherent.

Writing Topics:

1. Write a narrative in which you, like Kernan, begin your essay with a person performing a great feat, interrupt the action with a short biography of this person, and end by returning to the feat.
2. Recount the story of an old person who becomes vibrant when performing a task he loves.
3. After library research, write a story about Stokowski the motion-picture star.

115

weel
third of
en years old. On
ay, I stood on the
essed vaguely from
rying to and so i
I was about chap
waited on the step
the mass of honeys
and fell on my upt
unconsciously
ch had just c
I did no
surprise fo
rvel or suprise fo
upon me conti
ceeded

THE DESCRIPTIVE ESSAY

3

INTRODUCTION TO DESCRIPTION

When you try to tell a friend about an accident you saw on the way to school or about someone you recently met at a party, you are engaging in description. Description is the use of words to re-create an experience you have had so that your listener or reader feels that he too has had that experience. People who are unable to bring to life the person, object, or event they are trying to describe often end in frustration, saying, "Well, you just had to be there to understand." A few simple guidelines could help them to make their subjects seem quite real and close to their audience.

The writer of description wants to take you through an experience so that you sense it just as the writer did when it happened. He wants you to see it, hear it, feel it, even smell and taste it if those senses are involved. He does not tell you what the experience was like; he shows you what it was. A skillful writer of description would not write: "The girl was beautiful." Such a statement would present judgment, but you still would not know what she looked like. Was she tall or short? Blonde or brunette? Smiling or serious? You need to see for yourself. For example, notice how in "Memories of the Old South," Katherine Anne Porter shows you that the biscuits of her childhood were good. She says: "My father never forgot the taste of those biscuits, the big, crusty tender kind made with buttermilk and soda, with melted butter and honey, every blessed Sunday that came."

Sometimes a writer helps you to see and hear (or feel, taste, and smell) by comparing one thing to another or by speaking of one thing as if it were another. (See *Figurative Language,* Handbook.) In "The Big Sur" Henry Miller speaks of clouds as "huge iridescent soap bubbles." Because you know the impression the image of soap bubbles makes, you know what Miller wants you to sense about "a sea of clouds floating listlessly above the ocean."

118

The thesis statement of a descriptive essay is usually a sentence that summarizes the main impression the writer wants you to form about the subject. While reading the essay, you not only experience the subject being described, you also develop an attitude toward it. Each sensory detail provided by the writer helps you to arrive at an opinion about the nature of his subject.

Descriptive essays are much rarer than the other types of essays. Description more often supports and develops exposition, argumentation, and narration (particularly narration). Even when used in other types of discourse, description is not merely ornamentation. It is not included simply for the purpose of making one's writing appear to be more attractive. Whenever it is used, it has two purposes: to make the subject seem real and alive for the reader, and to express an attitude about that subject.

BIG BASH AT BILLY'S PLACE

STANLEY CLOUD

Stanley Cloud's description of the wedding of Billy Carter's daughter was written after Cloud had spent nearly three years covering the Carters for Time *magazine. He presents here an eyewitness account of the family gathering.*

Two Styrofoam swans, in full ostrich-feather plumage, floated serenely in the swimming pool, flanked by bouquets of roses and magnolia blossoms, at Billy Carter's place north of Plains. To the strains of the wedding march, Billy and his daughter Jana strode over a bridge built across the pool for the occasion. The bride wore white. Billy outdid the swans in his ruffled shirt and his pale, cream-colored tuxedo with brown piping and a broad brown stripe down each trouser leg. His hair is rapidly turning gray now, and he wept a little as he gave his 18-year-old daughter away to 19-year-old Johnny Theus, who works in an Americus mobile-home factory.

The President was there, with the First Lady and the First Child. So were 1,000 or so other folks. In the background were the rolling farm land and pine forests of south Georgia. In the foreground was Billy's new and modest mansion, 19 long miles from Plains, a kind

119

of post-bellum Tara, built out of brick and grit and Billy's determination to be an altogether different sort of person from his brother.

There were a few who were not there. The White House press corps, by and large, was not. Cousin Hugh Carter, who had just published a gossipy little book called *Cousin Beedie and Cousin Hot,* which prompted Billy to describe Hugh as "a self-made son of a bitch," was in San Francisco. And where was Sister Gloria, who prefers to march to her own drummer? Billy exhaled some cigarette smoke, sucked on his beer can and said, "How do I know? You know I haven't spoken to Gloria in 2½ years."

It didn't matter, Billy was in his element, reveling in himself, his nouveau wealth, his friends—good old boys and all—and the members of his family about whom he still cares. Actually Billy cares about a lot of people and things, but he chooses, for reasons Freud could explain even if Billy could not, to express his caring through outrageous behavior and flamboyantly bad taste. Jana's wedding was more than simply a wedding; it was Billy's great work of art, his moment of total self-expression.

From the isolated knoll on which his house is perched, one can scan the Georgia countryside. Billy wanted to be alone with his family when Plains became a place to see and now he is. For the wedding, cars jammed the farm land below the house and vans hauled guests up the hill. Beyond the pool were tables of food (roast beef, lobster balls) and booze (California pink champagne, Blue Nun wine, Billy Beer and gallons of harder stuff). A large aluminum boat was packed with ice and jammed with wine and champagne.

Not until after the Rev. Earl Duke had said "I now pronounce you man and wife" and the last strains of organ music had faded, did it start to rain. Everybody ran for cover, the ladies lifting their long dresses to avoid splattering them with red mud. In 30 or 40 minutes the skies began to clear. "It's stopped raining," the President announced. As if on signal, people began to return to poolside.

But Jimmy Carter evidently sensed that something was wrong and that he was it. After a respectable interval, he and Rosalynn and Amy said their goodbyes and headed home in their limousine. Now the real party could begin. The country-music band started to saw away. Some of the teen-agers complained that pot had been forbidden and so went after the booze as a poor substitute. Billy ripped off his tie and jacket and continued the binge that had begun the night before when he had thrown a party for 800 people at the local Best Western motel.

At the wedding, the drinkers went at it as if they were in a contest. Within an hour, 85 cases of beer had been consumed. Within two hours, the boat full of wine and champagne was empty. The glasses became scarce and people started drinking what was left directly from the bottles. They whooped and cheered and sang—and the sound rolled over the farm land that somehow had created it all.

A full moon hung in a damp mist overhead. Country-and-Western Singer Tom T. Hall sang at poolside. "Whisky's too rough," he sang, "champagne costs too much . . . as a matter of fact, I like beer." The guests cheered. The mother of the bride joined Tom T. Hall, and they sang a duet. "It may be peanuts to you," they warbled, "but it's love to us."

Finally, the party was ending. But not for Billy. He and a few friends drove over to the Best Western where a free bar had been set up. Everyone was tired. For the most part they drank silently. When he had had enough, Billy went home to bed. By the time he awoke, his brother, the President, was long gone from Plains, headed for an appearance in Tennessee.

Billy was alone again.

AN ANALYSIS OF "BIG BASH AT BILLY'S PLACE"

"Big Bash at Billy's Place" is not so much a description of a wedding as it is a particular portrait of Billy Carter—his unique behavior and bad taste. Both this behavior and bad taste establish the flippant tone that exists throughout most of the essay: "Two Styrofoam [with a capital *S*] swans, in full ostrich-feather plumage . . ."; "Billy outdid the swans in his ruffled shirt. . . ." Author Cloud has set the scene for buffoonery, accented by the presence of Jimmy Carter, "the First Lady and the First Child."

Basically there is a chronological organization in this essay. First we are given a description of the wedding place itself with, among other gaudy trappings, a "bridge built across the pool for the occasion." Then the hosts are depicted, together with the invited (in the case of Hugh Carter and Sister Gloria, the seemingly uninvited) guests. There follows a digression from the order of time. Correspondent Cloud gives a psychological brief of the man Billy, which states the thesis of the essay: Billy cares

121

about people and things, "but he chooses . . . to express his caring through outrageous behavior and flamboyantly bad taste." The wedding was "his moment of total self-expression."

After a short description of the isolated hill on which Billy lives and can be alone with his family, Cloud continues his march through time with a rather detailed account of food, booze, the marriage ceremony, and the rain that chased the guests into the house. Prophet Jimmy Carter announced that the rain had ceased. "As if on signal, people began to return to poolside." We are not certain here if Cloud is satirizing the shepherd, the sheep, or both. At any rate the incident is amusing and becomes more so when Jimmy realized that his eminent presence was perhaps affecting the party. So he left. Then the bash takes on monumental proportions. When most of the other guests have left, it even extends to the "Best Western."

Time has continued to mark organizational technique, but the concluding paragraph—one sentence—once again carries with it psychological overtones: "Billy was alone again."

The diction is essentially informal: Billy "sucked on his beer can"; his friends are "good ole boys and all"; country musicians began to "saw away"; teenagers went "after the booze." But these informal expressions are perfectly consistent with both the intimacy and tone of the essay.

And the strength of this essay lies in its tone and intimacy. But of the two, the intimate touch that Cloud bestows on Billy is significant and moving. Amid all this pompous display, a kind but perhaps unhappy man is momentarily glimpsed without his clown makeup.

THE WORLD OF MY APPLE TREE

ROBERT F. SISSON

Robert F. Sisson is a photographer for National Geographic. *This brief description shows how the most common objects of our world are fit subjects for observation.*

November 10   It has snowed all night. The ground is covered with about a foot of wet snow. The apple tree bows beneath the heavy white blanket. Here and there a red-faced York peers through. One large apple wears a cap of melting snow, and drops of water trickle down its sides.

Reprinted by permission of *National Geographic* magazine, June 1972, Vol. 141, No. 6.

A sow just plowed her way past the tree like a big tank, looking for fallen apples. Only a few hardy ones are left on the limbs, as if each is trying to be the last one.

I shake wet snow from some of the branches before they break, then head homeward for a good hot cup of tea. The old tree once again has come through a storm safely. But how many more can she ride out? Sleet coats her to the breaking point; summer sun bakes her, drying her to the roots. In spite of it all, she stands there on the hill, shelter and food to all. Good luck, old girl.

April 30   The morning sun comes skipping down the mountainside, pushing light and warmth into Harmony Hollow. Father Robin perches on a nest in my York Imperial apple tree, waiting for his mate to swoop in with breakfast for two greedy babies.

The old tree, on its Virginia hillside overlooking the barnyard, is a bit slow in dressing up. But after 70 years, being a little out of style is forgivable. Just today does she begin to blossom.

I come by my love for the tree in many ways. We both sit on the hill and watch. I watch the animals and birds that visit or live in the tree, and she watches over them for me.

I have another connection. My fourth great-uncle—so my grandmother said—was John Chapman, better known as Johnny Appleseed.

One Point for Analysis: Because the writer feels that the apple tree has a distinctive personality, he speaks of it as if it were a human being.

Writing Topics:
1. Write a description of the apple tree which is similar to these two, but dated August 1.
2. Describe some part of nature with which you feel a close kinship.
3. Describe a scene of nature as it appears in two contrasting seasons of the year.

PSYCHOLOGICAL PROFILES

NATHAN F. LEOPOLD

Now an ornithologist and medical researcher, Nathan F. Leo- pold shocked the world in the 1920's by committing a heinous Terrible *crime for which he was convicted and imprisoned.*

Dick was in high spirits. The main part of the scheme he had lived with and lived for for months was accomplished. The difficult part, the risky part. Now there remained only the collection of the ransom.

"That'll be a snap, Nate. Nothing to it. You saw how smooth this all went off. Just like I told you over and over it would. Are you convinced now that it was easy as falling off a log? And the rest will be even easier. We don't have to get within a hundred yards of any- body. Just sit safe and snug in that alley and wait for them to toss us the dough. Those rubes have about as much chance of catching up with us as a snowball in hell. What do you say, Butch, let's go out and have a few drinks after we make the phone call and mail the letter?"

"Wish I could, Dick. I could use a drink. But you know I have to go home and drive Aunt Birdie and Uncle Al home. And then I have to stay home, at least until after Dad goes to bed. It's my night to be home. Tell you what, though. I can probably sneak out later, when I'm sure Dad's asleep. Say about midnight or twelve-thirty."

"Naw, that's too late. Skip it. What would I do with myself till then? Those coppers will be getting a good night's sleep. We better too, so's to be in top form tomorrow to stay ahead of 'em. About two miles ahead!"

It seems like a nightmare now. Even then there was something feverish about conversation with Dick.

There it was again, that thought I'd had about Dick so often. You just couldn't figure the fellow out. Those quick alternations of mood, those sudden changes of mind. But then that was nothing compared to the real, fundamental contradiction in his character. Everybody went for the guy—and rightly so. There wasn't a sun-

124

nier, pleasanter, more likable fellow in the world. Why, I thought more of Dick than of all the rest of my friends put together. His charm was magnetic—maybe mesmeric is the better word. He could charm anybody he had a mind to. Lots of people who thought the world of him would be surprised to know his real thoughts about them. He looked down on nearly everybody. But they never knew it.

And he was at home with everybody. College presidents or hobos, it was all the same to Dick. He fitted in with everybody, became instantly a charter member of any group. He blended with his environment as some moths and butterflies do.

And all this he did so effortlessly. He seemed to have the inborn knack of making friends, of winning everyone's affection. I'd try deliberately to copy his mannerisms, to be consciously charming. I couldn't come close. More often than not I'd just alienate people, more so than if I hadn't made a conscious effort. But Dick didn't have to try. He just seemed able to push an imaginary button and turn on the charm.

And he could be generous to a fault.

But then there was that other side to him. In the crime, for instance, he didn't have a single scruple of any kind. He wasn't immoral; he was just plain amoral—unmoral, that is. Right and wrong didn't exist. He'd do anything—anything. And it was all a game to him. He reminded me of an eight-year-old all wrapped up in a game of cops and robbers. Dick, with his brilliant mind, with his sophistication!

And it wasn't only in big things like this crime we had just committed together. In little things too. Didn't he realize that I knew he was lying about his grades at school, for instance? "All A's," my foot. I had stolen a peek at his card in the registrar's office. Yet in spite of what I had seen with my own eyes, I still more than half believed him. Was he a little nuts—to lie about little things where he was almost sure to be caught in the lie? But what about me then? I must be a lot more nuts to let him get away with it. What power did he have over me? Was it hypnotism? Oh, bunk; that's for the birds. I just liked the guy so darn much, admired him so darn much, that my mind closed automatically to anything unpleasant about him. It just didn't register.

But how could a contradiction like that live in one body?

125

One Point for Analysis: Despite an abundance of clichés, the essay is an effective description of a sociopath.

Writing Topics:

1. Describe a complex person you know, introducing him by an example that employs dialogue.
2. Write, like Leopold, a description of another person in which you also reveal some part of your own personality.
3. Rewrite the description of Dick as a policeman would see him.

CANNIBALISM

LEWIS COTLOW

Cotlow's experiences as an explorer won for him the Gold Medal of the Adventurers' Club in 1937. Following his interest in primitive people, he has conducted numerous expeditions to the Upper Amazon and other parts of South America, as well as to Africa, New Guinea, and Ellesmere Island.

Tom Bozeman, who went into the Baliem as a missionary in 1956, has had many close brushes with death. Although he ascribed his safety to divine intervention, I was aware of considerable courage, quick thinking, and determination on his part—and, in similar circumstances, on that of other missionaries there. Perhaps the most deeply disturbing of Bozeman's experiences was his witnessing the eating of human flesh.

"Of course, it is ritualistic cannibalism," he told me. "They do not eat humans for food, although they say the meat tastes good, a lot like pork. They eat only the bodies of slain enemies, that being considered the worst insult one can give to his enemy. They don't eat every enemy by any means, but do it only when they are so angry and aroused that they must be as insulting as possible."

One day he and a fellow missionary saw some Dani warriors on their way past their station, returning from a big battle. They reported that they had won, and that they had killed one of the bravest warriors of the enemy group. They were going to cook him the next day, at the scene of the battle.

Reprinted with permission of Louis Cotlow from *In Search of the Primitive*, © 1966, Little, Brown and Company, Boston.

"When we got to the scene of the celebration the next day," Bozeman said, "there were hundreds already there, running around, chanting and singing their victory songs. Some women were beating the dead body viciously with their digging sticks, and hurling insults at it. It was very hot that day, so they had put some grass over the body in an effort to keep the sun from spoiling it too fast, but I could see enough to know that the enemy warrior had been speared many times."

The missionaries treated the wounded from the battle, and some others who were sick—and all the time the dancing and chanting went on, growing in force and madness. After about four hours, around noon, one man cut a long pole and laid it across the body. Other men got vines, with which they tied the body to the pole. Then they picked up the pole to carry the body back to the fighting area, about a mile and a half away. To carry out the insult properly, the enemy group had to see them cooking and eating the fallen warrior.

The enemy group was waiting on its side of a deep gulch that served as a boundary, in the hope that the body would be flung into the gulch so they could retrieve it. When they saw the huge crowd with the victors, they set up a tremendous wailing and moaning, calling and pleading for the return of the body. But those with the body called back that they were going to eat the hated enemy in view of his relatives and friends.

"While the fire was being built," Bozeman continued, "there was another hour or so of dancing and chanting which grew wilder and wilder. Women jumped up and down on the body; their hatred of it was something awful to see. And by this time the body was spoiling badly and the smell was terrible. I began to get sick at my stomach, but I had to see. I could not really believe what was happening before my eyes, and I still had to be convinced. I wanted to remonstrate, to stop them, but I knew that they were all so frenzied they would not hear me.

"Finally the men chased the women away and started the business of carving up the body. Some had bamboo knives, some steel knives they'd traded from us. Some had stone axes, a few had steel axes, while a few could find only jagged sharp rocks. First they cut off the toes, then the feet, and then the calves of the legs. Then they stripped the meat away from the bones. It was a reddish-purple color and I saw it plainly, for I was standing only a few feet away.

127

Next some men cut off the hands and went to work on the arms. One man couldn't get an arm off, so he draped it over a sharp rock, took up another rock and banged away at it until he got it free; a long strip of meat was left, clinging to the shoulder.

"A good deal of the meat was roasted there over the fire, cut up into small pieces and distributed through the crowd. No one person ate very much—that was not the point. As many people as possible wanted to participate in the insult to the enemy. Some of the meat was wrapped in leaves, to be taken home and cooked there for the old folks who couldn't travel. Every single bit of meat was used."

One Point for Analysis: The subject of this essay, like most bizarre subjects, fascinates many people.
Writing Topics:
1. After library research, describe a Voodoo ceremony.
2. Describe some rite of passage in which you move from one stage of your life to another by participating in a ceremony.
3. Describe a drunken party you have witnessed as the only sober person there.

THE DEATH OF A MOTHER

ST. AUGUSTINE

Born in Africa of a pagan father and Christian mother, Augustine marks a transition from Classical Rome to the early Middle Ages.

I closed her eyes, and a great flood of sorrow swept into my heart and would have overflowed in tears. But my eyes obeyed the forcible dictate of my mind and seemed to drink that fountain dry. Terrible indeed was my state as I struggled so. And then, when she had breathed her last, the boy Adeodatus burst out into loud cries until all the rest of us checked him, and he became silent. In the same way something childish in me which was bringing me to the brink of tears was, when I heard the young man's voice, the voice of the heart, brought under control and silenced. For we did not

From *The Confessions of St. Augustine,* translated by Rex Warner. Copyright © 1963 by Rex Warner. Reprinted by arrangement with The New American Library, Inc., New York, N.Y.

think it right that a funeral such as hers should be celebrated with tears and groans and lamentations. These are ways in which people grieve for an utter wretchedness in death or a kind of total extinction. But she did not die in misery, nor was she altogether dead. Of this we had good reason to be certain from the evidence of her character and from a faith that was not feigned.

Why, then, did I feel such pain within me? It was because the wound was still fresh, the wound caused by the sudden breaking off of our old way of living together in such sweet affection. I was glad indeed to have the testimony which she gave me in these very last days of her illness when, as I was doing what service I could for her, she spoke so affectionately to me, calling me her good and dutiful son, and, with such great love, she told me that she had never once heard me say a word to her that was hard or bitter. And yet, my God who made us, what comparison was there between the respect I paid to her and the slavery she offered to me? And so, now that I had lost that great comfort of her, my soul was wounded and my life was, as it were, torn apart, since it had been a life made up of hers and mine together.

One Point for Analysis: The subject of the description is not merely the death of St. Monica but also St. Augustine's emotional and intellectual reaction to it.

Writing Topics:
1. Recall some crisis you have faced and describe both your emotional and intellectual reaction to it.
2. By describing some occasion of grief, imply the thesis that grief is essentially selfish.
3. Describe the contrasting responses of a child and an adult to the same important event.

THE GOLDEN EAGLE

WALTER R. SPOFFORD

Walter R. Spofford's admiration for the golden eagle is evident in his description of its mating ritual.

Cresting the low pass, first one eagle and then the second sailed on partly flexed wings—two dark shapes as silent as their shadows that raced along the slope below. . . . Now they wheeled in an updraft of air, spiraled, and topped the ridge. Their circles of flight tightened, crossed, and recrossed. At times the long-feathered legs and feet of the male seemed to touch the back of his larger mate.

Suddenly the eagles interlocked talons, and with wings outspread, they cartwheeled down the sky in a breathtaking spectacle.

Separating from his mate, the male shot upward and dropped. With wings folded close to his body, his speed quickened. A dark wedge, he hurtled earthward at nearly 200 miles an hour. Just as he seemed about to crash into the treetops below, his wings opened, spread hard, and he banked steeply upward. With powerful thrusts he bounded high until, closing his wings again into a flying wedge, he made an arc against the sky. . . . Slowing, like a spent rocket, he folded backward into a second headlong plunge.

The nuptial flight was reaching its climax. The female followed her mate in each figure of the sky dance. At times the pair tumbled backward over and over, slid sideways down the sky, and then rose again in great continuing arcs.

No longer silent, the eagles chittered excitedly down long spans of air. After a half hour of ecstatic display, one eagle shallowed out of a steep descent and landed gently on a grassy knoll of the ridge. Immediately the other followed, and the great birds with their golden hackles rested. Then for a few seconds, the cock mounted the hen and spread his wings slightly. Afterward, side by side, they stood, looking off into the distance for nearly half an hour.

One Point for Analysis: Many of the words used in this description of the mating of two eagles are sexually oriented.

From "The Golden Eagles" by Walter R. Spofford. From the book, *Alive in the Wild*, edited by Victor H. Calahane. © 1960 by Prentice-Hall, Inc. Published by Prentice-Hall, Inc., Englewood Cliffs, New Jersey.

Writing Topics:

1. After library research, write a descriptive essay about the bald eagle.
2. Observe for an uninterrupted period of time one insect or animal. Write a descriptive essay about its behavior.
3. Throughout the ages animals have worked with people to carry out human activities. Write a descriptive essay about one such relationship.

MORNING ON THE SAVANNA

COLIN FLETCHER

Explorer and man of many trades, Colin Fletcher has seen much of the world in unorthodox ways. He is the author of The Man Who Walked Through Time, *an account of a two-month solitary hike through the Grand Canyon.*

You can become aware that something has stirred at the back of your mind long before a shape emerges. And after it is all over and you can look back down the floodlit tunnel of hindsight you may well see that what finally emerged was big enough and solid enough to deflect the tide race of your life. But all you know at the time, to begin with, are the minutes and hours of another day.

The first morning at Keekorok we left the lodge early and drove north across the pale savanna. At least, I think we went north. It is something of a surprise, the way I know that corner of the Mara now, to find that I am not at all sure where we were, just after sunrise, when I touched our driver on his arm and nodded toward a big herd of zebras. But I can still remember the grass, all around us, when he swung the Volkswagen minibus off the track and up an open slope. The grass was long and dry and it glowed golden in the slanting sunlight.

We stopped sixty yards from the zebras and stood up, heads and shoulders out above the sliding roof. The air was still cold but the sun struck warm and welcome where it found bare skin. The other three vehicles of my party pulled up alongside so that we formed an

From *The Winds of Mara,* by Colin Fletcher. Copyright © 1972 by Colin Fletcher. Reprinted by permission of Alfred A. Knopf, Inc.

131

impromptu little grandstand out there in the open. I could smell the grass now, with its blend of dust and life. It rustled, very faintly.

The sunlight, slanting forward over our shoulders, fell full on the zebras. Their stripes stood out sharp as test patterns on a TV screen. There were eighty or a hundred of them, bunched tight, midway between us and a wedge of dark trees. We stood watching them through binoculars.

And then the lions came out of the trees.

They came in loose line abreast, making no attempt to conceal themselves. They walked slowly and lazily, low-slung bodies dark gold against the pale golden grass, all twenty of them moving steadily toward the zebras.

The zebras bunched tighter still, every animal alert and facing the danger. The lions kept coming. The zebras edged away to the left, out of the lions' path. The lions held the course. The zebras, reassured, halted.

The lions continued their slow and lazy passage, directly toward us. Once a lioness stopped and turned her head to look briefly at the zebras, then walked on. A trio of cubs began to romp and tumble; an adult cuffed them into order. The gap between us narrowed. Soon we could see magnificently self-assured expressions on golden faces; then rib cages showing faintly, sculpturally; then muscles rippling beneath powerful haunches. Eventually it seemed as if we could see each hair adjusting to the animals' slow and lazy movements. Before long the whole pride, somewhat scattered now, was threading its way among our vehicles. Several of the beasts passed so close that you felt you could reach out and touch the long, lean, golden bodies. Then they were moving away from us, into the sun, and the detail had gone. I could almost hear my people let our their collective breath.

It would be difficult, I think, to say just what had held us. After all, there had been no drama—no ferocious snarling, no skirmish in the dust, no sudden slaughter. And the quiet scene had lasted, I suppose, less than ten minutes. But there had been more to it than the lions' perfectly timed entrance. More to it than their languid and graceful and arrogant passage across the stage. More to it, even, than the vivid morning sunlight. But perhaps the light was the essence: it touched the scene with a freshness that seemed to have been distilled from the dawn of more than one perfect and passing day.

132

We drove slowly after the lions, taking care not to disturb them. All of us, I think, were conscious of that warm sense of privilege you get when you are lucky enough to watch, close up, as truly wild animals go about their quiet business. And something may have stirred in my mind, even then.

Soon we were watching the pride drink in small groups from a grass-fringed pool. We were so close that we could see their tongues curl into pink, flexile ladles that lapped up the water with the same deft and astonishing motion by which a house cat's tongue annexes milk. When they raised their heads from the pool we could see water glistening on pale whiskers.

An old male, ignoring our vehicles in the extraordinary way that lions nearly always do, walked slowly over to the bus I was in. He moved with an aloof, languid kind of arrogance that is rarely achieved anywhere outside England. Still ignoring us, he lay down in the bus's shadow. His huge, regally maned head was less than six feet from mine and I could see the outline of every scar on his broad nose, the mottled inlay of pink on the black skin of his nostrils, and the parallel lines of neat black dots along the roots of his whiskers. When he deigned to look up at us—with an uncomprehending and curiously inefficient kind of stare—I found myself looking down into golden eyes with pupils that were not large and elliptical but small and round and quite uncatlike.

One Point for Analysis: The images used in this essay are strong, clear, visual pictures.

Writing Topics:

1. Write a description of a scene from nature that relies exclusively on visual images.
2. Write a description that relies on images that appeal solely to one of the senses besides the visual.
3. Describe an experience in which you felt close to an animal or person of whom you would ordinarily be afraid.

WILD HORSES

J. FRANK DOBIE

J. Frank Dobie was a noted folklorist of the Southwest. He taught at Cambridge University and at the University of Texas. One of his most important works is The Longhorns.

Although wild horses cooperated in many ways, mareless stallions did not combine with each other to overcome a possessor of mares. Sometimes while two herd-masters were contending midway between their passive bands, a bachelor tried to steal a mare, but as soon as her master became aware of the thief he broke away from the fight to retrieve his property.

Immediately before an engagement, the stallions, tails straight out or raised to an angle of about forty-five degrees, would prance, rush back and forth, nicker and whistle with a shrillness that could be heard a mile away. The combatants met each other walking on hind legs striking with forefeet, ears laid back, mouths open, teeth bared. They raked the hide from each other, made deep cuts. They screamed. Their teeth slipping off firm flesh clicked together. They sought jugular veins. They lunged their whole weight against each other. Now one or both whirled with catlike rapidity and kicked like a pile-driver. A pair of flying heels hitting against another pair of flying heels cracked like a whipsnap of lightning. Those heels could crash a hock or cave in a rib. Unless the weaker ran—and he often chose the better part of valor—he went to the ground, there to be pounded with iron-hard clubs and lacerated between steel-strong, ivory-spiked jaws.

After going to the ground, a stallion was lucky if he could regain his feet and run. The victor might follow a runaway for a mile, tearing at him with every jump. If the runaway had mares, some might escape with him, but the conqueror was likely to take some. Sometimes the fighters were evenly matched. Cheyenne warriors once rode up on two stallions, each the dominator of a band of mares, too exhausted from long fighting to run away. Great strips had been jerked from their hides, and the nostrils of one had been torn off.

Perhaps no wild animal had to stay on guard more unremittingly than the mustang stallion. On approaching water, he tested the ground around it before allowing the mares and colts to drink. He smelled for the dung of a competing stallion, for sign of lurking panther or man. If something aroused his faintest suspicion, he stood, advanced, retreated, waited, looked a long time. If assured of danger, he ordered immediate retreat. Only at his signal did the band enter the water. They came eagerly, drank deep; some pawed and rolled. Their monarch gave the signal to race to clear ground.

One Point for Analysis: In the description of the fight, Dobie uses words which by their sounds make the struggle more vivid—e.g., *striking, clicked, cracked, whip-snap, crash.*

Writing Topics:

1. Describe a fight you have witnessed between two animals.
2. Describe a dispute between two people that parallels that of the stallions.
3. Write a description that uses words that help to create the effect by their sounds.

MEMORIES OF THE OLD SOUTH

KATHERINE ANNE PORTER

A native-born Texan, Katherine Anne Porter sometimes reveals her Southern background in her writing. She is principally a short story writer interested in portraying the psychology of human relations.

I am the grandchild of a lost War, and I have blood-knowledge of what life can be in a defeated country on the bare bones of privation. The older people in my family used to tell such amusing little stories about it. One time, several years after the War ended, two small brothers (one of them was my father) set out by themselves on foot from their new home in south Texas, and when neighbors picked them up three miles from home, hundreds of miles from their goal, and asked them where they thought they were going, they answered confidently, "To Louisiana, to eat sugar cane," for they hadn't tasted sugar for months and remembered the happy times in my grandmother's cane fields there.

"Portrait: Old South" excerpted from the book *The Collected Essays and Occasional Writings of Katherine Anne Porter*. Originally published in *Mademoiselle*. Copyright © 1944 by Katherine Anne Porter. Reprinted by permission of Delacorte Press/Seymour Lawrence.

Does anyone remember the excitement when for a few months we had rationed coffee? In my grandmother's day, in Texas, everybody seemed to remember that man who had a way of showing up with a dozen grains of real coffee in his hand, which he exchanged for a month's supply of corn meal. My grandmother parched a mixture of sweet potato and dried corn until it was black, ground it up and boiled it, because her family couldn't get over its yearning for a dark hot drink in the mornings. But she would never allow them to call it coffee. It was known as That Brew. Bread was a question, too. Wheat flour, during the period euphemistically described as Reconstruction, ran about $100 a barrel. Naturally my family ate corn bread, day in, day out, for years. Finally Hard Times eased up a little, and they had hot biscuits, nearly all they could eat, once a week for Sunday breakfast. My father never forgot the taste of those biscuits, the big, crusty tender kind made with buttermilk and soda, with melted butter and honey, every blessed Sunday that came. "They almost made a Christian of me," he said.

My grandfather, a soldier, toward the end of the War was riding along one very cold morning, and he saw, out of all reason, a fine big thick slice of raw bacon rind lying beside the road. He dismounted, picked it up, dusted it off and made a hearty breakfast of it. "The best piece of bacon rind I ever ate in my life," said my grandfather. These little yarns are the first that come to mind out of hundreds; they were the merest surface ripples over limitless deeps of bitter memory. My elders all remained nobly unreconstructed to their last moments, and my feet rest firmly on this rock of their strength to this day.

The woman who made That Brew and the soldier who ate the bacon rind had been bride and groom in a Kentucky wedding somewhere around 1850. Only a few years ago a cousin of mine showed me a letter from a lady then rising ninety-five who remembered that wedding as if it had been only yesterday. She was one of the flower girls, carrying a gilded basket of white roses and ferns, tied with white watered-silk ribbon. She couldn't remember whether the bride's skirt had been twenty-five feet or twenty-five yards around, but she inclined to the latter figure; it was of white satin brocade with slippers to match.

The flower girl was allowed a glimpse of the table set for the bridal banquet. There were silver branched candlesticks everywhere, each holding seven white candles, and a crystal chandelier holding fifty white candles, all lighted. There was a white lace tablecloth reaching to the floor all around, over white satin. The wedding cake was tall as the flower girl and of astonishing circumference, festooned all over with white sugar roses and green leaves. The room, she wrote, was a perfect bower of southern smilax and white dogwood. And there was butter. This is a bizarre note, but there was an enormous silver butter dish, *with feet* (italics mine), containing at least ten pounds of butter. The dish had cupids and some sort of fruit around the rim, and the butter was molded or carved, to resemble a set-piece of roses and lilies, every petal and leaf standing out sharply, natural as life. The flower girl, after the lapse of nearly a century, remembered no more than this, but I think it does well for a glimpse.

That butter. She couldn't get over it, and neither can I. It seems as late-Roman and decadent as anything ever thought up in Hollywood. Her memory came back with a rush when she thought of the food. All the children had their own table in a small parlor, and ate just what the grownups had: Kentucky ham, roast turkey, partridges in wine jelly, fried chicken, dove pie, half a dozen sweet and hot sauces, peach pickle, watermelon pickle and spiced mangoes. A dozen different fruits, four kinds of cake and at last a chilled custard in tall glasses with whipped cream capped by a brandied cherry. She lived to boast of it, and she lived along with other guests of that feast to eat corn pone and bacon fat, and yes, to be proud of that also. Why not? She was in the best of company, and quite a large gathering too.

In my childhood we ate, my father remarked, "as if there were no God." By then my grandmother, her brocaded wedding gown cut up and made over to the last scrap for a dozen later brides in the connection, had become such a famous cook it was mentioned in her funeral eulogies. There was nobody like her for getting up a party, for the idea of food was inseparably connected in her mind with social occasions of a delightful nature, and though she loved to celebrate birthdays and holidays, still any day was quite good enough to her. Several venerable old gentlemen, lifelong friends of my grandmother, sat down, pen in hand, after her death and out of their grateful recollection of her bountiful hospitality—their very words—wrote long accounts of her life and works for the local newspapers of their several communities, and each declared that at one time or another he had eaten the best dinner of his life at her table. The furnishings of her table were just what were left over from times past, good and bad; a mixture of thin old silver and bone-handled knives, delicate porcelain, treasured but not hoarded, and such crockery as she had been able to replace with; fine old linen worn thin and mended, and stout cotton napery with fringed borders; no silver candlesticks at all, and a pound of sweet butter with a bouquet of roses stamped upon it, in a plain dish—plain for the times; it was really a large opal-glass hen seated on a woven nest, rearing aloft her scarlet comb and beady eye.

Grandmother was by nature lavish, she loved leisure and calm, she loved luxury, she loved dress and adornment, she loved to sit and talk with friends or listen to music; she did not in the least like pinching or saving and mending and making things do, and she had no patience with the kind of slackness that tried to say second-best was best, or half good enough. But the evil turn of fortune in her life tapped the bottomless reserves of her character, and her life was truly heroic. She had no such romantic notion of herself. The long difficulties of her life she regarded as temporary, an unnatural interruption to her normal fate, which required simply firmness, a good deal of will-power and energy and the proper aims to re-establish finally once more. That no such change took place during her long life did not in the least disturb her theory. Though we had no money and no prospects of any, and were land-poor in the most typical way, we never really faced this fact as long as our grandmother lived because she would not hear of such a thing. We had been a good old family of solid wealth and property in Kentucky, Louisiana and Virginia, and we remained that in Texas, even though due to a temporary decline for the most honorable reasons, appearances were entirely to the contrary. This accounted for our fragmentary, but strangely useless and ornamental education, appropriate to our history and our station in life, neither of which could be in the least altered by the accident of straitened circumstances.

AN ANALYSIS OF "MEMORIES OF THE OLD SOUTH"

The remembrances Katherine Anne Porter shares in "Memories of the Old South" appear to be presented in random order, without any overall design or purpose. Such is not the case, however. They are, in fact, carefully structured to leave the reader with a picture of far more than the writer has actually discussed. Through a description of her grandmother at three separate periods of her life, Porter gives a sense of an entire family's background and, even more generally, of the people of a region and an era.

Porter suggests her intention of describing a collective identity in the introduction when she says she has "blood-knowledge," and she mentions the "amusing little stories" her family told of the South after the defeat of the Confederacy. Because the brief anecdote she cites about the small brothers who wanted to walk to Louisiana suggests not only something about her family but also about a time and a place, the reader recognizes that her description is to be on several levels.

The first scene described is set during Reconstruction in Texas. It is characterized by privation and hardship, answered by strength of character from the family. The second scene, in contrast, is a depiction of an elegant, opulent wedding. The two settings are tied together by the transition in the opening sentence of paragraph four: "The woman who made That Brew and the soldier who ate the bacon rind had been bride and groom in a Kentucky wedding somewhere around 1850."

Another reference to the grandmother, in the second sentence of the seventh paragraph, makes a transition to the third descriptive sketch, this one concerned with family traditions and habits of the author's own childhood. The three scenes are not set in chronological order, but the reader follows them easily because the last two are introduced by references to the experiences and attitudes of the grandmother.

A second technique Porter uses to create coherence is that of food imagery. In the first scene there is makeshift coffee and corn bread, and, at long last, crusty buttermilk biscuits. In the second she mentions a footed silver dish filled with ten pounds of sculpted butter, Kentucky ham, roast turkey, spiced mangoes, and more. The third sketch does not name specific dishes but speaks of the "bountiful hospitality" of her grandmother's table and the occasions filled with her gaiety, warmth, and, of course, her cooking. In addition, the food images guide the reader into seeing, smelling, and tasting—in other words, into sharing the experiences being described.

The final paragraph of the essay returns to the broad view of the introduction. It continues the focus on Porter's grandmother, but at this point she becomes a symbol of the entire family. Her strength has become theirs; her faith in the temporary nature of hard times, which persisted despite the evidence of the years, has created their own affirmations. And because the family that she came to typify was in its way typical of other families of "solid wealth and property" who found themselves in a "temporary decline," the description is, at its most general level, concerned with picturing members of the Old South as they moved toward the New. Porter's affection and admiration for her grandmother are transferred to those people, who, she suggests, were nothing less than heroic. Although she says little of anyone but her grandparents, and speaks mostly of her grandmother, she says a great deal about the Old South as she remembers it through personal experience and family tradition.

GRAY MANHATTAN

ANONYMOUS

New York is a city that wears many faces. In this description Manhattan is a bleak place where the viewer has a sense of hopeless desolation.

Standing on a concrete jetty at seven-thirty of a drizzly morning, looking across the gray Hudson at the shore softened by fog, one can just make out an endless miniature procession of Manhattan-bound cars going down the ramp to the Lincoln Tunnel. They vanish under the river and come up on New York's streets: a chain of them is moving now a hundred yards away along the road under the old West Side Highway, and soon they will be searching for a place to park. Here they are passing Pier 76, at Thirty-seventh Street—the Police Department Parking Enforcement depot—where another parade of cars, these without drivers, and hauled by tow trucks, is moving toward a huge building. The cars pass under a damp flag shifting restlessly in the wind above a doorway where a Dantesque sign says, "To Redeem Auto Enter Here." Inside, four hundred cars are currently captive, waiting for owners with license, registration, and sixty-five dollars in cash or check. (Cash or certified check is the rule for scofflaws.) Nobody is picking up a car right now; late at night, however, the lines at the windows are long and slow. On a wall by some pay phones, a notice has been posted: "Generous Reward. Dog Stolen with Red Station Wagon . . . Answers to name of Susie . . . We only want the dog back—no questions asked—she is very frightened." On the jetty outside is a scattering of old French-fried potatoes; just offshore, ancient pilings—green above the low-tide line, then gray, then brown at the top—stand ready for ships that will never come again. Inland, across the roadway, there are abandoned factories of brick, and collapsed sheds. On a bleak morning like this, the city can look hopelessly desolate—a ruin devoid of grandeur. The nomads come and go in their cars, rerouted around the devastation. In a field to the south of Thirty-eighth Street, old railroad tracks are buried under weeds and grass and wild flowers. There are masses of small white asters with yellow centers—it looks as if fresh snow had started to fall—and they toss in the wind.

We get into our own car, to head north and then east. Near Ninth Avenue and Forty-fourth Street, pedestrians are watching something: a one-legged woman in a wheelchair is struggling with a man who is standing over her. She is trying to hit him with a cane. People stare, not knowing what to do. But the woman and the man apparently know each other: he holds her arm; he is trying to calm her down. Her face is full of rage and resentment. We drive by, another nomad slipping through this city of frightened lost dogs and forever departed ships and rusting hopes. Then, as we look back in the rear-view mirror, we see that the woman has grown quiet, at least for now, and the man is kissing her on the forehead.

One Point for Analysis: The images of this essay are almost all visual ones.

Writing Topics:

1. Using visual images, describe from a fixed point of observation some part of a city that you know.
2. Using visual images, describe some part of a city that you know as you travel through it.
3. In this essay the author states: "just offshore, ancient pilings—green above the low-tide line, then gray, then brown at the top—stand ready for ships that will never come again." Describe a deserted landmark you know that, like the pilings, stands as evidence of a time that will never come again.

THE BIG SUR

HENRY MILLER

Henry Miller is known not only for his fiction and essays but also for his fight to liberalize the use of the English language. His usage of "obscenities" has shocked many conventional readers.

Big Sur has a climate of its own and a character all its own. It is a region where extremes meet, a region where one is always conscious of weather, of space, of grandeur, and of eloquent silence. Among other things, it is the meeting place of migratory birds coming from north and south. It is said, in fact, that there is a greater variety of birds to be found in this region than in any other part of the United States. It is also the home of the redwoods; one encounters them on entering from the north and one leaves them on passing southward. At night one can still hear the coyote howling, and if one ventures beyond the first ridge of mountains one can meet up with mountain lions and other beasts of the wild. The grizzly bear is no longer to be found here, but the rattlesnake is still to be reckoned with. On a clear, bright day, when the blue of the sea rivals the blue of the sky, one sees the hawk, the eagle, the buzzard soaring above the still, hushed canyons. In summer, when the fogs roll in, one can look down upon a sea of clouds floating listlessly above the ocean; they have the appearance, at times, of huge iridescent soap bubbles, over which, now and then, may be seen a double rainbow. In January and February the hills are greenest, almost as green as the Emerald Isle. From November to February are the best months, the air fresh and invigorating, the skies clear, the sun still warm enough to take a sun bath.

From our perch, which is about a thousand feet above the sea, one can look up and down the coast a distance of twenty miles in either direction. The highway zigzags like the Grande Corniche. . . . It now forms part of the great international highway which will one day extend from the northern part of Alaska to Tierra del Fuego. By the time it is finished the automobile, like the mastodon, may be extinct. But the Big Sur will be here forever, and perhaps in the year A.D. 2000 the population may still number only a few hundred souls. Perhaps, like Andorra and Monaco, it will become a Republic all its own. Perhaps the dread invaders will not come from other parts of this continent but from across the ocean, as the American aborigines are said to have come. And if they do, it will not be in boats or in airplanes.

And who can say when this region will once again be covered by the waters of the deep? Geologically speaking, it is not so long ago that it rose from the sea. Its mountain slopes are almost as treacherous as the icy sea in which, by the way, one scarcely ever sees a sail boat or a hardy swimmer, though one does occasionally spot a seal, an otter or a sperm whale. The sea, which looks so near and so tempting, is often difficult to reach. We know that the Conquistadores were unable to make their way along the coast, neither could they cut through the brush which covers the mountain slopes. An inviting land, but hard to conquer. It seeks to remain unspoiled, uninhabited by man.

Often, when following the trail which meanders over the hills, I pull myself up in an effort to encompass the glory and the grandeur which envelops the whole horizon. Often, when the clouds pile up in the north and the sea is churned with white caps, I say to myself: "This is the California that men dreamed of years ago, this is the Pacific that Balboa looked out on from the Peak of Darien, this is the face of the earth as the Creator intended it to look."

One Point for Analysis: The last paragraph of the essay is a series of widening generalizations growing out of the specific information that precedes it.

Writing Topics:
1. Describe a place by presenting specific information about it. End with generalizations concerning the nature of that place.
2. Miller says of the Big Sur, "Perhaps, like Andorra and Monaco, it will become a Republic all its own." Describe a republic as you would imagine it to be.
3. How would you describe " 'the face of the earth as the Creator intended it to look' "? Answer by writing an essay.

A BIG, BIG MAN

NICHOLAS VON HOFFMAN

Nicholas von Hoffman writes an informal apostrophe to the former President in this descriptive essay. It was published shortly after Lyndon Johnson's death.

Ah, Lyndon, you're not cold yet and they're calling you great. That's what happens when one politician dies: The rest of them call him great, but, Lyndon, you deserve better than patriotic hagiography. You were better than the eulogistic junk they're saying at the memorial services.

Lyndon, you got your teeth into us and we got our teeth into you. Those five years of you in the White House were a barroom brawl, and, just four years ago almost to the day, when we staggered out of the saloon, dusty and bloody, we didn't hate you anymore. We understood better how you got us into Vietnam than how Nixon got us out and we liked you more, you cussed, cussing, bullheaded, impossible, roaring, wild coot.

You had your credibility gaps and your silent sullennesses, but we read you. Oh, man, Lyndon, did we know you! You were the best and the worst of ourselves, the personification of our national deliriums. You were always so completely, so absolutely you. Kennedy had Pablo Casals to play for him, Nixon's got Pat Boone to pray for him, but you, Lyndon, you had Country Joe and the Fish singing songs soaked in four-letter words at you.

They're not bringing it up at your funeral, but you had a famous dirty mouth. By most accounts the only man in the history of the White House who could cuss better than you was Andrew Jackson. We on the outside knew how to make obscenity a tool of eloquence, too. We could recognize you, not as a Great American, but as an American man. But you did your own hating and your own cussing, not like these stiffs they've got in there now who import Sinatra and the dregs of Las Vegas to call people filthy names for them.

That wasn't your style, Lyndon. You let it all hang out; but then, man, even when we hated you most, we knew you at least had something. Your dogs had names and you pulled their ears. No official court photograph animal for you to have its picture taken as

Reprinted by permission of King Features.

144

you asked the mutt's name. Sure, you could be gross. Getting your picture taken in the hospital bed, pulling up your pj's so we could all see the scar on your belly, and they still whisper around Washington that you used to receive ambassadors from foreign countries stepping out of the shower bath nekkid as a jaybird, as they say where you came from.

And still you kept your dignity. Maybe because everything you did, good, bad, indifferent or just funny, was so big. You were Andy Jackson's boy. Immoderate and big. No rein on yourself. They say even after the second heart attack you couldn't bring yourself to quit smoking.

Lyndon, you were immoderate, and greedy. You outdid all the rest of us hungry Americans for reaching out and grabbing, fingers always stretched for grasping, but now they're saying after your death that you divided America, left her all split and bleeding. It is true that if ever a man had a reach which exceeded his grasp, it was you, you wicked old devil, but you redeemed this country even while dropping us, plop!, in the middle of the Vietnam Big Muddy.

You fought our Second Civil War and carried out our Second Reconstruction. The credit has gone to John Kennedy but he doesn't deserve it. He had the speechwriters to say fair, promising things, while he and his brother appointed racist judges to the federal bench. Lyndon, it isn't fair to you that Jack Kennedy's picture should be tacked up on the walls of so many poor black homes, Kennedy who regarded blacks as but another pressure group to be tricked or placated.

But some of us remember. Some of us who were in a room in the public housing project across the street from Brown's Chapel in Selma, Ala., that night you talked to a joint session of Congress in your rich, half-Southern accent and we saw you on TV say to them, "We shall overcome." Lyndon, you did you best to overcome. Where Jack Kennedy reacted with official indifference to what happened to black people, you shook and threatened the federal bureaucracy from the FBI to the Department of Agriculture to make them redeem the pledge of equal protection.

Much of what you started is being abandoned, discarded and attacked, and much of it ought to be. You were so impulsive. You tried to solve social problems like a drunken hardware wholesaler trying to snag girls in a Paris nightclub. You drank so much of the social betterment bubbly the nation woke up with a hangover, but

145

God bless you for it. Every right-living nation ought to go on that kind of a drunk every so often, and even if you went about it the wrong way, you got us thinking about what we should be doing. Your Medicare and Medicaid aren't exactly winners, but thanks to you our people will have the health protection.

You were a big 'un, Lyndon. We're going to miss you, you old booger, and we're going to know, regardless of official proclamations, you deserve better than to be saluted, left at half-mast and forgotten.

One Point for Analysis: Von Hoffman uses ellipsis, the omission of understood words, to create the conversational tone.

Writing Topics:

1. Write a description of a well-known public figure by addressing it to him, as von Hoffman addresses his essay to Lyndon Johnson.
2. Write an informal essay in which you make negative statements about a person but in which your affection or admiration for him is always apparent.
3. Write a humorous description of a public official.

A SON'S EDUCATION

E. B. WHITE

For many years, E. B. White wrote essays and stories for The New Yorker. *His experience with the city and his love for the country are reflected in this descriptive piece.*

I have an increasing admiration for the teacher in the country school where we have a third-grade scholar in attendance. She not only undertakes to instruct her charges in all the subjects of the first three grades, but she manages to function quietly and effectively as a guardian of their health, their clothes, their habits, their mothers, and their snowball engagements. She has been doing this sort of Augean task for twenty years, and is both kind and wise. She cooks for the children on the stove that heats the room, and she can cool

"Education—March 1939" (pp. 52–57) from *One Man's Meat* by E. B. White. Copyright 1939 by E. B. White. Reprinted by permission of Harper & Row Publishers, Inc.

their passions or warm their soup with equal competence. She conceives their costumes, cleans up their messes, and shares their confidences. My boy already regards his teacher as his great friend, and I think tells her a great deal more than he tells us.

The shift from city school to country school was something we worried about quietly all last summer. I have always rather favored public school over private school, if only because in public school you meet a greater variety of children. This bias of mine, I suspect, is partly an attempt to justify my own past (I never knew anything but public schools) and partly an involuntary defense against getting kicked in the shins by a young ceramist on his way to the kiln. My wife was unacquainted with public schools, never having been exposed (in her early life) to anything more public than the washroom of Miss Winsor's. Regardless of our backgrounds, we both knew that the change in schools was something that concerned not us but the scholar himself. We hoped it would work out all right. In New York our son went to a medium-priced private institution with semi-progressive ideas of education, and modern plumbing. He learned fast, kept well, and we were satisfied. It was an electric, colorful, regimented existence with moments of pleasurable pause and giddy incident. The day the Christmas angel fainted and had to be carried out by one of the Wise Men was educational in the highest sense of the term. Our scholar gave imitations of it around the house for weeks afterward, and I doubt if it ever goes completely out of his mind.

His days were rich in formal experience. Wearing overalls and an old sweater (the accepted uniform of the private seminary), he sallied forth at morn accompanied by a nurse or a parent and walked (or was pulled) two blocks to a corner where the school bus made a flag stop. This flashy vehicle was as punctual as death: seeing us waiting at the cold curb, it would sweep to a halt, open its mouth, suck the boy in, and spring away with an angry growl. It was a good deal like a train picking up a bag of mail. At school the scholar was worked on for six or seven hours by half a dozen teachers and a nurse, and was revived on orange juice in mid-morning. In a cinder court he played games supervised by an athletic instructor, and in a cafeteria he ate lunch worked out by a dietitian. He soon learned to read with gratifying facility and discernment and to make Indian weapons of a semi-deadly nature. Whenever one of his classmates fell low of a fever the news was put on the wires and there were

147

breathless phone calls to physicians, discussing periods of incuba-
tion and allied magic.

In the country all one can say is that the situation is different, and
somehow more casual. Dressed in corduroys, sweatshirt, and short
rubber boots, and carrying a tin dinner-pail, our scholar departs at
crack of dawn for the village school, two and a half miles down the
road, next to the cemetery. When the road is open and the car will
start, he makes the journey by motor, courtesy of his old man.
When the snow is deep or the motor is dead or both, he makes it on
the hoof. In the afternoons he walks or hitches all or part of the way
home in fair weather, gets transported in foul. The schoolhouse is a
two-room frame building, bungalow type, shingles stained a burnt
brown with weather-resistant stain. It has a chemical toilet in the
basement and two teachers above stairs. One takes the first three
grades, the other the fourth, fifth, and sixth. They have little or no
time for individual instruction, and no time at all for the esoteric.
They teach what they know themselves, just as fast and as hard as
they can manage. The pupils sit still at their desks in class, and do
their milling around outdoors during recess.

There is no supervised play. They play cops and robbers (only
they call it "Jail") and throw things at one another—snowballs in
winter, rose hips in fall. It seems to satisfy them. They also construct darts, pinwheels, and "pick-up sticks" (jackstraws), and the
school itself does a brisk trade in penny candy, which is for sale
right in the classroom and which contains "surprises." The most
highly prized surprise is a fake cigarette, made of cardboard, fiend-
ishly lifelike.

The memory of how apprehensive we were at the beginning is
still strong. The boy was nervous about the change too. The tension, on that first fair morning in September when we drove him to
school, almost blew the windows out of the sedan. And when later
we picked him up on the road, wandering along with his little blue
lunch-pail, and got his laconic report "All right" in answer to our
inquiry about how the day had gone, our relief was vast. Now,
after almost a year of it, the only difference we can discover in the
two school experiences is that in the country he sleeps better at
night—and *that* probably is more the air than the education. When
grilled on the subject of school-in-country *vs.* school-in-city, he
replied that the chief difference is that the day seems to go so much
quicker in the country. "Just like lightning," he reported.

148

One Point for Analysis: White's description divides neatly into two
comparative parts: the city school and the country school.
Writing Topics:
1. Compare by description dating practices in your hometown
   and on the college campus.
2. Describe the physical plant and emotional impact of one elementary school you attended.
3. Describe your best friend in high school.

MARRAKECH

GEORGE ORWELL

*Orwell was a British writer who was born in India. After his
formal education in England, he went to Burma, where he
served with Indian Imperial Police. His acquaintance with the
East is evident in this essay.*

As the corpse went past the flies left the restaurant table in a
cloud and rushed after it, but they came back a few minutes later.

The little crowd of mourners—all men and boys, no women—
threaded their way across the market place between the piles of
pomegranates and the taxis and the camels, wailing a short chant
over and over again. What really appeals to the flies is that the
corpses here are never put into coffins, they are merely wrapped in
a piece of rag and carried on a rough wooden bier on the shoulders
of four friends. When the friends get to the burying-ground they
hack an oblong hole a foot or two deep, dump the body in it and
fling over it a little of the dried-up, lumpy earth, which is like
broken brick. No gravestone, no name, no identifying mark of any
kind. The burying-ground is merely a huge waste of hummocky
earth, like a derelict building-lot. After a month or two no one can
even be certain where his own relatives are buried.

When you walk through a town like this—two hundred thousand
inhabitants, of whom at least twenty thousand own literally nothing except the rags they stand up in—when you see how the people
live, and still more how easily they die, it is always difficult to

believe that you are walking among human beings. All colonial empires are in reality founded upon that fact. The people have brown faces—besides, there are so many of them! Are they really the same flesh as yourself? Do they even have names? Or are they merely a kind of undifferentiated brown stuff, about as individual as bees or coral insects? They rise out of the earth, they sweat and starve for a few years, and then they sink back into the nameless mounds of the graveyard and nobody notices that they are gone. And even the graves themselves soon fade back into the soil.

Sometimes, out for a walk, as you break your way through the prickly pear, you notice that it is rather bumpy underfoot, and only a certain regularity in the bumps tells you that you are walking over skeletons.

One Point for Analysis: Orwell uses description to lead up to a statement that directly indicts colonialism.

Writing Topics:

1. Construct a scene by which you intend to make the reader experience a sense of revulsion.
2. Describe a scene that you think stands as an indictment of your society.
3. Describe a "civilized" cemetery.

MY WOOD

E. M. FORSTER

E. M. Forster was an English writer who in 1969 was awarded the Order of Merit in recognition of his work. His best-known novels are A Passage to India *and* Howards End.

A few years ago I wrote a book which dealt in part with the difficulties of the English in India. Feeling that they would have had no difficulties in India themselves, the Americans read the book freely. The more they read it the better it made them feel, and a cheque to the author was the result. I bought a wood with the cheque. It is not a large wood—it contains scarcely any trees, and it is intersected, blast it, by a public footpath. Still, it is the first prop-

From *Abinger Harvest*, copyright 1936, 1964, by E. M. Forster. Reprinted by permission of Harcourt Brace Jovanovich, Inc.

erty that I have owned, so it is right that other people should participate in my shame, and should ask themselves, in accents that will
vary in horror, this very important question: What is the effect of
property upon the character? Don't let's touch economics; the effect
of private ownership upon the community as a whole is another
question—a more important question, perhaps, but another one.
Let's keep to psychology. If you own things, what's their effect on
you? What's the effect on me of my wood?

In the first place, it makes me feel heavy. Property does have this
effect. Property produces men of weight, and it was a man of
weight who failed to get into the Kingdom of Heaven. He was not
wicked, that unfortunate millionaire in the parable, he was only
stout; he stuck out in front, not to mention behind, and as he
wedged himself this way and that in the crystalline entrance and
bruised his well-fed flanks, he saw beneath him a comparatively
slim camel passing through the eye of a needle and being woven
into the robe of God. The Gospels all through couple stoutness and
slowness. They point out what is perfectly obvious, yet seldom
realized: that if you have a lot of things you cannot move about a
lot, that furniture requires dusting, dusters require servants, servants require insurance stamps, and the whole tangle of them
makes you think twice before you accept an invitation to dinner or
go for a bathe in the Jordan. Sometimes the Gospels proceed further
and say with Tolstoy that property is sinful; they approach the difficult ground of asceticism here, where I cannot follow them. But as
to the immediate effects of property on people, they just show
straightforward logic. It produces men of weight. Men of weight
cannot, by definition, move like the lightning from the East unto
the West, and the ascent of a fourteen-stone bishop into a pulpit is
thus the exact antithesis of the coming of the Son of Man. My wood
makes me feel heavy.

In the second place, it makes me feel it ought to be larger.

The other day I heard a twig snap in it. I was annoyed at first, for
I thought that someone was blackberrying, and depreciating the
value of the undergrowth. On coming nearer, I saw it was not a
man who had trodden on the twig and snapped it, but a bird, and I
felt pleased. My bird. The bird was not equally pleased. Ignoring
the relation between us, it took fright as soon as it saw the shape of
my face, and flew straight over the boundary hedge into a field, the
property of Mrs. Henessy, where it sat down with a loud squawk. It

had become Mrs. Henessy's bird. Something seemed grossly amiss here, something that would not have occurred had the wood been larger. I could not afford to buy Mrs. Henessy out, I dared not murder her, and limitations of this sort beset me on every side. Ahab did not want that vineyard—he only needed it to round off his property, preparatory to plotting a new curve—and all the land around my wood has become necessary to me in order to round off the wood. A boundary protects. But—poor little thing—the boundary ought in its turn to be protected. Noises on the edge of it. Children throw stones. A little more, and then a little more, until we reach the sea. Happy Canute! Happier Alexander! And after all, why should even the world be the limit of possession? A rocket containing a Union Jack, will, it is hoped, be shortly fired at the moon. Mrs. Sirius. Beyond which . . . But these immensities ended by saddening me. I could not suppose that my wood was the destined nucleus of universal dominion—it is so very small and contains no mineral wealth beyond the blackberries. Nor was I comforted when Mrs. Henessy's bird took alarm for the second time and flew clean away from us all, under the belief that it belonged to itself.

In the third place, property makes its owner feel that he ought to do something to it. Yet he isn't sure what. A restlessness comes over him, a vague sense that he has a personality to express—the same sense which, without any vagueness, leads the artist to an act of creation. Sometimes I think I will cut down such trees as remain in the wood, at other times I want to fill up the gaps between them with new trees. Both impulses are pretentious and empty. They are not honest movements towards money-making or beauty. They spring from a foolish desire to express myself and from an inability to enjoy what I have got. Creation, property, enjoyment form a sinister trinity in the human mind. Creation and enjoyment are both very, very good, yet they are often unattainable without a material basis, and at such moments property pushes itself in as a substitute, saying, "Accept me instead—I'm good enough for all three." It is not enough. It is, as Shakespeare said of lust, "The expense of spirit in a waste of shame"; it is "Before, a joy proposed; behind, a dream." Yet we don't know how to shun it. It is forced on us by our economic system as the alternative to starvation. It is also forced on us by an internal defect in the soul, by the feeling that in property may lie the germs of self-development and of exquisite or heroic

152

deeds. Our life on earth is, and ought to be, material and carnal. But we have not yet learned to manage our materialism and carnality properly; they are still entangled with the desire for ownership, where (in the words of Dante) "Possession is one with loss."

And this brings us to our fourth and final point: the blackberries.

Blackberries are not plentiful in this meagre grove, but they are easily seen from the public footpath which traverses it, and all too easily gathered. Foxgloves, too—people will pull up the foxgloves, and ladies of an educational tendency even grub for toadstools to show them on the Monday in class. Other ladies, less educated, roll down the bracken in the arms of their gentlemen friends. There is paper, there are tins. Pray, does my wood belong to me or doesn't it? And, if it does, should I not own it best by allowing no one else to walk there? There is a wood near Lyme Regis, also cursed by a public footpath, where the owner has not hesitated on this point. He has built high stone walls each side of the path, and has spanned it by bridges, so that the public circulate like termites while he gorges on the blackberries unseen. He really does own his wood, this able chap. Dives in Hell did pretty well, but the gulf dividing him from Lazarus could be traversed by vision, and nothing traverses it here. And perhaps I shall come to this in time. I shall wall in and fence out until I really taste the sweets of property. Enormously stout, endlessly avaricious, pseudo-creative, intensely selfish, I shall weave upon my forehead the quadruple crown of possession until those nasty Bolshies come and take it off again and thrust me aside into the outer darkness.

One Point for Analysis: Through the description of the effect that his wood has had on him, Forster moves to an argumentative thesis, that the owning of property produces undesirable effects on a person.

Writing Topics:

1. Describe something you have wanted badly; then discuss its effect on you after obtaining it.
2. Forster used his wood as a place where he thought he could escape the world. Describe a place, real or imaginary, that furnishes an escape for you.
3. Describe a person who fits some part of a biblical story or parable.

THE BLOCK AND BEYOND

ALFRED KAZIN

In this selection from his longer work A Walker in the City, *Alfred Kazin remembers the expanding horizons of childhood.*

The block: *my* block. It was on the Chester Street side of our house, between the grocery and the back wall of the old drugstore, that I was hammered into the shape of the streets. Everything beginning at Blake Avenue would always wear for me some delightful strangeness and mildness, simply because it was not of my block, *the* block where the clang of your head sounded against the pavement when you fell in a fist fight, and the rows of storelights on each side were pitiless, watching you. Anything away from the block was good: even a school you never went to, two blocks away: there were vegetable gardens in the park across the street. Returning from "New York," I would take the longest routes home from the subway, get off a station ahead of our own, only for the unexpectedness of walking through Betsy Head Park and hearing the gravel crunch under my feet as I went beyond the vegetable gardens, smelling the sweaty sweet dampness from the pool in summer and the dust on the leaves as I passed under the ailanthus trees. On the block itself everything rose up only to test me.

We worked every inch of it, from the cellars and the backyards to the sickening space between the roofs. Any wall, any stoop, any curving metal edge on a billboard sign made a place against which to knock a ball; any bottom rung of a fire escape ladder a goal in basketball; any sewer cover a base; any crack in the pavement a "net" for the tense sharp tennis that we played by beating a soft ball back and forth with our hands between the squares. Betsy Head Park two blocks away would always feel slightly foreign, for it belonged to the Amboys and the Bristols and the Hopkinsons as much as it did to us. *Our* life every day was fought out on the pavement and in the gutter, up against the walls of the houses and the glass fronts of the drugstore and the grocery, in and out of the fresh steaming piles of horse manure, the wheels of passing carts and automobiles, along the iron spikes of the stairway to the cellar, the jagged edge of the open garbage cans, the crumbly steps of the old farmhouses still left on one side of the street.

As I go back to the block now, and for a moment fold my body up again in its narrow arena—there, just there, between the black of the asphalt and the old women in their kerchiefs and flowered house dresses sitting on the tawny kitchen chairs—the back wall of the drugstore still rises up to test me. Every day we smashed a small black viciously hard regulation handball against it with fanatical cuts and drives and slams, beating and slashing at it almost in hatred for the blind strength of the wall itself. I was never good enough at handball, was always practicing some trick shot that might earn me esteem, and when I was weary of trying, would often bat a ball down Chester Street just to get myself to Blake Avenue. I have this memory of playing one-o'-cat by myself in the sleepy twilight, at a moment when everyone else had left the block. The sparrows floated down from the telephone wires to peck at every fresh pile of horse manure, and there was a smell of brine from the delicatessen store, of egg crates and of the milk scum left in the great metal cans outside the grocery, of the thick white paste oozing out from behind the fresh Hecker's Flour ad on the metal signboard. I would throw the ball in the air, hit it with my bat, then with perfect satisfaction drop the bat to the ground and run to the next sewer cover. Over and over I did this, from sewer cover to sewer cover, until I had worked my way to Blake Avenue and could see the park.

With each clean triumphant ring of my bat against the gutter leading me on, I did the whole length of our block up and down, and never knew how happy I was just watching the asphalt rise and fall, the curve of the steps up to an old farmhouse. The farmhouses themselves were streaked red on one side, brown on the other, but the steps themselves were always gray. There was a tremor of pleasure at one place; I held my breath in nausea at another. As I ran after my ball with the bat heavy in my hand, the odd successiveness of things in myself almost choked me, the world was so full as I ran—past the cobblestoned yards into the old farmhouses, where stray chickens still waddled along the stones; past the little candy store where we went only if the big one on our side of the block was out of Eskimo Pies; past the three neighboring tenements where the last of the old women sat on their kitchen chairs yawning before they went up to make supper. Then came Mrs. Rosenwasser's house, the place on the block I first identified with what was farthest from home, and strangest, because it was a "private" house; then the fences around the monument works, where black cranes rose up above the yard and you could see the smooth gray slabs that would be cut and carved into tombstones, some of them already engraved with the names and dates and family virtues of the dead.

Beyond Blake Avenue was the pool parlor outside which we waited all through the tense September afternoons of the World's Series to hear the latest scores called off the ticker tape—and where as we waited, banging a ball against the bottom of the wall and drinking water out of empty coke bottles, I breathed the chalk off the cues and listened to the clocks ringing in the fire station across the street. There was an old warehouse next to the pool parlor; the oil on the barrels and the iron staves had the same rusty smell. A block away was the park, thick with the dusty gravel I liked to hear my shoes crunch in as I ran around and round the track; then a great open pavilion, the inside mysteriously dark, chill even in summer; there I would wait in the sweaty coolness before pushing on to the wading ring where they put up a shower on the hottest days.

Beyond the park the "fields" began, all those still unused lots where we could still play hard ball in perfect peace—first shooing away the goats and then tearing up goldenrod before laying our bases. The smell and touch of those "fields," with their wild compost under the billboards of weeds, goldenrod, bricks, goat droppings, rusty cans, empty beer bottles, fresh new lumber, and damp cement, live in my mind as Brownsville's great open door, the wastes that took us through to the west. I used to go round them in summer with my cousins selling near-beer to the carpenters, but always in a daze, would stare so long as the fibrous stalks of the goldenrod as I felt their harshness in my hand that I would forget to make a sale, and usually go off sick on the beer I drank up myself. Beyond! Beyond! Only to see something new, to get away from each day's narrow battleground between the grocery and the back wall of the drugstore! Even the other end of our block, when you got to Mrs. Rosenwasser's house and the monument works, was dear to me for the contrast. On summer nights, when we played Indian trail, running away from each other on prearranged signals, the greatest moment came when I could plunge into the darkness down the block for myself and hide behind the slabs in the monument works. I remember the air whistling around me as I ran, the panicky thud of my bones in my sneakers, and then the slabs rising in the light from the street lamps as I sped past the little candy store and crept under the fence.

In the darkness you could never see where the crane began. We liked to trap the enemy between the slabs and sometimes jumped them from great mounds of rock just in from the quarry. A boy once fell to his death that way, and they put a watchman there to keep us out. This made the slabs all the more impressive to me, and I always aimed first for that yard whenever we played follow-the-leader. Day after day the monument works became oppressively more mysterious and remote, though it was only just down the block; I stood in front of it every afternoon on my way back from school, filling it with my fears. It was not death I felt there—the slabs were usually faceless. It was the darkness itself, and the wind howling around me whenever I stood poised on the edge of a high slab waiting to jump. Then I would take in, along with the fear, some amazement of joy that I had found my way out that far.

One Point for Analysis: By describing the physical elements of his block and beyond, Kazin implies the nature of his childhood experiences.

Writing Topics:

1. Select some inanimate object, like Kazin's wall or monument works, and describe the force it came to represent for you in childhood.
2. Recall in a descriptive essay how you used your imagination to devise childhood games.
3. Describe your feelings on first leaving home to engage in another pursuit.

TOWARDS AN EASTERN LANDFALL

LAWRENCE DURRELL

Lawrence Durrell is an English poet and novelist whose most celebrated four novels compose his Alexandria Quartet. *He is the brother of Gerald Durrell (see "Knee Deep in Scorpions") and good friend of Henry Miller (see "The Big Sur").*

Journeys, like artists, are born and not made. A thousand differing circumstances contribute to them, few of them willed or determined by the will—whatever we may think. They flower spontaneously out of the demands of our natures—and the best of them lead us not only outwards in space, but inwards as well. Travel can be one of the most rewarding forms of introspection. . . .

These thoughts belong to Venice at dawn, seen from the deck of the ship which is to carry me down through the islands to Cyprus; a Venice wobbling in a thousand fresh-water reflections, cool as a jelly. It was as if some great master, stricken by dementia, had burst his whole colour-box against the sky to deafen the inner eye of the world. Cloud and water mixed into each other, dripping with colours, merging, overlapping, liquefying, with steeples and balconies and roofs floating in space, like the fragments of some stained-glass window seen through a dozen veils of rice-paper. Fragments of history touched with the colours of wine, tar, ochre, blood, fire-opal and ripening grain. The whole at the same time being rinsed softly back at the edges into a dawn sky as softly as circumspectly blue as a pigeon's egg.

Mentally I held it all, softly as an abstract painting, cradling it in my thoughts—the whole encampment of cathedrals and palaces, against the sharply-focused face of Stendhal as he sits forever upon a stiff-backed chair at Florian's sipping wine: or on that of a Corvo, flitting like some huge fruit-bat down these light-bewitched alleys. . . .

The pigeons swarm the belfries. I can hear their wings across the water like the beating of fans in a great summer ballroom. The *vaporetto* on the Grand Canal beats too, softly as a human pulse, faltering and renewing itself after every hesitation which marks a landing-stage. The glass palaces of the Doges are being pounded in a crystal mortar, strained through a prism. Venice will never be far from me in Cyprus—for the lion of Saint Mark still rides the humid airs of Famagusta, of Kyrenia.

It is an appropriate point of departure for the traveller to the eastern Levant. . . .

But heavens, it was cold. Down on the grey flagged quay I had noticed a coffee-stall which sold glasses of warm milk and *croissants*. It was immediately opposite the gang-plank, so that I was in no danger of losing my ship. A small dark man with a birdy eye served me wordlessly, yawning in my face, so that in sympathy I was forced to yawn too. I gave him the last of my liras.

There were no seats, but I made myself comfortable on an up-ended barrel and, breaking my bread into the hot milk, fell into a sleepy contemplation of Venice from this unfamiliar angle of vision across the outer harbour.

A tug sighed and spouted a milky jet upon the nearest cloud. The cabin-steward joined me for a glass of milk; he was an agreeable man, rotund and sleek, with a costly set of dimples round his smile—like expensive cuff-links in a well-laundered shirt. "Beautiful," he agreed, looking at Venice, "beautiful": but it was a reluctant admission, for he was from Bologna, and it was hard to let the side down by admiring a foreign city. He plunged into a pipe full of scented shag. "You are going to Cyprus?" he said at last, politely, but with the faintest hint of commiseration.

"Yes. To Cyprus."

"To work?"

"To work."

It seemed immodest to add that I was intending to live in Cyprus, to buy a house if possible. . . . After five years of Serbia I had begun to doubt whether, in wanting to live in the Mediterranean at all, I was not guilty of some fearful aberration; indeed the whole of this adventure had begun to smell of improbability. I was glad that I was touching wood.

"It is not much of a place," he said.

"So I believe."

"Arid and without water. The people drink to excess."

This sounded rather better. I have always been prepared, where water was scarce, to wash in wine if necessary. "How is the wine?" I asked.

"Heavy and sweet." This was not so good. A Bolognese is always worth listening to on the subject of wine. No matter. (I should buy a small peasant house and settle in the island for four or five years.) The most arid and waterless of islands would be a rest after the heartless dusty Serbian plains.

"But why not Athens?" he said softly, echoing my own thoughts.

"Money restrictions."

"Ah! Then you are going to live in Cyprus for some time?"

My secret was out. His manner changed, and his picture of Cyprus changed with it, for politeness does not permit an Italian to decry another's plans, or run down his native country. Cyprus was to become mine by adoption—therefore he must try to see it through my eyes. At once it became fertile, full of goddesses and mineral springs; ancient castles and monasteries; fruit and grain and verdant grasslands; priests and gipsies and brigands. . . . He gave it a swift Sicilian travel-poster varnish, beaming at me approvingly as he did so. "And the girls?" I said at last.

But here he stuck; politeness battled with male pride for a long moment. He would have to tell the truth lest later on, in the field, so to speak, I might convict him—a Bolognese, above all!—of having no standards of female beauty. "Very ugly," he said at last, in geniune regret. "Very ugly indeed." This was disheartening. We sat there in silence for a while until the steamer towering above us gave a loud lisp of steam *fffff*, while beaded bubbles of condensing steam trickled down the siren.

AN ANALYSIS OF "TOWARDS AN EASTERN LANDFALL"

In the opening sentence of "Towards an Eastern Landfall," Lawrence Durrell compares journeys and artists. The reader realizes soon thereafter that in this descriptive essay the author is both traveler and artist. As such he is led, as he points out in the third sentence, to introspection. Durrell the traveler questions his feelings and decisions as he leaves the familiar beauty of Venice and anticipates the unknown and possibly inhospitable ambiance of Cyprus. Durrell the artist describes the physical qualities of both places as well as the feelings of the traveler. He calls upon the reader's sensory responses to participate in the physical and emotional experience.

Venice is a painter's delight. In the second paragraph Durrell confirms,

"It was as if some great master, stricken by dementia, had burst his whole colour-box against the sky to deafen the inner eye of the world." In this sentence Durrell makes use of synesthesia, a combination of sensory appeals. Sometimes he uses words as a painter uses brushes and paints, trying to give shape and color to a scene so that the reader can see it. For example, he says that the whole picture of Venice as he leaves is "being rinsed softly back at the edges into a dawn sky as softly as circumspectly blue as a pigeon's egg."

Like a musician Durrell tries to capture the sounds of Venice in the euphony of his diction. He speaks of the pigeons, "their wings across the water like the beating of fans in a great summer ballroom." When the traveler is cold, the artist-writer pleases the reader by the gustatory appeal of glasses of warm milk and croissants.

Durrell goes a step beyond simple images, appeals to the reader's senses, and uses a number of figures of speech. He speaks of "a Venice wobbling in a thousand fresh-water reflections, *cool as a jelly.*" "Cloud and water mixed into each other dripping with colours . . . *like the fragments of some stained-glass window seen through a dozen veils of rice-paper.*" The *vaporetto* beats "softly as *a human pulse. . . .*" And, in general, it is all beheld "softly *as an abstract painting. . . .*" The description, like the subject, is a work of art.

If Venice and its images are lush, Cyprus, the end of the journey, is its opposite. The brief contrast of the aridity of the destination and the sensuality of the point of departure heightens the nature of each. Venice is richer for Cyprus; Cyprus is more arid for Venice.

Durrell's sensual images and figures of speech allow the reader to experience the journey through the eyes and ears and feelings of an artist. The linguistic paintings and music, the tastes and touchings, give the reader Venice, the sea, and a destination—only slightly at second hand.

THE AWFUL CONDITIONS AT FORT DELAWARE
RANDOLPH A. SHOTWELL

Randolph A. Shotwell was a Confederate soldier captured on the eve of the battle of Cold Harbor. He was a prisoner at Point Lookout and later at Fort Delaware, which is the subject of this description.

August 10th:—How strange a thing it is to be hungry! actually craving something to eat, and constantly thinking about it from morning till night, from day to day; for weeks and months!

161

It did not seem possible for a man thus to worry over lack of nourishment, keeping his mind continually engrossed with anger against those who starve us, and with longing for food, the German philosopher's "earnest aspirations after the unattainable."

For the past month our rations have been six, sometimes four hard crackers and $1/10$ of a pound of rusty bacon (a piece the size of a hen's egg) for the twenty-four hours.

But for five days past we have not had a morsel of meat of any kind; the cooks alleging that the supply ran short and "spoiled." (For a fortnight before it ceased to be issued, the rations were so full of worms, and stank so that one had to hold his nose while eating it!) But now we receive *none at all!* Talk about Andersonville! We would gladly exchange rations with the Yankees there!

For my part I cannot swallow very fat meat, or any that is in the very least tainted, so that for a long time I have subsisted on little else than hard tack and water. And such water! There has been no rain for some time; the tanks are no longer adequate for the supply of the pen even when full; therefore the Yankees have a small vessel that is used as a water boat, and is designed to ascend the creek sufficiently far to obtain fresh water. But the boat doesn't go above tide water, hence brings back a brackish *briny* fluid scarcely one whit better than the water from the Delaware, which oozes through the ditches in the pen.

The standing rain water of course breeds a dense swarm of animalculae, and when the hose pipes from the water boat are turned into the tanks the interior sediment is stirred up, and the whole contents become a turgid, salty, jellified mass of waggle tails, worms, dead leaves, dead fishes, and other putrescent abominations, most of which is visible to the eye in a cup of it.

The *smell* of it is enough to revolt the stomach of a fastidious person; to say nothing of the thought of making one's throat a channel for such stuff. Yet, when the tanks are empty—as they are for half a day once or oftener in the week—the cry for this briny liquid is universal, because it creates a thirst equally as much as it quenches it, but if it were not so, the intense heat which beats upon this flat, parched island would make us swallow soluble salts for temporary relief.

The surface of the Pea Patch being of alluvial mud, becomes very porous and damp in wet weather, but parched and as hard as rock in the long dry season. No shade is there, no elevation, no breeze;

only a low, flat, sultry, burning oven! Today the heat is so intense that men by hundreds are seen sweltering on their backs, fairly gasping for breath, like fish dying on a sand beach.

One Point for Analysis: The tone of desperation is created by the catalogue of unpleasant images.

Writing Topics:

1. Describe a prison experience that you know of.
2. Write a descriptive essay on a topic affected by one of your biases. Do not be objective.
3. After library research, describe one of the modern penal institutions.

SUFFERING IN ANDERSONVILLE PRISON

ELIZA ANDREWS

In her book The War-Time Journal of a Georgia Girl, *Eliza Andrews recorded scenes of the Confederacy during the Civil War. After the war she wrote two books on botany and three novels.*

January 27, 1865.—While going our rounds in the morning we found a very important person in Peter Louis, a paroled Yankee prisoner, in the employ of Captain Bonham. The captain keeps him out of the stockade, feeds and clothes him, and in return reaps the benefit of his skill. Peter is a French Yankee, a shoemaker by trade, and makes as beautiful shoes as I ever saw imported from France. My heart quite softened toward him when I saw his handiwork, and little Mrs. Sims was so overcome that she gave him a huge slice of her Confederate fruitcake. I talked French with him, which pleased him greatly, and Mett and I engaged him to make us each a pair of shoes. I will feel like a lady once more, with good shoes on my feet. I expect the poor Yank is glad to get away from Anderson on any terms. Although matters have improved somewhat with the cool weather, the tales that are told of the condition of things there last summer are appalling. Mrs. Brisbane heard all about it from Father Hamilton, a Roman Catholic priest from Macon, who has been working like a good Samaritan in those dens of filth and misery. It is a shame to us Protestants that we have let a Roman Catholic get so far ahead of us in this work of charity and mercy. Mrs. Brisbane says Father Hamilton told her that during the summer the wretched prisoners burrowed in the ground like moles to protect themselves from the sun. It was not safe to give them material to build shanties as they might use it for clubs to overcome the guard. These underground huts, he said, were alive with vermin and stank like charnel houses. Many of the prisoners were stark naked, having not so much as a shirt to their backs. He told a pitiful story of a Pole who had no garment but a shirt, and to make it cover him better, he put his legs into the sleeves and tied the tail around his neck. The others guyed him so on his appearance and the poor wretch was so disheartened by suffering that one day he deliberately stepped over the dead line and stood there till the guard was forced to shoot him. But what I can't understand is that a Pole, of all people in the world, should come over here and try to take away our liberty when his own country is in the hands of oppressors. One would think that the Poles, of all nations in the world, ought to sympathize with a people fighting for their liberties.

Father Hamilton said that at one time the prisoners died at the rate of a hundred and fifty a day, and he saw some of them die on the ground without a rag to lie on or a garment to cover them. Dysentery was the most fatal disease, and as they lay on the ground in their own excrements, the smell was so horrible that the good father says he was often obliged to rush from their presence to get a breath of pure air. It is dreadful. My heart aches for the poor wretches, Yankees though they are, and I am afraid God will suffer some terrible retribution to fall upon us for letting such things happen. If the Yankees ever should come to southwest Georgia and go to Anderson and see the graves there, God have mercy on the land! And yet what can we do? The Yankees themselves are really more to blame than we, for they won't exchange these prisoners, and our poor, hard-pressed Confederacy has not the means to provide for them when our own soldiers are starving in the field. Oh, what a horrible thing war is when stripped of all its pomp and circumstance!

One Point for Analysis: The author's presence in this essay is directly evident.

Writing Topics:
1. Describe an unfortunate situation and justify its existence, as the author does here.
2. Gather information on your local prison and describe it.
3. Describe a situation generally considered to be glamorous or noble and show its other side as the author of this essay shows the other side of war.

A CHRISTMAS MEMORY

TRUMAN CAPOTE

One of the country's best-known contemporary fiction writers, Truman Capote is the author of In Cold Blood *and* Breakfast at Tiffany's, *as well as many short stories.*

Morning. Frozen rime lusters the grass; the sun, round as an orange and orange as hot-weather moons, balances on the horizon, burnishes the silvered winter woods. A wild turkey calls. A renegade hog grunts in the undergrowth. Soon, by the edge of knee-deep, rapid-running water, we have to abandon the buggy. Queenie wades the stream first, paddles across barking complaints at the swiftness of the current, the pneumonia-making coldness of it. We follow, holding our shoes and equipment (a hatchet, a burlap sack) above our heads. A mile more: of chastising thorns, burs and briers that catch at our clothes; of rusty pine needles brilliant with gaudy fungus and molted feathers. Here, there, a flash, a flutter, an ecstasy of shrillings remind us that not all the birds have flown south. Always, the path unwinds through lemony sun pools and pitch vine tunnels. Another creek to cross: a disturbed armada of speckled trout froths the water round us, and frogs the size of plates practice belly flops; beaver workmen are building a dam. On the farther shore, Queenie shakes herself and trembles. My friend shivers, too: not with cold but enthusiasm. One of her hat's ragged roses sheds a petal as she lifts her head and inhales the pine-heavy air. "We're almost there; can you smell it, Buddy?" she says, as though we were approaching an ocean.

And, indeed, it is a kind of ocean. Scented acres of holiday trees, prickly leafed holly. Red berries shiny as Chinese bells: black crows swoop upon them screaming. Having stuffed our burlap sacks with enough greenery and crimson to garland a dozen windows, we set about choosing a tree. "It should be," muses my friend, "twice as tall as a boy. So a boy can't steal the star." The one we pick is twice as tall as me. A brave handsome brute that survives thirty hatchet strokes before it keels with a creaking rending cry. Lugging it like a kill, we commence the long trek out. Every few yards we abandon the struggle, sit down and pant. But we have the strength of triumphant huntsmen; that and the tree's virile, icy perfume revive us, goad us on. Many compliments accompany our sunset return along the red clay road to town; but my friend is sly and noncommittal when passers-by praise the treasure perched on our buggy: what a fine tree and where did it come from? "Yonderways," she murmurs vaguely. Once a car stops and the rich mill owner's lazy wife leans out and whines: "Giveya two-bits cash for that ol tree." Ordinarily my friend is afraid of saying no; but on this occasion she promptly shakes her head: "We wouldn't take a dollar." The mill owner's wife persists. "A dollar, my foot! Fifty cents. That's my last offer. Goodness, woman, you can get another one." In answer, my friend gently reflects: "I doubt it. There's never two of anything."

One Point for Analysis: The title of this descriptive piece announces that the tone will be nostalgic.

Writing Topics:
1. Remember and describe a particular holiday tradition of your family.
2. Using Capote's essay as a model, describe some experience that for you is associated with a particular smell.
3. Describe something that to you would fit the friend's comment: "There's never two of anything."

MOSCOW

LEONA P. SCHECTER

With her husband as coauthor, Leona P. Schecter wrote An
American Family in Moscow. *It was based on their life there
with their five children.*

Muscovites are uneasy at the end of autumn, before winter takes
hold. They say they feel better when the real freeze comes, the
hard-edged cold that clears the air of vapors and dangerous viruses.
There is nothing ambiguous about a Russian winter once the temperature drops. For weeks on end the thermometer may vary only
between 15 below and 8 below zero Farenheit; the winter's steely
edge doesn't permit leisurely walks outdoors.

On a clear day the winter sun plays on the deep pastels of old
Moscow. Streets of prerevolutionary yellow row houses, the ochre
plaster walls of old churches, the crumbling sea-green mansions
now occupied by government offices—all seem in sharper focus,
with their defects hidden by the snow. Here and there a half-forgot-
ten church has been revitalized with a coat of white paint, dec-
orated with bright orange and green trim, and its domes refur-
bished with squares of gold leaf.

To be reasonably comfortable for even short walks outdoors it is
necessary to wear coats of natural fur. Russians love fake-fur coats
and man-made fur linings because they are novelties, but they
aren't warm enough for Moscow winters. Everyone wears two pairs
of gloves, one heavier and one lighter, inside each other. Fur hats,
preferably with earflaps, and a scarf underneath, protect heads from
the piercing continental winds. Fleece-lined boots or thick felt
valenki, designed for powdery Siberian snow, keep Russians' feet
warm. Children have only a slit for their eyes left open between
layers of scarves and sheepskin coats. The little ones often have a
rope tied around their coats at the waistline to keep their body
warmth from escaping. The handsome blue suede of policemen's
coats is the reverse side of sheepskin, which makes the men appear
bulky, but keeps them warm while they walk the Moscow beat.

. . .

Moscow is, of course, greener and warmer in summer, but to
enter the real spirit of Russia it is necessary to visit in winter. In the

sparkle of a winter's noonday sun, or even in the impressionistic outlines of a street scene in the fog of a sudden thaw, a visitor can be enveloped in the romantic arms of that strength that survives all adversity. Walking the streets of Moscow are the same Russians who laughed at winter and used it to turn back Napoleon and Hitler.

One Point for Analysis: The second paragraph uses colors to make the description vivid.
Writing Topics:
1. Write a description of a region that seems to exhibit its real self at a particular season of the year.
2. Following the example of the second paragraph, describe a city scene by references to the colors of the place.
3. Describe the methods people use to survive and be comfortable in either an extremely cold region or an extremely hot region.

A PLAIN MEAL

VIRGINIA WOOLF

In the early part of this century, Virginia Woolf and her friends were the center of a London literary circle known as the Bloomsbury Group. She is known for her impressionistic style of description and narration.

Here was my soup. Dinner was being served in the great dining-hall. Far from being spring it was in fact an evening in October. Everybody was assembled in the big dining-room. Dinner was ready. Here was the soup. It was a plain gravy soup. There was nothing to stir the fancy in that. One could have seen through the transparent liquid any pattern that there might have been on the plate itself. But there was no pattern. The plate was plain. Next came beef with its attendant greens and potatoes—a homely trinity, suggesting the rumps of cattle in a muddy market, and sprouts curled and yellowed at the edge, and bargaining and cheapening, and women with string bags on Monday morning. There was no reason to complain of human nature's daily food, seeing that the supply was sufficient and coal-miners doubtless were sitting down to less. Prunes and custard followed. And if any one complains that prunes, even when mitigated by custard, are an uncharitable vegetable (fruit they are not), stringy as a miser's heart and exuding a fluid such as might run in misers' veins who have denied themselves wine and warmth for eighty years and yet not given to the poor, he should reflect that there are people whose charity embraces even the prune. Biscuits and cheese came next, and here the water-jug was liberally passed round, for it is the nature of biscuits to be dry, and these were biscuits to the core. That was all. The meal was over. Everybody scraped their chairs back; the swing-doors swung violently to and fro; soon the hall was emptied of every sign of food and made ready no doubt for breakfast next morning. Down corridors and up staircases the youth of England went banging and singing. And was it for a guest, a stranger (for I had no more right here in Fernham than in Trinity or Somerville or Girton or Newnham or Christchurch), to say, "The dinner was not good," or to say (we were now, Mary Seton and I, in her sitting-room), "Could we not have dined up here alone?" for if I had said anything of the kind I should have been prying and searching into the secret economies of a house which to the stranger wears so fine a front of gaiety and courage. No, one could say nothing of the sort. Indeed conversation for a moment flagged. The human frame being what it is, heart, body and brain all mixed together, and not contained in separate compartments as they will be no doubt in another million years, a good dinner is of great importance to good talk. One cannot think well, love well, sleep well, if one has not dined well. The lamp in the spine does not light on beef and prunes. We are all *probably* going to heaven, and Vandyck is, we *hope,* to meet us round the next corner—that is the dubious and qualifying state of mind that beef and prunes at the end of the day's work breed between them. Happily my friend, who taught science, had a cupboard where there was a squat bottle and little glasses—(but there should have been sole and partridge to begin with)—so that we were able to draw up to the fire and repair some of the damages of the day's living.

One Point for Analysis: Highly complex metaphors carry the burden
of this description.
Writing Topics:
  1. Describe your sensual, emotional, and intellectual reactions to
     a sumptuous feast.
  2. Describe a meal by speaking of the various dishes in meta-
     phors.
  3. In a humorous way describe your reaction to a formal dinner
     at which you were uncomfortable.

THE INCOMING TIDE

ELIZABETH BOWEN

The Heat of the Day, *the novel from which this selection is
taken, has sometimes been called a "woman's novel." Elizabeth
Bowen has also written literary criticism and book reviews for*
The Tatler *and other journals.*

That Sunday, from six o'clock in the evening, it was a Viennese
orchestra that played. The season was late for an outdoor concert;
already leaves were drifting on to the grass stage—here and there
one turned over, crepitating as though in the act of dying, and during the music some more fell.

The open-air theatre, shelving below the level of the surrounding
lawns, was walled by thickets and a few high trees; along the top
ran a wattle fence with gates. Now the two gates stood open. The
rows of chairs down the slope, facing the orchestra, still only filled
up slowly. From here, from where it was being played at the base of
this muffled hollow, the music could not travel far through the
park—but hints of it that did escape were disturbing: from the
mound, from the rose gardens, from the walks round the lakes,
people were being slowly drawn to the theatre by the sensation that
they were missing something. Many of them paused in the gate-
ways doubtfully—all they had left behind was in sunshine, while
this hollow which was the source of music was found to be also the
source of dusk. War had made them idolise day and summer; night
and autumn were enemies. And, at the start of the concert, this tar-

nished bosky theatre, in which no plays had been acted for some time, held a feeling of sequestration, of emptiness the music had not had time to fill. It was not completely in shadow—here and there blades of sunset crossed it, firing branches through which they travelled, and lay along ranks of chairs and faces and hands. Gnats quivered, cigarette smoke dissolved. But the light was so low, so theatrical and so yellow that it was evident it would soon be gone. The incoming tide was evening. Glass-clear darkness, in which each leaf was defined, already formed in the thicket behind the orchestra and was the other element of the stage.

The Sunday had been brilliant, without a stain of cloud. Now, the burning turquoise sky of the afternoon began to gain in transparency as it lost colour: from above the trees round the theatre there stole away not only colour but time. Music—the waltzes, the marches, the gay overtures—now began to command this hourless place. The people lost their look of uncertainty. The heroic marches made them lift up their heads; recollections of opera moulded their faces into unconscious smiles, and during the waltzes women's eyes glittered with delicious tears about nothing. First note by note, drop by drop, then steadily, the music entered senses, nerves and fancies that had been parched. What first was a mirage strengthened into a universe, for the shabby Londoners and the exiled foreigners sitting in this worn glade in the middle of Regent's park. This Sunday on which the sun set was the first Sunday of September 1942.

Pairs of lovers, fatigued by their day alone with each other, were glad to enter this element not themselves: when their looks once more met, it was with refreshed love. Mothers tired by being mothers forgot their children as their children forgot them—one held her baby as though it had been a doll. Married couples who had sat down in apathetic closeness to one another could be seen to begin to draw a little apart, each recapturing some virginal inner dream. Such elderly people as had not been driven home by the disappearance of sun from the last chair fearlessly exposed their years to the dusk, in a lassitude they could have shown at no other time.

These were the English. As for the foreigners, some were so intimate with the music that you could feel them anticipate every note; some sat with eyes closed; others, as though aroused by some unbearable movement inside the breast, glanced behind them or

171

quickly up at the sky. Incredulity, as when waking up from a deep sleep, appeared once or twice in faces. But in most of them, as they continued to sit and listen, stoicism only intensified.

A proportion of the listeners were solitary; and, of the solitary, those who came every Sunday, by habit, could be told from those who had come this Sunday by chance. Surprise at having stumbled upon the music was written on the faces of first-timers. For many, chiefly, the concert was the solution of where to be: one felt eased by this place where something was going on. To be sitting packed among other people was better than walking about alone. At the last moment, this crowned the day with meaning. For there had been moments, heightening towards the end, when the Sunday's beauty—for those with no ambition to cherish, no friend to turn to, no love to contemplate—drove its lack of meaning into the heart.

One Point for Analysis: The author uses images of light and shadow (chiaroscuro) throughout the essay.

Writing Topics:
1. Describe some experience with art that has taken you out of yourself and into something larger.
2. Describe a situation that was at first frightening, but later pleasing.
3. Describe how two different groups react differently to the same event.

OF MAN AND ISLANDS

CASKIE STINNETT

Caskie Stinnett is a frequent contributor to magazines such as Atlantic, Holiday, Esquire, *and* Saturday Review. *Stinnett is a former executive editor of* Ladies' Home Journal, *and was appointed travel editor of* Holiday *in 1965.*

The Latin word for island is *insula,* and the word itself breathes the spirit of island life. Here, surrounded on all sides by a protective moat, one is insulated from the grosser absurdities of an irrational world, from the wearisome conflicts of a restless society, from

172

the relentless sweep of a century that often seems more freighted with fear than with hope. The island offers once more the great prize of passionate individualism, a steady constant in a shifting universe. It is no wonder that possession of an island is the central fantasy of man's dreams.

I am thinking of small islands, I suppose, not something as large as Corfu or Cyprus or Hawaii or Sicily. There—on large islands— the problems of the mainland have intruded, and although one is constantly aware of being on an island, some of the delights of island life have been diminished by traffic and noise and commerce. What I have in mind is an island somewhat the size of the one off the coast of Maine, where I spend five months of every year; an island of three-and-a-half acres, heavily wooded with spruce and fir and with thickets of bayberry growing in the open spaces and with a rocky coastline to which mussels and starfish cling. There the mornings are serene and the nights are compounded of stars, and lamplight, and silence that is broken only by the sound of water lapping against the pilings of the dock. Darkness brings mystery, the mysterious blending of wind whispering through the spruce boughs, of woodsmoke hanging in the evening air, of a gull's raucous screech shattering the stillness of the night. Far away, from the mainland, the sound of an automobile horn is borne on the sea wind, but it is muffled and indistinct and seems part of another world.

For reasons that strike me as odd, I am constantly asked if I am not uneasy about living on an island alone and if I am not bored. I feel more protected by the water than I do by the doorman of the apartment house where I live during the winter months, and while I must confess to occasional boredom, I am less frequently bored on the island than in the city. There is always a changing tide to divert me, a fog-bank lifting to reveal a lobster boat cautiously working its way through the rock ledges, a totally unbelievable moon lighting up the cove, or a summer thunderstorm that rages with terrifying violence for a few minutes and then subsides apologetically into a rainbow. The man who lives on an island builds his isolation without meaning to, and sooner or later it begins to take possession of his soul; but it brings him a serenity and a sureness, a trust in himself that he may never have known before. Whether he desires it or not, he becomes the monarch of a miniature kingdom, the keeper of peace and the protector of lives, and he soon learns that he must

173

deal with fretful winds and fickle seas and lightning and drought. This, I think, is why most island dwellers are innately humble people: They quickly learn their dependence upon nature, a lesson that is the beginning of wisdom for us all.

Fantasies die slowly on an island, and perhaps the last to succumb is the dream of self-sufficiency. I have never known an island dweller who didn't cling stubbornly to the notion that sooner or later he could cut himself adrift from the rest of the world if he cared to. This is a foolish thought, but it nibbles like mischievous mice at the mind of the true islander, and he derives great satisfaction from contemplating it. True sovereignty is the most wistful dream of all, but it does little harm by occupying one's thoughts.

On an island, the quality of life reflects the tastes of the owner, and the corruptive fallout from the mainland is as great as he will tolerate, and no greater. That fragment of land offers the rare opportunity of creating a world of one's own, and the blame for failure can be pinpointed with terrible accuracy. This is probably the unspoken promise that draws twentieth-century man to islands—not that he wants to run on ahead of the rest of the human race, but quite the contrary, to run back to the beginning and make sure the same mistakes are not repeated. This is the true lure of islands, whether they are large or small.

One Point for Analysis: Stinnett uses the etymology of *island* to define it and introduce the thesis.

Writing Topics:
1. Describe a passionate person who is a "steady constant in a shifting universe."
2. Stinnett describes the lure of island life. Describe in your essay the lure of city life.
3. Describe a *missile* by making reference to its etymology (its root meaning).

REFLECTIONS ON THE GUILLOTINE

ALBERT CAMUS

*Albert Camus was a French novelist, essayist, and playwright.
In his writing man is often pictured as alone in a hostile, illogi-
cal, absurd world.*

Instead of boasting, with the pretentious thoughtlessness characteristic of us, of having invented this rapid and humane method of
killing condemned men, we should publish thousands of copies of
the eyewitness accounts and medical reports describing the state of
the body after the execution, to be read in schools and universities.
Particularly suitable for this purpose is the recent report to the
Academy of Medicine made by Doctors Piedelièvre and Fournier.
Those courageous doctors, invited in the interest of science to examine the bodies of the guillotined after the execution, considered
it their duty to sum up their dreadful observations: "If we may be
permitted to give our opinion, such sights are frightfully painful.
The blood flows from the blood vessels at the speed of the severed
carotids, then it coagulates. The muscles contract and their fibrilla-
tion is stupefying; the intestines ripple and the heart moves ir-
regularly, incompletely, fascinatingly. The mouth puckers at certain
moments in a terrible pout. It is true that in that severed head the
eyes are motionless with dilated pupils; fortunately they look at
nothing and, if they are devoid of the cloudiness and opalescence of
the corpse, they have no motion; their transparence belongs to life,
but their fixity belongs to death. All this can last minutes, even
hours, in sound specimens: death is not immediate. . . . Thus,
every vital element survives decapitation. The doctor is left with
this impression of a horrible experience, of a murderous vivisec-
tion, followed by a premature burial."

I doubt that there are many readers who can read that terrifying
report without blanching. Consequently, its exemplary power and
its capacity to intimidate can be counted on. There is no reason not
to add to it eyewitness accounts that confirm the doctors' observations. Charlotte Corday's severed head blushed, it is said, under
the executioner's slap. This will not shock anyone who listens to
more recent observers. An executioner's assistant (hence hardly

175

suspect of indulging in romanticizing and sentimentality) describes in these terms what he was forced to see: "It was a madman undergoing a real attack of *delirium tremens* that we dropped under the blade. The head dies at once. But the body literally jumps about in the basket, straining on the cords. Twenty minutes later, at the cemetery, it is still quivering." The present chaplain of the Santé prison, Father Devoyod (who does not seem opposed to capital punishment), gives in his book, *Les Délinquants,* an account that goes rather far and renews the story of Languille, whose decapitated head answered the call of his name: "The morning of the execution, the condemned man was in a very bad mood and refused the consolations of religion. Knowing his heart of hearts and the affection he had for his wife, who was very devout, we said to him: 'Come now, out of love for your wife, commune with yourself a moment before dying,' and the condemned man accepted. He communed at length before the crucifix, then he seemed to pay no further attention to our presence. When he was executed, we were a short distance from him. His head fell into the trough in front of the guillotine and the body was immediately put into the basket; but, by some mistake, the basket was closed before the head was put in. The assistant who was carrying the head had to wait a moment until the basket was opened again; now, during that brief space of time we could see the condemned man's eyes fixed on me with a look of supplication, as if to ask forgiveness. Instinctively we made the sign of the cross to bless the head, and then the lids blinked, the expression of the eyes softened, and finally the look, that had remained full of expression, became vague. . . ." The reader may or may not, according to his faith, accept the explanation provided by the priest. At least those eyes that "had remained full of expression" need no interpretation.

AN ANALYSIS OF "REFLECTIONS ON THE GUILLOTINE"

Camus' essay "Reflections on the Guillotine" is essentially a descriptive horror-piece that argues against capital punishment. By forcing the reader to experience vicariously a number of severed heads and quivering torsos, the author hopes to dissuade his countrymen from continuing to use what he ironically calls "this rapid and humane method of killing condemned men."

Each detailed picture of a head separated from its body enforces the rhetorical irony implied in the words *rapid* and *humane*. One medical description says, "All this can last minutes, even hours." An executioner's assistant describes a guillotined victim in this way: "Twenty minutes later, at the cemetery, it [the body] is still quivering." Camus even resorts to accounts of executions that are, at best, nonscientific. A chaplain tells the story of a severed head that "answered the call of his name." Rapid? Humane? After reading Camus' essay, it would be hard to answer yes.

The organization of the essay is effective. It is essentially a tableau of one guillotined victim after another, but each descriptive picture becomes progressively more shocking. Finally, Camus' argument peaks in the simple repetition of a phrase from an account he has already used. He says, "At least those eyes that 'had remained full of expression' need no interpretation." In the somber, often gory language of this essay, he closes his case, and the reader is left with the mental picture of a head separated from its quivering body—"then the lids blinked, the expression of the eyes softened."

THE ENDURING SEA

RACHEL CARSON

Rachel Carson was a marine biologist who loved life and people. She was the winner of the National Book Award in 1951 for The Sea Around Us.

Now I hear the sea sounds about me; the night high tide is rising, swirling with a confused rush of waters against the rocks below my study window. Fog has come into the bay from the open sea, and it lies over water and over the land's edge, seeping back into the spruces and stealing softly among the juniper and the bayberry. The restive waters, the cold wet breath of the fog, are of a world in which man is an uneasy trespasser; he punctuates the night with the complaining groan and grunt of a foghorn, sensing the power and menace of the sea.

Hearing the rising tide, I think how it is pressing also against other shores I know—rising on a southern beach where there is no fog, but a moon edging all the waves with silver and touching the wet sands with lambent sheen, and on a still more distant shore

From *The Edge of the Sea* by Rachel Carson. Copyright © 1955 by Rachel L. Carson. Reprinted by permission of Houghton Mifflin Company.

sending its streaming currents against the moonlit pinnacles and the dark caves of the coral rock.

Then in my thoughts these shores, so different in their nature and in the inhabitants they support, are made one by the unifying touch of the sea. For the differences I sense in this particular instant of time that is mine are but the differences of a moment, determined by our place in the stream of time and in the long rhythms of the sea. Once this rocky coast beneath me was a plain of sand; then the sea rose and found a new shore line. And again in some shadowy future the surf will have ground these rocks to sand and will have returned the coast to its earlier state. And so in my mind's eye these coastal forms merge and blend in a shifting, kaleidoscopic pattern in which there is no finality, no ultimate and fixed reality—earth becoming fluid as the sea itself.

On all these shores there are echoes of past and future: of the flow of time, obliterating yet containing all that has gone before; of the sea's eternal rhythms—the tides, the beat of surf, the pressing rivers of the currents—shaping, changing, dominating; of the stream of life, flowing as inexorably as any ocean current, from past to unknown future. For as the shore configuration changes in the flow of time, the pattern of life changes, never static, never quite the same from year to year. Whenever the sea builds a new coast, waves of living creatures surge against it, seeking a foothold, establishing their colonies. And so we come to perceive life as a force as tangible as any of the physical realities of the sea, a force strong and purposeful, as incapable of being crushed or diverted from its end as the rising tide.

Contemplating the teeming life of the shore, we have an uneasy sense of the communication of some universal truth that lies just beyond our grasp. What is the message signaled by the hordes of diatoms, flashing their microscopic lights in the night sea? What truth is expressed by the legions of the barnacles, whitening the rocks with their habitations, each small creature within finding the necessities of its existence in the sweep of the surf? And what is the meaning of so tiny a being as the transparent wisp of protoplasm that is a sea lace, existing for some reason inscrutable to us—a reason that demands its presence by the trillion amid the rocks and weeds of the shore? The meaning haunts and ever eludes us, and in its very pursuit we approach the ultimate mystery of Life itself.

178

One Point for Analysis: The words of the essay flow with a rhythm like that of the sea—in particular, the opening of the fourth paragraph.

Writing Topics:

1. Describe an experience in which you have come into contact with "some universal truth that lies just beyond. . . ."
2. Following the description of some phenomenon, conclude, like Carson, with a series of questions that cannot be answered.
3. Describe your feelings on seeing the ocean for the first time.

HITLER THE DICTATOR

ALAN BULLOCK

Bullock was Vice-Chancellor of Oxford University. His works include The Liberal Tradition *and* The Life and Times of Ernest Bevin.

In his Munich days Hitler always carried a heavy riding-whip, made of hippopotamus hide. The impression he wanted to convey was one of force, decision, will. Yet Hitler had nothing of the easy, assured toughness of a condottiere like Göring. His strength of personality, far from being natural to him, was the product of an exertion of will: from this sprang a harsh, jerky and over-emphatic manner which was very noticeable in his early days as a politician.

To say that Hitler was ambitious scarcely describes the intensity of the lust for power and the craving to dominate which consumed him. It was the will to power in its crudest and purest form, not identifying itself with the triumph of a principle as with Lenin or Robespierre—for the only principle of Nazism was power and domination for its own sake—nor finding satisfaction in the fruits of power, for, by comparison with other Nazi leaders like Göring, Hitler lived an ascetic life. For a long time Hitler succeeded in identifying his own power with the recovery of Germany's old position in the world, but as soon as the interests of Germany began to diverge from his own, his patriotism was seen at its true value— Germany, like everything else in the world, was only a means, a

179

vehicle for his own power, which he would sacrifice with the same indifference as the lives of those he sent to the Eastern Front.

Although, looking backwards, it is possible to detect anticipations of this monstrous will to power in Hitler's early years, it remained latent until the end of the First World War and only began to appear noticeably when he reached his thirties. From the account in *Mein Kampf* it appears that the shock of defeat and the Revolution of November 1918 produced a crisis in which hitherto dormant faculties were awakened and directed towards the goal of becoming a politician and founding a new movement.

Resentment is marked in Hitler's attitude, and hatred intoxicated him. Many of his speeches are long diatribes of hate—against the Jews, the Marxists, the Czechs, the Poles, the intellectuals and the educated middle-classes who belonged to that comfortable bourgeois world which had once rejected him and which he was determined to destroy in revenge.

No less striking was his constant need of praise. The atmosphere of adulation in which he lived seems to have deadened the critical faculties of all who came into it. The most banal platitudes and the most grotesque errors of taste and judgement, if uttered by the Führer, were accepted as the words of inspired genius. It is to the credit of Röhm and Gregor Strasser, who had known Hitler for a long time, that they were irritated and totally unimpressed by this Byzantine attitude towards the Führer; no doubt, this was among the reasons why they were murdered.

One Point for Analysis: The sentence structure used in this essay is sophisticated.

Writing Topics:
1. After library research, describe another well-known tyrant from history.
2. A number of organizations exist in America today that are characterized by hatred of and opposition to another ethnic or political group. Describe one such organization.
3. Describe a mob you have seen swayed by a particularly effective speaker or leader.

AT THE FORKS

JAMES AGEE

James Agee was reared in Tennessee, where he developed a love of the land and the people who live in the rural areas. "At the Forks" is from his longer descriptive work Let Us Now Praise Famous Men.

On a road between the flying shadows of loose woods toward the middle of an afternoon, far enough thrust forward between towns that we had lost intuition of our balance between them, we came to a fork where the sunlight opened a little more widely, but not on cultivated land, and stopped a minute to decide.

Marion would lie some miles over beyond the road on our left; some other county seat, Centerville most likely, out beyond the road on our right; but on which road the woods might give way to any extension of farm country there was no deducing: for we were somewhere toward the middle of one of the wider of the gaps on the road map, and had seen nothing but woods, and infrequent woods farms, for a good while now.

Just a little behind us on our left and close on the road was a house, the first we had passed in several miles, and we decided to ask directions of the people on the porch, whom, in the car mirror, I could see still watching us. We backed slowly, stopping the car a little short of the house, and I got slowly out and walked back toward them, watching them quietly and carefully, and preparing my demeanors and my words for the two hundredth time.

There were three on the porch, watching me, and they must not have spoken twice in an hour while they watched beyond the rarely traveled road the changes of daylight along the recessions of the woods, and while, in the short field that sank behind their house, their two crops died silently in the sun: a young man, a young woman, and an older man; and the two younger, their chins drawn inward and their heads tall against the grained wall of the house, watched me steadily and sternly as if from beneath the brows of helmets, in the candor of young warriors or of children.

They were of a kind not safely to be described in an account claiming to be unimaginative or trustworthy, for they had too much and too outlandish beauty not to be legendary. Since, however, they existed quite irrelevant to myth, it will be necessary to tell a little of them.

The young man's eyes had the opal lightings of dark oil and, though he was watching me in a way that relaxed me to cold weakness of ignobility, they fed too strongly inward to draw to a focus: whereas those of the young woman had each the splendor of a monstrance, and were brass. Her body also was brass or bitter gold, strong to stridency beneath the unbleached clayed cotton dress, and her arms and bare legs were sharp with metal down. The blenched hair drew her face tight to her skull as a tied mask; her features were baltic. The young man's face was deeply shaded with soft short beard, and luminous with death. He had the scornfully ornate nostrils and lips of an aegean exquisite. The fine wood body was ill strung, and sick even as he sat there to look at, and the bone hands roped with vein; they rose, then sank, and lay palms upward in his groins. There was in their eyes so quiet and ultimate a quality of hatred, and contempt, and anger, toward every creature in existence beyond themselves, and toward the damages they sustained, as shone scarcely short of a state of beatitude; nor did this at any time modify itself.

These two sat as if formally, or as if sculptured, one in wood and one in metal, or as if enthroned, about three feet apart in straight chairs tilted to the wall, and constantly watched me, all the while communicating thoroughly with each other by no outward sign of word or glance or turning, but by emanation.

The other man might have been fifty by appearance, yet, through a particular kind of delicateness upon his hands, and hair, and skin—they were almost infantine—I was sure he was still young, hardly out of his twenties, though again the face was seamed and short as a fetus. This man, small-built and heavy jointed, and wandering in his motions like a little child, had the thorny beard of a cartoon bolshevik, but suggested rather a hopelessly deranged and weeping prophet, a D. H. Lawrence whom male nurses have just managed to subdue into a straitjacket. A broken felt hat struck through with grass hair was banged on flat above his furious and leaky eyes, and from beneath its rascally brim as if from ambush he pored at me walleyed while, clenching himself back against the wall, he sank along it trembling and slowly to a squat, and watched up at me.

One Point for Analysis: Two prevailing metaphors are used to develop the descriptions of the younger man and woman. She is spoken of in terms of metal, he, less extensively in terms of wood.

Writing Topics:

1. Write a descriptive essay on a "hopelessly deranged and weeping prophet" whom you have known through either literature or experience.
2. Describe two people, one in terms of lead, the other in terms of gold.
3. Write a description of an underprivileged group in which suffering has produced wisdom.

AGAINST GLUTTONY AND GOURMANDS

GIOVANNI BOCCACCIO

Boccaccio was an Italian writer and humanist of the fourteenth century. His masterpiece The Decameron *has amused and entertained readers since it was written around 1348.*

To be sure, gluttony is an abominable vice, and—like lust, sloth, and avarice—should be avoided; and wrath and blind fury must, as well, be condemned. Gluttony is bestial and deadly. In gluttony we use immoderately what nature has given us for our sustenance, and to avoid the vice, we should not readily slacken the reins of temperance in our appetite. Nature, uncomplicated, is content with moderation, and rejects what is prepared with human cunning. The present age, the Saturnine age of gold, gives shameful testimony of this. To alleviate their hunger and thirst, most ancient people relate that for them acorns and brook-water sufficed. Diogenes, in more recent times, approved this repast with the addition of wild greens and roots. And much more famous, the Most Glorious One, He who was sanctified in the womb, was nourished on locusts and honey in the wilderness. In place of this diet our younger and wanton age not only discovered the flesh of harmless animals and wine, but in addition substituted artificiality instead of letting nature provide. It is now considered wise to incite the calm appetite by introducing spice or mulling wine with outside flavors. Would that the discovery of these things had been enough to satisfy us! But much that was gluttonous went beyond this to an extreme, without mentioning those vices that excessive gormandizing allowed or how many diseases it introduced into the troubled body. But while we do not plan to enumerate all these, still we do not wish to pass over them in silence.

When the voracious glutton sits down at a loaded table, devouring now this, now that, and greedily draining the overflowing mug, he does not do this to satisfy the wants of nature, but to stuff the chasm of his corpulent belly, warmed with the strong vapors of steaming platters. Instantly, from ecstasy he goes into frenzy, and imagines he has achieved greatness. An immense ostentation follows; than an easy credulousness, the revelation of secrets, the miserable deprecation of whatever occurs. Ears now respond to flattery, the heart to any kind of confidence, and the mind rejects nothing except what is worthwhile. The brain, stupefied, suffers with dizziness; there is frequent gaping, forgetfulness, indecent talk, conflict of the senses, a floundering step. Finally there is repulsive belching and vomiting, because what he devoured and what the gullet forced down into it, the stomach did not have the strength to support.

Sometimes, in contrast, the stomach retains all the food. The gourmand very painfully begins putrefying, and by this putrefaction of the blood the body's whole organization of nature is brought out of balance. This results in the disfiguration of the eyes and the mouth as well as in tremors, paralysis, staggers, stammering, dropsy, consumption, gout, a feverish itching, filthy scabs, a violent fever, and nausea, for the stomach refuses all food. In addition to these, very often even an untimely death results. Verifying what the most learned doctors have told us, more people have died from banquets than from battles.

Most of these gluttons will, therefore, be seen among the drowsy, the delirious, the diseased, those dying shamefully, the slaves of their stomachs. The glutton is constantly arranging meals. Inspired by his oversized goblets, he thinks he can get out of any kind of work.

Oh, too degrading a life! How satisfying it would be—if the acorns of the ancients are too sparse—to follow the moderation of the men of history. With moderation, the vices are indeed suppressed and the virtues maintained, and the minds of men easily raised to higher things. The whole strength of the body is conserved for the best habits. When Vitellius on the royal throne spurned these, his satiety did not take away disgrace from his person nor pain from his body.

One Point for Analysis: The moralistic tone of this essay reflects the writer's concern with virtue and vice.

Writing Topics:
1. Describe a party you have attended at which the guests ate and drank too much.
2. Describe your own efforts at dieting.
3. Omitting the moralistic judgments, rewrite this essay as a modern person concerned with the effect of eating habits on health.

THURSDAY MORNING IN A NEW YORK SUBWAY STATION

TOM WOLFE

Tom Wolfe is a careful observer of social groups and movements in contemporary America. He is noted for his fast-paced and innovative descriptions.

Love! Attar of libido in the air! It is 8:45 A.M. Thursday morning in the IRT subway station at 50th Street and Broadway and already two kids are hung up in a kind of herringbone weave of arms and legs, which proves, one has to admit, that love is not *confined* to Sunday in New York. Still, the odds! All the faces come popping in clots out of the Seventh Avenue local, past the King Size Ice Cream machine, and the turnstiles start whacking away as if the world were breaking up on the reefs. Four steps past the turnstiles everybody is already backed up haunch to paunch for the climb up the ramp and the stairs to the surface, a great funnel of flesh, wool, felt, leather, rubber and steaming alumicron, with the blood squeezing through everybody's old sclerotic arteries in hopped-up spurts from too much coffee and the effort of surfacing from the subway at the rush hour. Yet there on the landing are a boy and a girl, both about eighteen, in one of those utter, My Sin, backbreaking embraces.

He envelops her not only with his arms but with his chest, which has the American teen-ager concave shape to it. She has her head cocked at a 90-degree angle and they both have their eyes pressed shut for all they are worth and some incredibly feverish action going with each other's mouths. All round them, ten, scores, it seems like hundreds, of faces and bodies are perspiring, trooping and bellying up the stairs with arteriosclerotic grimaces past a showcase full of such novel items as Joy Buzzers, Squirting Nickels, Finger Rats, Scary Tarantulas and spoons with realistic dead flies on them, past Fred's barbershop, which is just off the landing and has glossy photographs of young men with the kind of baroque haircuts one can get in there, and up onto 50th Street into a madhouse of traffic and shops with weird lingerie and gray hair-dyeing displays in the windows, signs for free teacup readings and a pool-playing match between the Playboy Bunnies and Downey's Showgirls, and then everybody pounds on toward the Time-Life Building, the Brill Building or NBC.

The boy and the girl just keep on writhing in their embroilment. Her hand is sliding up the back of his neck, which he turns when her fingers wander into the intricate formal gardens of his Chicago Boxcar hairdo at the base of the skull. The turn causes his face to start to mash in the ciliated hull of her beehive hairdo, and so she rolls her head 180 degrees to the other side, using their mouths for the pivot. But aside from good hair grooming, they are oblivious to everything but each other. Everybody gives them a once-over. Disgusting! Amusing! How touching! A few kids pass by and say things like "Swing it, baby." But the great majority in that heaving funnel up the stairs seem to be as much astounded as anything else. The vision of love at rush hour cannot strike anyone exactly as romance. It is a feat, like a fat man crossing the English Channel in a barrel. It is an earnest accomplishment against the tide. It is a piece of slightly gross heroics, after the manner of those knobby, varicose old men who come out from some place in baggy shorts every year and run through the streets of Boston in the Marathon race. And somehow that is the gaffe against love all week long in New York, for everybody, not just two kids writhing under their coiffures in the 50th Street subway station; too hurried, too crowded, too hard, and no time for dalliance.

One Point for Analysis: The long sentence in the second paragraph gives the feeling of motion like that of the crowd as it emerges from the subway, surfaces on the street, and merges with the traffic.

Writing Topics:
1. Describe a person or persons who are out of place in a particular setting.
2. Write a humorous description of someone who is comical not because of himself but because of his surroundings.
3. Rewrite Wolfe's description, making the lovers serious figures instead of laughable ones.

THE BOY'S AMBITION

SAMUEL L. CLEMENS

Samuel L. Clemens, who wrote under the familiar name Mark Twain, was a lifelong lover of the Mississippi River and the steamboats that traveled it. His affection for both is recorded in this essay.

When I was a boy, there was but one permanent ambition among my comrades in our village on the west bank of the Mississippi River. That was, to be a steamboatman. We had transient ambitions of other sorts, but they were only transient. When a circus came and went, it left us all burning to become clowns; the first negro minstrel show that ever came to our section left us all suffering to try that kind of life; now and then we had a hope that, if we lived and were good, God would permit us to be pirates. These ambi-

"The Boy's Ambition" from *Life on the Mississippi* by Mark Twain. Harper & Row.

tions faded out, each in its turn; but the ambition to be a steamboatman always remained.

Once a day a cheap, gaudy packet arrived upward from St. Louis,
and another downward from Keokuk. Before these events, the day
was glorious with expectancy; after them, the day was a dead and
empty thing. Not only the boys, but the whole village, felt this.
After all these years I can picture that old time to myself now, just
as it was then: the white town drowsing in the sunshine of a summer's morning; the streets empty, or pretty nearly so; one or two
clerks sitting in front of the Water Street stores, with their splint-
bottomed chairs tilted back against the wall, chins on breasts, hats
slouched over their faces, asleep—with shingle-shavings enough
around to show what broke them down; a sow and a litter of pigs
loafing along the sidewalk, doing a good business in watermelon
rinds and seeds; two or three lonely little freight piles scattered
about the "levee"; a pile of "skids" on the slope of the stone-paved
wharf, and the fragrant town drunkard asleep in the shadow of
them; two or three wood flats at the head of the wharf, but nobody
to listen to the peaceful lapping of the wavelets against them; the
great Mississippi, the majestic, the magnificent Mississippi, rolling
its mile-wide tide along, shining in the sun; the dense forest away
on the other side; the "point" above the town, and the "point"
below, bounding the river-glimpse and turning it into a sort of sea,
and withal a very still and brilliant and lonely one. Presently a film
of dark smoke appears above one of those remote "points"; instantly a negro drayman, famous for his quick eye and prodigious
voice, lifts up the cry, "S-t-e-a-m-boat a-comin'!" and the scene
changes! The town drunkard stirs, the clerks wake up, a furious
clatter of drays follows, every house and store pours out a human
contribution, and all in a twinkling the dead town is alive and moving. Drays, carts, men, boys, all go hurrying from many quarters to
a common centre, the wharf. Assembled there, the people fasten
their eyes upon the coming boat as upon a wonder they are seeing
for the first time. And the boat *is* rather a handsome sight, too. She
is long and sharp and trim and pretty; she has two tall, fancy-
topped chimneys, with a gilded device of some kind swung between them; a fanciful pilot-house, all glass and "gingerbread,"
perched on top of the "texas" deck behind them; the paddle-boxes
are gorgeous with a picture or with gilded rays above the boat's
name: the boiler deck, the hurricane deck, and the texas deck are

fenced and ornamented with clean white railings; there is a flag gallantly flying from the jack-staff; the furnace doors are open and the fires glaring bravely; the upper decks are black with passengers; the captain stands by the big bell, calm, imposing, the envy of all: great volumes of the blackest smoke are rolling and tumbling out of the chimneys—a husbanded grandeur created with a bit of pitch pine just before arriving at a town; the crew are grouped on the forecastle; the broad stage is run far out over the port bow, and an envied deck-hand stands picturesquely on the end of it with a coil of rope in his hand; the pent steam is screaming through the gauge-cocks; the captain lifts his hand, a bell rings, the wheels stop; then they turn back, churning the water to foam, and the steamer is at rest. Then such a scramble as there is to get aboard, and to get ashore, and to take in freight and to discharge freight, all at one and the same time; and such a yelling and cursing as the mates facilitate it all with! Ten minutes later the steamer is under way again, with no flag on the jack-staff and no black smoke issuing from the chimneys. After ten more minutes the town is dead again, and the town drunkard asleep by the skids once more.

One Point for Analysis: The diction used before the steamboat is seen is slow and heavy; the pace quickens with the arrival of the steamboat and grows slow again after its departure.

Writing Topics:
1. Describe some person or object that represented glamour or adventure to you in childhood.
2. The drunkard on television and in films is usually a laughable character. Write a descriptive essay in which you give a serious picture of the drunkard.
3. Imitating Clemens's essay, describe a setting that begins lazily, livens quickly, and returns finally to its original drowsiness.

SUFFERINGS AND GREATNESS OF RICHARD WAGNER

THOMAS MANN

Thomas Mann was a German writer who left Nazi Germany in 1933 to settle in Switzerland and then in the United States. He was awarded the Nobel Prize for Literature in 1929.

The general tone, psychologically speaking, of Wagner's music is heavy, pessimistic, laden with sluggish yearning, broken in rhythm; it seems to be wrestling up out of darkness and confusion to redemption in the beautiful; it is the music of a burdened soul, it has no dancing appeal to the muscles, it struggles, urges, and drives most labouredly, most unsouthernly—Lenbach's quick wit characterized it aptly when he said to Wagner one day: "Your music—dear me, it is a sort of luggage van to the kingdom of heaven." But it is not that alone.

Its soul-heaviness must not make one forget that it can also produce the sprightly, the blithe, and the stately—as in the themes of the knights, the motifs of Lohengrin, Stolzing, and Parsifal, the natural mischievousness and loveliness of the terzetto of the Rhine maidens, the burlesque humour and learned arrogance of the overture to the *Meistersinger,* the jolly folk-music of the dance in the second act. Wagner can do anything. In the art of characterization he is incomparable; to understand his music as a method of characterization is to admire it without stint. It is picturesque, it is even grotesque; it is all based upon the perspective required by the theatre. But it has a richness of inventiveness even in small matters, a flexible capacity of entering into character, speech, and gesture such as was never seen in so marked a degree.

In the single roles it is triumphant: take the figure of the Flying Dutchman, musically and poetically encompassed by doom and destruction, wrapped round by the wild raging of the lonely seas. Or Loki with his elemental incalculableness and malicious charm, or Siegfried's dwarf foster-father, knock-kneed and blinking; or Beckmesser's silly spite. It is the Dionysiac play-actor and his art—his arts, if you like—revealing themselves in his omnipotent, ubiquitous power of depiction and transformation. He changes not only his human mask; he enters into nature and speaks in the tempest and the thunderbolt, in the rustling leaf and the sparkling wave, in the rainbow and the dancing flame. Alberic's tarn-cap is the comprehensive symbol of this genius for disguise, this imitative all— pervasiveness: that can enter as well into the spongy hopping, and crawling of the lowly toad as into the care-free, cloud-swinging existence of the old Norse gods.

It is this characteristic versatility that could encompass works of such absolute heterogeneity as the *Meistersinger,* sturdy and German as Luther himself, and *Tristan's* death-drunken, death-yearning world. It marks off each of the operas from the others, develops each out of one fundamental note that distinguishes it from all the rest; so that—within the entire product, which after all is a personal cosmos—each single work forms a closed and starry cosmos of its own.

One Point for Analysis: Paragraph indentations help the reader to follow the organization of this essay.

Writing Topics:
1. Describe, following the example of Mann, the music (not song lyrics) of one composer (not performer) you have listened to at length.
2. Listen to a recording of Wagner for an hour. Describe what it sounds like to you.
3. Describe how an individual song by your favorite composer is related musically or by lyrics to other songs he has written.

4

THE EXPOSITORY ESSAY

INTRODUCTION TO EXPOSITION

The reader who looks carefully at the word *exposition* will find another word, one that states the purpose of exposition: to *expose*. In other words, you write expository prose when you want to explain what something is or how it operates, how to do something, or why one thing causes another. When you write an expository essay, you are primarily interested in stating facts about the subject.

Exposition is helpful when you are writing other types of essays. For example, if you are arguing that the municipal government should extend the city limits, you need to present some background information if your case is to have any meaning for someone who is uninformed about the issue. Such background is expository. Sometimes description presents factual information about a subject at the same time it helps the reader to sense the kind of experience being described.

If, however, your purpose is simply to explain, not essentially to argue a point or describe an experience or tell a story, you can choose to arrange your information in a number of different ways. You can define your subject by stating what kind of thing it is, then go on to list its particular characteristics. You can compare and contrast it with something else, discuss what caused it and what effect it will have, divide it into its parts, or list the steps involved in carrying it out. Whatever form your expository essay takes, each point should be illustrated with examples. They make your explanation easier for the reader to understand. And understanding is the main purpose of exposition.

THE SYMPHONY AND HAYDN

JEAN SELIGMANN AND JULIET DANZIGER

"The Symphony and Haydn" is expository rather than narrative because it presents information concerning the symphony and how Haydn influenced its development, instead of telling the story of the composer's life.

In the days of Joseph Haydn noblemen employed composers just as they did cooks and coachmen. The various members of the family as well as the household servants usually played some musical instrument, and it was generally the custom of noblemen to give many informal concerts in their palaces. And just as the cook had to prepare food for the table, so the composer had to provide music for these private concerts.

Joseph Haydn was employed by Prince Esterházy, who maintained at his estate in Austria a very fine orchestra of fourteen performers. It was Haydn's duty not only to take charge of all the music for this orchestra, but also to see that the musicians appeared in white stockings and with their wigs thoroughly powdered, and "to compose such music as His Highness shall order, divulge these new compositions to no one, and compose nothing for anybody without His Highness' knowledge and gracious permission."

For his orchestra, which contained most of the instruments of our present-day orchestra, Haydn composed many works built on the same musical framework. These works are called symphonies. You may be familiar with Haydn's "Surprise Symphony" and the "Clock Symphony." These names were given to the symphonies by Haydn's admirers, and not by Haydn himself. They were not composed with the idea of telling a story.

At most orchestral concerts you will hear a symphony played. One of the things you will notice about a symphony is that it is comparatively long; it usually lasts over a half hour. Another thing you will notice is that it is divided into separate sections, in most cases four. These sections are called movements. In the concert hall you can usually both see and hear that there are separate movements. You *see* that there are separate movements because at the end of each one the orchestra stops playing and the conductor drops his arms and waits before continuing with the next movement. And even with only slight experience in listening to music you will also *hear* that there are different movements. Each movement is usually a complete piece in itself, and the movements of the symphony sound like four different pieces by one composer.

Haydn composed over a hundred works in a form which almost all the great composers of symphonies after him used as a framework for their symphonic works. Each composer altered the form in some way, but the general structure remained the same.

The term "symphony" is used to describe all four movements together. But each individual movement has its own form too.

What is the form of the first movement of a symphony? The first movement is almost always written in a form known as the sonata form. Form in music is the structure or design of a piece of music, that is, its framework. What we mean when we say that the first movements of most symphonies are in the sonata form is that, no matter how different they may seem, they have all been constructed around the same framework.

A fugue is built up around one theme (musical idea). The sonata form is built up around at least two themes, often more, seldom less. A big advantage of working with two or more themes instead of one is the greater possibility of contrast. One theme, for example, can be vigorous and forceful, another gentle and song-like. Contrast makes music more interesting. That is one reason the sonata form has been used by so many composers.

The first movement of a symphony—a work for orchestra in four movements—is written in the sonata form, which uses as its subject several themes. The second movement in a Haydn symphony is frequently built upon one theme used over and over again in varied ways. These different ways of treating the same theme are called variations. The second movement of a symphony, when it employs this form, is called Theme and Variations.

There are many ways of varying the theme: changing its rhythm, making it faster or slower, decorating the outline of the theme with additional notes, changing the tone color by giving the theme to different combinations of instruments, passing the tune from one instrument to another in turn. In most instances some element of the theme—its melody, harmony, or form—remains recognizable. Listening to a theme and variations can be most rewarding if you know your theme. But you should not regard variations as puzzles challenging you to find the theme. There are some instances in which the relationship of a variation to its parent theme becomes apparent only after you have heard it several times.

The third movement of a Haydn symphony is almost always written in a dance form of lively tempo called a minuet. The rhythm of the minuet is probably familiar to you: three beats to the measure, the first one accented. The form of the minuet is a simple one: three sections, the first and third alike, the center section (called the trio) different. The gay, fresh, sprightly qualities of the minuets are part of what we mean when we say "typically Haydn." Mozart also used the minuet form for the third movements of his symphonies, and it is found, too, in some of the works of Beethoven.

After using the sonata form for the first movement of his symphonies, a theme and variations or three-part form for his second movement, and the minuet for his third movement, Haydn often returns to the sonata form for his fourth movement. A well-known English critic calls Haydn's fourth movements "kittenish," for they are almost always fast and full of fun.

Besides more than one hundred symphonies, Haydn also composed over seventy-five string quartets.

He remained in the employ of the Esterházy family for almost thirty years. During this time he composed a vast quantity of works, and achieved fame throughout most of Europe. Oxford University in England honored him with a degree of Doctor of Music.

AN ANALYSIS OF "THE SYMPHONY AND HAYDN"

The authors of "The Symphony and Haydn" announce to the reader in the title that they intend to discuss two subjects, not just one. Because Haydn exerted a great deal of influence on the development of the symphony, the topics help to explain each other. Some parts of the essay are devoted solely to presenting information about the symphony, some solely about Haydn. In other places they are examined together.

The three opening paragraphs explain who Joseph Haydn was and what he did. Although this essay is expository, beginning with the presentation of biographical information about the composer allows the authors to create the sense that one is reading a story, not just a collection of facts. By so doing, they build the reader's interest in going on.

The fourth paragraph makes an abrupt change of subject, with no attempt at providing the reader with a transition. Instead, it suddenly takes up the essay's second subject, the symphony. The paragraph is purely expository, explaining how a symphony is organized, what a "movement" is, and how one movement is related to the others.

After a brief comment about Haydn's influence on the development of symphonic form, to remind the reader that the two subjects are closely related, the authors continue their discussion of the symphony. The sixth through eighth paragraphs define the sonata form and the fugue, then explain the importance of contrasts in music.

After the separate discussions of Haydn and the symphony, the topics are brought together for simultaneous consideration. The ninth through twelfth paragraphs, composing the longest single section of the essay, explain in detail each of the four movements of the traditional symphony. Interwoven with that explanation is information about how Haydn treated each of the movements. As the authors point out, they are clarifying what a person means when he says that music is "typically Haydn."

The final two brief paragraphs employ the same device as the introduction. They too focus primarily on Haydn's life, specifically the end of his life. The essay's conclusion stresses not only the composer's relationship with his musical patrons, the Esterházy family, but also the worldwide fame he had by the time of his death.

This essay is a good example of exposition written for a nonprofessional audience about a technical subject. The authors, who use a number of terms likely to be unfamiliar to the reader who is not a musician, are careful to define any word or phrase that may be confusing. Sometimes they call the reader's attention to the fact thay they are using an unusual term. For example, the opening sentence of the seventh paragraph asks, "What is the form of the first movement of a symphony?" Such a question, known as a rhetorical question, signals the reader that an explanation of *form* will immediately follow.

The clear presentation of historical and biographical data, the careful use of definitions, and the lucid explanations make this essay an effective piece of exposition. It is interesting and informative even to one whose musical background is limited, because the authors considered their purpose and the audience as well as their subject before they sat down to write.

SATCHEL PAIGE: BASEBALL'S PITCHING WONDER

STEVE M. BARKIN

Satchel Paige has in the course of his long career in baseball been the subject of many newspaper columns and magazine articles. Steve M. Barkin presents in this essay a brief account of Paige's career.

Even if you're a baseball fan, you may never have heard of the Kansas City Monarchs, the Pittsburgh Crawfords, or the Birmingham Black Barons. But one man who played with those teams may have been the greatest pitcher in all of baseball—a man named LeRoy "Satchel" Paige.

Because he was black, Satchel Paige was not allowed to pitch in the major leagues until he was in his forties. By that time he had lost much of the blinding speed that had made him famous. Paige had pitched for more than twenty years in the organized Negro leagues before becoming the oldest rookie in major-league history.

It is difficult to measure how great Satchel Paige really was. Statistics were not carefully kept in the Negro leagues, so we can only estimate what he accomplished. Even educated guesses are astounding: Paige probably pitched in 3,000 games, won at least 2,000, and hurled about 100 no-hitters. Cy Young holds the major-league record for pitching victories with 511. Yet Paige won perhaps four times as many games. Remarkably, he was still capable of pitching three scoreless innings for the Kansas city Athletics at the age of fity-nine.

LeRoy Paige was the seventh of eleven children born to John and Lula Paige. The family lived in a small four-room house in Mobile, Alabama. John Paige was a gardener, and his wife Lula worked as a maid. Because there were thirteen mouths to feed, all the children had to start working when they were very young. "By the time I was about six," Satchel wrote many years later, "all my older brothers and sisters had steady jobs—even Wilson, who was about nine or ten. We all gave our money to Mom, so she could get food."

Amid such poverty, there was no money for toys. Satchel and his friends played in the dirt, and then raced to the nearby bay to wash off. A favorite game was knocking cans off tree stumps with stones.

LeRoy Paige's first job was looking for empty bottles he could return for cash. But by the time he was seven, his parents thought he could earn more money. He was put to work carrying luggage at the railroad station for a nickel or dime per bag. He rigged up a pole and ropes that enabled him to carry three or four bags at once. When one of the other young porters said he "looked like a walking satchel tree," LeRoy Paige acquired a nickname that would become legendary.

Wilbur Hines, the baseball coach at Mobile's W. H. Council School, was the first person to recognize Satchel's extraordinary talent. He noticed that Satchel was a fine hitter and played him in the outfield and at first base. Hines let the skinny ten-year-old pitch in a game midway through the season, but only after two other pitchers had given up six runs in the first inning. Satchel did not give up a hit and struck out sixteen. Satchel's team won the game 11 to 6, and Wilbur Hines had found a pitcher.

Throwing rocks developed Satchel's speed and control, but it often got him into trouble when he and his friends had rock fights with boys from a rival school. When he was twelve, he was caught stealing a handful of toy rings from a store. He was sent to a reform school in Mt. Meigs, Alabama. Satchel would later say that the five years he spent at Mt. Meigs changed the direction of his life. He became choir leader at the school and a member of the drum and bugle corps. Away from Mobile's street gangs, he took more interest in his school work and developed his growing baseball skills.

In 1923, Satchel Paige was released from the reform school and returned home to Mobile. He was seventeen years old, stood 6 feet 3½ inches, and weighed only 140 pounds. Although he added weight in later years, the sight of a lean and lanky Paige walking to the pitcher's mound is remembered by many fans to this day.

The next year Satchel joined the semi-pro Mobile Tigers. If a good number of people turned out for a game, he would earn a dollar; if gate receipts were poor, he might have to settle for some lemonade. Ten years later he was the most famous black baseball player in America, pitching on exhibition tours around the country. One of the teams he played with had a season record of 104 wins and only one loss.

From the very beginning, Satchel Paige was a master showman as well as a superb pitcher. He once ordered the outfield to come in and pitched without them, when even a lazy pop fly would have won for the other team. Other times he would promise to strike out the first six or nine men he faced—and do so. Satchel could pitch strikes using a handkerchief as home plate. He called his fast ball a variety of colorful names—the "sneaky pitch," "bee ball," "jump ball," "trouble ball," and "Long Tom."

Even before he was allowed to play in the majors, Satchel's abilities were respected by the great players of his day. The famous Dizzy Dean of the St. Louis Cardinals called him "the best pitcher I ever saw." In one exhibition game, Paige allowed no runs against a team of major-league all-stars. In another game, he struck out the great Rogers Hornsby five times.

Paige was able to pitch for so many years because he kept himself in top physical condition. He exercised and practiced during whatever spare time he could find. He usually played baseball twelve months a year, pitching part of the season in Latin America.

At the age of forty-two, Satchel finally realized his dream of playing in the majors. He joined the Cleveland Indians in July of 1948. He was certainly old for a "rookie," and some people thought he was too old to be an effective pitcher. But Satchel wasn't worried. "Maybe I'll pitch forever," he said. He won six of his seven games, helping Cleveland win that year's World Series.

In 1971, Satchel was awarded a place in baseball's Hall of Fame in Cooperstown, New York. It is certain he would have rewritten the record books if he had been given a chance to play in the major leagues earlier in his life. Still, Satchel Paige left his mark as one of the great athletes of this century.

One Point for Analysis: Following general statements about Paige's accomplishments, the essayist moves chronologically through an account of his life.

Writing Topics:
1. Compare two professional athletes engaged in the same sport.
2. Write an expository essay about someone who reached the height of his fame in his later years.
3. Following the model of Barkin's essay, make general statements about some well-known person's accomplishments, and then give a chronological account of his life.

STRANGE EVENTS ARE MEASURED BY THE YARDSTICK OF SCIENCE

ERWIN STEINKAMP

"Strange Events" manages to convey a considerable amount of information and at the same time to cause the reader to feel that he is reading solely for pleasure.

The plant certainly can't scream in the true sense of the word. But according to engineer Cleve Backster, plants and even single cells may be able to give off distress signals that can be picked up by an instrument called a polygraph (lie detector). Now before you fall out of your chair, there's more.

Would you believe that onions and carrots, give off distress signals while being chopped up for a salad; and your mother's favorite African violet reacts when someone in the house strikes a match?

Ridiculous? Unscientific? Maybe but according to Mr. Backster a plant may actually emit distress signals because it is afraid of fire.

One day while watering an office plant, Mr. Backster wondered if his polygraph could measure how fast water moves up the plant stems to the leaves. The engineer attached the polygraph electrodes to the plant leaves and waited.

After a time he noticed something unusual. The polygraph tracing was similar to the ones humans make when emotionally upset.

He decided to test this observation further. Mr. Backster dipped a plant leaf into a cup of hot coffee. Nothing happened. He decided to strike a match in front of the plant.

The moment this *thought* crossed his mind, the polygraph needle jumped to a high peak similar to those formed when a person tells a lie. The actual striking of the match produced the same response.

Could it be that the plant was able to read the experimenter's mind and respond emotionally? Mr. Backster thinks it could be. He is spending a great deal of time and money trying to find out.

After reading this account, you are probably shaking your head in disbelief. Come on now, plants just don't behave this way! How would other scientists view these findings?

Mr. Backster is *guessing* that the plant response revealed by his polygraph is a distress signal. He is basing his experiments on this guess, or hypothesis. To him this hypothesis seems to be the most reasonable one because what he sees indicates a clear case of cause and effect.

But as Mr. Backster and all other scientists know, his hypothesis could be wrong. The hypothesis will have to be tested by other scientists in other laboratories.

One Point for Analysis: The introduction states a shocking concept to attract the reader's attention.

Writing Topics:

1. After library research, write an expository paper on how plants respond to different kinds of music or how they respond to human speech.
2. Explain another strange event measured by the yardstick of science.
3. Write a report of a strange phenomenon *not* explainable by science.

GIRAFFES

GEORGE W. FRAME

George W. Frame frequently writes about nature, particularly about animals. His nature essays are usually based on personal observations.

The tall giraffe suddenly stopped eating and stared intently with big brown eyes at some distant object. He slowly turned his ears, one at a time, in search of a sound. And his nose wriggled to catch a scent in the cool morning breeze.

I turned my binoculars to where the giraffe was looking and saw seven big lions moving slowly and quietly toward him through the tall grass. The giraffe knew the danger, and he gave a loud snort. With head and neck leaning forward and tail twisted over his back like a corkscrew, he galloped away between the thorny bushes. The rhythm of his long neck and legs gave me the impression that he was moving in slow motion, but I knew that he was really running at a fast 25 to 35 miles per hour.

This giraffe escaped from the predators because he was alert. But sometimes giraffes are not so fortunate, and they become a meal for lions, leopards, spotted hyenas, or crocodiles. If attacked, giraffes can defend themselves by kicking. However, their best defense is their great height, which enables them to see predators at a great distance.

Once I was watching a giraffe in the bushes about 30 yards away, and suddenly I noticed an ear flicker a few yards to the right. I looked and saw another giraffe who was looking at me. Then, to the left another's jaw moved as he chewed a mouthful of tiny green leaves. Soon another ear twitched, and a tail swished, and before long I could see eight giraffes! They had been in plain sight all the time, but their spots and colors provided them with very effective camouflage.

Each giraffe's spot pattern remains the same throughout its life, but the colors become darker with age. Scientists studying giraffes can easily identify individuals by photographing the spot pattern on the neck. Later, when a giraffe is seen again in a different place, the scientist compares it to the photographs, and then knows which giraffe it is. All sorts of interesting information can be gathered in this way. For example, a scientist can learn how far one giraffe travels in search of food.

All giraffes have horns. However, the number and size of the horns depend upon the sex and age of the individual. Giraffe horns are different from the horns of any other animal. They are unlike deer antlers in that they are never shed. And they differ from true horns, such as those of cattle, by having a covering of thick hairy skin.

The giraffe has four pairs of horns on its skull. The largest pair is on top, and smaller pairs lie behind the ears, behind the eyes, and on the side of the head. Adult males have an additional horn (sometimes well developed) in the center of the forehead. The big males also have an extra layer of bone over the entire top of the skull.

Mostly, giraffes go together in small groups of three to fifteen, but sometimes a hundred or more join together. The large herds continually change as giraffes come and go. Males join together in bachelor herds. Young males join these bachelor herds when they reach about three years old, and they stay until fully grown at about seven years of age, when they are about 17 to 19 feet tall and weigh a ton or more. Other herds consist of mothers and baby giraffes, and sometimes one adult male who accompanies them.

Newborn giraffes are nearly 6 feet in height and weigh about 120 pounds. When one week old, they begin eating the leaves of thorn-bushes, but they usually continue to drink some milk until they are more than a year old. Older calves often wander away from their mothers and join up with other calves, or even with adult males.

Like many other animals, giraffes have a social rank order. One male is dominant over all the others. Each of the others is dominant over some and gives way to others.

Normally giraffes live together very peacefully, but sometimes the males fight in order to determine their rank. The loser admits defeat by retreating several paces, and the winner (or dominant male) follows with his head raised. After the fight both winner and loser know their rank, and they live together in a completely friendly way.

Giraffes eat the leaves of bushes and thorny acacia trees. Some trees are eaten so often that they are made into the shape of an hourglass by having a band eaten away around their middle about 15 feet above the ground. Giraffes feed by taking a branch into the mouth and pulling until the leaves tear off. Both the long, tough upper lip and the 18-inch-long tongue can wrap around objects in much the same way that a hand can. This enables giraffes to hold stems tightly while feeding. Giraffes are ruminants, like cattle, so after feeding they lie or stand around for hours chewing their cud.

Drinking is difficult for animals as tall and lanky as giraffes. They manage to drink by stretching their forelegs apart, or else by bending their front knees forward until they can reach the water.

People have long believed that giraffes are silent, but this is not so. Besides the loud snort they make when alarmed, they can produce several other sounds. One is described as a "hunh" or flute-like grunt. The second sound is like a sneeze. And a third is a loud breathing or blowing sound.

Giraffes have declined in numbers over most of Africa. In many areas they were hunted until few or none were left. People ate giraffe meat and sold the hides and bones. The tails were used as fly whisks. Also, large areas of land formerly used by giraffes were taken for cities, towns, farms, and roads. Now many African countries have established national parks and nature reserves where thousands of giraffes can live in their natural way.

One Point for Analysis: In the introduction the essayist focuses on a single giraffe to move into a discussion of giraffes in general. His transition occurs in the first sentence of the third paragraph.

Writing Topics:

1. Discuss the habits of another animal that lives as part of a group.
2. Report on what is being done in the United States to perpetuate endangered species.
3. Writing an account of the experiences of one college freshman, explain the process of registration at your university.

THE OLYMPIC GAMES

HAL HIGDON

Hal Higdon's interest in sports is evident in many of his published works such as The Electronic Olympics *(1971) and* Heroes of the Olympics *(1965). It is also evident in his own lifestyle, as he competes as a long-distance runner and was the first American to finish in the 1964 Boston Marathon.*

The *Olympic Games* began in Greece thousands of years ago. Then, after not being held for many centuries, the Olympics came alive again in Greece in 1896. And the hero of that first modern Olympics in Athens was a Greek shepherd named Spiridon Loues.

Today the Olympics have become the world's greatest sporting event. Once every four years, the top runners, swimmers, boxers, wrestlers, weight-lifters, boaters, and other athletes meet in one place to compete for the title of champion of the world in their sport.

The top sport of the summer Olympics is track and field. A separate Olympics for skiing, skating, and sledding is held during the winter in another area.

Each winner in the Olympic Games receives a gold medal as an

From the book, *Heroes of the Olympics,* by Hal Higdon. © 1965 by Prentice-Hall, Inc. Published by Prentice-Hall, Inc., Englewood Cliffs, New Jersey.

emblem of victory. Millions will hear of his exploits in the newspapers or on radio and television.

But in 1896, the Olympic Games were just beginning again after a lapse of 1500 years.

The Olympic Games started long before the birth of Christ, and they were celebrated by the ancient Greeks in honor of the God Zeus. Greek sportsmen used to compete once every fourth year on a plain called *Olympia* in southwestern Greece. The first recorded Olympic winner was a cook named Coroebos, who won a race about 200 yards long in 776 B.C. The symbol of victory was then a laurel wreath instead of today's gold medal. The top sculptors of the day carved statues of the Olympic champions, and poets composed songs in praise of them.

To the Greeks the training of the body was equally as important as the training of the mind, and so highly did they value the Olympic Games that even wars were often postponed to allow the Olympics to begin on time. The Games continued for more than a thousand years—until finally, after the Romans came into power, the Roman emperor, Theodosius, abolished the Olympic Games, in 394 A.D.

Toward the end of the nineteenth century, a Frenchman, named Baron Pierre de Coubertin, suggested reviving the Olympic Games. "It will promote good will among nations," he insisted. Since Greece had founded the ancient Olympic Games, Athens became the site of the first modern Olympics.

Sixty thousand people, including the king of Greece, jammed the Olympic stadium on the first day of the Games. Almost as many people watched from the surrounding hills. Ten countries sent teams to this first modern Olympics. America had the strongest track squad. But the home fans counted on their champion, Panayotis Paraskevopoulos, to win the discus throw, normally a Greek event.

Robert Garrett, a Princeton shot putter, had never seen a discus before leaving America. Someone had told him its size. He had a discus made of iron, and it weighed twenty pounds. He decided to forget the event.

But when Garrett arrived in Athens, he discovered the Greek discus was made of wood and weighed only a few pounds.

Greek hopes were high when Paraskevopoulos stepped into the

throwing ring on the first day. A cheer rang through the stadium after he sailed the discus 94 feet 11⅔ inches to take the lead.

Then Bob Garrett stepped up for his last throw. His discus thudded to the ground a foot beyond his rival's mark. The Greek crowd sighed in disappointment. The American Garrett had won—with 95 feet 7½ inches.

The American runners and jumpers matched Garrett's skill. By the last day of the Games, Americans had won nine out of eleven events. Only E. H. Flack, an Australian, was able to halt the American victory rush. He won the 800 and 1500 meter runs.

The Greeks had not won a single event on their home track. Their only hope was in the final event: the *marathon*.

This was to be the first marathon ever run. The origin of the event goes back, however, to ancient Greek history. In 490 B.C. the Persians invaded Greece. They hoped to capture Athens. To stop them, the Athenian general sent an Olympic champion named Pheidippides to Sparta for more troops.

Pheidippides ran through fields, swam rivers, and climbed mountains to get help. Then he returned and fought with the Greek troops at the plains of Marathon, where thousands of Persians were killed.

The Athenian general sent the already exhausted Pheidippides to Athens with news of the victory. According to legend, he ran the twenty-six miles from Marathon to Athens. "Rejoice. We conquer!" he shouted arriving in the city. Then he fell dead.

In memory of Pheidippides, the Olympic sponsors proposed a twenty-six-mile race from Marathon to Athens. Twenty runners lined up at the starting line near the site of the old battle. Among them was Spiridon Loues, a Greek shepherd. He had prepared for his race the previous night by praying and fasting. He must have done some training too.

A French runner named Lemursiaux led in the early stages. The Australian, E. H. Flack, stayed close to the front for a while. The American, Arthur Blake, second to Flack in the 1500 meters, led at eighteen miles. He soon dropped out.

As the lead runner neared the stadium, the cheers told those inside that the winner would be Greek. Spiridon Loues trotted onto the track to finish the last few hundred yards, and the crowd went wild, Greece's honor had been saved.

Loues crossed the finish line. He was grabbed by the crown

prince and his brother, who carried him on their shoulders to the royal box to see the king. Never before had a lowly shepherd been so honored. Finishing in second and third far behind him came two other Greeks.

Overnight Spiridon Loues became a national hero just as the Olympic champions had in ancient Greece. A barber promised free haircuts for life. A restaurant owner promised free meals.

The time recorded by Spiridon Loues in that first marathon of the first modern Olympics has many times been outdone, but the excitement of his victory has never been matched.

One Point for Analysis: The essayist moves back and forth between accounts of the ancient Olympics and the first Olympic revival in 1896.

Writing Topics:
   1. Write an account of the high point of the last Olympic Games.
   2. Write a biographical sketch of some Olympic gold medal winner.
   3. Write an expository essay about some contemporary custom that, like the Olympic Games, honors an event in history.

ABOUT THUNDER AND LIGHTNING

JACK MYERS

The weather, particularly its most powerful aspects, is a subject always interesting to people. Jack Myers has written about two of weather's most spectacular elements.

I recently read an article about thunder. Since we all get to see lightning and hear thunder in one of nature's great performances, I thought you might like to know something about this.

Usually the performance starts near the base of a big cloud. Inside that cloud all sorts of violent air movements and temperature changes are going on. Water droplets and ice pellets are being bounced around in the swirling air. Such tiny particles usually carry electric charges on their surfaces. One result is that a great concentration of negative electric charges (electrons) is built up just above the base of the cloud. That place may get charged up to 300 million volts.

The discharge of that great electrical voltage seems to happen very rapidly, but really it does not happen "all at once." It may take a tenth of a second, and a series of events occur. A lightning flash is born as a leader stroke which works its way across the cloud and downward in a jerky path. The leader forms a channel of hot and conducting gas. Then, wham-o, the first big return stroke follows that channel to make a big flash. Often the leader may extend its channel farther into the cloud. Then there may be more big return strokes quickly following each other through that same channel.

The flash we see comes from hot glowing gas in the lightning channel. Its color tells about its temperature, about 30,000° Celsius. That high temperature, which is reached in a fraction of a second, means that the air in the channel rapidly reaches 10 to 100 times its usual pressure. It expands like a blown-up balloon and then collapses as if the balloon had burst. That makes the noise we call thunder.

Drawings often show a lightning flash as a big zig-zag. That is exaggeration. Photographs show the flash as short line segments, each a few hundred feet long, but with only small angles between them. The channel is jerky but not really zig-zaggy like the letter Z. The exploding noise of the hot expanding gas happens at each little segment of the channel. Much of the lightning channel may be up in the cloud where we cannot see it. So the noise of thunder comes from different places and not all at once.

Thunder has been studied by taking photographs of the lightning and also using microphones to record the sounds. Doing this has helped to answer a question I have wondered about. Maybe you have, too. Why does thunder have such different kinds of sounds? Sometimes it seems like a long roll or rumble, sometimes a short, sharp clap.

When microphones are put in different places they do not record the same sounds. The sound records together with the photographs tell why thunder has different sounds. Light travels very rapidly to your eyes but sound travels more slowly, about 1,000 feet per second. If the lightning channel is going crosswise as you see it, most of its noise-making is just about the same distance away. Most of the noise reaches your ear all at once. That seems like a short clap. If the lightning channel is slanted toward you or away from you, then some of its noises may reach you long before the others. That gives a sequence of sounds like the roll of big drums. I guess no two people ever hear exactly the same thunder. How it sounds depends on where you are.

One Point for Analysis: Myers uses several words that suggest their own meaning: *rumble; a short, sharp clap; zig-zaggy.*
Writing Topics:
1. Following this essay as a model, write an explanation of another of nature's great performances.
2. Explain several ways in which man uses nature's power to his benefit.
3. Write an expository essay about how at times nature becomes man's enemy.

ELECTRONIC EYES HELP BLIND SEE

JACQUELINE HARRIS

Despite the technical nature of the subject of "Electronic Eyes," the exposition is interesting to the nonscientist as well as the scientist.

The scene was a California laboratory.

A blind man sat bolt upright in his chair. Suddenly a scientist thrust his hand in front of the man's eyes. A TV camera whirred into action.

"I see a hand! I see a hand!" the blind man exclaimed.

The scientist was just as excited. For his idea was working. The lens of the TV camera could give vision to the blind.

The TV camera is only one of several new research projects that offer the promise of sight to the hopelessly blind. For example, a scientist in England helps the blind to see by stimulating the visual center of the brain with radio transmitters. Another British doctor has invented a tiny eye tube that will allow persons with scarred outer layers of the eye to see.

. . .

The TV research is being conducted by Dr. Paul Bach-y-Rita and Dr. Carter Collins in their laboratories at San Francisco's Pacific Medical Center. They have a blind person sit in a chair with the bare skin of his back resting against a special 10-inch-square metal panel. Mounted in the panel are 400 tiny plastic-tipped cones.

A TV camera is attached to the chair's arm. The camera records the image of an object in front of it. This image is converted into a pattern of large dots. The position of each dot is transmitted to a matching cone in the chair's panel. The stimulated cones begin to vibrate against the person's back. He feels the pattern on his skin. And, like the person with normal sight, he perceives an image in his mind.

The blind person literally "sees" with his skin. For his skin takes over the job of the retina of the eye. The retina is that area lining the back of the eye that converts an image made up of dots of light into nerve impulses. Like the retina, the skin translates an image made up of tiny vibrating cones into nerve impulses. These impulses are then transmitted to the brain, where they are decoded.

It takes a little practice to learn to see with your skin. But after a while, the blind person can see many different objects. The experienced skin "see-er" soon forgets that the images are being transmitted through his back. They seem to be in front of him.

The two scientists are now working to perfect their system. They hope to develop an 8-ounce camera that can be worn on the head like a miner's lamp. A special undershirt holding 10,000 stimulators would transmit the image to the skin.

The skin seeing system you have just read about involves using the nerves of the skin to send images to the brain. But is there a way to bypass nerves and give the blind sight through direct stimulation of the brain? Dr. Giles S. Brindley, a British scientist, thinks so.

Dr. Brindley's goal is a kind of map of the visual center of the brain. Such a map would tell the scientists the exact spot within the visual center to stimulate in order to produce a particular point of light. From those points of light, images could be made.

The scientist has already implanted a set of electrodes on the surface of the brain of a blind volunteer. The electrodes are activated by remote-control radio.

Now Dr. Brindley is in the process of testing his electrodes. So far, he has mapped 37 scattered locations in the volunteer's visual center. The 37 points aren't enough to produce many images. But Dr. Brindley has proved that the idea will work. He and other scientists are working to map other points.

How could the map be used? Scientists at Albert Einstein College of Medicine in New York City think a tiny TV camera might be the answer. The camera would pick up the image and transmit it to a tiny computer. The computer would decode the image and activate the proper electrodes implanted in the person's visual center. Camera and computer together could be fitted into the eye socket.

"Skin sight" and direct brain stimulation are two ideas that will take over the entire function of the eye. But there is yet another idea that will give vision back to the person who still has a functioning retina.

Such persons are usually blinded when chemicals or fire damage the cornea, or "window" of the eye. The cornea is the thick transparent covering of the lens of the eye. When damage fogs the cornea, it can no longer transfer light from an object through to the retina.

A British surgeon has invented a tiny tube that will allow light to pass through the damaged cornea to the retina. The tube resembles a tiny microscope eyepiece. Installing the tube requires a series of operations. But when the final bandages come off, the patient can see.

While some scientists are working to give the blind vision, others are looking for substitutes for the Seeing Eye dog.

A group of New Zealand scientists have devised sonar glasses. Mounted in the bridge of the glasses are three disks that send and receive ultrasound—sound pitched so high it can't be heard. Barriers in the path of the blind person change the way the sound is echoed back. A small box worn at the waist converts the echoes to audible sounds that are relayed to the person through the frames of the glasses.

Other such electronic seeing aids for the blind include carpenter's levels and footballs that beep. This age of electronics could prove to be a bright one for the blind.

One Point for Analysis: The introduction presents a dramatic event to attract the reader's attention.

Writing Topics:
1. After library research, write an explanation of current scientific efforts to improve the hearing of the deaf.
2. Write a humorous account of a friend or relative discussing his recent operation.
3. Report on various methods blind people use to go about their daily business.

THE GREEK CITIES

HENDRIK VAN LOON

The excellence of the civilization known as Classical Greece has been examined by many writers. In "The Greek Cities" Hendrik van Loon discusses the spirit of that culture.

We modern people love the sound of the word "big." We pride ourselves upon the fact that we belong to the "biggest" country in the world and possess the "biggest" navy and grow the "biggest" oranges and potatoes, and we love to live in cities of "millions" of inhabitants and when we are dead we are buried in the "biggest" cemetery of the whole state."

A citizen of ancient Greece, could he have heard us talk, would not have known what we meant. "Moderation in all things" was the ideal of his life and mere bulk did not impress him at all. And this love of moderation was not merely a hollow phrase used upon special occasions: it influenced the life of the Greeks from the day of their birth to the hour of their death. It was part of their literature and it made them build small but perfect temples. It found expression in the clothes which the men wore and in the rings and the bracelets of their wives. It followed the crowds that went to the theatre and made them hoot down any playwright who dared to sin against the iron law of good taste or good sense.

The Greeks even insisted upon this quality in their politicians and in their most popular athletes. When a powerful runner came to Sparta and boasted that he could stand longer on one foot than any other man in Hellas the people drove him from the city because he

Selection is reprinted from *The Story of Mankind* by Hendrik Willem van Loon, with the permission of Liveright Publishing Corporation. Revised Edition Copyright © 1972 by Henry B. van Loon and Gerard W. van Loon.

prided himself upon an accomplishment at which he could be beaten by any common goose.

"That is all very well," you will say, "and no doubt it is a great virtue to care so much for moderation and perfection, but why should the Greeks have been the only people to develop this quality in olden times?" For an answer I shall point to the way in which the Greeks lived.

The people of Egypt or Mesopotamia had been the "subjects" of a mysterious Supreme Ruler who lived miles and miles away in a dark palace and who was rarely seen by the masses of the population. The Greeks on the other hand, were "free citizens" of a hundred independent little "cities" the largest of which counted fewer inhabitants than a large modern village. When a peasant who lived in Ur said that he was a Babylonian he meant that he was one of millions of other people who paid tribute to the king who at that particular moment happened to be master of western Asia. But when a Greek said proudly that he was an Athenian or a Theban he spoke of a small town, which was both his home and his country and which recognised no master but the will of the people in the market-place.

To the Greek, his fatherland was the place where he was born; where he had spent his earliest years playing hide and seek amidst the forbidden rocks of the Acropolis; where he had grown into manhood with a thousand other boys and girls, whose nicknames were as familiar to him as those of your own schoolmates. His Fatherland was the holy soil where his father and mother lay buried. It was the small house within the high city-walls where his wife and children lived in safety. It was a complete world which covered no more than four or five acres of rocky land. Don't you see how these surroundings must have influenced a man in everything he did and said and thought? The people of Babylon and Assyria and Egypt had been part of a vast mob. They had been lost in the multitude. The Greek on the other hand had never lost touch with his immediate surroundings. He never ceased to be part of a little town where everybody knew every one else. He felt that his intelligent neighbours were watching him. Whatever he did, whether he wrote plays or made statues out of marble or composed songs, he remembered that his efforts were going to be judged by all the free-born citizens of his home-town who knew about such things. This knowledge forced him to strive after perfection, and perfection, as

215

he had been taught from childhood, was not possible without moderation.

In this hard school, the Greeks learned to excel in many things. They created new forms of government and new forms of literature and new ideals in art which we have never been able to surpass. They performed these miracles in little villages that covered less ground than four or five modern city blocks.

And look, what finally happened!

In the fourth century before our era, Alexander of Macedonia conquered the world. As soon as he had done with fighting, Alexander decided that he must bestow the benefits of the true Greek genius upon all mankind. He took it away from the little cities and the little villages and tried to make it blossom and bear fruit amidst the vast royal residences of his newly acquired Empire. But the Greeks, removed from the familiar sight of their own temples, removed from the well-known sounds and smells of their own crooked streets, at once lost the cheerful joy and the marvelous sense of moderation which had inspired the work of their hands and brains while they laboured for the glory of their old city-states. They became cheap artisans, content with second-rate work. The day the little city-states of old Hellas lost their independence and were forced to become part of a big nation, the old Greek spirit died. And it has been dead ever since.

One Point for Analysis: This essay compares and contrasts several ancient civilizations.

Writing Topics:

1. Compare and contrast two spans of time in your life.
2. An ancient Greek saying is, "Know Thyself." Discuss two essential aspects of yourself.
3. Covering some of the same points as those found in this essay, write an essay entitled "The American City."

THE SPIDER AND THE WASP

ALEXANDER PETRUNKEVITCH

A zoologist whose special field of interest is spiders, Petrunkevitch published Index Catalogue of Spiders of North, Central, and South America *in 1911. He has also translated English poetry into Russian and Russian poetry into English.*

In the feeding and safeguarding of their progeny insects and spiders exhibit some interesting analogies to reasoning and some crass examples of blind instinct. The case I propose to describe here is that of the tarantula spiders and their archenemy, the digger wasps of the genus Pepsis. It is a classic example of what looks like intelligence pitted against instinct—a strange situation in which the victim, though fully able to defend itself, submits unwittingly to its destruction.

Most tarantulas live in the tropics, but several species occur in the temperate zone and a few are common in the southern U.S. Some varieties are large and have powerful fangs with which they can inflict a deep wound. These formidable looking spiders do not, however, attack man; you can hold one in your hand, if you are gentle, without being bitten. Their bite is dangerous only to insects and small mammals such as mice; for man it is no worse than a hornet's sting.

Tarantulas customarily live in deep cylindrical burrows, from which they emerge at dusk and into which they retire at dawn. Mature males wander about after dark in search of females and occasionally stray into houses. After mating, the male dies in a few weeks, but a female lives much longer and can mate several years in succession. In a Paris museum is a tropical specimen which is said to have been living in captivity for 25 years.

A fertilized female tarantula lays from 200 to 400 eggs at a time; thus it is possible for a single tarantula to produce several thousand young. She takes no care of them beyond weaving a cocoon of silk to enclose the eggs. After they hatch, the young walk away, find convenient places in which to dig their burrows and spend the rest of their lives in solitude. The eyesight of tarantulas is poor, being

217

limited to a sensing of change in the intensity of light and to the perception of moving objects. They apparently have little or no sense of hearing, for a hungry tarantula will pay no attention to a loudly chirping cricket placed in its cage unless the insect happens to touch one of its legs.

But all spiders, and especially hairy ones, have an extremely delicate sense of touch. Laboratory experiments prove that tarantulas can distinguish three types of touch: pressure against the body wall, stroking of the body hair, and riffling of certain very fine hairs on the legs called trichobothria. Pressure against the body, by the finger or the end of a pencil, causes the tarantula to move off slowly for a short distance. The touch excites no defensive response unless the approach is from above where the spider can see the motion, in which case it rises on its hind legs, lifts its front legs, opens it fangs and holds this threatening posture as long as the object continues to move.

The entire body of a tarantula, especially its legs, is thickly clothed with hair. Some of it is short and wooly, some long and stiff. Touching this body hair produces one of two distinct reactions. When the spider is hungry, it responds with an immediate and swift attack. At the touch of a cricket's antennae the tarantula seizes the insect so swiftly that a motion picture taken at the rate of 64 frames per second shows only the result and not the process of capture. But when the spider is not hungry, the stimulation of its hairs merely causes it to shake the touched limb. An insect can walk under its hairy belly unharmed.

The trichobothria, very fine hairs growing from disklike membranes on the legs, are sensitive only to air movement. A light breeze makes them vibrate slowly, without disturbing the common hair. When one blows gently on the trichobothria, the tarantula reacts with a quick jerk of its four front legs. If the front and hind legs are stimulated at the same time, the spider makes a sudden jump. This reaction is quite independent of the state of its appetite.

These three tactile responses—to pressure on the body wall, to moving of the common hair, and to flexing of the trichobothria—are so different from one another that there is no possibility of confusing them. They serve the tarantula adequately for most of its needs and enable it to avoid most annoyances and dangers. But they fail the spider completely when it meets its deadly enemy, the digger wasp Pepsis.

218

These solitary wasps are beautiful and formidable creatures. Most species are either a deep shiny blue all over, or deep blue with rusty wings. The largest have a wing span of about four inches. They live on nectar. When excited, they give off a pungent odor—a warning that they are ready to attack. The sting is much worse than that of a bee or common wasp, and the pain and swelling last longer. In the adult stage the wasp lives only a few months. The female produces but a few eggs, one at a time at intervals of two or three days. For each egg the mother must provide one adult tarantula, alive but paralyzed. The mother wasp attaches the egg to the paralyzed spider's abdomen. Upon hatching from the egg, the larva is many hundreds of times smaller than its living but helpless victim. It eats no other food and drinks no water. By the time it has finished its single Gargantuan meal and become ready for wasphood, nothing remains of the tarantula but its indigestible chitinous skeleton.

The mother wasp goes tarantula-hunting when the egg in her ovary is almost ready to be laid. Flying low over the ground late on a sunny afternoon, the wasp looks for its victim or for the mouth of a tarantula burrow, a round hole edged by a bit of silk. The sex of the spider makes no difference, but the mother is highly discriminating as to species. Each species of Pepsis requires a certain species of tarantula, and the wasp will not attack the wrong species. In a cage with a tarantula which is not its normal prey, the wasp avoids the spider and is usually killed by it in the night.

Yet when a wasp finds the correct species, it is the other way about. To identify the species the wasp apparently must explore the spider with her antennae. The tarantula shows an amazing tolerance to this exploration. The wasp crawls under it and walks over it without evoking any hostile response. The molestation is so great and so persistent that the tarantula often rises on all eight legs, as if it were on stilts. It may stand this way for several minutes. Meanwhile the wasp, having satisfied itself that the victim is of the right species, moves off a few inches to dig the spider's grave. Working vigorously with legs and jaws, it excavates a hole 8 to 10 inches deep with a diameter slightly larger than the spider's girth. Now and again the wasp pops out of the hole to make sure that the spider is still there.

When the grave is finished, the wasp returns to the tarantula to complete her ghastly enterprise. First she feels it all over once more

219

with her antennae. Then her behavior becomes more aggressive. She bends her abdomen, protruding her sting, and searches for the soft membrane at the point where the spider's legs join its body—the only spot where she can penetrate the horny skeleton. From time to time, as the exasperated spider slowly shifts ground, the wasp turns on her back and slides along with the aid of her wings, trying to get under the tarantula for a shot at the vital spot. During all this maneuvering, which can last for several minutes, the tarantula makes no move to save itself. Finally the wasp corners it against some obstruction and grasps one of its legs in her powerful jaws. Now at last the harassed spider tries a desperate but vain defense. The two contestants roll over and over on the ground. It is a terrifying sight and the outcome is always the same. The wasp finally manages to thrust her sting into the soft spot and holds it there for a few seconds while she pumps in the poison. Almost immediately the tarantula falls paralyzed on its back. Its legs stop twitching; its heart stops beating. Yet it is not dead, as is shown by the fact that if taken from the wasp it can be restored to some sensitivity by being kept in a moist chamber for several months.

After paralyzing the tarantula, the wasp cleans herself by dragging her body along the ground and rubbing her feet, sucks the drop of blood oozing from the wound in the spider's abdomen, then grabs a leg of the flabby, helpless animal in her jaws and drags it down to the bottom of the grave. She stays there for many minutes, sometimes for several hours, and what she does all that time in the dark we do not know. Eventually she lays her egg and attaches it to the side of the spider's abdomen with a sticky secretion. Then she emerges, fills the grave with soil carried bit by bit in her jaws, and finally tramples the ground all around to hide any trace of the grave from prowlers. Then she flies away, leaving her descendant safely started in life.

In all this the behavior of the wasp evidently is qualitatively different from that of the spider. The wasp acts like an intelligent animal. This is not to say that instinct plays no part or that she reasons as man does. But her actions are to the point; they are not automatic and can be modified to fit the situation. We do not know for certain how she identifies the tarantula—probably it is by some olfactory or chemo-tactile sense—but she does it purposefully and does not blindly tackle a wrong species.

On the other hand, the tarantula's behavior shows only confusion. Evidently the wasp's pawing gives it no pleasure, for it tries to move away. That the wasp is not simulating sexual stimulation is certain because male and female tarantulas react in the same way to its advances. That the spider is not anesthetized by some odorless secretion is easily shown by blowing lightly at the tarantula and making it jump suddenly. What, then, makes the tarantula behave as stupidly as it does?

No clear, simple answer is available. Possibly the stimulation by the wasp's antennae is masked by a heavier pressure on the spider's body, so that it reacts as when prodded by a pencil. But the explanation may be much more complex. Initiative in attack is not in the nature of tarantulas; most species fight only when cornered so that escape is impossible. Their inherited patterns of behavior apparently prompt them to avoid problems rather than attack them. For example, spiders always weave their webs in three dimensions, and when a spider finds that there is insufficient space to attach certain threads in the third dimension, it leaves the place and seeks another, instead of finishing the web in a single plane. This urge to escape seems to arise under all circumstances, in all phases of life, and to take the place of reasoning. For a spider to change the pattern of its web is as impossible as for an inexperienced man to build a bridge across a chasm obstructing his way.

In a way the instinctive urge to escape is not only easier but often more efficient than reasoning. The tarantula does exactly what is most efficient in all cases except in an encounter with a ruthless and determined attacker dependent for the existence of her own species on killing as many tarantulas as she can lay eggs. Perhaps in this case the spider follows its usual pattern of trying to escape, instead of seizing and killing the wasp, because it is not aware of its danger. In any case, the survival of the tarantula species as a whole is protected by the fact that the spider is much more fertile than the wasp.

AN ANALYSIS OF "THE SPIDER AND THE WASP"

The thesis of Alexander Petrunkevitch's "The Spider and the Wasp" is both fascinating and disturbing: the Pepsis wasp, acting "like an intelligent animal," kills a tarantula, reacting like an arachnid whose instinctual drives are confused. The fascination arises from observing an elaborate ritual of life and death involving the "dreaded" tarantula and its archenemy the Pepsis. The disturbance comes from the fact that the Pepsis appears to make a series of judgments not unlike those of man.

The author states his thesis in the introductory paragraph, and develops it first by a lengthy explanation of the nature and physical characteristics of the tarantula; then by a short exposition of the Pepsis; finally by the dramatic interaction of the two "insects." The wasp appears to act deliberately ("her actions are to the point"; they "can be modified to fit the situation"; she identified the species of tarantula purposefully "and does no blindly tackle a wrong species"). The spider, normally an efficient being, seems to give up, despite instinctual drives, "in an encounter with a ruthless and determined attacker dependent for the existence of her own species on killing as many tarantulas as she can lay eggs." In the concluding paragraph Petrunkevitch offers a possible explanation of the peculiarly cooperative behavior of the tarantula being prepared by Pepsis for a "living" death. His explanation is pale because it is somewhat contradicted by the drama that has preceded it.

The weakness of the conclusion, however, is by no means reflected in the body of the essay. Suspense is there, and it is achieved for a non-scientific audience by means of diction that is, on the one hand, emotionally charged and generally understandable to the layman; on the other hand, interspersed with enough technical terms (*trichbothria, chitinous, chemo-tactile*) to give it an air of scientific authenticity. Petrunkevitch's style reflects a genuine feeling of awe at the mystery of nature in one of her ritualistic performances. The wasps are "beautiful and formidable creatures"; its larva eats a "Gargantuan meal"; Pepsis walks "to dig the spider's grave." Expressions such as these help establish the sense-of-the-wonderful tone of "The Spider and the Wasp." But tone alone cannot account for the success of this essay.

A sense of coherence (for instance, the last sentence of the eighth paragraph is picked up in the first sentence of the ninth paragraph), a personal approach to a scientific event (for instance, "When the grave is finished, the wasp returns to the tarantula to complete her ghastly enterprise"), a skillful interweaving of the various types of prose (essentially exposition, description, narration, and some argumentation)—all contribute to a suspenseful, awesome, mysterious look at a process of nature that suggests more than sheer instinct as the guiding force for the actions of lower creatures.

A VICTIM OF THE CONSUMER CRUSADERS

JOANNA WOLPER

Joanna Wolper is a New York television producer-director and a filmmaker. She specializes in television documentaries.

I can't eat or drink anything. I can't go anywhere. I have become a victim of the consumer reporter. Ever since Ralph Nader and his pals started investigating, I have gradually become an anorexia nervosa[1] hermit. My friends warn me that I've been taking the news too seriously. But if you read the paper and watch television every night, you begin to get the feeling that if the mugger doesn't kill you—BOTULISM will!

I have ceased eating from a can. The tiniest dent sends me into fits of terror. After all, the *New York Times* said that seven ounces of botulism bacteria could kill the entire human race. Tuna fish is double jeopardy. You might avoid the toxic bacteria—but beware of maggots.

I started eating hamburgers instead of tuna for lunch, but then I read a story in the *New York Post* that hamburger meat tested around town showed particles of animal shit mashed in it, and the spices were spiked with rodent hairs. Hot dogs were vanished from the luncheon fare following features of franks filled with cancerous chicken wings. If carcinogenic agents don't phase you, one doctor wrote that the nitrate in hot dogs inhibits one's sexual hormones.

Hormones are another horror. If you're afraid of blood clots and cancer from ingesting birth control or morning after pills—just think what happens when you devour a juicy steak from a cow chock full of hormones to fatten her up.

Sausage can cause trichinosis. It said so right on the package I bought at the D'Agostino Supermarket. Eggs can give you a heart attack. If this story is making you nervous, don't take a drink—cirrhosis of the liver—and don't pick up that cigarette—you know what the Surgeon General said. It's on the side of the pack.

Reach for a tomato, and it's filled with gas and covered with

---

[1] A loss of appetite due to nerves.

223

DDT. The frozen food has preservatives and the milk you are feeding your baby could be watered down. And you know what they've been saying about the water in New Orleans. It might just be causing THE BIG C!

Mortal fear of the refrigerator drives me from the apartment. But I freeze at the elevator remembering too many tales of elevator rapes. I dash through the vestibule with visions of vestibule murders. Subways are out. Too much of a risk for a woman alone. I'm afraid to wait for a bus or a cab, because I might get mugged while I'm waiting or choke from the pollution.

The National Safety Council says someone dies in a car crash every nine minutes. There is no way I'm going to get on a plane after what happened in Guatemala, Venezuela, Tunisia and Paris. Even waving good-by to a daring traveller is fraught with peril. You never know where a Palestinian guerrilla will strike next.

So I'm lying under the covers in my apartment, freezing. I've turned off the steam heat, because it's bad for my complexion. I can't use the electric heater, because it might catch on fire. I'm lying flat on my back. I can't even get comfortable. I threw out my pillow last week. You see, it's because I read in a magazine that sleeping on a pillow gives you wrinkles on your neck.

So I turned over to watch the late movie on my color TV—and than I remembered—THE RAYS . . . THE RAYS . . . THE RAYS . . .

One Point for Analysis: The brief conclusion humorously reinforces to the plight of Wolper's "victim" by appealing to the truth on the one hand and a "science fiction" stock concept on the other.

Writing Topics:
1. Write a humorous expository essay on twentieth-century man and his fear of the hydrogen bomb.
2. By first discussing the organism that causes *botulism*, write a cause-effect essay on the progress and treatment of the disease.
3. In a nonhumorous expository essay, discuss the positive knowledge that we have acquired through the "Consumer Crusaders."

224

A FEW WORLD SERIES SINKERS

JIM BOUTON

During the 1960's Jim Bouton was a pitcher for the New York Yankees. He has since that time become a television sportscaster.

The dedicated baseball fan is a man who likes to kid himself. He'll get to a World Series game early, see a ballplayer yawning and take it as a sign of nervousness. He'll see a nervelessly relaxed body leaning against the batting cage and consider it merely feigned indifference. He'll watch an outfielder casually scratching his nose and count it as a tic. He's wrong. In fact, what looks like boredom on behalf of the people involved in the World Series is most often just that.

In the years when I was involved in series competition, the only thing that really got to me was the pennant race. A great deal of psychic energy was expended while the pennant was being won. After that, there was maybe a $3,000 difference between winning and losing.

Now things are even tougher. Winning a divisional title and the World Series can be worth $20,000. Finishing second in the division or losing the league playoff is worth virtually zilch. So the stakes are even higher. Just watch the guys around the batting cage. If they were any looser, they'd fall down.

Another thing you might keep your eye on is the baseball pants. It tells a lot about a player. There is a new uniform in every locker as the World Series begins. The trouble with new uniforms is that most often the pants aren't tight enough. There are players who swear they can't run if their trousers aren't skin tight. In the minor leagues there have been instances of players refusing to take the field because a pencil would fit between the cloth of their trousers and the skin of their thighs.

So what happens in the series is this: a lot of the players wear new blouses and old trousers. Old trousers can be recognized because they've been laundered many times and show evidence of fading. It's easier to detect this in the grey road uniforms than the home whites. In any case, a good pair of glasses and a keen eye can spot the tight pants men.

Another thing to watch during one of the little delays that make up such a big part of the game is what the pitcher is up to. I don't mean when he's looking in to get the sign, winding up, throwing the ball. I mean during the time he steps off the mound and seems to be looking out at his outfielders or into the stands at girls. What he's really doing is rubbing up the ball and under the latest rules he has to walk off the mound to do so.

This gives him some marvelous opportunities. He can, for one thing, stick a finger between his belt and trousers and come up with a gob of previously concealed vaseline. This while he has his back to the plate umpire. And what good is vaseline? Well, it's slippery like spit. This means you can throw the ball exactly as hard as you would a fastball and have it come off your hand behaving like a curve. This is very confusing for the hitter.

Sometimes the sharp observer will see the batter shouting out at the pitcher. He will wonder what the batter is saying, and well he might. Because chances are he's not saying anything to the pitcher at all; he's shouting at the umpire, probably because he didn't like the last called strike. The reason for the confusion is that umpires don't like to be showed up, which is their word for having a player arguing with them openly. So long as the batter looks out at the pitcher he can call the umpire almost every name in the book. Your best chance of getting the full flavor of this from the stands is to bring along a lip reader.

Finally, there is feet watching. Routine ground balls are not exactly the most thrilling things that ever happen in a baseball game. But a bit of spice can be added if you watch a good first baseman in action. The big thing is to catch him taking his foot off first base before the ball actually arrives in his glove. Gil Hodges, late manager of the Mets, was a master of this deception. It's an important move because the umpires watch the feet, too. But if the first baseman takes his foot off the bag with proper aplomb the umpire can easily delude himself into thinking he heard the sound of the ball in glove at the same time. Thus many runners who are actually safe at first base are called out.

There are other little cheats going on (like the umpire who sneaks into the dugout ostensibly to use the WC but actually to grab a

226

smoke). But there are some things that are better left unsaid. Watch for them today.

One Point for Analysis: The tone of the essay is established in the last sentence of the first paragraph: a rather cynical, humorous notion of a World Series game.

Writing Topics:

1. In an expository essay, discuss the inflated salaries of professional sportsmen and the response these salaries evoke in dedicated sports viewers.
2. Report on an important sports event that you have witnessed.
3. "Tight pants" are a necessity for some baseball players. Explain how specific clothing is essential in the execution of other sports.

PUBLIC FRIENDSHIPS

JANE JACOBS

Jane Jacobs has for many years been interested in how cities affect the people who live there. She has served as an associate editor of Architectural Forum *and is the author of* The Economy of Cities.

Anthropologist Elena Padilla, author of *Up from Puerto Rico,* describing Puerto Rican life in a poor and squalid district of New York, tells how much people know about each other—who is to be trusted and who not, who is defiant of the law and who upholds it, who is competent and well informed and who is inept and ignorant—and how these things are known from the public life of the sidewalk and its associated enterprises. These are matters of public character. But she also tells how select are those permitted to drop into the kitchen for a cup of coffee, how strong are the ties and how limited the number of a person's genuine confidants, those who share in a person's private life and private affairs. She tells how it is not considered dignified for everyone to know one's affairs. Nor is

From *The Death and Life of Great American Cities,* by Jane Jacobs. Copyright © 1961 by Jane Jacobs. Reprinted by permission of Random House, Inc.

it considered dignified to snoop on others beyond the face presented in public. It does violence to a person's privacy and rights. In this, the people she describes are essentially the same as the people of the mixed, Americanized city street on which I live, and essentially the same as the people who live in high-income apartments or fine town houses, too.

A good city street neighborhood achieves a marvel of balance between its people's determination to have essential privacy and their simultaneous wishes for differing degrees of contact, enjoyment or help from the people around. This balance is largely made up of small, sensitively managed details, practiced and accepted so casually that they are normally taken for granted.

Perhaps I can best explain this subtle but all-important balance in terms of the stores where people leave keys for their friends, a common custom in New York. In our family, for example, when a friend wants to use our place while we are away for a week end or everyone happens to be out during the day, or a visitor for whom we do not wish to wait up is spending the night, we tell such a friend that he can pick up the key at the delicatessen across the street. Joe Cornacchia, who keeps the delicatesssen, usually has a dozen or so keys at a time for handing out like this. He has a special drawer for them.

Now why do I, and many others, select Joe as a logical custodian for keys? Because we trust him, first, to be a responsible custodian, but equally important because we know that he combines a feeling of good will with a feeling of no personal responsibility about our private affairs. Joe considers it no concern of his whom we choose to permit in our places and why.

Around on the other side of our block, people leave their keys at a Spanish grocery. On the other side of Joe's block, people leave them at the candy store. Down a block they leave them at the coffee shop, and a few hundred feet around the corner from that, in a barber shop. Around one corner from two fashionable blocks of town houses and apartments in the Upper East Side, people leave their keys in a butcher shop and a bookshop; around another corner they leave them in a cleaner's and a drug store. In unfashionable East Harlem keys are left with at least one florist, in bakeries, in luncheonettes, in Spanish and Italian groceries.

The point, wherever they are left, is not the kind of ostensible service that the enterprise offers, but the kind of proprietor it has.

A service like this cannot be formalized. Identifications . . . questions . . . insurance against mishaps. The all-essential line between public service and privacy would be transgressed by institutionalization. Nobody in his right mind would leave his key in such a place. The service must be given as a favor by someone with an unshakable understanding of the difference between a person's key and a person's private life, or it cannot be given at all.

Or consider the line drawn by Mr. Jaffe at the candy store around our corner—a line so well understood by his customers and by other storekeepers too that they can spend their whole lives in its presence and never think about it consciously. One ordinary morning last winter, Mr. Jaffe, whose formal business name is Bernie, and his wife, whose formal business name is Ann, supervised the small children crossing at the corner on the way to P.S. 41, as Bernie always does because he sees the need; lent an umbrella to one customer and a dollar to another; took custody of two keys; took in some packages for people in the next building who were away; lectured two youngsters who asked for cigarettes; gave street directions; took custody of a watch to give the repair man across the street when he opened later; gave out information on the range of rents in the neighborhood to an apartment seeker; listened to a tale of domestic difficulty and offered reassurance; told some rowdies they could not come in unless they behaved and then defined (and got) good behavior; provided an incidental forum for half a dozen conversations among customers who dropped in for oddments; set aside certain newly arrived papers and magazines for regular customers who would depend on getting them; advised a mother who came for a birthday present not to get the ship-model kit because another child going to the same birthday party was giving that; and got a back copy (this was for me) of the previous day's newspaper out of the deliverer's surplus returns when he came by.

After considering this multiplicity of extra-merchandising services I asked Bernie, "Do you ever introduce your customers to each other?"

He looked startled at the idea, even dismayed. "No," he said thoughtfully. "That would just not be advisable. Sometimes, if I know two customers who are in at the same time have an interest in common, I bring up the subject in conversation and let them carry it on from there if they want to. But oh no, I wouldn't introduce them."

229

When I told this to an acquaintance in a suburb, she promptly assumed that Mr. Jaffe felt that to make an introduction would be to step above his social class. Not at all. In our neighborhood, storekeepers like the Jaffes enjoy an excellent social status, that of businessmen. In income they are apt to be the peers of the general run of customers and in independence they are the superiors. Their advice, as men or women of common sense and experience, is sought and respected. They are well known as individuals, rather than unknown as class symbols. No; this is that almost unconsciously enforced, well-balanced line showing, the line between the city public world and the world of privacy.

This line can be maintained, without awkwardness to anyone, because of the great plenty of opportunities for public contact in the enterprises along the sidewalks, or on the sidewalks themselves as people move to and fro or deliberately loiter when they feel like it, and also because of the presence of many public hosts, so to speak, proprietors of meeting places like Bernie's where one is free either to hang around or dash in and out, no strings attached.

Under this system, it is possible in a city street neighborhood to know all kinds of people without unwelcome entanglements, without boredom, necessity for excuses, explanations, fears of giving offense, embarrassments respecting impositions or commitments, and all such paraphernalia of obligations which can accompany less limited relationships. It is possible to be on excellent sidewalk terms with people who are very different from oneself, and even, as time passes, on familiar public terms with them. Such relationships can, and do, endure for many years, for decades; they could never have formed without that line, much less endured. They form precisely because they are by-the-way to people's normal public sorties.

One Point for Analysis: The essayist presents information in the fifth paragraph by making a catalogue, a list, of where people leave their keys in New York neighborhoods.

Writing Topics:
1. Write an account of how people in your neighborhood or town help each other, using, like Jacobs, a number of examples.
2. Write an explanation of what characterizes the public world you live in and the private world that is yours.

230

3. Explain your relationship to someone you know only by street contact, not through personal friendship.

CONFESSIONS OF AN UNPUBLISHED WRITER
BABETTE BLAUSHILD

When Babette Blaushild published her "confession," she left the ranks of those she was writing about. She became a published writer.

Without being too pompous about it, I think I can say I speak for one of the largest unorganized groups in the world—the unpublished authors. We write as though our lives depended on it—yet we have long since adapted ourselves to the icy truth that we will never get into print. Why do we do it? Because it happens to please us. In my own case I enjoy it.

People who know I write for love and not money probably feel there's something wrong with my moorings. They don't quite comprehend that writing can be an end in itself—and a profoundly rewarding one. In fact, it goes into the making of a good life.

A good life, for me at least, means making all sorts of connections with the world around me. It means a heightened awareness of people and their moods, a sensitivity to all sorts of subtle shadings. It means an existence without murkiness. The discipline of writing conditions the mind for this kind of life. It has enabled me to develop the tri-dimensional or stereoscopic habit. People at a dinner party, who used to fade one into the other with a flat sameness, now take on sharp forms and colors. Women at a committee meeting, or children and their mothers at the school play, now become defined in their own elements of uniqueness. And, as I try to understand them, I find myself liking them better. Take the committee chairman. Why should she be officious and small-minded? After the meeting I talked to her over coffee. Something about her reminded me of my mother's friend when I was small. Doors began to open in my mind; I could go exploring through rooms filled with old memories and feelings. Next: A man seated next to me at dinner. He has always been a bore. But now I look at him through different eyes. He fascinates me; he is literary fodder. True, he is a stereotype: the golf-playing, cigar-smoking, back-slapping businessman who inevitably sits next to you at dinner. But now I talk to him, draw him out, and he lets me have a glimpse now and then of the part of him that is not a cliché. Before I started to write, this kind of evening would numb me; now it excites my imagination.

I remember my first visit to a symphony concert after I took to writing as an important part of my life. I left the hall moved, though not really understanding why. What was I feeling? My ears had become newly alive. Thereafter I was struck with the difference between live and recorded music. It was as if I had been color blind all my life, seeing everything in grays and blacks, and then suddenly found I could see vivid hues. But there was more. I had a feeling of peace, and of wonder, too: If man is capable of creating this beauty and truth, I thought, here is our supreme elevation, and here is our hope.

As I find myself getting closer to human beings through my writing, I find myself becoming more patient and compassionate, never finding "answers," but perhaps stumbling on small truths. Not for me the novelist who ties up and polishes off the human problem he has posed, who says in effect: that's that. I feel that the novel can only be a search for human truths; and that along the way, some self-discovery is inevitable. In this view, it is not important that my writing be successful. I would of course like to be successful, but even if I do not create best-sellers or "successes of esteem," other rewards are open to me.

When I sit down to write, I change places with fate. I am its master at last. For a little while I am no longer one of millions dominated by forces quite outside my control: I become truly omnipotent. What could be sweeter? I create my characters, I make things happen or not happen to them, I make them happy or sad. I look at life from a few steps back, as if viewing a painting. I manipulate, maneuver, and fashion. I know what is going to happen, because I make it happen.

But if writing has its pleasures it also has its pain, as when I see my own handwriting on the self-addressed, manuscript envelope the mailman tosses casually on the doorstep. Inside, the melancholy printed rejection slip is clipped to the top page: "Thank you for

232

submitting your work which has been read with interest, *but. . . ."* Sometimes there is a little note of cheer: a "sorry" written across the bottom. Better yet, you may find enclosed a note scribbled on a memo pad by an editor.

Sometimes the manuscript is kept a tantalizingly long time. You then wonder, is this a good omen? Are they passing it up the hierarchy of editors at the magazine, actually liking it? Or is it lying on the desk of an editor who is home sick with the flu? Or is it home with him, not read because his kids are making too much noise? *What is taking so long?* Finally, the mailman brings the story back and there is a crazy kind of relief; you are temporarily liberated from your daily mailbox-vigil. But, full of hope and paper clips, you send another story out, and it starts all over again.

When you get frustrated, you look around and borrow strength from others who have been there, too. Eugene O'Neill, for instance, who said about the writer's task, "I know what you are up against and how you feel. The only thing is, keep up your confidence that sooner or later you'll come through . . . and keep on writing, no matter what. . . ." Then there is always the Old Harry Truman brand of philosophy, "If you can't stand the heat, get out of the kitchen."

We humans are a mixed lot: scared and lonely and foolish, inhuman and humane, graceful and graceless, full of hope and hopeless. Out of the conflict between reality and our fantasies, art can bring understanding and illuminate truth. To me, this is the supreme function of writing. It is no easy calling, but its rewards go so far beyond the mundane that I expect to practice it for as many years as I have left on earth.

One Point for Analysis: The beginning of the third paragraph furnishes a transition by repeating the end of the second paragraph.
Writing Topics:
  1. Write an expository essay discussing something you do that has no rewards beyond the pleasure it brings you.
  2. Define what the phrase the good life *means to you.*
  3. Following the example of Blaushild, discuss an activity that brings you pleasure, then explain how it brings you pain.

MAN-MADE TWISTERS

ANONYMOUS

The old saying that "everybody talks about the weather, but no-body does anything about it" is to some degree disproved in "Man-Made Twisters."

When an area is threatened, a tornado watch goes out via radio and television. When one of the terrifying funnels is sighted, or when radar picks up an echo with the shape of a hook or a flying eagle, characteristic of a tornado-producing cloud, every means of communication is mobilized to warn people to take shelter immediately.

Allen Pearson, who for years has headed the forecast center in Kansas City, tells about an encounter with a lady who was displeased with the warning system.

"She called me up to protest that the tornado watch had kept her in her basement for five hours, and nothing happened," says Al. "I tried to explain that we didn't want to alarm her; we just wanted her to be aware. Unfortunately, the same thing happened again five months later. She was really angry that time; we had given a warning but there was no tornado.

"Two years later, we had a really big storm. The lady came up out of her shelter to find her house blown away. She got me on the phone and said, 'Now, that's more like it!' "

If anyone ever figures out how to mitigate the fury of a tornado, that man may be Dr. T. Theodore Fujita of the Department of Geophysical Sciences at the University of Chicago. His intensive studies during the past 20 years of the behavior of these devastating funnels have earned him the sobriquet "Mr. Tornado."

A visit to Dr. Fujita's laboratory is a fascinating experience. With the aid of skilled machinist Vincent Ankus, he has built a wondrous tornado machine. A few minutes' preparation and the flick of a switch—and before your eyes miniature funnels dance and spin as do their lethal counterparts on the plains of Texas.

Wind force for the machine comes from an overlapping series of rotating cups, turning slowly at the outside but more rapidly toward the center, so that the suction is greatest in the middle.

Several feet below this apparatus sits a large tray filled with water. Dr. Fujita adds chunks of dry ice. The water bubbles like a devil's caldron, with "smoke" from the dry ice writhing and flowing above it.

Mr. Ankus turns on the machine. Instantly the smoke whips into a dazzling funnel, dancing erratically about the pan as it feeds into the exhaust fan above.

Now Dr. Fujita experiments to see what will affect his miniature maelstrom. He positions a framework of electrical wires so that they extend through the funnel; nothing happens. But when he turns on the current and the wires glow red, the funnel seems bewildered and tends to break up. Heat is poison to it.

Next he pokes a ruler into the spinning cloud. If held out flat, there is little effect; if turned on edge, the funnel falters. Similarly, if suction is made uniform over the area of whirling motions, the action is damped.

Says Dr. Fujita, "I hope that within ten years we will learn from experiments like these how to modify real tornadoes."

Dr. Fujita shows visitors a picture of a tornado aftermath in which one house is totally destroyed and the next is virtually undisturbed. Such variable damage is common, supposedly because the tornado skips and jumps. That may not be the answer at all, the scientist believes. Instead, the heaviest destruction may be caused by areas called "suction spots" in the funnel wall, which Dr. Fujita was the first to explain.

"A tornado moves across country at an average speed of about 30 miles an hour," he says. "The funnel itself rotates at speeds that may vary from 50 to 200 miles an hour. But carried along in the wall are three or four, sometimes five spots, that have an additional rotation of as much as 100 miles an hour. They may measure only a twentieth of the diameter of the funnel, but the suction in that small area is much greater than within the tornado as a whole."

Dr. Fujita discovered this phenomenon when he noticed in his voluminous file of photographs of tornado destruction that the worst damage often appeared along spiral lines. Each series of loops marked the devastating track of a suction spot.

Remarkably enough, this brilliant scientist, who has contributed so much to our knowledge of tornadoes, has yet to see one of the storms in action!

235

One Point for Analysis: The introduction leads into the subject by presentation of a humorous anecdote.

Writing Topics:

1. Dr. Fujita is called "Mr. Tornado." Describe someone you know who is called by a similar title—for example, "Miss University."
2. Write a description of a technical process following the example of the essay given here.
3. Describe some natural phenomenon you have witnessed.

MAN OR ROBOT?

ERWIN STEINKAMP

The discoveries of medical science are prolonging our lives but also beginning to make us partly mechanical. Some of the recent developments in the field of medicine are explained in this essay.

A plastic heart will soon take over after surgeons remove a diseased heart. Artificial blood will carry food and oxygen to body cells and carry wastes away. Bone, made of the same materials as pottery, will enclose the brain. Artificial glands will secrete chemicals necessary to keep the body alive. The list is practically endless.

All this hasn't happened yet. But there is no doubt that doctors of the future will have access to organ banks where they can pick up parts for their patients.

. . .

Fascinating research in this area is taking place at Harvard University. Here Dr. Robert Geyer is keeping rats alive on artificial blood.

The chemicals are called fluorocarbons. Dr. Geyer has proved that the fluorocarbons can supply animal tissues with oxygen and carry away poisonous carbon dioxide. His experiments were performed on white rats.

The scientist drained all the blood from a rat and replaced the blood with fluorocarbons. Ordinarily a white rat has pink ears and

Special permission granted by *Current Science,* published by Xerox Education Publications, © Xerox Corp., 1971.

red eyes. But as the milky colored chemical moved through the animal's body, the rat's eyes and ears became white.

Even though there was complete replacement of blood, the rat acted normally. It ran around; washed its face; and responded to light and sound.

The rat stayed alive for as long as eight hours. Precisely what caused its death is still not known.

While these experiments were going on at Harvard, scientists at other universities built and tested another artificial part for the circulatory system—the heart. Of all the organs of the body that suffer the most damage, the heart ranks first.

Each year 600,000 people die of heart attacks. Heart transplants using real hearts are not the answer to the problem. There are not enough heart donors to go around. On the other hand, artificial hearts, once perfected, could be made in unlimited quantities.

But heart researchers are faced with several problems. One problem is to find a material that the body will not reject as foreign material.

The artificial heart must also be able to pump 6 to 7 quarts of blood a minute without damaging delicate blood cells.

And most of all, the heart should be able to function perfectly inside the body and need no outside connections. Such a perfect organ is still a long way off. But tests are under way.

One of the materials being tested for the heart is a kind of plastic called silicone rubber. This substance has been found useful for building artificial noses, ears, and finger joints.

A heart made of this material was recently tried out for the first time in a human being. The heart pulsed for 63 hours in the chest of a 47-year-old man while doctors waited for a real heart to implant in the patient. A day after the real heart was implanted, the man died.

Dr. Denton Cooley who performed the operation considers the artificial heart implant a success. It bought time for the patient while he waited for the real heart.

But the artificial heart is at least five years away from being a practical answer. It now takes an instrument the size of a piano to regulate its beat.

The circulatory system is not the only body system that is receiving an assist from scientists. An artificial lung developed at the Chicago Wesley Memorial Hospital kept a dog alive for eight days. The lung is composed of the same material as the artificial heart.

237

At Clemson University artificial bones and teeth made from pottery material (ceramics) are being tried in dogs. Scientists are using this material because it is strong and porous. Bone cells grow into the pores much as they do in the real bones.

The use of artificial parts raises an interesting question. For example, if you were outfitted with a whole line of spare parts, would your identity suffer? When would you stop becoming a "who," and start becoming a "what"?

But in spite of these questions artificial body parts hold out a promise toward the future. That is, they will brighten and extend the lives of those who would have otherwise suffered or died.

One Point for Analysis: Difficult terms are explained within the essay.

Writing Topics:

1. After library research, write a brief history of Dr. Christiaan Barnard's transplants of human hearts.
2. One hundred years ago this essay on the human anatomy and what is being done to sustain it would have been considered science fiction. Discuss another phenomenon, now within the range of possibility, that a few years ago would have been considered sheer fantasy.
3. In an expository piece, discuss the effect on population that new lifesaving techniques will produce.

THE BURNING OF THE GLOBE

ANONYMOUS

The fire at the theater where many of Shakespeare's plays were originally produced furnished a show that was as exciting as some of his dramas.

Shortly after 2 o'clock on a Monday afternoon in June, 1613, an eager crowd filled the Globe theater for the first production of a new Shakespeare play, *Henry VIII*. Near the end of the first act, the actor playing the king made his entrance, announced by the thunder of a cannon fired from a cupola over the theater's thatched roof. No one seemed to notice or care that sparks from the cannon landed on the thatch. The sparks smouldered, smoked, flamed and in moments spectators were rushing for the two exits. "Some lost their hats, and some their swords," said a ballad on sale the next day in St. Paul's. The fire blazed wildly and although everybody escaped unscathed—one man doused his burning britches with a bottle of ale—the Globe was done for. It burned to the ground in two hours, the finest fire London had seen since St. Paul's steeple burned up in 1561.

The Globe had been built in 1599 with the lumber from another theater, London's first, which had been torn down because the man who owned the land on which it stood refused to renew the lease. The theater's owners boated the lumber across the Thames. With money raised by selling shares to a group of actors, they rebuilt the theater and named it the Globe.

The new theater was located in a disreputable borough, officially named The Clink, famed for its profusion of brothels, tenements, theaters and prisons. The Clink was chosen because it was outside the jurisdiction of the London council. The Council, composed of businessmen, politicians and Puritans, had railed against the Globe and other theaters as vile breeding places of "seditious matters, and many other corruptions of youth." The Clink, however, was ruled directly by Queen Elizabeth, who had little patience with the council's puritanical views.

Though the Globe was completely destroyed by the 1613 fire, it had made its owners—including Shakespeare—so prosperous that they rebuilt it within the year "in a fairer manner than before."

One Point for Analysis: Toward the end of the first paragraph, a humorous anecdote is inserted to counterbalance the potential horror of this tragedy.

Writing Topics:

1. In an expository essay discuss another or other historical locations as "vile breeding places of 'seditious matters, and many other corruptions of youth.'"
2. After library research, discuss the closing of the English theater in the seventeenth century.
3. Numerous buildings have burned or been bombed, killing scores of people. Like the author of this essay, discuss one of

these catastrophes by beginning with the state of events immediately preceding it.

CAN PEOPLE BE JUDGED BY THEIR APPEARANCE?

ERIC BERNE

Berne is a psychiatrist whose book Games People Play, *which is a study of human relationships, has been read by many lay readers. He is also the author of* A Layman's Guide to Psychiatry and Psychoanalysis, *from which this essay is taken.*

Everyone knows that a human being, like a chicken, comes from an egg. At a very early stage, the human embryo forms a three-layered tube, the inside layer of which grows into the stomach and lungs, the middle layer into bones, muscles, joints, and blood vessels, and the outside layer into the skin and nervous system.

Usually these three grow about equally, so that the average human being is a fair mixture of brains, muscles, and inward organs. In some eggs, however, one layer grows more than the others, and when the angels have finished putting the child together, he may have more gut than brain, or more brain than muscle. When this happens, the individual's activities will often be mostly with the overgrown layer.

We can thus say that while the average human being is a mixture, some people are mainly "digestion-minded," some "muscle-minded," and some "brain-minded," and correspondingly digestion-bodied, muscle-bodied, or brain-bodied. The digestion-bodied people look thick; the muscle-bodied people look wide; and the brain-bodied people look long. This does not mean the taller a man is the brainier he will be. It means that if a man, even a short man, looks long rather than wide or thick, he will often be more concerned about what goes on in his mind than about what he does or what he eats; but the key factor is slenderness and not height. On the other hand, a man who gives the impression of being thick rather than long or wide will usually be more interested in a good steak than in a good idea or a good long walk.

Medical men use Greek words to describe these types of body-build. For the man whose body shape mostly depends on the inside layer of the egg, they use the word *endomorph*. If it depends mostly upon the middle layer, they call him a *mesomorph*. If it depends upon the outside layer, they call him an *ectomorph*. We can see the same roots in our English words "enter," "medium," and "exit," which might just as easily have been spelled "ender," "mesium," and "ectit."

Since the inside skin of the human egg, or endoderm, forms the inner organs of the belly, the viscera, the endomroph is usually belly-minded; since the middle skin forms the body tissues, or soma, the mesomorph is usually muscle-minded; and since the outside skin forms the brain, or cerebrum, the ectomorph is usually brain-minded. Translating this into Greek, we have the viscerotonic endormorph, the somatotonic mesomorph, and the cerebrotonic ectomorph.

Words are beautiful things to a cerebrotonic, but a viscerotonic knows you cannot eat a menu no matter what language it is printed in, and a somatotonic knows you cannot increase your chest expansion by reading a dictionary. So it is advisable to leave these words and see what kinds of people they actually apply to, remembering again that most individuals are fairly equal mixtures and that what we have to say concerns only the extremes. Up to the present, these types have been thoroughly studied only in the male sex.

Viscerotonic Endomorph. If a man is definitely a thick type rather than a broad or long type, he is likely to be round and soft, with a big chest but a bigger belly. He would rather eat than breathe comfortably. He is likely to have a wide face, short, thick neck, big thighs and upper arms, and small hands and feet. He has over-developed breasts and looks as though he were blown up a little like a balloon. His skin is soft and smooth, and when he gets bald, as he does usually quite early, he loses the hair in the middle of his head first.

The short, jolly, thickset, red-faced politician with a cigar in his mouth, who always looks as though he were about to have a stroke, is the best example of this type. The reason he often makes a good

241

politician is that he likes people, banquets, baths, and sleep; he is easygoing, soothing, and his feelings are easy to understand.

His abdomen is big because he has lots of intestines. He likes to take in things. He likes to take in food, and affection and approval as well. Going to a banquet with people who like him is his idea of a fine time. It is important for a psychiatrist to understand the natures of such men when they come to him for advice.

Somatotonic Mesomorph. If a man is definitely a broad type rather than a thick or long type, he is likely to be rugged and have lots of muscle. He is apt to have big forearms and legs, and his chest and belly are well formed and firm, with the chest bigger than the belly. He would rather breathe than eat. He has a bony head, big shoulders, and a square jaw. His skin is thick, coarse, and elastic, and tans easily. If he gets bald, it usually starts on the front of the head.

Dick Tracy, Li'l Abner, and other men of action belong to this type. Such people make good lifeguards and construction workers. They like to put out energy. They have lots of muscles and they like to use them. They go in for adventure, exercise, fighting, and getting the upper hand. They are bold and unrestrained, and love to master the people and things around them. If the psychiatrist knows the things which give such people satisfaction, he is able to understand why they may be unhappy in certain situations.

Cerebrotonic Ectomorph. The man who is definitely a long type is likely to have thin bones and muscles. His shoulders are apt to sag and he has a flat belly with a dropped stomach, and long, weak legs. His neck and fingers are long, and his face is shaped like a long egg. His skin is thin, dry, and pale, and he rarely gets bald. He looks like an absent-minded professor and often is one.

Though such people are jumpy, they like to keep their energy and don't fancy moving around much. They would rather sit quietly by themselves and keep out of difficulties. Trouble upsets them, and they run away from it. Their friends don't understand them very well. They move jerkily and feel jerkily. The psychiatrist who understands how easily they become anxious is often able to help them get along better in the sociable and aggressive world of endomorphs and mesmorphs.

In the special cases where people definitely belong to one type or another, then, one can tell a good deal about their personalities from their appearance. When the human mind is engaged in one of its struggles with itself or with the world outside, the individual's way of handling the struggle will be partly determined by his type. If he is a viscerotonic he will often want to go to a party where he can eat and drink and be in good company at a time when he might be better off attending to business; the somatotonic will want to go out and do something about it, master the situation, even if what he does is foolish and not properly figured out, while the cerebrotonic will go off by himself and think it over, when perhaps he would be better off doing something about it or seeking good company to try to forget it.

Since these personality characteristics depend on the growth of the layers of the little egg from which the person developed, they are very difficult to change. Nevertheless, it is important for the individual to know about these types, so that he can have at least an inkling of what to expect from those around him, and can make allowances for the different kinds of human nature, and so that he can become aware of and learn to control his own natural tendencies, which may sometimes guide him into making the same mistakes over and over again in handling his difficulties.

AN ANALYSIS OF "CAN PEOPLE BE JUDGED BY THEIR APPEARANCE?"

The reason for Eric Berne's success with such books as *Games People Play* is easy to understand after reading "Can People Be Judged by Their Appearance?" In this essay he is concerned with scientific matters, and even uses scientific terminology. Nevertheless, his clearly organized explanation and his vivid examples interest and instruct even the reader who is not usually excited by discussions of medicine and biology.

The essay is organized into three distinct parts. The first six paragraphs establish definitions, the next seven present examples, and the final two summarize the information that has been presented and explain why knowing such information is important.

Recognizing that scientific expressions are intimidating to most people, Berne leads up to citing *endomorph, mesomorph,* and *ectomorph* by first defining them in terms that are easily grasped by the layman. Only after the reader understands the concepts does Berne introduce the foreign words that denote them. Even then (fourth paragraph) he relates each of them to common English words so that their strangeness is less pronounced. He treats the additional terms *viscera, soma,* and *cerebrum* (fifth paragraph) in the same way. By explaining their etymologies and associating them with more familiar terms, Berne makes the reader feel relatively comfortable with *viscerotononic endomorph, somatotonic mesomorph,* and *cerebrotonic ectomorph* in a surprisingly short amount of space. The sixth paragraph neatly summarizes the explanations presented up to that point and provides a transition into the second part of the essay.

In the second section Berne helps the reader by providing a heading for each of the three categories he has defined and for which he will now give examples and descriptions. In addition, each of the three discussions follows the same pattern. First, Berne describes a person typical of the category under discussion. He follows the description with an example that the reader will be quick to recognize and connect with the description. Finally, he notes how a psychiatrist can profit from being aware of that particular body type.

The vivid examples scattered throughout the piece are to a large degree responsible for the clarity of the presentation. The essay begins with a comparison of the human egg to the egg of a chicken and then to a three-layer tube. Later on, Berne's examples grow more extended. For instance, in the eighth paragraph he states: "The short, jolly, thickset, red-faced politician with a cigar in his mouth, who always looks as though he were about to have a stroke, is the best example of this type." The reader is made to see the example and thus understand the type and the terminology. The essay ends with a final reference to the egg with which the explanation began.

Eric Berne has handled technical explanations in a manner that makes them not only simple to understand but also interesting to discover and easy to remember.

REVERENCE FOR LIFE

ALBERT SCHWEITZER

Dr. Schweitzer spent the last fifty-three years of his life at the hospital he founded in Lambarene, Africa. During the first part of his life he was known for his philosophical and theological writings, as well as for his musicianship. He was awarded the Nobel Peace Prize in 1952.

Explore everything around you, penetrate to the furthest limits of human knowledge, and always you will come up against something inexplicable in the end. It is called life. It is a mystery so inexplicable that the knowledge of the educated and the ignorant is purely relative when contemplating it.

But what is the difference between the scientist who observes in his microscope the most minute and unexpected signs of life; and the old farmer who by contrast can barely read or write, who stands in springtime in his garden and contemplates the buds opening on the branches of his trees? Both are confronted with the riddle of life. One may be able to describe life in greater detail, but for both it remains equally inscrutable. All knowledge is, in the final analysis, the knowledge of life. All realization is amazement at this riddle of life—a reverence for life in its infinite and yet ever-fresh manifestations. How amazing this coming into being, living, and dying! How fantastic that in other existences something comes into being, passes away again, comes into being once more, and so forth from eternity to eternity! How can it be? We can do all things, and we can do nothing. For in all our wisdom we cannot create life. What we create is dead.

Life means strength, will, arising from the abyss, dissolving into the abyss again. Life is feeling, experience, suffering. If you study life deeply, looking with perceptive eyes into the vast animated chaos of this creation, its profundity will seize you suddenly with dizziness. In everything you recognize yourself. The tiny beetle that lies dead in your path—it was a living creature, struggling for existence like yourself, rejoicing in the sun like you, knowing fear and

Pp. 114–117 in *Reverence for Life* by Albert Schweitzer, translated by Reginald H. Fuller. Copyright © 1969 by Rhena Eckert-Schweitzer. Reprinted by permission of Harper & Row Publishers, Inc.

pain like you. And now it is no more than decaying matter—which is what you will be sooner or later, too. . . .

What is this recognition, this knowledge within the reach of the most scientific and the most childlike? It is reverence for life, reverence for the unfathomable mystery we confront in our universe, an existence different in its outward appearance and yet inwardly of the same character as our own, terribly similar, awesomely related. The strangeness between us and other creatures is here removed.

Reverence for the infinity of life means removal of the alienation, restoration of empathy, compassion, sympathy. And so the final result of knowledge is the same as that required of us by the commandment of love. Heart and reason agree together when we desire and dare to be men who seek to fathom the depths of the universe.

Reason discovers the bridge between love for God and love for men, love for all creatures, reverence for all being, compassion with all life, however dissimilar to our own.

I cannot but have reverence for all that is called life. I cannot avoid compassion for everything that is called life. That is the beginning and foundation of morality. Once a man has experienced it and continues to do so—and he who has once experienced it will continue to do so—he is ethical. He carries his morality within him and can never lose it, for it continues to develop within him. He who has never experienced this has only a set of superficial principles. These theories have no root in him, they do not belong to him, and they fall off him. The worst is that the whole of our generation had only such a set of superficial principles. Then the time came to put the ethical code to the test, and it evaporated. For centuries the human race had been educated with only a set of superficial principles. We were brutal, ignorant, and heartless without being aware of it. We had no scale of values, for we had no reverence for life.

It is our duty to share and maintain life. Reverence concerning all life is the greatest commandment in its most elementary form. Or expressed in negative terms: "Thou shalt not kill." We take this prohibition so lightly, thoughtlessly plucking a flower, thoughtlessly stepping on a poor insect, thoughtlessly, in terrible blindness because everything takes its revenge, disregarding the suffering and lives of our fellow men, sacrificing them to trivial earthly goals.

Much talk is heard in our times about building a new human race. How are we to build a new humanity? Only by leading men toward a true, inalienable ethic of our own, which is capable of further development. But this goal cannot be reached unless countless individuals will transform themselves from blind men into seeing ones and begin to spell out the great commandment which is: Reverence for Life. Existence depends more on reverence for life than the law and the prophets. Reverence for life comprises the whole ethic of love in its deepest and highest sense. It is the source of constant renewal for the individual and for mankind.

One Point for Analysis: Schweitzer in this essay attempts the definition of a highly complex mystery: life.
Writing Topics:
1. Write an essay that defines another "unfathomable mystery," such as love.
2. Discuss what you conceive to be ethical behavior in a classroom or in a job.
3. Whereas Schweitzer expresses reverence for life, explain your reverence for an institution.

UN-AMERICAN PEEVES

LARRY L. KING

King is a native Texan who contributes essays to journals in that state as well as to national publications. He has also written a novel, The One-Eyed Man, *and longer works of nonfiction.*

There are certain things an American is not permitted to hate. Americans may, without social ostracism or penalty of law, hate their partisan or ideological opposites. They may hate someone because of race or religion or class so long as they show selective decorum and speak in coded euphemisms. It is permissible to hate anybody you accuse of beating you out of money or stealing your girl. You may hate your career rivals, former spouses or the neighboring town without losing public sympathy. You may hate the Hottentots until you turn blue, especially if Dr. Kissinger happens not to be getting along with them, and you'd damn well *better* hate the Godless communists, for who knows when or where the next Joe McCarthy may appear. But there is a tyranny of the mind not permitting one to hate, for example, dogs.

I very much hate dogs. Some weeks ago in this space I made an excellent case for hating dogs. From the vituperative qualities of my mail, one might have thought I'd sold atomic secrets and repealed Mother's Day. Up with this I shall not put: if George Wallace got the right to hate black folks and others got the right to hate George Wallace, then I got the right to hate dogs. Because the Constitution protects my First Amendment liberties, I hereby claim my right to be as honestly hateful as my nature allows. Fasten your seatbelts while I prepare to land four-square on some very un-American pet peeves:

The Star Spangled Banner. To avoid burdening you with terms of expertise, trust me when I simply say that—musically—it's a piece of shit. No American, native-born or naturalized, has been discovered who properly can sing it. Instrumentally, it's perfectly suited to public executions. Its lyrics, when not bellicose, are nonsensical. I make the motion that we substitute in lieu thereof "Three Blind Mice." Plaintiff contends that it is as logical to get a chill up your spine on hearing "They all ran after the farmer's wife" as on hearing "O'er the ramparts we watched were so gallantly streaming."

Baseball. When the masses rise and restore me to my destined place, justice quickly shall dictate that baseball fanatics draw stiffer terms than dope addicts; baseball players themselves will be dealt with more harshly than pushers. As a former sports writer I attest that the representative baseball player's I.Q. averages a full digit less than his hat size. The baseball player alternately occupies himself by attempting to smite a cowhide spheroid with a wooden injector and preventing others from doing same. When he is unsuccessful, he sulks and kicks inanimate objects. The average baseball game consumes more than two hours. All but nine minutes consists of people standing around chewing tobacco and rubbing dirt on their hands. Once I am in power, baseball shall be abolished from the Little League up.

Little Kids. More expensive than yachts, more clamorous than street parades, naturally grubbier than your average hobo, they rise at ungodly hours for the sole purpose of providing their parents a long day. In addition to encouraging dogs in the home and playing baseball, they keep far too many bad marriages going. They are

248

permitted excessive holidays from school and spend perfectly good whiskey money on such fluff as dental work and bicycles. Even the Internal Revenue Service values the best of them at no more than $1,000. The outraged reader is reminded that Howard Cosell, Spiro Agnew and Jack the Ripper began as little kids: The obvious moral lesson is "Stomp 'em before they grow."

Public Prayer. The presumption of those who rise before audiences to address Heaven is that God is so much at leisure He may trouble Himself to assure the fates of football teams, Rotary Club speakers, political candidates or beauty queens. Personally, I resent His being called away from keeping a wary eye on the North Koreans and the John Birchers. Besides, public prayer violates the civil rights of all us good atheists—especially if we've paid to get in.

Vegetables. Nobody respecting good health should eat anything green except guacamole. The prudent will be suspicious of all yellows. Red is not to be trusted when superimposed on tomatoes or radishes. Ditto for orange when applied to carrots and white as it influences cauliflower. Stick with browns and grays. As to liquids, don't drink nothing that won't make you giggle.

Space being short, you must trust me without explanations in being cautioned against TV sit-coms, suburban shopping centers, academicians, musical comedies, charities and foundations, neckties, women who keep cats, people who enjoy the telephone, the out-of-doors and any mother not your own. Don't question my Americanism, now. I'm a plumb damn fool about football and Mom's apple pie.

One Point for Analysis: The disparity between the way people usually treat the subjects under discussion here and the way King treats them creates humor.

Writing Topics:
1. Like King, write an essay discussing your objections to some practice generally enjoyed by your friends.
2. Rewrite King's essay, omitting all humorous references. In other words, be serious.
3. Write a humorous essay by treating a serious subject frivolously, as King does, or by treating a trivial subject with great seriousness.

WHO IS A CHICANO?

RUBEN SALAZAR

During the past decade Americans have become increasingly concerned with ethnic origins. Salazar examines some of the problems involved in the use of labels.

A Chicano is a Mexican-American with a non-Anglo image of himself. He resents being told Columbus "discovered" America when the Chicano's ancestors, the Mayans and the Aztecs, founded highly sophisticated civilizations centuries before Spain financed the Italian explorer's trip to the "New World."

Chicanos resent also Anglo pronouncements that Chicanos are "culturally deprived" or that the fact that they speak Spanish is a "problem."

Having told you that, the Chicano will then contend that Anglos are Spanish-oriented at the expense of the Mexicans.

When you think you know what Chicanos are getting at, a Mexican-American will tell you that Chicano is an insulting term and may even quote the Spanish Academy to prove that Chicano derives from chicanery.

A Chicano will scoff at this and say that such Mexican-Americans have been brainwashed by Anglos and that they're Tio Tacos (Uncle Toms). This type of Mexican-American, Chicanos will agree, don't like the word Chicano because it's abrasive to their Anglo-oriented minds.

These poor people are brown Anglos, Chicanos will smirk— What, then, is a Chicano? Chicanos say that if you have to ask you'll never understand, much less become a Chicano.

Actually, the word Chicano is as difficult to define as "soul."

For those who like simplistic answers, Chicano can be defined as short for Mexicano. For those who prefer complicated answers, it has been suggested that Chicano may have come from the word Chihuahua—the name of a Mexican state bordering on the United States.

Getting trickier, this version then contends that Mexicans who migrated to Texas call themselves Chicanos because having crossed into the United States from Chihuahua they adopted the first three letters of that state, *Chi,* and then added *cano,* for the latter part of Texano.

Such explanations, however, tend to miss the whole point as to why Mexican-American activists call themselves Chicanos.

Mexican-Americans, the second largest minority in the country and the largest in the Southwestern states (California, Texas, Arizona, New Mexico and Colorado), have always had difficulty making up their minds what to call themselves.

Why, ask some Mexican-Americans, can't we just call ourselves Americans?

Chicanos are trying to explain why not. Mexican-Americans, though indigenous to the Southwest, are on the lowest rung scholastically, economically, socially and politically.

Mexican-Americans average eight years of schooling compared to the Negroes' 10 years. Farm workers, most of whom are Mexican-Americans in the Southwest, are excluded from the National Labor Relations Act unlike other workers. Also Mexican-Americans often have to compete for low-paying jobs with their Mexican brothers from across the border who are willing to work for even less.

Mexican-Americans have to live with the stinging fact that the word Mexican is the synonym for inferior in many parts of the Southwest.

That is why Mexican-American activists flaunt the barrio word Chicano—as an act of defiance and a badge of honor. Mexican-Americans, though large in numbers, are so politically impotent that in Los Angeles, where the country's largest single concentration of Spanish-speaking live, they have not one of their own on the City Council. This, in a city politically sophisticated enough to have three Negro councilmen. Chicanos, then, are merely fighting to become "Americans." Yes, but with a Chicano outlook.

One Point for Analysis: Originally written for publication in a newspaper, this essay is journalistic in its paragraphing.

Writing Topics:

1. Define another ethnic group, using as your title "Who Is a _____?"
2. Salazar says that "Chicano is as difficult to define as "soul.' " Write an essay in which you define *soul.*
3. Explain how some other term has been used by a dissatisfied

251

group in the same way *Chicano* has been, as "an act of defiance and a badge of honor."

A BABY LEARNS TO SMILE

DESMOND MORRIS

Desmond Morris's book The Naked Ape, *from which this essay is taken, was a popular bestseller. It explores, in a witty as well as scholarly manner, man, who "in acquiring lofty new motives . . . has lost none of the earthy old ones."*

Smiling begins during the first few weeks of life, but to start with it is not directed at anything in particular. By about the fifth week it is being given as a definite reaction to certain stimuli. The baby's eyes can now fixate objects. At first it is most responsive to a pair of eyes staring at it. Even two black spots on a piece of card will do. As the weeks pass, a mouth also becomes necessary. Two black spots with a mouth-line below them are now more efficient at eliciting the response. Soon a widening of the mouth becomes vital, and then the eyes begin to lose their significance as key stimuli. At this stage, around three to four months, the response starts to become more specific. It is narrowed down from any old face to the particular face of the mother. Parental imprinting is taking place.

The astonishing thing about the growth of this reaction is that, at the time when it is developing, the infant is hopeless at discriminating between such things as squares and triangles, or other sharp geometrical shapes. It seems as if there is a special advance in the maturing of the ability to recognize certain rather limited kinds of shapes—those related to human features—while other visual abilities lag behind. This ensures that the infant's vision is going to dwell on the right kind of object. It will avoid becoming imprinted on some near-by inanimate shape.

By the age of seven months the infant is completely imprinted on its mother. Whatever she does now, she will retain her mother-image for her offspring for the rest of its life. Young ducklings achieve this by the act of following the mother, young apes by clinging to her. We develop the vital bond of attachment via the smiling response.

As the visual stimulus the smile has attained its unique configuration principally by the simple act of turning up the mouth-corners. The mouth is opened to some extent and the lips pulled back, as in the face of fear, but by the addition of the curling up of the corners the character of the expression is radically changed. This development has in turn led to the possibility of another and contrasting facial posture—that of the down-turned mouth. By adopting a mouth-line that is the complete opposite of the smile shape, it is possible to signal an anti-smile. Just as laughing evolved out of crying and smiling out of laughing, so the unfriendly face has evolved, by a pendulum swing, from the friendly face.

But there is more to smiling than a mouth-line. As adults we may be able to convey our mood by a mere twist of the lips, but the infant throws much more into the battle. When smiling at full intensity, it also kicks and waves its arms about, stretches its hands out towards the stimulus and moves them about, produces babbling vocalizations, tilts back its head and protrudes its chin, leans its trunk forward or rolls it to one side, and exaggerates its respiration. Its eyes become brighter and may close slightly; wrinkles appear underneath or alongside the eyes and sometimes also on the bridge of the nose; the skin-fold between the sides of the nose and the sides of the mouth becomes more accentuated, and the tongue may be slightly protruded. Of these various elements the body movements seem to indicate a struggle on the infant's part to make contact with the mother. With its clumsy physique, the baby is probably showing us all that remains of the ancestral primate clinging response.

One Point for Analysis: The process by which the infant learns to smile is traced through a number of stages discussed in the sequence in which they occur.

Writing Topics:
  1. Trace the stages of another process, noting as Morris does the time period at which each step takes place.
  2. Write a report on what a good babysitter should know if he/she is called on to care for an infant.
  3. Explain how to teach a young child to acquire a new skill, such as riding a bicycle or swimming.

HOW TO READ A DICTIONARY

MORTIMER ADLER

Adler is an American philosopher and educator who was largely responsible for publication of the Great Books series, which he started while teaching at the University of Chicago. He has also written How to Read a Book *and* How to Think About War and Peace.

There is no more irritating fellow than the man who tries to settle an argument about communism, or justice, or liberty, by quoting from Webster. Webster and all his fellow lexicographers may be respected as authorities on word-usage, but they are not the ultimate founts of wisdom. They are no Supreme Court to which we can appeal for a decision of those fundamental controversies which, despite the warnings of semanticists, get us involved with abstract words. It is well to remember that the dictionary's authority can, for obvious reasons, be surer in the field of concrete words, and even in the field of the abstract technical words of science, than it ever can be with respect to philosophical words. Yet these words are indispensable if we are going to talk, read, or write about the things that matter most.

Another negative rule is: Don't swallow the dictionary. Don't try to get word-rich quick, by memorizing a lot of fancy words whose meanings are unconnected with any actual experience. Merely verbal knowledge is almost worse than no knowledge at all. If learning consisted in nothing but knowing the meanings of words, we could abolish all our courses of study, and substitute the dictionary for every other sort of book. But no one except a pedant or a fool would regard it as profitable or wise to read the dictionary from cover to cover.

In short, don't forget that the dictionary is a book about words, not about things. It can tell you how men have used words, but it does not define the nature of the things the words name. A Scandinavian university undertook a "linguistic experiment" to prove that human arguments always reduce to verbal differences. Seven lawyers were given seven dictionary definitions of truth and asked to defend them. They soon forgot to stick to the "verbal meanings" they had been assigned, and became vehemently involved in defending or opposing certain fundamental views about the nature of truth. The experiment showed that discussions may start about the meanings of words, but that, when interest in the problem is aroused, they seldom end there. Men pass from words to things, from names to natures. The dictionary can start an argument, but only thought or research can end it.

If we remember that a dictionary is a book about words, we can derive from that fact all the rules for reading a dictionary intelligently. Words can be looked at in four ways.

(1) *Words are physical things*—writable marks and speakable sounds. There must, therefore, be uniform ways of spelling and pronouncing them, though the uniformity is often spoiled by variations.

(2) *Words are parts of speech.* Each single word plays a grammatical role in the more complicated structure of a phrase or a sentence. According to the part it plays, we classify it as a certain part of speech—noun or verb, adjective or adverb, article or preposition. The same word can vary in different usages, shifting from one part of speech to another, as when we say "Man the boat" or "Take the jump." Another sort of grammatical variation in words arises from their inflection, but in a relatively uninflected language like English, we need pay attention only to the conjugation of the verb (infinitive, participle, past tense, etc.), the number of the noun (singular and plural), and the degree of the adjective (especially the comparative and superlative).

(3) *Words are signs.* They have meanings, not one but many. These meanings are related in various ways. Sometimes they shade from one into another; sometimes one word will have two or more sets of totally unrelated meanings. Through their meanings words are related to one another—as synonyms sharing in the same meaning even though they differ in its shading; or as antonyms through opposition or contrast of meanings. Furthermore, it is in their capacity as signs that we distinguish words as proper or common names (according as they name just one thing or many which are alike in some respect); and as concrete or abstract names (according as they point to some thing which we can sense, or refer to some aspect of things which we can understand by thought but not observe through our senses).

255

Finally, (4) *Words are conventional.* They mean or signify natural things, but they themselves are not natural. They are man-made signs. That is why every word has a history, just as everything else man makes has a time and place of origin, and a cultural career, in which it goes through certain transformations. The history of words is given by their etymological derivation from original word-roots, prefixes, and suffixes; it includes the account of their physical change, both in spelling and pronunciation; it tells of their shifting meanings, and which among them are archaic and obsolete, which are current and regular, which are idiomatic, colloquial, or slang.

A good dictionary will answer all your questions about words under these four heads. The art of reading a dictionary (as any other book) consists in knowing what questions to ask about words and how to find the answers. I have suggested the questions. The dictionary itself tells you how to find the answers. In this respect, it is a perfect self-help book, because it tells you what to pay attention to and how to interpret the various abbreviations and symbols it uses in giving you the four varieties of information about words. Anyone who fails to consult the explanatory notes and the list of abbreviations at the beginning of a dictionary can blame only himself for not being able to read the dictionary well. Unfortunately, many people fail here, as in the case of other books, because they insist upon neglecting the prefatory matter—as if the author were just amusing himself by including it.

I think these suggestions about how to read, and how not to misuse, a dictionary are easy to follow. But like all other rules they will be followed well only by the man who is rightly motivated in the first place. And, in the last place, they will be wisely applied only by the man who remembers that we are both *free* and *bound* in all our dealing with language, whether as writers or readers.

One Point for Analysis: The essayist first explains how *not* to use a
   dictionary, then discusses how it should be used.

Writing Topics:
1. Following the example of this essay, explain how to use one of your textbooks. That is, approach the explanation first negatively, then positively.
2. Compare the information presented in Adler's essay with the information given in the *Dictionary* section of the Handbook of this text.

3. Look up one word in a good dictionary. Using the information you find there, write an expository essay about the various meanings and levels of usage of the word.

TWINS' PRIVATE LANGUAGE BAFFLES SCIENTISTS

EVERETT R. HOLLES

The question of whether language is inherent or acquired has puzzled linguists and laymen for many centuries. Everett R. Holles presents information in this essay that may lead to some answers about the origins of language in human beings.

Playing with a doll house in the speech therapy center at Children's Hospitals here, Virginia and Grace Kennedy, identical twins who will be 7 years old next month, carried on an animated conversation broken by outbursts of childish laughter.

"Dugon, thosh yom kinchkin, duah?" asked Virginia, who is called "Cabenga" by her sister.

Grace, who is "Poto," nodded and replied with what sounded like "Snup aduk, chase die-dipanna." Both immediately set about removing the doll house's furniture.

Neither seemed to notice a tape recorder or voice-wave tracing equipment monitoring their gibberish, or a group of speech and language specialists watching and listening intently in a glass-windowed booth.

Scientists have been fascinated and baffled in recent weeks by the conversations of the pretty, black-haired twins, who understand English, German, sign language and a smattering of Spanish, but who for five years have spoken only in what appears to be a language of their own.

Their conversations are unintelligible, even to their parents, Thomas Kennedy and his German-born wife Christine, of San Diego. The Kennedys decided in January that the girls were mentally impaired and enrolled them in a school for retarded children.

But psychologists at the school concluded before the end of their first semester that the children had been misplaced. They were, the psychologists said, mentally alert, quick to learn and except for language, of normal intelligence. In June, the twins were referred to the speech therapy clinic at Children's Hospital.

Alexa Romain, the principal therapist working with the Kennedy twins, believes further observations and testing may disclose that "their jabberwocky may be really a comprehensive private language with a structured syntax.

"In the scientific literature on the subject over the last 50 years," she said, "there is only one other case that even comes close to what we are witnessing, that of triplets in Germany some years ago."

They could prove to be one of a very few documented cases of idioglossia, or twin speech, according to several of the linguistic experts trying to unscramble their conversations.

If the twins' jargon can be broken down and translated into a consistent, meaningful vocabulary and sentence structure, it may help to solve a longstanding scientific problem. Researchers have never been able to establish whether children are born with a genetic brain mechanism for developing language or whether they merely acquire speech communication by exposure to the spoken word.

Several speech experts have cautioned, however, that a neurological explanation may be found for the phenomenon.

Having suffered convulsive seizures soon after their birth in Columbus, Ga., the Kennedy girls underwent surgery at the age of 6 months because of excessive brain fluid.

Dr. Harlan Lane of Northwestern University is one of those who have suggested the twins may have suffered in infancy an obscure form of brain damage known as corticoanarthria.

The affliction, he explained, produces distorted, unarticulated speech, scrambling or even reversing normal language, while leaving unaffected that part of the brain that receives and comprehends normal conversation.

Linguists at the hospital said, however, that the twins have begun to respond with English words and sentences without any trace of distortion or vocal impediment.

Ann Koenecke of the speech therapy staff said that, with the affinity unique to twins, the evidence of "twin speech" rather than operative brain damage appears to be strong.

Idioglossia, she said, although extremely rare, is usually found in twins who, like Virginia and Grace Kennedy, have grown up in unusually close companionship largely isolated from the influence of other children.

Miss Romain explained the girls' conversation bore no resemblance to baby talk or to phonological distortions of the English and German spoken in their home.

"It appears at this point, but remains to be verified, that they have made up between themselves a language with a sentence structure, verbs, nouns and verb tenses within an ordered although still immature grammatical framework," she added.

Dr. Leonard Newmark, professor of linguistics at the University of California here, said the studies of the Kennedy twins "may help us in resolving one of the most intriguing and controversial enigmas of linguistic and cognitive science."

"We have never had an opportunity before to watch what appears to be a natural language being constructed," he said. "Studying these children may provide data that will help provide the answer as to whether language ability is inherited."

The twins were nearly 2 years old when the family came to California, living first in a rural community near Escondido, where the girls had little opportunity to play with other children. It was about that time they began developing their "private language."

Kennedy said: "You had only to watch and listen to them for a few minutes and it was quite clear they were carrying on what to them was an intelligible conversation in their own private language. It started when they were about 17 months old. One would hold up an object, suggest a name for it and the other would agree."

The class for the retarded that the twins attended included Mexican-American children, and Spanish words sometimes crept into their gibberish. It was arranged for the girls and Mr. and Mrs. Kennedy to study sign language, and the twins picked it up more readily than their parents.

For a large part of the twins' lives, both parents worked and they were under the care of their maternal grandmother, who came to this country from Germany about the time of their birth and speaks very little English.

"We brought in a German linguist and he could find only four of five words, such as milch for milk, that in any way resembled German," Miss Romain said. "We have found no evidence, thus far at least, that their speech is a complicated English-German dialect."

259

One Point for Analysis: The validity of the information in this essay is supported by frequent references to authorities in the field.

Writing Topics:

1. Explain a private language (slang, code, English variant) that you and a friend have used to communicate with each other while deceiving others.
2. Write a letter to a friend. Using the same subject, write a formal essay. Your two pieces of writing should employ different diction.
3. Report on some strange event, such as UFO's, giving your information validity by citing the statements of authorities and witnesses.

OLFACTION IN HUMANS

EDWARD T. HALL

Edward T. Hall is an anthropologist who has traveled widely to observe and analyze man's use of space and gestures. He is the author of The Hidden Dimension, *from which this essay is taken, and* The Silent Language.

Americans traveling abroad are apt to comment on the smell of strong colognes used by men living in Mediterranean countries. Because of their heritage of northern European culture, these Americans will find it difficult to be objective about such matters. Entering a taxicab, they are overwhelmed by the inescapable presence of the driver, whose olfactory aura fills the cab.

Arabs apparently recognize a relationship between disposition and smell. The intermediaries who arrange an Arab marriage usually take great precautions to insure a good match. They may even on occasion ask to smell the girl and will reject her if she "does not smell nice," not so much on esthetic grounds but possibly because of a residual smell of anger or discontent. Bathing the other person in one's breath is a common practice in Arab countries. The American is taught not to breathe on people. He experiences difficulty when he is within olfactory range of another person with whom he is not on close terms, particularly in public settings. He finds the intensity and sensuality overwhelming and has trouble paying attention to what is being said and at the same time coping with his feelings. In brief, he has been placed in a double bind and is pushed in two directions at once. The lack of congruence between U.S. and Arab olfactory systems affects both parties and has repercussions which extend beyond mere discomfort or annoyance. . . . By banishing all but a few odors from our public life, what have Americans done to themselves and what effect does this have on life in our cities?

In the northern European tradition most Americans have cut themselves off from a powerful communication channel: olfaction. Our cities lack both olfactory and visual variety. Anyone who has walked along the streets of almost any European village or town knows what is nearby. During World War II in France I observed that the aroma of French bread freshly removed from the oven at 4:00 A.M. could bring a speeding jeep to a screaming halt. The reader can ask himself what smells we have in the U.S. that can achieve such results. In the typical French town, one may savor the smell of coffee, spices, vegetables, freshly plucked fowl, clean laundry, and the characteristic odor of outdoor cafés. Olfactions of this type can provide a sense of life; the shifts and the transitions not only help to locate one in space but add zest to daily living.

One Point for Analysis: Hall is explaining a process by comparison and contrast instead of by the more usual method of noting stages of development.

Writing Topics:
1. Explain a cultural phenomenon of another society that you find to be surprising because it is different from what you are used to.
2. Explain a disagreement caused by misunderstanding of ethnic customs.
3. Write an expository essay discussing the process of taste, as Hall has discussed the process of olfaction.

WHY YOU WILL NOT BE BURIED ALIVE

JESSICA MITFORD

The American Way of Death, from which this essay is taken, was a popular bestseller in the 1960's. Jessica Mitford often takes as her subject practices of American life that, although well established, call for examination.

Embalming is indeed a most extraordinary procedure, and one must wonder at the docility of Americans who each year pay hundreds of millions of dollars for its perpetuation, blissfully ignorant of what it is all about, what is done, how it is done. Not one in ten thousand has any idea of what actually takes place. Books on the subject are extremely hard to come by. They are not to be found in most libraries or bookshops.

In an era when huge television audiences watch surgical operations in the comfort of their living rooms, when, thanks to the animated cartoon, the geography of the digestive system has become familiar territory even to the nursery school set, in a land where the satisfaction of curiosity about almost all matters is a national pastime, the secrecy surrounding embalming can, surely, hardly be attributed to the inherent gruesomeness of the subject. Custom in this regard has within this century suffered a complete reversal. In the early days of American embalming, when it was performed in the home of the deceased, it was almost mandatory for some relative to stay by the embalmer's side and witness the procedure. Today, family members who might wish to be in attendance would certainly be dissuaded by the funeral director. All others, except apprentices, are excluded by law from the preparation room.

A close look at what does actually take place may explain in large measure the undertaker's intractable reticence concerning a procedure that has become his major *raison d'être*. Is it possible he fears that public information about embalming might lead patrons to wonder if they really want this service? If the funeral men are loath to discuss the subject outside the trade, the reader may, understandably, be equally loath to go on reading at this point. For those who have the stomach for it, let us part the formaldehyde curtain. . . .

The body is first laid out in the undertaker's morgue—or rather, Mr. Jones is reposing in the preparation room—to be readied to bid the world farewell.

The preparation room in any of the better funeral establishments has the tiled and sterile look of a surgery, and indeed the embalmer-restorative artist who does his chores there is beginning to adopt the term "dermasurgeon" (appropriately corrupted by some mortician-writers as "demisurgeon") to describe his calling. His equipment, consisting of scalpels, scissors, augers, forceps, clamps, needles, pumps, tubes, bowls and basins, is crudely imitative of the surgeon's as is his technique, acquired in a nine- or twelve-month post-high-school course in an embalming school. He is supplied by an advanced chemical industry with a bewildering array of fluids, sprays, pastes, oils, powders, creams, to fix or soften tissue, shrink or distend it as needed, dry it here, restore the moisture there. There are cosmetics, waxes and paints to fill and cover features, even plaster of Paris to replace entire limbs. There are ingenious aids to prop and stabilize the cadaver: a Vari-Pose Head Rest, the Edwards Arm and Hand Positioner, the Repose Block (to support the shoulders during the embalming), and the Throop Foot Positioner, which resembles an old-fashioned stocks.

Mr. John H. Eckels, president of the Eckels College of Mortuary Science, thus describes the first part of the embalming procedure: "In the hands of a skilled practitioner, this work may be done in a comparatively short time and without mutilating the body other than by slight incision—so slight that it scarcely would cause serious inconvenience if made upon a living person. It is necessary to remove the blood, and doing this not only helps in the disinfecting, but removes the principal cause of disfigurements due to discoloration."

Another textbook discusses the all-important time element: "The earlier this is done, the better, for every hour that elapses between death and embalming will add to the problems and complications encountered. . . ." Just how soon should one get going on the embalming? The author tells us, "On the basis of such scanty information made available to this profession through its rudimentary and haphazard system of technical research, we must conclude that the best results are to be obtained if the subject is embalmed before life is completely extinct—that is, before cellular death has occurred. In the average case, this would mean within an hour after somatic death." For those who feel that there is something a little rudimentary, not to say haphazard, about this advice, a comforting thought is offered by another writer. Speaking of fears entertained in early days of premature burial, he points out, "One of the effects of embalming by chemical injection, however, has been to dispel fears of live burial." How true; once the blood is removed, chances of live burial are indeed remote.

To return to Mr. Jones, the blood is drained out through the veins and replaced by embalming fluid pumped in through the arteries. As noted in *The Principles and Practices of Embalming*, "every operator has a favorite injection and drainage point—a fact which becomes a handicap only if he fails or refuses to forsake his favorites when conditions demand it." Typical favorites are the carotid artery, femoral artery, jugular vein, subclavian vein. There are various choices of embalming fluid. If Flextone is used, it will produce a "mild, flexible rigidity. The skin retains a velvety softness, the tissues are rubbery and pliable. Ideal for women and children." It may be blended with B. and G. Products Company's Lyf-Lyk tint, which is guaranteed to reproduce "nature's own skin texture . . . the velvety appearance of living tissue." Suntone comes in three separate tints: Suntan; Special Cosmetic Tint, a pink shade "especially indicated for young female subjects"; and Regular Cosmetic Tint, moderately pink.

About three to six gallons of a dyed and perfumed solution of formaldehyde, glycerin, borax, phenol, alcohol and water is soon circulating through Mr. Jones, whose mouth has been sewn together with a "needle directed upward between the upper lip and gum and brought out through the left nostril," with the corners raised slightly "for a more pleasant expression." If he should be bucktoothed, his teeth are cleaned with Bon Ami and coated with colorless nail polish. His eyes, meanwhile, are closed with fleshtinted eye caps and eye cement.

The next step is to have at Mr. Jones with a thing called a trocar. This is a long, hollow needle attached to a tube. It is jabbed into the abdomen, poked around the entrails and chest cavity, the contents of which are pumped out and replaced with "cavity fluid." This done, and the hole in the abdomen sewn up, Mr. Jones's face is heavily creamed (to protect the skin from burns which may be caused by leakage of the chemicals), and he is covered with a sheet and left unmolested for a while. But not for long—there is more, much more, in store for him. He has been embalmed, but not yet restored, and the best time to start the restorative work is eight to ten hours after embalming, when the tissues have become firm and dry.

The object of all this attention to the corpse, it must be remembered, is to make it presentable for viewing in an attitude of healthy repose. "Our customs require the presentation of our dead in the semblence of normality . . . unmarred by the ravages of illness, disease or mutilation," says Mr. J. Sheridan Mayer in his *Restorative Art*. This is rather a large order since few people die in the full bloom of health, unravaged by illness and unmarked by some disfigurement. The funeral industry is equal to the challenge: "In some cases the gruesome appearance of a mutilated or disease-ridden subject may be quite discouraging. The task of restoration may seem impossible and shake the confidence of the embalmer. This is the time for intestinal fortitude and determination. Once the formative work is begun and affected tissues are cleaned or removed, all doubts of success vanish. It is surprising and gratifying to discover the results which may be obtained."

The embalmer, having allowed an appropriate interval to elapse, returns to the attack, but now he brings into play the skill and equipment of sculptor and cosmetician. Is a hand missing? Casting one in plaster of Paris is a simple matter. "For replacement purposes, only a cast of the back of the hand is necessary; this is within the ability of the average operator and is quite adequate." If a lip or two, a nose or an ear should be missing, the embalmer has at hand a variety of restorative waxes with which to model replacements. Pores and skin texture are simulated by stippling with a little brush, and over this cosmetics are laid on. Head off? Decapitation cases are rather routinely handled. Ragged edges are trimmed, and head joined to torso with a series of splints, wires and sutures. It is a good idea to have a little something at the neck—a scarf or high collar—when time for viewing comes. Swollen mouth? Cut out tissue as needed from inside the lips. If too much is removed, the surface contour can easily be restored by padding with cotton. Swollen necks and cheeks are reduced by removing tissue through vertical incisions made down each side of the neck. "When the deceased is casketed, the pillow will hide the suture incisions . . . as an extra

265

precaution against leakage, the suture may be painted with liquid sealer."

The opposite condition is more likely to present itself—that of emaciation. His hypodermic syringe now loaded with massage cream, the embalmer seeks out and fills the hollowed and sunken areas by injection. In this procedure the backs of the hands and fingers and the under-chin area should not be neglected.

Positioning the lips is a problem that recurrently challenges the ingenuity of the embalmer. Closed too tightly, they tend to give a stern, even disapproving expression. Ideally, embalmers feel, the lips should give the impression of being ever so slightly parted, the upper lip protruding slightly for a more youthful appearance. This takes some engineering, however, as the lips tend to drift apart. Lip drift can sometimes be remedied by pushing one or two straight pins through the inner margin of the lower lip and then inserting them between the two front upper teeth. If Mr. Jones happens to have no teeth, the pins can just as easily be anchored in his Armstrong Face Former and Denture replacer. Another method to maintain lip closure is to dislocate the lower jaw, which is then held in its new position by a wire run through holes which have been drilled through the upper and lower jaws at the midline. As the French are fond of saying, *il faut souffrir pour être belle*.

If Mr. Jones has died of jaundice, the embalming fluid will very likely turn him green. Does this deter the embalmer? Not if he has intestinal fortitude. Masking pastes and cosmetics are heavily laid on, burial garments and casket interiors are color-correlated with particular care, and Jones is displayed beneath rose-colored lights. Friends will say, "How *well* he looks." Death by carbon monoxide, on the other hand, can be rather a good thing from the embalmer's viewpoint: "One advantage is the fact that this type of discoloration is an exaggerated form of a natural pink coloration." This is nice because the healthy glow is already present and needs but little attention.

The patching and filling completed, Mr. Jones is now shaved, washed and dressed. Cream-based cosmetic, available in pink, flesh, suntan, brunette and blond, is applied to his hands and face, his hair is shampooed and combed (and, in the case of Mrs. Jones, set), his hands manicured. For the horny-handed son of toil special care must be taken; cream should be applied to remove ingrained grime, and the nails cleaned. "If he were not in the habit of having them manicured in life, trimming and shaping is advised for better appearance—never questioned by kin."

Jones is now ready for casketing (this is the present participle of the verb "to casket"). In this operation his right shoulder should be depressed slightly "to turn the body a bit to the right and soften the appearance of lying flat on the back." Positioning the hands is a matter of importance, and special rubber positioning blocks may be used. The hands should be cupped slightly for a more lifelike, relaxed appearance. Proper placement of the body requires a delicate sense of balance. It should lie as high as possible in the casket, yet not so high that the lid, when lowered, will hit the nose. On the other hand, we are cautioned, placing the body too low "creates the impression that the body is in a box."

Jones is next wheeled into the appointed slumber room where a few last touches may be added—his favorite pipe placed in his hand or, if he was a great reader, a book propped into position. (In the case of little Master Jones a Teddy bear may be clutched.) Here he will hold open house for a few days, visiting hours 10 A.M. to 9 P.M.

AN ANALYSIS OF "WHY YOU WILL NOT BE BURIED ALIVE"

Jessica Mitford's essay "Why You Will Not Be Buried Alive" is shocking because it deals with a subject that most of us do not want to face. It is somewhat toned down by her bitter humor, and on the whole it is excellent process analysis that reveals the steps an embalmer and restorative artist takes to make a corpse presentable for "viewing."

Mitford organizes her essay by explanation achieved through a step one, step two, etc. approach. Her general introduction, a discussion of why we avoid this subject, covers the first three paragraphs, and the transition that leads into the process itself firms the tone of her essay: "For those who have the stomach for it, let us part the formaldehyde curtain. . . ."

In analyzing the process of embalming, Mitford often makes "lists" (see fifth and eighth paragraphs). This device of cataloguing lends itself to a highly structured essay. And such an essay is precisely what Ms. Mitford has written: a tightly organized, graphically descriptive, emotionally disturbing view of the secrets one finds in the embalmer's room.

Mitford's tone seems a final touch in giving a sense of sanity to the whole operation. She plays with the entire procedure, always indirectly

267

asking, "Is this really necessary?" Perhaps her answer comes in her conclusion: "In the case of little Master Jones a teddy bear may be clutched."

TROUT HEAVEN
ROBERT TRAVER

Robert Traver, whose real name is John D. Voelker, has written short stories in addition to serving on the Supreme Court of Michigan. His love for fishing the streams of that state is evident in his essay.

There is a certain bass lake in these parts the water height of which is regulated by the whims of nature coupled with the variable needs of a certain incorporated benevolence known as an hydroelectric company. Since both parties are strangely uncommunicative and their moods are equally unpredictable, it is difficult for me to tell ahead of time just when the damn place will be ripe for fishing. I'm just not consulted. . . . But why, you may ask, why does this prideful fellow who dilates so interminably on being a trout-fishing purist—why should this untouchable take the slightest interest in waters inhabited by the miserable and lowly *bass*?

The reason, my friends, is that I am a member of a small secretive band of fishermen that knows that this so-called "bass" lake is also inhabited by trout—what is more, by big, savage, lantern-jawed, square-tailed, native brook trout! The gimmick—and the cross we must bear—is that one has a fighting chance to take these trout on flies *only* during those rare periods when the lake level is way down low. When that happens the usually flooded and submerged channel of a certain inlet becomes exposed; the banks become dried out; the mechanical aspects of fly-casting are then ideal; and for some mysterious reason that still baffles me—doubtless connected with food, temperatures, and protection—the big trout then come crowding pell-mell into this enchanted half-mile-long exposed channel in incredible numbers. Verily, it is so.

My theory is that as the lake waters continue to recede and the competition for food daily grows more keen, the trout perforce

From Robert Traver, *Trout Madness*, © 1960, by Robert Traver, St. Martin's Press., Inc.

leave the cool deeps (where I suspect they normally dwell) and range out not only in search of food but also to avoid the ever-narrowing proximity with the bass. (You see, even the trout hate 'em!) I also suspect that as the waters dwindle the lake temperatures doubtless rise, and the sensitive trout with their low toleration for rising temperatures, come crowding into the old river outlet to enjoy the concentrated coolness of fresh aerated waters pouring out of the deep woods. At any rate one thing is certain: given these conditions, the trout are *there;* and while the anguished and threadbare utility people prostrate themselves and beat their breasts and burn incense daily for rain, our little knot of initiated trout fishermen smile evilly and quietly foregather from miles around. For then it is we know that we are about to enter the very front door of trout heaven.

One Point for Analysis: The introductory paragraph is based on personification. (See *Figurative Language,* Handbook.)

Writing Topics:

1. Write an analysis of an ideal hunting or fishing situation.
2. Explain the equipment needed for participation in a specific outdoor sport.
3. Write a cause-and-effect essay about why a person enjoys some specific activity.

THE BLACK DEATH

PHILIP ZIEGLER

Philip Ziegler does not consider himself a professional historian. He writes about subjects from history because of his own interest in them.

The population that awaited the Black Death in Europe was ill equipped to resist it. The medieval peasant—distracted by war, weakened by malnutrition, exhausted by his struggle to win a living from his inadequate portion of ever less fertile land—was physically an easy prey for the disease. Intellectually and emotionally, he was prepared for disaster and ready to accept it if not actually welcome it.

The Europeans of the fourteenth century were convinced that the plague was an affliction laid on them by the Almighty, a retribution for the wickedness of the present generation. Credulous and superstitious, they believed without question in the direct participation of God on earth and were well versed in Old Testament precedents for the destruction of cities or whole races in an access of divine indignation. Because they were unable to see a natural explanation of this sudden holocaust, they took it for granted that they were the victims of God's wrath.

Given so grim a sense of destiny, it is to the credit of the medieval physicians that they devoted themselves to preventing or curing the infection. It is, however, hardly surprising that their efforts proved inadequate. Sudhoff's great archives of medical history, published in Germany in 1925, reproduce more than two hundred and eighty plague treatises; seventy-seven were written before 1400 and at least twenty before 1353. There is much windy nothingness in these, but also a certain amount of common sense and sound judgement. Certainly there was a depressing readiness to stress that flight or prayer was the only possible defense, but the patient was also given some guidance on how he should conduct himself.

There were frequent differences of opinion among the experts. Simon of Covino thought pregnant women and "those of fragile nature," like undernourished paupers would be the first to go—a conclusion the Medical Faculty of Paris rejected, claiming that those "whose bodies are replete with humors" were the most vulnerable. There was more agreement on the best place to live. Seclusion was the first priority. After that, the problem was how to avoid the infected air that carried death from land to land. A low site, sheltered from the wind, was desirable. The coast was to be shunned because of the corrupt mists that were creeping across the surface of the sea. Houses should be built facing north, and windows should be glazed or covered with waxed cloth.

If the infection was carried by corrupted air, something was needed to build up antibodies. Anything aromatic was considered of value. For example, it was good to burn dry and richly scented woods, like juniper, ash, vine, or rosemary. Diet was important, too. Fish from infected waters of the sea was prohibited, but eggs were authorized if eaten with vinegar.

It was bad to sleep by day and best to keep the heat of the liver steady by sleeping first on the right side and then on the left. To sleep on one's back was disastrous, since this would cause a stream of superfluities to descend on the palate and nostrils. These would flow to the brain and submerge the memory.

Bad drove out bad, and to imbibe foul odors was a useful protection. According to another contemporary writer, John Colle: "Attendants who take care of latrines are nearly all to be considered immune." It was not unknown for apprehensive citizens to spend hours each day crouched over a latrine absorbing the fetid smells.

These were mainly preventives; once the disease struck, the remedies became still more irrelevant.

One Point for Analysis: The second paragraph is developed by a series of causes and effects.
Writing Topics:
  1. Present a contemporary superstition that is used to explain an event inexplicable by logical reasoning.
  2. Explain a home remedy used in your family to combat illness or soothe pain.
  3. After library research, write an account of the Great Fire of London in 1666 in the style of Ziegler.

MARRYING ABSURD

JOAN DIDION

Joan Didion is a freelance writer whose essays and fiction have met with popular success over the past few years. Her best known work is Slouching Towards Bethlehem.

To be married in Las Vegas, Clark County, Nevada, a bride must swear that she is eighteen or has parental permission and a bridegroom that he is twenty-one or has parental permission. Someone must put up five dollars for the license. (On Sundays and holidays, fifteen dollars. The Clark County Courthouse issues marriage licenses at any time of the day or night except between noon and one in the afternoon, between eight and nine in the evening, and between four and five in the morning.) Nothing else is required. The State of Nevada, alone among these United States, demands neither a premarital blood test nor a waiting period before or after the issuance of a marriage license. Driving in across the Mojave from Los Angeles, one sees the signs way out on the desert, looming up from that moonscape of rattlesnakes and mesquite, even before the Las Vegan lights appear like a mirage on the horizon: "GETTING MARRIED? Free License Information First Strip Exit." Perhaps the Las Vegas wedding industry achieved its peak operational efficiency between 9:00 P.M. and midnight of August 26, 1965, an otherwise unremarkable Thursday which happened to be, by Presidential order, the last day on which anyone could improve his draft status merely by getting married. One hundred and seventy-one couples were pronounced man and wife in the name of Clark County and the State of Nevada that night, sixty-seven of them by a single justice of the peace, Mr. James A. Brennan. Mr. Brennan did one wedding at the Dunes and the sixty-six in his office, and charged each couple eight dollars. One bride lent her veil to six others. "I got it down from five to three minutes," Mr. Brennan said later of his feat. "I could've married them *en masse*, but they're people, not cattle. People expect more when they get married."

What people who get married in Las Vegas actually do expect—what, in the largest sense, their "expectations" are—strikes one as a curious and self-contradictory business. Las Vegas is the most extreme and allegorical of American settlements, bizarre and beautiful in its venality and in its devotion to immediate gratification, a place the tone of which is set by mobsters and call girls and ladies' room attendants with amyl nitrite poppers in their uniform pockets. Almost everyone notes that there is no "time" in Las Vegas, no night, and no day and no past and no future (no Las Vegas casino, however, has taken the obliteration of the ordinary time sense quite so far as Harold's Club in Reno, which for a while issued at odd intervals in the day and night, mimeographed "bulletins" carrying news from the world outside); neither is there any logical sense of where one is. One is standing on a highway in the middle of a vast hostile desert looking at an eighty-foot sign which blinks "STARDUST" or "CEASAR'S PALACE." Yes, but what does that explain? This geographical implausibility reinforces the sense that what happens there has no connection with "real" life; Nevada cities like Reno and Carson are ranch towns, Western towns, places behind which there is some historical imperative. But Las Vegas seems to exist only in the eye of the beholder. All of which makes it an extraordinarily stimulating and interesting place, but an odd one in which to want to wear a candlelight satin Priscilla of Boston wedding dress with Chantilly lace insets, tapered sleeves and a detachable modified train.

And yet the Las Vegas wedding business seems to appeal to precisely that impulse. "Sincere and Dignified Since 1954," one wedding chapel advertises. There are nineteen such wedding chapels in Las Vegas, intensely competitive, each offering better, faster, and, by implication, more sincere services than the next: Our Photos Best Anywhere, Your Wedding on A Phonograph Record, Candlelight with Your Ceremony, Honeymoon Accommodations, Free Transportation from Your Motel to Courthouse to Chapel and Return to Motel, Religious or Civil Ceremonies, Dressing Rooms, Flowers, Rings, Announcements, Witnesses Available, and Ample Parking. All of these services, like most others in Las Vegas (sauna baths, payroll-check cashing, chinchilla coats for sale or rent) are offered twenty-four hours a day, seven days a week, presumably on the premise that marriage, like craps, is a game to be played when the table seems hot.

But what strikes one most about the Strip chapels, with their wishing wells and stained-glass paper windows and their artificial bouvardia, is that so much of their business is by no means a matter of simple convenience, of late-night liaisons between show girls and baby Crosbys. Of course there is some of that. (One night about eleven o'clock in Las Vegas I watched a bride in an orange minidress and masses of flamecolored hair stumble from a Strip chapel on the arm of her bridegroom, who looked the part of the expendable nephew in movies like *Miami Syndicate*. "I gotta get the kids," the bride whimpered. "I gotta pick up the sitter, I gotta get to the midnight show." "What you gotta get," the bridegroom said, opening the door of a Cadillac Coupe de Ville and watching her crumple on the seat, "is sober.") But Las Vegas seems to offer something other than "convenience"; it is merchandising "niceness," the facsimile of proper ritual, to children who do not know how else to find it, how to make the arrangements, how to do it "right." All day and evening long on the Strip, one sees actual wedding parties, waiting under the harsh lights at a crosswalk, stand-

273

ing uneasily in the parking lot of the Frontier while the photographer hired by The Little Church of the West ("Wedding Place of the Stars") certifies the occasion, takes the picture: the bride in a veil and white satin pumps, the bridegroom usually in a white dinner jacket, and even an attendant or two, a sister or a best friend in a hot-pink *peau de soie,* a flirtation veil, a carnation nosegay. "When I Fall in Love It Will Be Forever," the organist plays, and then a few bars of Lohengrin. The mother cries; the stepfather, awkward in his role, invites the chapel hostess to join them for a drink at the Sands.The hostess declines with a professional smile; she has already transferred her interest to the group waiting outside. One bride out, another in, and again the sign goes up on the chapel door: "One moment please—Wedding."

I sat next to one such wedding party in a Strip restaurant the last time I was in Las Vegas. The marriage had just taken place; the bride still wore her dress, the mother her corsage. A bored waiter poured out a few swallows of pink champagne ("on the house") for everyone but the bride, who was too young to be served. "You'll need something with more kick than that," the bride's father said with heavy jocularity to his new son-in-law; the ritual jokes about the wedding night had a certain Panglossian character, since the bride was clearly several months pregnant. Another round of pink champagne, this time not on the house, and the bride began to cry. "It was just as nice," she sobbed, "as I hoped and dreamed it would be."

One Point for Analysis: In the midst of factual information about getting married, Didion makes the ironic statement, "Nothing more is required." The implication is that much more is needed.

Writing Topics:

1. Develop an expository essay on some aspect of war, using your introduction as ironic statement about the subject.
2. Trace the process of having a wedding, either your own or one you have been in.
3. Write an essay of cause and effect concerning why people get married.

STAR OF STARS

ALBERT ROSENFELD

Albert Rosenfeld is science editor of Saturday Review. *He says that he is "increasingly concerned with the communication of science and science policy to the general public."*

Perhaps it's just as well that, most of the time, we take the sun pretty much for granted. It's that friendly and familiar lamp up in the sky that provides us with warmth and daylight—with night-light, too, for that matter, its glow reflected off the moon. We do know, of course, that when it is shining at its brightest, it can scorch our skins; we squint and dare not look at it straight on. So we are not totally unaware of its power. But if we were able to comprehend, in anything remotely like their true dimensions, the incredible forces that play erratically within the fiery innards of the star that holds our planet prisoner in its gravitational field, we might be almost too awestruck to go about our daily business. We might live in terror of being vaporized at any moment without notice, just as the substance of the sun itself is vaporized by its own unimaginable temperatures, so that it is made of nothing but gases—all 2 billion billion billion tons of it.

Only in modern times have we come to understand that our sun *is* a star. Or, to put it another way, what we once believed to be stars—those pinpoint-sized twinkles of light all over the night sky—turned out to be distant suns (except for those few that turned out to be nearby planets), many of them mightier than our own. In fact, the sun is no great shakes of a star, as stars go. It is one of the ordinary stars of the family that astronomers call the "main sequence." It is about average in size and in luminosity—a so-called fifth-magnitude star. If we look out at the constellation Orion, for instance, and find the star Rigel, we discover that it is a "blue supergiant," burning with the luminosity of 40,000 suns! Its life span, however, will be much shorter than our sun's.

Yes, stars, too, have finite life spans. It stands to reason that they must, considering the prodigal rates at which they consume their fuel. The realization that stars do possess life cycles also brought the realization that many stars—such as the "red giants" and "white dwarfs"—that seemed to belong to entirely different families of stars are really main-sequence stars at later stages in their life cycle. The sun, now about 5 billion years old, has just about reached the prime of its middle age. As more billions of years go by, it, too, seems destined to age and die in the main-sequence pattern.

For this moment in cosmic time, our sun is a middle-sized run-of-the-mill star. Anyone who wishes to downgrade it further need only point out that it is one of hundreds of millions of stars in this lens-shaped galaxy we call the Milky Way. Moreover, instead of being in the galactic center, as was once believed, it is located out on the periphery of the lens, about three-quarters of the distance from the galaxy's core. (Just as the earth orbits the sun once a year, the entire solar system revolves around the hub of the galaxy in a majestic swing that takes some 200 million years.) To emphasize further the immensity of the universe we inhabit, this galaxy of ours is one of a "local cluster" of galaxies—there are millions of such clusters—and the *light* from our closest neighboring galaxy takes 2 *million years* to reach us. Thus, our sun, from this cosmic perspective, is an inconsequential lightspeck lost on the outskirts of a minor galaxy.

All that said and admitted, still, the sun is *our* star of stars—and anything much more impressive would soon render our planet uninhabitable. Its diameter measures 864,000 miles across—not so enormous—roughly 144 round trips between New York and Los Angeles, though traveled in a straight line, right *through* the sphere of the sun, not over its surface. On the other hand, the sun is almost a million times heavier than the earth (2 octillion tons versus 6.6 sextillion tons) and more than a million times as voluminous (335 quadrillion cubic miles versus 260 billion cubic miles). And all that is hot gas in ceaseless turmoil. The sun is not a rigid body; its gases seem to be in separate globs that don't even rotate in unison. For example, a given point on the rim of the sun's equator takes about twenty-five days to make a complete rotation, whereas a site in the polar regions may take thirty-five days. What holds it all together and makes it possible for the sun to retain its stability is precisely its main-sequence dimensionality; that is, it is just the right size so that there remains a delicate balance between the force of gravity pressing its mass inward and the fierce internal temperatures exerting a balancing force outward. This will not always be so, but, according to the astronomers, we can count on it for another few billion years anyway.

One Point for Analysis: The final paragraph includes startling information that makes it an effective conclusion.
Writing Topics:
1. Rosenfeld says, "We take the sun pretty much for granted." Write an expository essay about another vital element of our existence that we tend to take for granted.
2. After library research, write an essay about the moon using Rosenfeld's essay as a model.
3. Explain the effects of sunspots on the earth.

CLONING: A GENERATION MADE TO ORDER

CARYL RIVERS

Caryl Rivers has contributed essays to many well-known magazines, such as World, Saturday Review, Glamour, *and* Ms. *One of her longer works is* Aphrodite at Midcentury: Growing up Female and Catholic in Postwar America.

Human reproduction begins with the merger of the sex cells, sperm and egg. Since each contains only half a set of chromosomes, the joining of sperm with the egg is the first step in the creation of a new and unique individual, with traits inherited from both parents. But this is not the only possible way for life to begin.

The other type of cells in the human body already has a full set of chromosomes. All the genetic information necessary for an organism to reproduce itself is contained in the nucleus of every cell in that organism. If body cells could be made to divide, the result would be asexual reproduction—the production of offspring with only one parent. Such a process is already being used with other species—it is called cloning. It has been tried successfully with plants, fruit flies—and more significantly, with frogs.

In 1968, J. B. Gurdon at Oxford University produced a clonal frog. He took an unfertilized egg cell from an African clawed frog and destroyed its nucleus by ultraviolet radiation. He replaced it with the nucleus of an intestinal cell of another frog of the same species. The egg, suddenly finding itself with a full set of chromosomes, began to reproduce. It was "tricked" into starting the reproductive process. The result was a tadpole that was a genetic twin of the frog that donated the cell. The "mother" frog contributed nothing to the genetic identity of the tadpole, since her potential to pass on her traits was destroyed when the nucleus of her egg was obliterated.

How would it work with human beings? Roughly the same way. A healthy egg could be removed from a woman's body, in the same way that Edwards and Fowler obtain eggs for their work. But instead of fertilizing the egg with sperm, scientists could destroy the nucleus of the human egg and replace it with a cell taken from the arm or anywhere of a donor we'll call John X. The egg would be reimplanted in the uterus of a woman. Although its identity would be wiped out with the destruction of its nucleus, it could nonetheless start to divide, because it had received the proper signal—the presence of a full set of chromosomes. The baby that would be the result of that process would have only one parent—John X. It would, in fact, be a carbon copy of John X—his twin, a generation removed. (Or her twin, if the cell donor were female.)

In March of this year scientists announced major progress on the hunt for the substance that "switches on" the reproductive mechanisms of the cell. Gurdon's first experiments with the frog proved that such a mechanism exists and that all cells—not just sex cells—could be made to reproduce. Now, work done by Gurdon at Cambridge and by Ann Janice Brothers at the University of Indiana is moving science closer to discovering the identity of the "master switch."

Gurdon inserted the nuclei of human cancer cells into immature frogs eggs, and the human cell nuclei responded in dramatic fashion, swelling in size to as much as hundredfold.

Brothers, working with amphibians, axolotls, has observed that a molecule identified as the O+ factor appears to be the substance that signals the reproductive process to carry on. Eggs produced by axolotls that did not contain the O+ factor did not develop past very rudimentary stages until they were injected with O+ substance. Brothers and her colleagues at Indiana report that O+ appears to be a large protein molecule that is somewhat acidic. The scientists are working to isolate and define that molecule. The identification of the "master switch" would be a giant step toward understanding cancer and would bring the day of human cloning closer.

The consequences of human cloning are almost impossible to imagine. Widespread human cloning would alter human society beyond recognition. The family would no longer exist, sexuality would have no connection with reproduction. The idea of parenthood would be completely changed. The diversity of human beings provided by sexual reproduction would vanish. One could imagine entire communities of people who looked exactly the same, whose range of potential was identical. Some scientists have suggested that "clones and clonishness" could replace our present patterns of nation and race.

The misuses of cloning are not hard to predict. Would an aging dictator try to insure the continuance of his regime by an heir apparent who was his genetic double? Would women and men project their egos into the future by producing their own "carbon copies"? Would society choose to clone our most valued citizens? Artists? Generals? Members of elite groups? The capacity of our species to change and adapt may be rooted in the diversity of the gene pool. By tampering with that process we could be limiting our own ability to survive.

There are some who believe that current work in test-tube fertilization to extract eggs is a first step in the direction of cloning. There have been some estimates that human cloning will be a reality within the decade. Who will say where we draw the line?

One Point for Analysis: The diction of this essay is scientifically oriented, although the essay is written for a general readership.
Writing Topics:
1. Write an expository essay on a recent scientific breakthrough in which you speculate on possible future ramifications.
2. Write an essay in which you answer some of the questions posed in the ninth paragraph.
3. Explain why you would or would not want a clone of yourself.

NONVIOLENT RESISTANCE

MARTIN LUTHER KING, JR.

In his drive to gain civil rights for black people, Martin Luther King, Jr., urged his followers to use "nonviolent resistance."

Oppressed people deal with their oppression in three characteristic ways. One way is acquiescence: the oppressed resign themselves to their doom. They tacitly adjust themselves to oppression, and thereby become conditioned to it. In every movement toward freedom some of the oppressed prefer to remain oppressed. Almost 2800 years ago Moses set out to lead the children of Israel from the slavery of Egypt to the freedom of the promised land. He soon discovered that slaves do not always welcome their deliverers. They become accustomed to being slaves. They would rather bear those ills they have, as Shakespeare pointed out, than flee to others that they know not of. They prefer the "fleshpots of Egypt" to the ordeals of emancipation.

There is such a thing as the freedom of exhaustion. Some people are so worn down by the yoke of oppression that they give up. A few years ago in the slum areas of Atlanta, a Negro guitarist used to sing almost daily: "Ben down so long that down don't bother me." This is the type of negative freedom and resignation that often engulfs the life of the oppressed.

But this is not the way out. To accept passively an unjust system is to cooperate with that system; thereby the oppressed become as evil as the oppressor. Noncooperation with evil is as much a moral obligation as is cooperation with good. The oppressed must never allow the conscience of the oppressor to slumber. Religion reminds every man that he is his brother's keeper. To accept injustice or segregation passively is to say to the oppressor that his actions are morally right. It is a way of allowing his conscience to fall asleep. At this moment the oppressed fails to be his brother's keeper. So acquiescence—while often the easier way—is not the moral way. It is the way of the coward. The Negro cannot win the respect of his oppressor by acquiescing; he merely increases the oppressor's arrogance and contempt. Acquiescence is interpreted as proof of the

From pp. 211–214 (under the title "Nonviolent Resistance") in *Stride Toward Freedom* by Martin Luther King, Jr. Reprinted by permission of Harper & Row Publishers, Inc.

280

Negro's inferiority. The Negro cannot win the respect of the white people of the South or the peoples of the world if he is willing to sell the future of his children for his personal and immediate comfort and safety.

A second way that oppressed people sometimes deal with oppression is to resort to physical violence and corroding hatred. Violence often brings about momentary results. Nations have frequently won their independence in battle. But in spite of temporary victories, violence never brings permanent peace. It solves no social problem; it merely creates new and more complicated ones.

Violence as a way of achieving racial justice is both impractical and immoral. It is impractical because it is a descending spiral ending in destruction for all. The old law of an eye for an eye leaves everybody blind. It is immoral because it seeks to humiliate the opponent rather than win his understanding; it seeks to annihilate rather than to convert. Violence is immoral because it thrives on hatred rather than love. It destroys community and makes brotherhood impossible. It leaves society in monologue rather than dialogue. Violence ends by defeating itself. It creates bitterness in the survivors and brutality in the destroyers. A voice echoes through time saying to every potential Peter, "Put up your sword." History is cluttered with the wreckage of nations that failed to follow this command.

If the American Negro and other victims of oppression succumb to the temptation of using violence in the struggle for freedom, future generations will be the recipients of a desolate night of bitterness, and our chief legacy to them will be an endless reign of meaningless chaos. Violence is not the way.

The third way open to oppressed people in their quest for freedom is the way of nonviolent resistance. Like the synthesis in Hegelian philosophy, the principle of nonviolent resistance seeks to reconcile the truths of two opposites—acquiescence and violence—while avoiding the extremes and immoralities of both. The nonviolent resister agrees with the person who acquiesces that one should not be physically aggressive toward his opponent; but he balances the equation by agreeing with the person of violence that evil must be resisted. He avoids the nonresistance of the former and the violent resistance of the latter. With nonviolent resistance, no individual or group need submit to any wrong, nor need anyone resort to violence in order to right a wrong.

It seems to me that this is the method that must guide the actions

281

of the Negro in the present crisis in race relations. Through non-violent resistance the Negro will be able to rise to the noble height of opposing the unjust system while loving the perpetrators of the system. The Negro must work passionately and unrelentingly for full stature as a citizen, but he must not use inferior methods to gain it. He must never come to terms with falsehood, malice, hate, or destruction.

Nonviolent resistance makes it possible for the Negro to remain in the South and struggle for his rights. The Negro's problem will not be solved by running away. He cannot listen to the glib suggestion of those who would urge him to migrate en masse to other sections of the country. By grasping his great opportunity in the South he can make a lasting contribution to the moral strength of the nation and set a sublime example of courage for generations yet unborn.

By nonviolent resistance, the Negro can also enlist all men of good will in his struggle for equality. The problem is not a purely racial one, with Negroes set against whites. In the end, it is not a struggle between people at all, but a tension between justice and injustice. Nonviolent resistance is not aimed against oppressors but against oppression. Under its banner consciences, not racial groups, are enlisted.

If the Negro is to achieve the goal of integration, he must organize himself into a militant and nonviolent mass movement. All three elements are indispensable. The movement for equality and justice can only be a success if it has both a mass and militant character; the barriers to be overcome require both. Nonviolence is an imperative in order to bring about ultimate community.

A mass movement of militant quality that is not at the same time committed to nonviolence tends to generate conflict, which in turn breeds anarchy. The support of the participants and the sympathy of the uncommitted are both inhibited by the threat that bloodshed will engulf the community. This reaction in turn encourages the opposition to threaten and resort to force. When, however, the mass movement repudiates violence while moving resolutely toward its goal, its opponents are revealed as the instigators and practitioners of violence if it occurs. Then public support is magnetically attracted to the advocates of nonviolence, while those who employ violence are literally disarmed by overwhelming sentiment against their stand.

One Point for Analysis: In the introduction King states that there are three ways in which oppressed people can deal with their oppression. His essay is organized by discussing one after the other.

Writing Topics:

1. Explain several ways in which people face death.
2. Report on social changes that have come about in the United States as a result of Martin Luther King's concept of nonviolent resistance.
3. After library research, write an analysis of the Selma, Alabama, civil rights march.

THE WISDOM AND FORTITUDE OF MARCUS AURELIUS

HENRY CHAMBERLAIN

Chamberlain has been a contributing editor of the New Leader *and the* Wall Street Journal. *He has written often about political relations between the United States and the Soviet Union.*

It was said of Britain's great eighteenth-century statesman, William Pitt, and more recently of Winston Churchill, that none left his presence without feeling himself a braver man. Over a span of eighteen centuries this same observation holds good for the Roman Emperor Marcus Aurelius Antoninus, one of the very few absolute rulers who lived and thought as a philosopher and whose spirit still comes alive in his *Meditations*.

Marcus Aurelius (121–180 A.D.) was of patrician stock and Spanish origin. Adopted as the son and heir—and for many years the colleague of his mild and gentle predecessor, Antoninus Pius, whose name he took—Marcus Aurelius was the last and best of the five good Emperors, whose reign, in the opinion of Gibbon, was the period during which the condition of the human race was most happy and prosperous. While this is a dangerous generalization (for the Western world a good case could be made out for the century between the fall of Napoleon and the outbreak of the First World War) some solid reasons can be advanced in its behalf. The many

283

peoples of the Roman Empire enjoyed the benefits of internal peace and, with a few exceptions, of freedom from foreign invasion, under the rule of princes who remained immune to the usual association of absolute corruption with absolute power and ruled their vast realms in justice and order.

From childhood Marcus Aurelius had been attracted to the teaching of the Stoics, a school of Greek philosophers from whom he learned to submit the body to the mind and the passions to the reason, to endure bodily hardship, to pursue virtue as the only good, and to rise superior to all external vicissitudes. He spent many of his younger years in the famous Greek schools of the time and was familiar with the teachings of Plato and other Greek philosophers.

But there was a Roman cast to the mind and thought of Marcus Aurelius. He did not leave behind any elaborate system of speculative metaphysics. His *Meditations* represent rather a course in practical morality. Because of this work and because he was ruler of the greatest empire of his time, this Emperor-philosopher survives as the most impressive and vivid example of Stoicism, taken out of the study and put to the stern test of action and decision.

Marcus rejected hedonism, the pursuit of pleasure, as a goal. His ideal was rather tranquillity or equanimity, to be achieved by living in conformity with nature by cultivating four principal virtues. These are wisdom, knowing the difference between good and evil; justice, giving every man his due; fortitude, bearing labor and pain without complaint; and temperance, or moderation in all things.

With persuasive eloquence he advocates a code of conduct based on recognition of the fleeting quality of earthly honors and riches; the obligation to bear with patient firmness what is beyond one's control, while striving to shape for the best what is within one's control; the inner recess of one's soul as the surest refuge from petty vanities and vexations. Marcus Aurelius has no dogmatic convictions about such questions as the existence of a supreme deity or the possibility of life after death.

While many of his teachings correspond with the moral values of Christianity and other great religions, his writings are permeated with the resolute spirit of a man faced by ultimate mysteries which he cannot comprehend, but determined, with the aid of his reason, to order his life as best he may. If there are two qualities especially characteristic of this brooding Emperor of the second century, these are fortitude—a good word with an appropriate Latin derivation—and self-reliance.

. . .

Not a political innovator, Marcus Aurelius strove manfully to sustain and preserve the civilization and social order which he inherited, constantly conscious of the weight of the burden that rested on him, always trying to use his unlimited power justly and humanely. A triumphal column, erected in memory of Marcus Aurelius, with a record of his military victories and other achievements as Emperor, still stands in the Eternal City. A more enduring memorial is the spirit of calm courage and resolute self-reliance which breathes in such passages of his writings as: "Let thy chief fort and place of defense be, a mind free from passions. A stronger place and better fortified than this, hath no man."

For any human being in need of fortitude under the impact of grief or disappointment there is no better source than the grave and noble testament of the Emperor who was also a Stoic philosopher.

One Point for Analysis: The fifth paragraph consists of a series of definitions of difficult concepts.

Writing Topics:

1. Discuss by citing examples how one of the four principal virtues cultivated by Marcus Aurelius is practiced in America today.

2. Discuss by citing examples how one of the four principal virtues cultivated by Marcus Aurelius is ignored in America today.

3. In the serious style of Chamberlain, write an essay on the achievements of another great historical figure.

5

THE PERSUASIVE ESSAY

INTRODUCTION TO ARGUMENT AND PERSUASION

At one time or another, everyone gets into a disagreement with some-one else. If you find yourself trying to convince your friend that one polit-ical candidate is better than another, you are engaged in argument, the use of words to convince someone that your opinion is right. If you try to get him to cast his vote for the candidate, you are involved in persuasion, an attempt to involve someone in a particular action. Argument and per-suasion operate basically in the same way.

The thesis statement for an argumentative essay will be a statement of your opinion. Some writers feel that this type of thesis statement is the best kind because it results in a more interesting essay than does the thesis which is simply a statement of a noncontroversial fact. Similarly, the thesis statement for a persuasive essay will state the course of action you wish someone to follow and the reasons why he should do so. Aris-totle felt that all rhetoric had such a purpose.

Because your thesis statement is controversial, your reader will not necessarily agree with you readily. And the more controversial you are, the less likely he is to go along. You must, therefore, in your discussion, give evidence that supports your stand. At this point exposition enters your essay. Facts are stated that either prove your case or allow you to draw conclusions that strengthen your position. Sometimes you may want to list your pieces of evidence first, then draw a conclusion at the end. At other times you may prefer to state your opinion to begin with, following it with supporting facts and figures.

Although the rational approach just described goes far toward convinc-ing and persuading a reader, the effectiveness of an essay of argumenta-tion and persuasion can be enhanced by another element: emotion. If you feel strongly about an issue, you will want your reader to sense the urgency of your position. You will want him to share your enthusiasm and concern. Deeply held sentiments are rarely presented in the same way the changing of a tire is explained. Instead, these sentiments are set down with feeling, which gives the theme greater force. Think of some issue that you feel strongly about. Can you be totally unemotional when discussing it? Probably not. And it is your emotion that gives your rational argument its force.

Sometimes in argument and persuasion the major points of the side you are arguing against must be mentioned so that you can show them to be inaccurate, ineffective, or unimportant. Unless you do so, you leave your argument open to disagreement. If, however, you discredit the opposition, your thesis is relatively safe. Of course, when dealing with those opinions that disagree with yours, you should never be personal. All your points should deal with the subject, not with the personalities of those who hold different opinions. (See *Fallacies*, #5, Handbook.)

Argument and persuasion are all around us. Advertising seeks to persuade us to buy certain products. Parents and teenagers disagree about the need for a curfew. The United States Senate, the classroom, and even the church are filled with verbal controversy. And they should be in a democracy, for it is through argument and persuasion that we refine our ideas and opinions. Through argument and persuasion we move closer to determining what is right and what should be done.

TURNING FAILURE INTO SUCCESS

FREDELLE MAYNARD

Maynard offers words of comfort—and opportunity—for those whom success eludes.

"Vicky—beautiful, talented, very bright, voted "Most Likely to Succeed" in college—got a promising job with a large specialty store after graduation. Then, after two years without promotions, she was fired. She suffered a complete nervous breakdown. "It was panic," she told me later. "Everything had always gone so well for me that I had no experience in coping with rejection. I felt I was a failure."

Vicky's reaction is an extreme example of a common phenomenon. In a society that places so much emphasis on "making it," we fail to recognize that what looks like failure may, in the long run,

Reprinted with permission from the December 1977 *Reader's Digest*.

prove beneficial. When Vicky was able to think coolly about why she was fired, for example, she realized that she was simply not suited to a job dealing with people all the time. In her new position as a copy editor, she works independently, is happy and once again "successful."

People are generally prone to what semanticist S. I. Hayakawa calls "the two-valued orientation." We talk about seeing both sides of a question as if every question had *only* two sides. We assume that everyone is either a success or a failure when, in fact, infinite degrees of both are possible. As Hayakawa points out, there's a world of difference between "I have failed three times" and "I am a failure." Indeed, the words failure and success cannot be reasonably applied to a complex, living, changing human being. They can only describe the situation at a particular time and place.

Obviously no one can be a whiz at everything. In fact, success in one area often precludes success in another. An eminent politician once told me that his career had practically destroyed his marriage. "I have no time for my family," he explained. "I travel a lot. And even when I'm home, I hardly see my wife and kids. I've got power, money, prestige—but as a husband and father, I'm a flop."

Certain kinds of success can indeed be destructive. The danger of too early success is particularly acute whenever a child demonstrates special talent. I recall from my childhood a girl whose skill on ice skates marked her as "Olympic material." While the rest of us were playing, bicycling, reading, making things and just loafing, this girl skated—every day after school and all weekend. Her picture often appeared in the papers, and the rest of us envied her glamorous life. Years later, however, she spoke bitterly of those early triumphs. "I never prepared myself for anything but the ice," she said. "I peaked at 17—and it's been downhill ever since."

Success that comes too easily is also damaging. The child who wins a prize for a dashed-off essay, the adult who distinguishes himself at a first job by lucky accident faces probable disappointment when real challenges arise.

Success is also bad when it's achieved at the cost of the total quality of an experience. Successful students sometimes become so obsessed with grades that they never enjoy their school years. They never branch out into tempting new areas, because they don't want to risk their grade average.

Success may, quite simply, cost too much—in strain (infighting at

290

the job, keeping a cheerful public face while your personal life falls apart) or loss of integrity (flattering, lying, going along with questionable actions). Above all, it may be too costly if the end result is fear—fear of not repeating the success. One of the most successful hostesses I know has come to hate entertaining: "I've acquired such a reputation," she explains, "that my friends expect me to outdo myself. I can't disappoint them—and I'm worn out before my guests arrive."

Why are so many people so afraid of failure? Quite simply because no one tells us *how* to fail so that failure becomes a growing experience. We forget that failure is part of the human condition and that, as family therapist Virginia Satir observes, "every person has the *right* to fail."

Most parents work hard at either preventing failure or protecting their children from the knowledge that they *have* failed. One way is to lower standards. A mother describes her child's hastily made table as "perfect!" even though it wobbles on uneven legs. Another way is to shift blame. If John fails science, his teacher is unfair or stupid.

When one of my daughters was ten, she decided to raise money for charity by holding a carnival. Proud of her, we rashly allowed her to put posters all over town. We realized too late that she couldn't possibly handle all the refreshments, shows and games promised in the posters. The whole family pitched in to prevent embarrassing failure—and the next year she advertised an even more ambitious event. Why not? We had kept her from discovering her limitations.

The trouble with failure-prevention devices is that they leave a child unequipped for life in the real world. The young need to learn that no one can be best at everything, no one can win all the time— and that it's possible to enjoy a game even when you *don't* win. A child who's not invited to a birthday party, who doesn't make the honor roll or the baseball team feels terrible, of course. But parents should not offer a quick consolation prize or say, "It doesn't matter," because it does. The youngster should be allowed to experience disappointment—and then be helped to master it.

Failure is never pleasurable. It hurts adults and children alike. But it can make a positive contribution to your life once you learn to use it. Step one is to ask, "Why did I fail?" Resist the natural impulse to blame someone else. Ask yourself what *you* did wrong,

291

how *you* can improve. If someone else can help, don't be shy about inquiring.

When I was a teen-ager, I failed to get a job I'd counted on. I telephoned the interviewer to ask why. "Because you came ten minutes late," I was told. "We can't afford employes who waste other people's time." The explanation was reassuring (I hadn't been rejected as a person) and helpful, too. I don't think I've been late for anything since.

Success, which encourages repetition of old behavior, is not nearly as good a teacher as failure. You can learn from a disastrous party how to give a good one, from an ill-chosen first house what to look for in a second. Even a failure that seems definitive can prompt fresh thinking, a change of direction. After 12 years of studying ballet a friend of mine auditioned for a professional company. She was turned down. "Would further training help?" she asked. The ballet master shook his head. "You will never be a dancer," he said. "You haven't the body for it."

In such cases, the way to use failure is to take stock courageously, asking, "What have I left? What *else* can I do?" My friend put away her toe shoes and moved into dance therapy, a field where she's both competent and useful.

Oddly enough, failure often brings with it a peculiar kind of freedom. Even a major life failure can be followed by a sense of "It's happened. I wish it hadn't, but it's over now—and I survived."

Failure frees one to take risks because there's less to lose. Often there's a resurgence of energy—an awareness of new possibilities.

If faced, absorbed and accepted, failure contributes to personal growth and often leads to improved personal relationships. The officially "successful" person often remains closed off and self-protective, but simple human vulnerability is revealed in failure. A woman who recently ended what seemed like a perfect marriage says her friendships have a new closeness and warmth since her divorce. "I used to hear other people's troubles," she said, "but never tell my own. Now I can let it all out. The other day someone told me, 'I used to be put off by your superwoman act. You seem softer, more open now. I like you better this way.' "

Though we may envy the assurance that comes with success, most of us are attracted by gallantry in defeat—ideally exemplified by Adlai Stevenson's response after he lost the Presidential election in 1952; he said that he was "too old to cry, but it hurt too much to laugh." There is what might be called the noble failure—the special heroism of aiming high, doing your best and then, when that proves not enough, moving bravely on. As Ralph Waldo Emerson said: "A man's success is made up of failures, because he experiments and ventures every day, and the more falls he gets, moves faster on. . . . I have heard that in horsemanship he is not the good rider who never was thrown, but rather that a man will never be a good rider until he is thrown; then he will not be haunted any longer by the terror that he shall tumble, and will ride whither he is bound."

AN ANALYSIS OF "TURNING FAILURE INTO SUCCESS"

Because we have all been unsuccessful at something, we all want to know how to cope with discouragement and maybe even turn it to some positive end. The title "Turning Failure into Success," which suggests that this essay will argue that failure is manageable and can even be a profitable experience, makes us curious about what will follow. It entices us to find out what the author has to say.

The introduction maintains the interest stimulated by the title. Instead of immediately listing the steps in "how to deal with disappointing experiences," Maynard recounts a long example of a surprising failure, one that most readers can identify with. By commenting on Vicky's experience, the author is able to suggest the thesis that she will reiterate at several points throughout the discussion, that "what looks like failure may, in the long run, prove beneficial."

The development section of the essay is divided into two parts. In the first part, the fourth through twelfth paragraphs, Maynard disagrees with the commonly held opinion that success, or at least freedom from failure, is always good. She argues that success can, in contrast, be quite damaging. In the second section, the thirteenth through nineteenth paragraphs, she takes issue with the corresponding idea that failure is always bad. After the opening sentences of the thirteenth paragraph, which provide a transition from the first part to the second and at the same time remind the reader of the thesis of the essay, Maynard supports her argument by discussing several ways in which failure can "make a positive contribution to your life once you learn to use it."

The paragraphs of this essay have been designed to help the reader follow the course of the argument. Each point that supports her thesis is presented in a separate paragraph. The explanations of why success is

293

harmful or why failure is beneficial are arranged so that one reason provides the topic of one paragraph. The reader knows that with the beginning of a new paragraph new information supporting the generalization already stated will be presented. Sometimes a paragraph makes its point by example. For instance, the eleventh and fourteenth paragraphs recount short narratives that demonstrate the opinion Maynard has been advancing.

The conclusion of this essay summarizes what has been said, but it avoids simply repeating the major points. Maynard provides a brief reminder of her thesis by presenting one last example, that of Adlai Stevenson's comment on realizing that he had lost his bid for the Presidency, and by quoting from Emerson, a well-known and much admired American essayist. Use of two such widely respected men to confirm what Maynard has presented adds to the persuasiveness of her argument.

This essay addresses the reader in a rather personal way. Maynard speaks of "us" and "you." She mentions experiences that her friends have had. She even uses her own daughter as one of his examples. The reader feels that he is listening to a thoughtful friend rather than reading the advice of someone he does not know and will never meet. The personal tone also adds to the persuasive quality of the essay.

"Turning Failure into Success" is itself a success, for it attracts the reader's interest from the beginning, sustains it through a carefully ordered argument clarified by abundant use of examples, and stamps the whole with a seal of approval by references to Stevenson and Emerson. Not the least successful aspect of Maynard's essay is that she has offered us advice without patronizing us or offending us. We are disposed to agree with her for several reasons, not the least of which is that she has made us feel good about ourselves.

WAYS TO WORSHIP THE GREAT SPIRIT

CHIEF RED JACKET

Chief Red Jacket presented this essay in a speech delivered early in the nineteenth century.

Friend and Brother:

It was the will of the Great Spirit that we should meet together this day. He orders all things and has given us a fine day for our council. He has taken His garment from before the sun and caused it to shine with brightness upon us. Our eyes are open that we see clearly; our ears are unstopped that we have been able to hear distinctly the words you have spoken. For all these favors we thank the Great Spirit, and Him only. . . .

Brother, you say that you are sent to instruct us how to worship the Great Spirit agreeably to His mind; and, if we do not take hold of the religion which you white people teach we shall be unhappy hereafter. You say that you are right and we are lost. How do we know this to be true? We understand that your religion is written in a Book. If it was intended for us, as well as you, why has not the Great Spirit given to us, and not only to us, but why did He not give to our forefathers the knowledge of that Book, with the means of understanding it rightly? We only know what you tell us about it. How shall we know when to believe, being so often deceived by the white people?

Brother, you say there is but one way to worship and serve the Great Spirit. If there is but one religion, why do you white people differ so much about it? Why not all agree, as you can all read the Book?

Brother, we do not understand these things. We are told that your religion was given to your forefathers and has been handed down from father to son. We also have a religion which was given to our forefathers and has been handed down to us, their children. We worship in that way. It teaches us to be thankful for all the favors we receive, to love each other, and to be united. We never quarrel about religion.

295

Brother, the Great Spirit has made us all, but He has made a great difference between His white and His red children. He has given us different complexions and different customs. To you He has given the arts. To these He has not opened our eyes. We know these things to be true. Since He has made so great a difference between us in other things, why may we not conclude that He has given us a different religion according to our understanding? The Great Spirit does right. He knows what is best for His children; we are satisfied.

Brother, we do not wish to destroy your religion or take it from you. We only want to enjoy our own. . . . .

Brother, we are told that you have been preaching to the white people in this place. These people are our neighbors. We are acquainted with them. We will wait a little while and see what effect your preaching has upon them. If we find it does them good, makes them honest, and less disposed to cheat Indians, we will then consider again what you have said.

Brother, ... as we . . . part, we . . . take you by the hand, and hope the Great Spirit will protect you on your journey and return you safe to your friends.

One Point for Analysis: The thrust of Chief Red Jacket's argument is emotional.

Writing Topics:
1. Answer in an argumentative essay Chief Red Jacket's question: "If there is but one religion, why do you white people differ so much about it?"
2. Russia and the United States exist with two radically different forms of government. Argue that their coexistence can/cannot remain peaceful.
3. Using an emotional appeal, argue for the continuance of some institution or practice.

ON THE MERITS OF FOOTBALL

MIKE DOWTY

Mike Dowty is managing editor of the St. Tammany News-Banner. *He enjoys following high-school football teams, as well as more experienced and professional teams.*

I would like . . . to explain an opinion I've held for a long time. Perhaps it's just bias, but after examining most of the major sports played in America, I've come to the conclusion that none can compare with or measure up to football.

This is a drastic statement, I know, and one that is certain to raise disdainful eyebrows. So I'd like to justify it.

If you look closely, you will find that football is the only true team sport. A team sport does not mean a sport played by groups of athletes, but rather a sport in which each individual player has a specific task to perform so that his team might succeed.

In football tackles do not score touchdowns, but neither do tailbacks without the help of tackles. A quarterback is only as good as his blocking and his receivers. The best defense is a ball control offense. The best offense is the one that gets good field position from the defense.

In short, a good football team consists of a variety of types and styles of athletes and the most important attribute of any one of them is the ability to complement the play of all the others. While this is the kind of truism you generally see on every coach's bulletin board, it is surprising that very few teams realize this objective of total team play. Those that do are seen every year in playoffs and bowl games.

While every team sport requires some disciplined coordination among its players, not one approaches the level of team play required in football.

In baseball, a certain amount of teamwork is required, but winning and losing has more to do with the performance of individuals than of the team as a whole. Good pitching can win a baseball game. So can good hitting.

In basketball, team effort is required, but just as important is

Originally published in the St. Tammany News-Banner, November 6, 1977. Reprinted by permission of the author.

297

physical endowment of individuals—height, speed, passing and shooting ability.

In football, a good team must have all sorts of players. A kid with little coordination and speed, but 250 pounds of muscle can help you up front. Another kid with little size or strength, but 9.8 speed can give you a passing attack, if he can catch. Still another kid with some speed, some coordination, some brains, some leadership can make everything fit together as a quarterback.

This diversity of positions is just one way in which the sport of football mirrors life more than any other sport I know. Consider also the nature of losing and winning in football compared to other sports.

In baseball, for example, a team can be four games ahead one week, four behind the next, back and forth all season. The same with basketball.

In football, each game is more meaningful. To lose a game is almost like death. To win is to survive. The stakes are bigger.

That is why great moments of the game are remembered for a lifetime.

One Point for Analysis: Notice that Dowty tests his thesis (look at his title) by considering not only football but other sports as well.

Writing Topics:

1. Argue, in contrast to Dowty, that football is a primitive sport, one that confirms man's animal nature.
2. Dowty notes that the thesis of his essay is "the kind of truism you generally see on every coach's bulletin board." Choose for your topic another truism, one that you feel bears repetition or deserves dispute.
3. Argue that golf (or another non-team sport) is superior to team sports.

HOW BIRDS GOT OFF THE GROUND

VINCENT MARTEKA

"How Birds Got Off the Ground" examines some of the surprising ways in which scientific discoveries take place.

Several months ago, Yale scientist John H. Ostrom was touring a museum in the Dutch city of Haarlem. Since he was a paleontologist, Dr. Ostrom found the fossil section of the museum very interesting. Little did he guess, though, that the museum held an important clue to the origin of bird flight.

As the scientist examined the fossils, he found one labeled pterosaur. This prehistoric animal was one of many flying reptiles that lived over 120 million years ago.

But as Dr. Ostrom studied the bone structure of the fossil, he began to doubt the label. He removed the specimen from its case and held it up to the light.

In the limestone surrounding the fossil's bones, Dr. Ostrom saw the faint impression of *feathers*. The label *was* wrong. The fossil was actually that of the prehistoric bird archaeopteryx, a distant cousin of the flying reptile.

Although the fossil was not as complete as three other archaeopteryx fossils already found, one feature made it an extremely important find. Discovered were two remarkably preserved impressions of claws located on the forward edge of the bird's wing.

According to Dr. Ostrom, these claws have helped clear up the mystery surrounding the first flight of birds. For many years scientists have been trying to find out exactly how birds first learned to fly. Two theories have been developed.

One theory, the arboreal theory, states that the bird's lizard-like ancestors lived in trees. Eventually, as the animal leaped from branch to branch, its front legs evolved into wings. Soon the animal ventured beyond the tree and became an authentic feathered bird.

The other theory is called the cursorial or running theory. It claims that bird flight began at ground level. As the lizard-like animal ran along the ground it began to take long leaps. Eventually, the leaping became gliding and then flying.

But which of the two theories is supported by the new fossil find?

As Dr. Ostrom examined the claw imprints of the fossil, he noticed that the claws had a thin fingernail-like covering. Such claws are excellent tearing tools. And tearing claws are not very efficient for climbing trees. Any animal that lived in a tree would need claws less like razors and more like strong hooks.

Dr. Ostrom is still studying the fossil. But he believes that the running theory makes more sense.

One Point for Analysis: In this scientific essay technical terms are usually defined as they appear.

Writing Topics:

1. Argue that man will evolve into one big eye as a result of his fixation with television.
2. Argue that ants have never significantly evolved. (You will have to do some reading to acquire the technical information for this topic.)
3. Choose a phenomenon that, like this one, has two possible explanations. Argue the superiority of one of the explanations.

INDIAN GIVER'S COMEUPPANCE

ART BUCHWALD

Buchwald is a popular newspaper columnist whose satirical sketches of people in the news provide entertainment for a wide body of readers.

WASHINGTON—The United States made a terrible mistake many years ago when it gave the American Indians a lot of what it considered worthless land to live on. It now turns out that this land has on it—and under it—one-third of all the low-sulphur coal suitable for strip mining, about 55 percent of the nation's uranium and 3 or 4 percent of its oil and natural gas.

But the Indians, instead of offering to give the land back to the white man, have formed a Council of Energy Resources and are planning to play hard ball when it comes to leases and mining rights. No amount of persuasion can make the Indians realize that the white man had erred in giving them the *wrong* land.

A friend of mine went out to talk to an Indian council member the other day.

He said, "I come in peace. Many moons ago our forefathers did your tribe a terrible injustice. We gave you land on which nothing could grow and no animals could graze."

"We know about that," the Indian chief replied. "Our geologists recently reported that the reason nothing could grow on our land was that there was too much low-sulphur coal in it."

"Exactly. Since you are the descendants of these brave warriors we wish to make amends and give you land that really has some value."

"You are very kind, but we are happy with the land," the chief said. "The royalties from our uranium deposits will see us through many a cold winter."

"But mining uranium is so degrading for an American Indian," my friend said.

"We're not going to mine it," the Indian chief said. "We're going to let the white man do that. We're going into stock investments, bonds and real estate."

"But, Great Chief, wouldn't your people be happier living somewhere else besides this vast wasteland of parched earth?"

"Do you know what's under that parched earth? Three or 4 percent of all the oil reserves in the United States."

"But what does an Indian want with oil? Your horses and buffalo need fresh water."

"Our Cadillacs and Lincolns don't. They have fuel injection and once you put antifreeze in them they can go without water for a year. Actually, one of our plans is to open a string of gas stations with the brand name 'Fire Water' and start a multimillion-dollar advertising campaign with the slogan, 'Put an Apache in your tank.' How does that grab you?"

"Before you make these hasty decisions, O Mighty Chief, let me tell you what we are willing to trade for your grubby reservations."

"I'm listening."

"What would you say if I told you that the United States government is prepared to make up for the terrible treaties we made with you in the past by giving you in exchange for your land the follow-

301

ing: the South Bronx, most of Watts in Los Angeles, all the land on the SST approach to Kennedy Airport and part of downtown Cleveland."

"You would do that for the American Indian?"

"It's the least we can do for all the pain and anguish you have suffered through the years."

"I can't give you my answer now because I have to fly off to Washington in a few minutes."

"Why are you going to Washington?"

"I'm lobbying for the gas deregulation bill," the chief said. "How does Carter expect our people to drill for gas when he's only offering us $1.85 per 1,000 cubic feet?"

One Point for Analysis: Mike Royko's essay "President's Family in Everyone's Hair" (reprinted later in this section) develops its satire by using an unseen observer who makes statements about the subjects being ridiculed. Buchwald develops his satire, and thus his argument, by allowing two parties to satirize themselves through their dialogue.

Writing Topics:

1. In the manner of Buchwald, construct an essay in dialogue between two people of opposing viewpoints. Your thesis must emerge from their discussion.

2. As the white man invaded the land of the American Indian, so Cubans and Vietnamese have in recent years invaded the American job market. Argue for or against the justice of this situation.

3. Rewrite this satire by leaving out the dialogue.

ONE MOTHER'S BLAST AT MOTHERHOOD

SHIRLEY L. RADL

Shirley L. Radl has been active in groups working to curb the population explosion. She was Executive Director of Zero Population Growth and of the National Organization for Non-Parents.

The eight years before we had children were glorious. I had an enjoyable career, an idyllic home life. But friends pitied us, undoubtedly worried we would continue living hedonistic, meaningless but terribly comfortable lives unless we became parents.

When I was pregnant the first time, we celebrated our eighth wedding anniversary. My husband gave me an exquisite pearl bracelet. Six years later I was picking up the pearls in my vacuum cleaner. My son had destroyed it. It is a sad symbol of how two children affected a once-beautiful relationship.

It's hard to admit that my beautiful, wanted and planned children could arouse rage in me and could disturb my once-ideal marriage. I'd fallen for the Big Lie, that fulfillment automatically comes with motherhood. But now I'm confident there's enough love in our family to withstand a certain amount of truth.

A mother, according to TV and most women's magazines, is a happy person suited, without training, to one of the most formidable jobs in the world. But a mother is also *me*, and I'm a failure as one. I'm not cut out to be a service machine, laundress, PTA member, nurse. My kids deserve better than they got.

It's not enough for every child to be wanted as Planned Parenthood says. He must be wanted, not only at the start, but forever. Bearing children is a gamble with lives of innocents. The greatest failure is to have children and learn too late you're not equipped for that career. We who learned the truth must level with an unsuspecting generation of potential mothers. They must look beyond the myths, seek the truth, judge their capacities accordingly. Plan carefully: the life you save may be your own.

You don't have to justify deciding to be childless. It's no one's

"One Mother's Blast at Motherhood," *Life,* May, 1972; *Mother's Day Is Over,* Warner Paperback Library, 1974, 1978.

business if your ovaries don't work, or if they do. If you are pressured to "prove yourself," take it from one who has been there.

We don't tell others what jobs to take, whom they should marry, where to vacation. It's bad manners to ask how much money they make. Yet others' breeding habits, *if* they are childless, are considered fair game. The couples with children, who are miserable, don't hesitate to urge others to follow their examples.

When we started our family, it didn't occur to us we were succumbing to social pressure and the media. Now we see that all this couldn't fail to have conditioned us. We never discussed the matter thoroughly, and it never occurred to us we might not be cut out for parenthood. Why, we put more thought into buying a car than bringing two children into the world.

One Point for Analysis: Topics become increasingly controversial as they become attacks on "sacred cows"—one of which is motherhood.

Writing Topics:
1. Following Radl's model, write an essay in which you oppose a "sacred cow."
2. Turn Radl's essay into a gentle satire that makes the same point.
3. "Sacred cows" are the foundation on which society exists. Argue that to attack them is to damage society itself.

WHY I WANT A WIFE

JUDY SYFERS

Judy Syfers's own background, which she claims was hindered by the negative advice of male teachers, served as some of the motivation for writing this essay.

I belong to that classification of people known as wives. I am A Wife. And, not altogether incidentally, I am a mother.

Not too long ago a male friend of mine appeared on the scene fresh from a recent divorce. He had one child, who is, of course, with his ex-wife. He is looking for another wife. As I thought about

Reprinted from *Ms.* Magazine by permission of the author.

him while I was ironing one evening, it suddenly occurred to me that I, too, would like to have a wife. Why do I want a wife?

I would like to go back to school so that I can become economically independent, support myself, and, if need be, support those dependent upon me. I want a wife who will work and send me to school. And while I am going to school I want a wife to take care of my children. I want a wife to keep track of the children's doctor and dentist appointments. And to keep track of mine, too. I want a wife to make sure my children eat properly and are kept clean. I want a wife who will wash the children's clothes and keep them mended. I want a wife who is a good nurturant attendant to my children, who arranges for their schooling, makes sure that they have an adequate social life with their peers, takes them to the park, the zoo, etc. I want a wife who takes care of the children when they are sick, a wife who arranges to be around when the children need special care, because, of course, I cannot miss classes at school. My wife must arrange to lose time at work and not lose the job. It may mean a small cut in my wife's income from time to time, but I guess I can tolerate that. Needless to say, my wife will arrange and pay for the care of the children while my wife is working.

I want a wife who will take care of *my* physical needs. I want a wife who will keep my house clean. A wife who will pick up after my children, a wife who will pick up after me. I want a wife who will keep my clothes clean, ironed, mended, replaced when need be, and who will see to it that my personal things are kept in their proper place so that I can find what I need the minute I need it. I want a wife who cooks the meals, a wife who is a *good* cook. I want a wife who will plan the menus, do the necessary grocery shopping, prepare the meals, serve them pleasantly, and then do the cleaning up while I do my studying. I want a wife who will care for me when I am sick and sympathize with my pain and loss of time from school. I want a wife to go along when our family takes a vacation so that someone can continue to care for me and my children when I need a rest and change of scene.

I want a wife who will not bother me with rambling complaints about a wife's duties. But I want a wife who will listen to me when I feel the need to explain a rather difficult point I have come across in my course of studies. And I want a wife who will type my papers for me when I have written them.

I want a wife who will take care of the details of my social life.

305

When my wife and I are invited out by my friends, I want a wife who will take care of the babysitting arrangements. When I meet people at school that I like and want to entertain, I want a wife who will have the house clean, will prepare a special meal, serve it to me and my friends, and not interrupt when I talk about things that interest me and my friends. I want a wife who will have arranged that the children are fed and ready for bed before my guests arrive so that the children do not bother us. I want a wife who takes care of the needs of my guests so that they feel comfortable, who makes sure that they have an ashtray, that they are passed the hors d'oeuvres, that they are offered a second helping of the food, that their wine glasses are replenished when necessary, that their coffee is served to them as they like it. And I want a wife who knows that sometimes I need a night out by myself.

I want a wife who is sensitive to my sexual needs, a wife who makes love passionately and eagerly when I feel like it, a wife who makes sure that I am satisfied. And, of course, I want a wife who will not demand sexual attention when I am not in the mood for it. I want a wife who assumes the complete responsibility for birth control, because I do not want more children. I want a wife who will remain sexually faithful to me so that I do not have to clutter up my intellectual life with jealousies. And I want a wife who understands that *my* sexual needs may entail more than strict adherence to monogamy. I must, after all, be able to relate to people as fully as possible.

If, by chance, I find another person more suitable as a wife than the wife I already have, I want the liberty to replace my present wife with another one. Naturally, I will expect a fresh, new life; my wife will take the children and be solely responsible for them so that I am left free.

When I am through with school and have a job, I want my wife to quit working and remain at home so that my wife can more fully and completely take care of a wife's duties.

My God, who *wouldn't* want a wife?

One Point for Analysis: The humor in this essay prevents it from being bitter.

Writing Topics:
1. "Why I Want a Husband."
2. Almost every paragraph of this essay begins, "I want a wife

who . . .''. Write an essay in which you follow the same pattern, using another topic.

3. Write an essay that, like this one, uses a short incident as an introduction to an argument. You will be moving from the particular to the general.

PRESIDENT'S FAMILY IN EVERYONE'S HAIR

MIKE ROYKO

Mike Royko often comments in newspaper columns about current national events and concerns.

I voted for Jimmy Carter, but I've already made up my mind that it won't happen again.

It is not that I think he has done a bad job. I'm usually satisfied with almost anyone who isn't a complete disaster, which he hasn't been.

It is just that I think this country desperately needs a person with certain unique qualities that Carter doesn't have. None of today's major political figures has them. But I'm hoping the right person emerges and becomes President.

I've listed the rare qualities that I think are essential to any future President. Here is my list:

1. He should be unmarried and stay that way.
2. He should be an orphan.

Think of it. A President without any goofy relatives bumbling all over the country, the front pages and the cover of the newsmagazines. A President without a wife sticking her nose in affairs of state that nobody elected her to stick her nose into.

There has to be someone in a nation of 200 million people who is intelligent, honest, brave and without any relatives.

I didn't always feel this way. Eleanor Roosevelt didn't bother me because she basically limited herself to do-gooder activities that were outside of government.

Harry Truman's wife stayed out of sight most of the time, and his daughter didn't bang on the piano as often as the Republicans would have us believe.

Chicago Sun-Times, by Mike Royko. Reprinted with permission of *The Chicago Sun-Times.*

Mamie Eisenhower spent most of her day dealing canasta, which was fine with me. In fact, Ike was almost as invisible as Mamie.

It wasn't until the Kennedys came along that relatives became part of the presidential package, and their wives became semiofficial officers of government.

Jackie made good-will tours of several nations, causing foreign potentates to pant; Lady Bird chirped about all kinds of domestic issues and even Pat inspected nuclear plants.

But there has been nothing to compare with the Carters.

One sister, the faith healer, recently proclaimed that she had managed to make a born-again Christian out of Larry Flynt, the chief crud of Hustler magazine. This apparently meant that Flynt would shout hallelujah and only show the pubic hair of good Christians.

Flynt has since reconsidered his conversion, and has decided he would rather remain a rich creep than be a bankrupt Bible-thumper.

Another sister, the motorcycle rider, is running around the country pushing a book that is made up of letters written by her mother, Miz Lillian. If sales of the book lag, Miz Lillian probably will jump on a motorcycle herself to drum up interest.

And what more can be said about brother Billy, who began as an amusing sideshow, and has now turned into the National Carnival Barker?

The last time I looked, Billy was posing for pictures while wearing a crown made out of beer caps from Billy Beer cans. Before that, he was on the cover of Time, flexing his powerful belly muscles and smiling like a simple-minded chipmunk.

If you have enough money, you can probably hire Billy to bite the head off a chicken.

Then there is presidential partner Rosalynn. She already has gone to South America as a top-level representative of this country. I thought that was what we had a State Department for.

And she also has taken over some kind of National Mental Health Commission.

I would think she'd have enough to do, just concerning herself with the mental health of some of her in-laws.

Insiders at the White House have been saying that Rosalynn has become one of the most important figures in government, sharing in the making of big decisions and looking for even more moving and shaking to do.

Who elected her to do anything? If we are going to get presidential partners, then they should campaign for that office. They should debate the other presidential partners on the issues, reveal whether they have ever had lust in their hearts, and we should have an opportunity to vote for which presidential partner we prefer.

If they are going to act like ambassadors or Cabinet members, then they should appear before Congress and undergo confirmation hearings like everyone else.

And if they don't want to do that, then they should go upstairs and deal canasta.

Or spend their time knitting nets to throw over their in-laws.

One Point for Analysis: Gentle satire (ridicule) is an effective way of persuading a reader. Remember that the purpose of satire in general is to reform its subject.

Writing Topics:

1. Arguing for a particular reform, write a gentle satire on a well-known public figure.
2. Rewrite Royko's essay without the humor. (Notice how the quality of persuasion has changed.)
3. Argue the proposition that one of the marks of a good leader is the ability to delegate responsibility wisely.

THE THIN GREY LINE

MARYA MANNES

Marya Mannes has written poetry, novels, and plays in addition to essays. She also appears from time to time on television talk shows.

"Aw, they all do it," growled the cabdriver. He was talking about cops who took payoffs for winking at double parking, but his cynicism could as well have been directed at any of a dozen other in-

Reprinted by permission of Harold Ober Associates Incorporated. Copyright © 1963 by Marya Mannes.

stances of corruption, big-time and small-time. Moreover, the disgust in his voice was overlaid by an unspoken "So what?": the implication that since this was the way things were, there was nothing anybody could do.

Like millions of his fellow Americans, the cabdriver was probably a decent human being who had never stolen anything, broken any law or willfully injured another; somewhere, a knowledge of what was probably right had kept him from committing what was clearly wrong. But that knowledge had not kept a thin grey line that separates the two conditions from being daily greyer and thinner—to the point that it was hardly noticeable.

On one side of this line are They: the bribers, the cheaters, the chiselers, the swindlers, the extortioners. On the other side are We—both partners and victims. They and We are now so perilously close that the only mark distinguishing us is that They get caught and We don't.

The same citizen who voices his outrage at police corruption will slip the traffic cop on his block a handsome Christmas present in the belief that his car, nestled under a "No Parking" sign, will not be ticketed. The son of that nice woman next door has a habit of stealing cash from her purse because his allowance is smaller than his buddies'. Your son's friend admitted cheating at exams because "everybody does it."

Bit by bit, the resistance to and immunity against wrong that a healthy social body builds up by law and ethics and the dictation of conscience have broken down. And instead of the fighting indignation of a people outraged by those who prey on them, we have the admission of impotence: "They all do it."

Now, failure to uphold the law is no less corrupt than violation of the law. And the continuing shame of this country now is the growing number of Americans who fail to uphold and assist enforcement of the law, simply—and ignominiously—out of fear. Fear of "involvement," fear of reprisal, fear of "trouble." A man is beaten by hoodlums in plain daylight and in view of bystanders. These people not only fail to help the victim, but, like the hoodlums, flee before the police can question them. A city official knows of a colleague's bribe but does not report it. A pedestrian watches a car hit a woman but leaves the scene, to avoid giving testimony. It happens every day. And if the police get cynical at this irresponsibility, they are hardly to blame. Morale is a matter of giving support and having faith in one another; where both are lacking, "law" has become a worthless word.

How did we get this way? What started this blurring of what was once a thick black line between the lawful and the lawless? What makes a "regular guy," a decent fellow, accept a bribe? What makes a nice kid from a middle-class family take money for doing something he must know is not only illegal but wrong?

When you look into the background of an erring "kid" you will often find a comfortable home and a mother who will tell you, with tears in her eyes, that she "gave him everything." She probably did, to his everlasting damage. Fearing her son's disapproval, the indulgent mother denies him nothing except responsibility. Instead of growing up, he grows to believe that the world owes him everything.

The nice kid's father crosses the thin grey line himself in a dozen ways, day in and day out. He pads his expenses on his income-tax returns as a matter of course. As a landlord, he pays the local inspectors of the city housing authority to overlook violations in the houses he rents. When his son flunked his driving test, he gave him ten dollars to slip the inspector on his second test. "They all do it," he said.

The nice kid is brought up with boys and girls who have no heroes except people not much older than themselves who have made the Big Time, usually in show business or in sports. Publicity and money are the halos of their stars, who range from pop singers who can't sing to ballplayers who can't read: from teen-age starlets who can't act to television performers who can't think. They may be excited by the exploits of spacemen, but the work's too tough and dangerous.

The nice kids have no heroes because they don't believe in heroes. Heroes are suckers and squares. To be a hero you have to stand out, to excel, to take risks, and above all, not only choose between right and wrong, but defend the right and fight the wrong. This means responsibility—and who needs it?

Today, no one has to take any responsibility. The psychiatrists, the sociologists, the novelists, the playwrights have gone a long way to help promote irresponsibility. Nobody really is to blame for what he does. It's Society. It's Environment. It's a Broken Home. It's an Underprivileged Area. But it's hardly ever You.

Now we find a truckload of excuses to absolve the individual

311

from responsibility for his actions. A fellow commits a crime be-cause he's basically insecure, because he hated his stepmother at nine, or because his sister needs an operation. A policeman loots a store because his salary is too low. A city official accepts a payoff because it's offered to him. Members of minority groups, racial or otherwise, commit crimes because they can't get a job, or are unac-ceptable to the people living around them. The words "right" and "wrong" are foreign to these people.

But honesty is the best policy. Says who? Anyone willing to get laughed at. But the laugh is no laughing matter. It concerns the health and future of a nation. It involves the two-dollar illegal bettor as well as the corporation price-fixer, the college-examination cheater and the payroll-padding Congressman, the expense-account chiseler, the seller of pornography and his schoolboy reader, the bribed judge and the stealing delinquent. All these people may rep-resent a minority. But when, as it appears now, the majority excuse themselves from responsibility by accepting corruption as natural to society ("They all do it"), this society is bordering on total confu-sion. If the line between right and wrong is finally erased, there is no defense against the power of evil.

Before this happens—and it is by no means far away—it might be well for the schools of the nation to substitute for the much-argued issue of prayer a daily lesson in ethics, law, and responsibility to society that would strengthen the conscience as exercise strength-ens muscles. And it would be even better if parents were forced to attend it. For corruption is not something you read about in the papers and leave to courts. We are all involved.

AN ANALYSIS OF "THE THIN GREY LINE"

"They all do it!" is the key phrase in Marya Mannes's essay "The Thin Grey Line." Through this rationalization, the "thick black line" that di-vides the world of right from the world of wrong slowly disintegrates into a pale shadow, allowing the two worlds to intermingle and thus become indistinguishable one from the other. And Mannes's thesis, stated first in the fifth paragraph and restated in the fourteenth paragraph, is a cause-effect relationship emphasizing how a world which fails to distinguish be-tween right and wrong is eventually doomed to chaos: "when, as it ap-pears now, the majority excuse themselves from responsibility by accepting corruption as natural to society ('They all do it'), this society is bordering on total confusion."

Basically her argument is convincing because of its organization. In the first six paragraphs, there is mention of those who inhabit the world of "wrong." But more numerous and poignant are the concrete examples of "decent" people who commit irresponsible acts, sometimes of omission, and thus cause the line between right and wrong to grow thinner and greyer.

In the seventh paragraph she asks four questions, each searching for the same answer: the cause of the "blurred" line between the lawful and the lawless. A hypothetical "kid" and his "They all do it" parents provide in the next four paragraphs the reason for the blurring: a general lack of a sense of responsibility. So far, her argument is reasonable, but then she slips into a fallacy. (See *Fallacies*, Handbook.)

At the beginning of the twelfth paragraph, she indicts psychiatrists, sociologists, novelists, and playwrights who "have gone a long way to help promote irresponsibility." Her substantiation of such a large indictment is based on small and general evidence. Such a sweeping, insufficiently supported accusation, it seems, weakens an otherwise strong argument. Fortunately the essay recuperates in her concluding paragraph.

Here she offers a solution to the confusion that comes from a failure to discriminate between right and wrong. And her solution, although punctuated with abstract words like *ethics*, *law*, and *irresponsibility*, becomes possible and practical in light of strengthening "the conscience as exercise strengthens muscles."

OBITUARY FOR A HOUSEWIFE

MILDRED KAVANAUGH

In this hypothetical obituary Mildred Kavanaugh makes a point about the role of women in today's world.

Some feminists shout for equal pay for equal work, others want abortion on demand. All I am asking is that women be treated like men on the obituary page.

When a man fades away, he gets a write-up about all the things he has achieved and all the places he has been. When a housewife dies, if she gets even a line or two, the obituary is still about all the things her *husband* has achieved and all the places *he* has been.

As a suggestion I would like to present the following obituary for a housewife that is patterned after the hundreds of eulogies I have read for prominent men. This is an obituary for a prominent *housewife:*

Mrs. Ima Martar died following a brief illness of botulism poisoning contracted after eating some of her own home canning.

Those who knew her will recall that during the past twenty-five years, Mrs. Martar cooked three meals a day, plus snacks. Her laundry was always sunshine bright, and she will be remembered as an innovator since she was the first on her street to add a fabric softener to her wash. Never in her entire life did she scorch a garment while she ironed. No one excelled her when it came to mopping floors.

Before her death, Mrs. Martar was a national holder of the award that goes to the woman who for seven years never missed a single episode of *As the World Turns.* Mrs. Martar often remarked how thrilled she was the time she was approached to do a free testimonial for a detergent company.

Mrs. Martar's most admirable qualities were that she took a leading vitamin regularly so that her husband "would keep her," and she chose the brand of coffee that would repel her nosy neighbor, Mrs. Olsen. Thanks to hair coloring, there was not a single gray hair in Mrs. Martar's head, and one of the most welcome breaks in her day was when the traveling cosmetic woman came around.

Mrs. Martar is survived by two sons, both of whom are grown with wives of their own. They will barely notice that she is no longer here except when vacation time rolls around and they realize there is no free place to leave the kids.

She will be sorely missed by her husband until a respectable time has passed so that he can marry one of his former secretaries whom he has been supporting for years.

Mrs. Martar's final words, whispered into the ears of a nearby nurse, were that in lieu of flowers would her friends, *please,* send donations to a local, state, or national Women's Liberation group.

One Point for Analysis: The argument of this essay rests on narration.

Writing Topics:

1. Argue the importance of a group of usually ignored people by following Kavanaugh's model.
2. Argue that your role in life up to this point has not been sufficiently appreciated by your parents.

314

3. With women today often choosing nondomestic roles, argue that Kavanaugh's Mrs. Martar is an inaccurate picture of the contemporary female.

APPEARANCES

VOLTAIRE

Voltaire was an eighteenth-century French writer and philosopher. In translation he is particularly remembered for Candide.

Are all appearances deceptive? Have our senses been given us only to trick us? Is everything error? Do we live in a dream? We see the sun still setting when it is below the horizon. A square tower seems to be round. A straight stick in water seems to be bent. You see your face in a mirror; the image appears to be behind the glass when it is neither behind nor before it. The glass itself, seemingly so smooth and even, is made up of tiny projections and pits. The fairest skin is a bristling net of minute hairs. What is large to us is small to an elephant; what is small may be a whole world to an insect.

Nothing is either as it appears to be, or where we think it is. Philosophers, weary of being deceived, have in their petulance declared that nothing exists but what is in our mind. They might have gone all the way and concluded that, mind being as elusive as matter, there is nothing real either in matter or mind. Perhaps it is in this despair of ever knowing anything that certain Chinese philosophers say that Nothing is the beginning and end of all things.

You do not see the net of hairs of the white and delicate skin you idolize. Organisms a thousand times less than a mite perceive what escapes your vision; they lodge, feed, and travel about on it as in an extensive country; those on a right arm are ignorant that creatures of their own species exist on a left. If you were so unfortunate as to see what they see, this charming skin would transfix you with horror.

All is in due proportion. The laws of optics, which show you an object where it is not, make the sun appear two feet in diameter when it is a million times larger than the earth, a size impossible

Reprinted by permission of Peter Pauper Press.

315

for your eye to encompass. Our senses assist much more than they deceive us.

Motion, time, hardness, softness, size, distance, appearances, all are relative. And who has created the delicate adjustment of relativities?

One Point for Analysis: Voltaire uses many concrete examples to clarify the abstract subjects of reality and illusion.

Writing Topics:

1. Answering Voltaire's opening question, use the thesis that all appearances are deceptive.
2. In five brief paragraphs Voltaire wrestles with a philosophical problem. In an essay of similar length, discuss the existence of God. (Note the Point for Analysis.)
3. Assuming that God did not create "the delicate adjustment of relativities," discuss how they exist.

WE WERE NOT SKEPTICAL ENOUGH

JOSEPH WOOD KRUTCH

Joseph Wood Krutch wrote essays on subjects as diverse as philosophy and natural history. He was for some years drama critic of The Nation.

I was born in what was called "An Age of Unbelief." When I was young I took that description seriously, and I thought that I was an intellectual because of the number of things I did not believe.

Only very slowly did I come to realize that what was really characteristic of myself and my age was not that we did not believe anything but that we believed very firmly in a number of things which are not really so.

We believed, for example, in the exclusive importance of the material, the measurable, and the controllable. We had no doubts about "what science proves" and we took it for granted that whatever science did not prove was certainly false.

When, for example, "science proved" that man had risen from

the lower animals, we believed, as I still do, that this is a fact. But when science found it difficult to define, or measure, or deal with the ways in which a man's mind, and character and motives differ from those of the lower animals, we believed that there was no important difference between them. The trouble was not that we were skeptical but that we were not skeptical enough.

We studied man by the methods which had proved fruitful for the study of animals and machines. We learned a great deal about his reflexes, animal drives, the ways in which he could be conditioned to behave. And then, because our methods did not permit us to learn anything else about him, we came to the conclusion that there was nothing else to be learned.

We came to believe, to take the most familiar example, that love was "nothing but" the biological impulses connected with sex. What is even more important, we came also to believe that his thinking was "nothing but" his power of rationalization and that his ideals and values were "nothing but" the results of his early conditioning. We began to assume that what he believed to be his free choices were not really anything of the sort; that he was not the captain of his soul but only what the dialectic of society or perhaps his infantile fixations had made him. He was, we tended to believe, not a cause but an effect.

Seldom before in the history of civilization has the world been in so parlous a state and not often before have men seemed to believe less in a God who would save them. Yet it is at this moment that we have lost faith in man himself as a prime mover of events.

What I believe in most firmly is *man himself*. And by that I mean something quite specific. I believe that he descended from the animals but that he has powers which animals share but little, if at all. I believe that he is something in himself. I believe that he can will, and choose and prefer.

That means, for example, that society is what he makes it, not that he is what society makes him. It means that he can be permitted to think, not merely conditioned by good or bad propaganda. I believe, therefore, that he can be freed, and that means a good deal more than given the vote or permitted civil liberties. The difference between a totalitarian and a democratic society is the difference between those who believe the individual man capable of being the captain of his soul and those who believe that he is merely the creature of the society in which he lives.

317

I believe that we cannot set the world free until we believe that the individual himself is free.

One Point for Analysis: The introductory paragrah states what the author did not believe in his youth. The eighth, ninth, and tenth paragraphs, the thrust of his argument, state what he does believe in his maturity.

Writing Topics:
1. In the opening paragraph Krutch states that in his youth he thought he was an intellectual because of the number of things he did not believe. Argue whether this attitude does or does not generally exist among young people today.
2. Argue that too much skepticism can lead to discontent.
3. Argue that there are those in a democracy who are not free. Make your conclusion "echo" your introduction, as in Krutch's essay.

A MODEST PROPOSAL

GENE LEES

Lees has been a reporter for Canadian newspapers, a classical music critic, and film drama editor for the Louisville Times. *He has been an editor for* Down Beat *and* Hi Fi/Stereo Review.

Jonathan Swift once made what he called a Modest Proposal: since the Irish could not grow enough food to feed themselves but had no trouble producing babies, he suggested that babies should be made the prime Irish export (perhaps served as a table delicacy in England). There were those who thought he meant it. Perhaps, in a bitter and angry way, he did.

I wish to make a Modest Proposal myself. It relates to two serious contemporary problems: narcotics addiction and overpopulation. I feel that it is incumbent upon me as a man who makes his living from the record industry to offer this proposal. For the record industry is as responsible as any sector of our society for the growing number of deaths from the use of heroin and other drugs.

318

Now don't be hasty in condemning them. They've done no more than other industries have. Detroit finds 40,000 deaths a year in crashworthy cars an acceptable price for profits. Why shouldn't the record industry too be allowed to kill its quota of people for profit?

Ten years ago I devoted an issue of *Down Beat* to the drug problem. At the time only a few music-business people thought addiction was an important issue. A Negro singer I know said to me recently, "Nobody gave a damn about it when only black kids were dying in the doorways of Harlem. Nobody gave a damn until the well-to-do middle-class white kids started dying." *Touché.*

There is a great deal of criminal money invested in the music business, both in groups and in some record labels. Rock groups began pushing drug use. The kids bought it. The kids are dying. The underworld is making money on it. This is all coincidence, right? Oh sure.

Drug education in the schools is only going to make the problem worse, I am convinced. It will increase fascination, or even cause it, among youngsters who had never even thought much about using drugs. Watch it happen in the next two years.

And so I have come around to another view of the matter. I modestly propose that to all our other welfare programs we add free narcotics for the kids, including heroin. If your're a parent, this may shock you. But it shouldn't. You have been permitting your kids to take dope intellectually for years—from Bob Dylan, the Jefferson Airplane, the Lovin' Spoonful, the Beatles. When your five-year-old was wandering around the house singing, "I get by with a little help from my friends, I get high with a little help from my friends," didn't you say, "Isn't that cute? He's singing a Beatles song." All right, so now he's a few years older, and you're startled at the circulation of drugs in his school, and fearful that he'll start using them. (Maybe he's already started.) Why? You permitted it.

Now the main thing wrong with junkies is that they steal. Sometimes they go farther than that: in desperation for money, they *kill* and steal. This is a great social inconvenience, tying up the time of all kinds of policemen whom we need for such things as messing up traffic.

If I get my way, and the government subsidizes addiction the way it now subsidizes lethargy, all this will stop. It is useless to tell young people that the Beatles and heroin are bad for them. It simply is not so: the kids have told us this. And they are the wisest and

319

most honest and idealistic and decent and loving and unprejudiced and well-informed generation of Americans in history. We know it because they have told us this too. And the advertising industry and Marshall McLuhan have confirmed it. Who in his right mind would doubt the combined wisdom of Marshall McLuhan, the advertising industry, and our wonderful young people?

Now, if we supply them with all the heroin they can use—and I am talking about the pure, uncut stuff, not the powdered sugar that's floating around in many places these days—it will have immediate and far-reaching social benefits.

First, they'll stop rioting. Heroin makes you terribly passive. They'll start nodding out all over the place, and this will permit the police to catch up on *their* sleep in parked cruisers.

Then a lot of them will start dropping out of school. This will reduce the overload on our schools and universities. It will stop the building program, thus braking the felling of trees which give us our oxygen. Our air will improve.

Third, it will increase the food supply, since junkies don't eat much even when they can get it.

Fourth (and here is the real genius of my plan), ultimately the program will end the population explosion. One junkie I know told me that he and his strung-out wife hadn't had sexual relations in two years. Heroin produces profound sexual indifference, and impotence. But that isn't the end of it. Junkies die. In the late 1940s and early 1950s, a great many jazz musicians were on heroin. None of them are now. They are either in their graves or they are off drugs. There is no middle road, apparently.

Kids constitute nearly fifty per cent of the population. The population explosion, then, *is them*. Now since anyone forty years old is going to be around only for another thirty years or so tops, *they're* not going to be much of a problem. They're starting to die off now, from working too hard to make enough money for their kids to buy the Doors' records and acid and junk. But that eighteen-year-old over there—man, he's going to be around breathing air, using up food, making garbage for another forty or fifty years. Even a kid can grasp that he himself is the real enemy.

Now when we begin the widespread free distribution of drugs, this group will start dying like flies. And still more benefits will accrue to society as a whole.

Junk music will fade from the radio. There won't be so many cars on the highway, and those that are there won't be in such steady use. Air pollution will be further reduced. Since we won't need so many highways, the grass and trees will grow again, making more oxygen. Drug use, incidentally, including acid, is becoming as common a cause of traffic deaths as alcohol. So we get a bonus here too.

I know there are those out there in Readerland who will write me letters telling me I've got it all wrong—like the people who wrote me letters telling me New York is not dying. They'll say my proposal is heartless and cruel. But it isn't, I assure you. We have given the young what they want until now. Why should we draw the line at death?

To young people I would say this: don't believe old squares when they tell you that drugs, even grass, are damn dangerous. Don't believe the growing reports that the grass available now is often spiked with heroin to hook you on hard narcotics. Don't believe those who tell you that heroin is evil stuff. You know all those people are just trying to keep you from having a hip kind of good time.

And don't think about death. Think instead how you will be reducing the pressures of population on the rest of us. Think what a noble deed you'll be doing. Think Zen thoughts about eternity and the continuum of consciousness and about astrology and how mortal existence is a mere passing cloud. Think not of going into a valley of blackness. Think instead how you are going to join the great All-Consciousness and rest forever in nirvana. As you sit there, listening to John and Yoko with a needle in your arm, reflect not on the dying you're about to do. Just think how high you're going to be as you go.

And to the record industry I would say: keep up the good work, gentlemen. You've done a hell of a job thus far.

One Point for Analysis: This essay is classically organized by introduction, survey of background, presentation of the author's argument, refutation of those readers who will disagree, and a conclusion. Because of this careful organization, one part flows smoothly into the next.

Writing Topics:
1. Write a précis of Jonathan Swift's "A Modest Proposal."
2. Compare the effectiveness of the bitter argument offered by Lees and the more gentle one presented by Royko, "President's Family in Everyone's Hair."

3. Discuss whether efforts to curb drug abuse have been effective or ineffective. Enumerate your points as you present your argument, as Lees does beginning in the eleventh paragraph.

IF IT'S WORTH HAVING

ANDREW J. HIRT

Published in a number of scholarly journals, Andrew J. Hirt is associate professor of English at the University of Southwestern Louisiana. He is also coauthor of Comprehension and Composition: An Introduction to the Essay.

I can still hear my mother's voice, pleasant without frills and curlicues, loudly calling my name through a window that looked on Derbigny Street. She summoned me with tones of finality, calling my two-syllable name in a glissando pattern from the inconspicuous first to the rounded, melodic second—An-dréw. She might have been an opera singer, but I don't think she ever heard an opera. She was a "mama," unliberated, washing clothes in an old wringer washer, walking to Pardo's grocery with her credit book, occasionally going to the Keno house, cooking Saturday red beans, loving her husband and children, and forever calling, it seems, through the window that looked on Derbigny Street.

It was late afternoon and hers was the voice of my father, a grand policeman whose greatest virtue was uncompromising devotion to his family. It was a strong voice proclaiming practice time. I dropped my football game, usually played on the mud street that paralleled the side of our corner house, ran into the last room of our "shot-gun," removed my mellophone from its black, scarred, heavy cardboard case, and began to practice one of the many scales in my étude book.

Jumbo, my oldest brother, Gerald the second, and our only sister Rosemary had all heard the same daily voice. And although we didn't know it at the time, it summoned us to the beginning of a transcendental encounter with the glory of music: Practice might not make us great musicians, but it would teach us to appreciate music eventually, even though scales and études interfered with our recreation. At times we balked, but we always followed orders—we practiced, and practiced, and practiced.

322

My parents were poor, but not too poor to buy used musical instruments. Jumbo's trumpet came from a pawn shop on Rampart Street and had to be straightened by Cousin Pete, a boilermaker. I'm convinced Jumbo's breath control is the direct result of practicing on a somewhat flattened trumpet that required the help of Aeolus to make it toot. Gerald's trombone was bought through a newspaper ad. Its former owner must have had long arms because the curve of the slide was bent as if from repeated blows on a nearby wall, through extended, wrong positions. Gerald managed but he also had to impose a surfeit of air to obtain, from an imperfect instrument, a normal tone. My mellophone was a gift from a friend of my father, and Rosemary's piano was a family heirloom, the flatness of which was obvious but the origin obscure.

The daily practicing was dreary, often tear provoking. But on Saturday evening all got together to play. (My father was the fifth on a snare drum; my mother the next on spoons.) Our "band" was an attraction for the neighbors who gathered outside the window that looked on Derbigny Street. They joined us, clapping, even dancing joyously like the second line in a jazz funeral. Dreariness had turned into Dixieland, and love, and a sense of accomplishment.

The years have passed, almost forty of them, and though my father and mother are dead, we the children are deeply grateful to them for making us aware of what music can mean in someone's life. While I no longer play the mellophone, I still hear what it sings at symphonies. Rosemary plays simple tunes for her son Noah; more complex ones in her mind as she attends the ballet. Gerald played his trombone for years in Jumbo's band; a back operation stopped that, but he amuses his grand children and those friends that can bear it with a rinky-dink piano. Jumbo (his real name is Al Hirt) makes a good living with his trumpet and, like all of us, feels the fullness that our parents gave us. It all began with the fullness of the voice that daily called us to task.

One Point for Analysis: The tone is nostalgic.
Writing Topics:
1. Argue that some things worth having do not require work.
2. Persuade others to the worth of a particular course of action, basing your discussion on an episode from your own life.
3. Argue that being a participant in an activity increases one's enjoyment as a spectator of that activity.

WHO KILLED BENNY PARET?

NORMAN COUSINS

Norman Cousins was for many years the executive editor of
Saturday Review *(under several titles). In 1948 he received the*
Thomas Jefferson Award for the Advancement of Democracy in
Journalism.

Sometime about 1935 or 1936 I had an interview with Mike Jacobs, the prize-fight promoter. I was a fledgling reporter at that
time; my beat was education but during the vacation season I found
myself on varied assignments, all the way from ship news to sports
reporting. In this way I found myself sitting opposite the most
powerful figure in the boxing world.

There was nothing spectacular in Mr. Jacobs' manner or appearance; but when he spoke about prize fights, he was no longer a
bland little man but a colossus who sounded the way Napoleon
must have sounded when he reviewed a battle. You knew you were
listening to Number One. His saying something made it true.

We discussed what to him was the only important element in
successful promoting—how to please the crowd. So far as he was
concerned, there was no mystery to it. You put killers in the ring
and the people filled your arena. You hire boxing artists—men who
are adroit at feinting, parrying, weaving, jabbing, and dancing, but
who don't pack dynamite in their fists—and you wind up counting
your empty seats. So you searched for the killers and sluggers and
maulers—fellows who could hit with the force of a baseball bat.

I asked Mr. Jacobs if he was speaking literally when he said people came out to see the killer.

"They don't come out to see a tea party," he said evenly. "They
come out to see the knockout. They come out to see a man hurt. If
they think anything else, they're kidding themselves."

Recently, a young man by the name of Benny Paret was killed in
the ring. The killing was seen by millions; it was on television. In
the twelfth round, he was hit hard in the head several times, went
down, was counted out, and never came out of the coma.

The Paret fight produced a flurry of investigations. Governor

Rockefeller was shocked by what happened and appointed a committee to assess the responsibility. The New York State Boxing Commission decided to find out what was wrong. The District Attorney's office expressed its concern. One question that was solemnly studied in all three probes concerned the action of the referee. Did he act in time to stop the fight? Another question had to do with the role of the examining doctors who certified the physical fitness of the fighters before the bout. Still another question involved Mr. Paret's manager; did he rush his boy into the fight without adequate time to recuperate from the previous one?

In short, the investigators looked into every possible cause except the real one. Benny Paret was killed because of human fist delivers enough impact, when directed against the head, to produce a massive hemorrhage in the brain. The human brain is the most delicate and complex mechanism in all creation. It has a lacework of millions of highly fragile nerve connections. Nature attempts to protect this exquisitely intricate machinery by encasing it in a hard shell. Fortunately, the shell is thick enough to withstand a great deal of pounding. Nature, however, can protect man against everything except man himself. Not every blow to the head will kill a man—but there is always the risk of concussion and damage to the brain. A prize fighter may be able to survive even repeated brain concussions and go on fighting, but the damage to his brain may be permanent.

In any event, it is futile to investigate the referee's role and seek to determine whether he should have intervened to stop the fight earlier. That is not where the primary responsibility lies. The primary responsibility lies with the people who pay to see a man hurt. The referee who stops a fight too soon from the crowd's viewpoint can expect to be booed. The crowd wants the knockout; it wants to see a man stretched out on the canvas. This is the supreme moment in boxing. It is nonsense to talk about prize fighting as a test of boxing skills. No crowd was ever brought to its feet screaming and cheering at the sight of two men beautifully dodging and weaving out of each other's jabs. The time the crowd comes alive is when a man is hit hard over the heart or the head, when his mouthpiece flies out, when the blood squirts out of his nose or eyes, when he wobbles under the attack and his pursuer continues to smash at him with pole-axe impact.

Don't blame it on the referee. Don't even blame it on the fight managers. Put the blame where it belongs—on the prevailing mores

325

that regard prize fighting as a perfectly proper enterprise and vehicle of entertainment. No one doubts that many people enjoy prize fighting and will miss it if it should be thrown out. And that is precisely the point.

One Point for Analysis: This essay is a stinging argument because Cousins lays the blame for a man's death directly on our society.
Writing Topics:
  1. Argue that because boxing is legal, bullfighting should also be legal.
  2. Argue that boxing is a legitimate sport.
  3. Like Cousins, use an anecdote to introduce your subject, an argument against some currently accepted form of entertainment.

JEW-CONSCIOUSNESS

E. M. FORSTER

E. M. Forster was an English writer who attended King's College, Cambridge, to which he retired as an honorary fellow in 1946. In all his works Forster is interested in the importance of human feeling over social convention.

Long, long ago, while Queen Victoria reigned, I attended two preparatory schools. At the first of these, it was held to be a disgrace to have a sister. Any little boy who possessed one was liable to get teased. The word would go round: "Oh, you men, have you seen the Picktoes' sister?" The men would then reel about with sideway motions, uttering cries of "sucks" and pretending to faint with horror, while the Picktoes, who had hitherto held their own socially in spite of their name, found themselves banished into the wilderness, where they mourned, Major with Minor, in common shame. Naturally anyone who had a sister hid her as far as possible, and forbade her to sit with him at a Prizegiving or to speak to him except in passing and in a very formal manner. Public opinion was not bitter on the point, but it was quite definite. Sisters were disgraceful. I got through all right myself, because my conscience was clear, and though charges were brought against me from time to time they always fell through.

It was a very different story at my second school. Here, sisters were negligible, but it was a disgrace to have a mother. Crabbe's mother, Gob's mother, eeugh! No words were too strong, no sounds too shrill. And since mothers at that time of life are commoner than sisters, and also less biddable, the atmosphere of this school was less pleasant, and the sense of guilt stronger. Nearly every little boy had a mother in a cupboard, and dreadful revelations occurred. A boy would fall ill and a mother would swoop and drive him away in a cab. A parcel would arrive with "From Mummy for her darling" branded upon it. Many tried to divert suspicion by being aggressive and fastening female parents upon the weak. One or two, who were good at games and had a large popularity-surplus, took up a really heroic line, acknowledged their mother brazenly, and would even be seen walking with her across the playing-field, like King Carol with Madame Lupescu. We admired such boys and envied them, but durst not imitate them. The margin of safety was too narrow. The convention was established that a mother spelt disgrace, and no individual triumph could reverse this.

Those preparatory schools prepared me for life better than I realised, for having passed through two imbecile societies, a sister-conscious and a mother-conscious, I am now invited to enter a third. I am asked to consider whether the people I meet and talk about are or are not Jews, and to form no opinion on them until this fundamental point has been settled. What revolting tosh! Neither science nor religion nor common sense has one word to say in its favour. All the same, Jew-consciousness is in the air, and it remains to be seen how far it will succeed in poisoning it. I don't think we shall ever reintroduce ghettos into England; I wouldn't say for certain, since no one knows what wickedness may not develop in his country or in himself if circumstances change. I don't think we shall go savage. But I do think we shall go silly. Many people have gone so already. Today, the average man suspects the people he dislikes of being Jews, and is surprised when the people he likes are Jews. Having been a Gentile at my first preparatory school and a Jew at my second, I know what I am talking about. I know how the poison works, and I know too that if the average man is anyone in particular he is a preparatory school boy. On the surface, things do not look too bad. Labour and Liberalism behave with their expected decency and denounce persecution, and respectability generally follows suit. But beneath the surface things are not so good, and anyone who keeps his ears open in railway carriages or pubs or country lanes can hear a very different story. A nasty side of our nation's character has been scratched up—the sniggering side. People who would not ill-treat Jews themselves, or even be rude to them, enjoy tittering over their misfortunes; they giggle when pogroms are instituted by someone else and synagogues defiled vicariously. "Serve them right really, Jews." This makes unpleasant reading, but anyone who cares to move out of his own enlightened little corner will discover that it is true. The grand Nordic argument, "He's a bloody capitalist so he must be a Jew, and as he's a Jew he must be a Red," has already taken root in our filling-stations and farms. Men employ it more frequently than women, and young men more frequently than old ones. The best way of confuting it is to say sneeringly, "That's propaganda." When "That's propaganda" has been repeated several times, the sniggering stops, for no goose likes to think that he has been got at. There is another reply which is more intellectual but which requires more courage. It is to say, "Are you sure you're not a Jew yourself? Do you know who your eight great-grandparents were? Can you swear that all the eight are Aryan?" Cool reasonableness would be best of all, of course, but it does not work in the world of today any better than in my preparatory schools. The only effective check to silliness is silliness of a cleverer type.

Jew-mania was the one evil which no one foretold at the close of the last war. All sorts of troubles were discerned and discernible—nationalism, class-warfare, the split between the haves and the have-nots, the general lowering of cultural values. But no prophet, so far as I know, had foreseen this anti-Jew horror, wheras today no one can see the end of it. There had been warnings, of course, but they seemed no more ominous than a poem by Hilaire Belloc. Back in India, in 1921, a Colonel lent me the Protocols of the Elders of Zion, and it was such an obvious fake that I did not worry. I had forgotten my preparatory schools, and did not see that they were about to come into their own. To me, anti-Semitism is now the most shocking of all things. It is destroying much more than the Jews; it is assailing the human mind at its source, and inviting it to create false categories before exercising judgment. I am sure we shall win through. But it will take a long time. Perhaps a hundred years must pass before men can think back to the mentality of 1918, or can say with the Prophet Malachi, "Have we not all one father? Hath not one God created us?" For the moment, all that we can do is to dig in our heels, and prevent silliness from sliding into insanity.

One Point for Analysis: The wisdom of this essay is demonstrated by the fact that shortly after its 1939 publication the insanity that Forster feared became a reality.

Writing Topics:
1. Argue the legitimacy of labeling an individual by his race or religion.
2. Argue against some contemporary "silliness" that could possibly slide into "insanity."
3. Following Forster's pattern, write an argumentative essay entitled "Gay Consciousness."

SOCIABLE PONG

CARLL TUCKER

Carll Tucker is currently editor of Saturday Review.

Recently a friend gave me an electronic game called "Pong." By some manner of wizardry, the game turns the television screen into a playing field, with a stationary white line in the middle representing the net; shorter, movable white lines representing rackets; and a white dot in the role of the ball. A bleep when the ball "hits" the racket makes the game sound like a physical sport. The special features on my set include a dial that enables me to accelerate or retard the ball's speed and a switch with which I can transform the opposite player into either a backboard or a fiendish nonmissing opponent.

Although not generally a fan of nonathletic games, I cottoned to Pong immediately. Instead of merely talking to me, the television screen was challenging me, inviting me to participate. Moreover, the television was proving a social medium, a playground where two people could meet and relate to each other. For a change, it mattered whether or not I was paying attention to what was taking place on screen. Unless I was involved, the action on screen was meaningless.

Like most literate Americans, I suffer from a love-hate relationship with conventional television. Television is so easy to watch. One must force oneself to slog through a dull book, while the most insipid television program or commercial can be absorbed without difficulty. Particularly after a day's work, when one is tired, television is addictive. I can spend two valuable hours in an evening watching TV, not see anything of interest, and scarcely notice the passage of time.

Sometimes, while whistling one of the catchy tunes insinuated into my brain by advertisers, I assess the ways in which I could have spent those two hours a night, or perhaps six hours a week, more profitably. I could have exercised my mind by reading one of the dozens of nonwork-related books on my must-read shelf. I could have written letters to friends or family. I could have written a more explicit critique of a piece I was evaluating and could possibly have been of assistance to an aspiring freelancer. I could have thought more thoroughly about the next day's work, about how to publicize *Saturday Review* and bring articles to the attention of those whom they might interest. I could have done a dozen more productive or sociable things, or both. Yet, despite that knowledge, I continue to turn on the television and get hooked by its prattle.

In a way, my not atypical situation is comic: Am I so weak-willed that I can be defeated by a talking piece of furniture? In another way, my situation is troubling—because it is typical.

Whenever something is gained, something is lost. Dazzled by the magic of television, we tend to forget what we might have been doing without television. We might have read more, thought more, written more. We might have filled the hours with games like bridge or Scrabble. We might have played more musical instruments, spent more time outdoors, embroidered, knitted, whittled. We might also have consumed more spirits and drugs, to relieve boredom. What is certain is that we would have spent more time relating and learning to relate to other people. Without the instant smile at the touch of our dial, we would have felt more urgency about creating a more sociable environment for ourselves, and we would have worked harder to achieve it.

Perhaps the most lamentable victim of television is the art of conversation, the art of reaching out to a stranger through the medium of speech and forming a bond. In college I remember friends, weaned on television, who were so incapable of communicating with strangers that they refused to meet them. They called their fears shyness, as if it were a condition like red hair or a cleft palate. No one had told them that shyness can be overcome, like an infant's inability to walk, that shyness (to quote my late grandmother) "is a form of selfishness." Deafening music, drugs, and a nonjudgmental acceptance of each other as fellow travelers have to some extent compensated for my generation's lack of conversational competence. The fact remains: Television isolated us from each other; it collected the world into a global village and locked each of the villagers in cells.

Pong obviously is not the solution to this, but it is a hopeful sign. If, for a few hours, instead of the isolating TV fare, you have a playing field where live (as opposed to "live") people deal with each other, *communicate,* the world is that much more intimate and real.

AN ANALYSIS OF "SOCIABLE PONG"

"Sociable Pong" by Carll Tucker is an essay that reserves the statement of its thesis until the end of the discussion. The author gives the impression that he cannot be certain of his opinion until he has turned the question this way and that, examining it from all sides before reaching a judgement. Finally, at the end of the seventh paragraph, the last paragraph of the body of the essay, he takes his stand as a critic of television's impact on society. He writes: "Television isolated us from each other; it collected the world into a global village and locked each of the villagers in cells."

The delayed statement of thesis is appropriate in this essay because the author treats the subject as a paradox, one that he must resolve before he can know what he really feels about the subject. Television is a paradox because it has both good and bad effects on its viewers. Tucker's own attitudes are paradoxical because they constitute a "love-hate relationship" with the medium.

The third paragraph explores the "love" part of that relationship.

Tucker comments on how television offers the viewer something that he wants. In many cases it is not the actual programs that are desirable, but the mindless ease of simply watching.

The fourth paragraph discusses the "hate" aspect of the relationship. If television offers simple relaxation, it also takes one away from more fruitful pursuits, some of them professional duties, some only personal pleasures. These two paragraphs are essentially expository as they set up the positive and negative aspects of the topic under consideration. Following the brief transitional fifth paragraph, the argument itself begins.

Once Tucker has reached an opinion, he states it with clarity and certainty. He states it in part in the opening sentence of the seventh paragraph. He more generally states it at the end of the paragraph by playing with the metaphor of "a global village," a phrase first used by Marshall McLuhan, one of television's most astute analysts. Tucker supports his thesis by examples drawn from his own experience. He also cites specific activities that might have led us to "a more sociable environment" had television not intervened.

The device of mentioning the electronic game of "Pong" provides a frame for the central discussion. It allows Tucker to introduce the subject of television with a personal, almost informal tone. It also helps him to establish the paradox he goes on to examine. That is, he states that he is not fond of nonathletic games, and soon thereafter announces his antipathy for television, but he likes "Pong." Reference to the game also provides a convenient way to reiterate the thesis in the conclusion: "If, for a few hours, instead of the isolating TV fare, you have a playing field where live . . . people deal with each other, *communicate,* the world is that much more intimate and real."

Carll Tucker's persuasion is gentle. It indulges none of the techniques of a "hard sell." It abjures use of complex logic. It is a thoughtful look at several sides of a subject, leading to a carefully supported judgment.

MAN WILL PREVAIL

WILLIAM FAULKNER

William Faulkner was a Southern writer who delivered this address on the occasion of his acceptance of the Nobel Prize for Literature.

I feel that this award was not made to me as a man, but to my work—a life's work in the agony and sweat of the human spirit, not for glory and least of all for profit, but to create out of the materials of the human spirit something which did not exist before. So this award is only mine in trust. It will not be difficult to find a dedication for the money part of it commensurate with the purpose and significance of its origin. But I would like to do the same with the acclaim too, by using this moment as a pinnacle from which I might be listened to by the young men and women already dedicated to the same anguish and travail, among whom is already that one who will some day stand here where I am standing.

Our tragedy today is a general and universal physical fear so long sustained by now that we can even bear it. There are no longer problems of the spirit. There is only the question: When will I be blown up? Because of this, the young man or woman writing today has forgotten the problems of the human heart in conflict with itself which alone can make good writing because only that is worth writing about, worth the agony and the sweat.

He must learn them again. He must teach himself that the basest of all things is to be afraid; and, teaching himself that, forget it forever, leaving no room in his workshop for anything but the old verities and truths of the heart, the old universal truths lacking which any story is ephemeral and doomed—love and honor and pity and pride and compassion and sacrifice. Until he does so, he labors under a curse. He writes not of love but of lust, of defeats in which nobody loses anything of value, of victories without hope and, worst of all, without pity or compassion. His griefs grieve on no universal bones, leaving no scars, He writes not of the heart but of the glands.

Until he relearns these things, he will write as though he stood among and watched the end of man. I decline to accept the end of

Reprinted by permission of Random House, Inc.

man. It is easy enough to say that man is immortal simply because he will endure: that when the last ding-dong of doom has clanged and faded from the last worthless rock hanging tideless in the last red and dying evening, that even then there will still be one more sound: that of his puny inexhaustible voice, still talking. I refuse to accept this. I believe that man will not merely endure: he will prevail. He is immortal, not because he alone among creatures has an inexhaustible voice, but because he has a soul, a spirit capable of compassion and sacrifice and endurance. The poet's, the writer's, duty is to write about these things. It is his privilege to help man endure by lifting his heart, by reminding him of the courage and honor and hope and pride and compassion and pity and sacrifice which have been the glory of his past. The poet's voice need not merely be the record of man, it can be one of the props, the pillars to help him endure and prevail.

One Point for Analysis: When making a point about man's "puny, inexhaustible voice," Faulkner uses words that are memorable for their sounds: For example, "ding-dong of doom has clanged."

Writing Topics:

1. Faulkner says that the Nobel Prize was given not to him as a man but to his work. Argue that a person cannot be separated from his work.

2. Argue that the threat of nuclear destruction does or does not limit a person's capacity to love or to act.

3. After library research, argue how three Nobel laureates have affected your life.

KILLING FOR SPORT

JOSEPH WOOD KRUTCH

Among the numerous publications of Joseph Wood Krutch are
The Modern Temper, The Measure of Man, *and* The Great
Chain of Life.

It wouldn't be quite true to say that "some of my best friends are
hunters." Still, I do number among my respected acquaintances
some who not only kill for the sake of killing but count it among
their keenest pleasures. And I can think of no better illustration of
the fact that men may be separated at some point by a fathomless
abyss yet share elsewhere much common ground. To me, it is inconceivable that anyone can think an animal more interesting dead
than alive. I can also easily prove, to my own satisfaction, that
killing "for sport" is the perfect type of that pure evil for which
metaphysicians have sometimes sought.

Most wicked deeds are done because the doer proposes some
good for himself. The liar lies to gain some end; the swindler and
the thief want things which, if honestly got, might be good in
themselves. Even the murderer is usually removing some impediment to normal desires. Though all of these are selfish or unscrupu-
lous, their deeds are not gratuitously evil. But the killer for sport
seems to have no such excusable motive. He seems merely to prefer
death to life, darkness to light. He seems to get nothing other than
the satisfaction of saying: "Something which wanted to live is
dead. Because I can bring terror and agony, I assure myself that I
have power. Because of me there is that much less vitality, consciousness and perhaps joy in the universe. I am the spirit that denies." When a man wantonly destroys one of the works of man, we
call him "Vandal." When he wantonly destroys one of the works of
God, we call him "Sportsman."

The hunter-for-food may be as wicked and as misguided as vege-
tarians sometimes say, but he does not kill for the sake of killing.
The ranchers and the farmers who exterminate all living things not
immediately profitable to them may sometimes be working against
their own best interests; but whether they are or are not, they hope

335

to achieve some supposed good by the exterminations. If to do evil, not in the hope of gain but for evil's sake, involves the deepest guilt by which man can be stained, then killing for killing's sake is a terrifying phenomenon and as strong a proof as we could have of that "reality of evil" with which present-day theologians are again concerned.

One Point for Analysis: The second paragraph is organized by comparison and contrast, signaled by the word *but* in the middle.
Writing Topics:
   1. Argue that some human activity (other than the one discussed by Krutch) qualifies as "the perfect type of pure evil for which metaphysicians have sometimes sought."
   2. Argue the benefits of killing for sport.
   3. Write an argumentative essay which begins: "Some of my best friends are _____, but . . .".

AWAY WITH BIG-TIME ATHLETICS

ROGER M. WILLIAMS

Roger M. Williams has written for Sports Illustrated *and* Time *and is an editor of* Saturday Review.

At their mid-January annual meeting, members of the National Collegiate Athletic Association were locked in anguished discussion over twin threats to big-time college athletic programs: rapidly rising costs and federal regulations forcing the allocation of some funds to women's competition. The members ignored, as they always have, the basic issue concerning intercollegiate athletics. That is the need to overhaul the entire bloated, hypocritical athletic system and return athletics to a sensible place in the educational process.

A complete overhaul of the athletic programs, not the fiscal repair now being attempted by the NCAA, is what is necessary. For decades now big-time football, and to a lesser degree basketball, have commanded absurdly high priorities at our colleges and universities. Football stands at the center of the big-time system, both symbolically and financially; the income from football has long supported other, less glamorous sports.

Many American universities are known more for the teams they field than for the education they impart. Each year they pour hundreds of thousands of dollars apiece into athletic programs whose success is measured in games won and dollars earned—standards that bear no relation to the business of education and offer nothing to the vast majority of students.

The waste of resources is not the only lamentable result of the overemphasis of intercollegiate athletics. The skewing of values is at least as damaging. Everyone involved in the big-time system—players, coaches, alumni and other boosters, school officials, trustees, even legislators—is persuaded that a good football team is a mark of the real worth of an educational institution. Some of the most successful coaches elevate that bizarre notion to a sort of philosophy. Woody Hayes of Ohio State has said that the most important part of a young man's college education is the football he plays. Jim Kehoe, athletic director at the University of Maryland, has said of the games played by Maryland: "You do anything to win. I believe completely, totally, and absolutely in winning."

Anyone doubtful of the broad psychic satisfaction provided by winning teams need only observe who it is that shouts, "We're number one!" It is seldom the players and only sometimes other students. The hard core of team boosters is composed of middle-aged men—mainly alumni but also legions of lawyers, doctors, and businessmen with no tangible connection to the school.

In the South, where football mania rides at a shrill and steady peak, winning seems to offer a special reward: an opportunity to claim the parity with other regions that has been so conspicuously lacking in more important areas of endeavor. In Alabama in the late Sixties, when Coach Bear Bryant was fielding the first of his remarkable series of national championship teams, both Bear and team were the objects of outright public adulation: that is, *white* public adulation. White Alabamians, reacting to the assaults on George Wallace and other bastions of segregation, took a grim, almost vengeful pride in "their" team. During those years, when I covered the South as a reporter, one could hardly meet a white Alabamian who didn't talk football or display, on an office or den wall, a picture of Bryant and the Crimson Tide squad.

337

The disease of bigtime-ism seems to run rampant in provincial places where there is little else to do or cheer for: Tuscaloosa and Knoxville, Columbus and Lincoln, Norman and Fayetteville. But everywhere, always, it feeds on a need to win—not just win a fair share of games but win almost all of them, and surely all of the "big" ones.

At the University of Tennessee last fall, coach Bill Battle nearly lost his job because the Volunteers won a mere 7 out of 12 games. Never mind that Battle's Tennessee teams had previously amassed a five-year record of 46 victories, 12 defeats, and 2 ties and had been to a bowl in each of those years. Although Battle was eventually rehired, he received no public support from a university administration which seemed to agree with the fanatics that, outstanding as his record was, it was not good enough.

Everyone knows something about the excess of recruiting high-school players and something about the other trappings of the big-time system: the athletic dormitory and training table, where the "jocks" or "animals" are segregated in the interests of conformity and control, the "brain coaches" hired to keep athletes from flunking out of school; the full scholarships ("grants in aid"), worth several thousand dollars apiece, that big-time schools can give to 243 athletes each year. (Conference regulations restrict the size of football traveling squads to about 60, while the NCAA permits 95 players to be on football scholarships. This means that some three dozen football players at each big-time school are getting what's called a full ride without earning it.)

What a few people realize is that these are only the visible workings of a system that feeds on higher education and diverts it from its true purposes. The solution, therefore, is not to deliver slaps on the wrist to the most zealous recruiters, as the NCAA often does, or to make modest reductions in the permissible number of athletic scholarships, as it did last year. The solution is to banish big-time athletics from American colleges and universities.

Specifically, we should:

(1) Eliminate all scholarships awarded on the basis of athletic ability *and* those given to athletes in financial need. Every school should form its teams from a student body drawn there to pursue academic interests.

(2) Eliminate athletic dormitories and training tables, which keep athletes out of the mainstream of college life and further their image

338

as hired guns. Also eliminate special tutoring, which is a preferential treatment of athletes, and "red shirting," the practice of keeping players in school an additional year in the hope that they'll improve enough to make the varsity.

(3) Cut drastically the size and the cost of the coaching staffs. Football staffs at Division I schools typically number 12 or 14, so that they are larger than those employed by professional teams. With practice squads numbering 80 or 50, the present staff size creates a "teacher-pupil" ratio that permits far more individualized instruction on the playing field than in the classroom. The salaries paid to assistant coaches should be spent to hire additional faculty members. The salaries of head coaches, who in some states earn more than the governor, should be reduced to a point where no head coach is paid more than a full professor.

(4) Work to eliminate all recruiting of high-school athletes. It has produced horrendous cases of misrepresentation, illegal payments, and trauma for the young man involved.

The worst of the abuses is the athletic scholarship, because it is central to all the others. If members of a college team are not principally athletes, there is no need to lure them to the school by offering special treatment and platoons of coaches. They should be students to whom football or basketball is the season's major extracurricular activity.

What will happen if these changes are made? The games will go on. In fact, they may well be more like real games than the present clashes between hired, supertrained, and sometimes brutalized gladiators. Will the caliber of play suffer? Of course, but every school will be producing the same lower caliber. Given a certain proficiency, which the best of any random selection of student-athletes always possesses, the games will be as competitive and as exciting for spectators as they are today. Is a 70-yard run by a non-scholarship halfback less exciting than the same run by Bear Bryant's best pro prospect? For spectators who crave top athletic performance, it is available from a myriad of professional teams. We need not demand it of students.

Certainly, the counter-argument runs, alumni and other influential supporters would not stand for such changes. There would indeed be ill feeling among—and diminished contributions from—old grads who think of their alma mater primarily as a football team. Let them stew in their own pot of distorted values. Those legislators

339

whose goodwill toward a state university depends on winning seasons and free tickets can stew with them. A serious institution is well rid of such "supporters." They may discover the pleasures of a game played enthusiastically by moderately skilled students who are not in effect paid performers.

Will athletic-program revenues drop? They undoubtedly will, at least for a while; not many people will pay seven dollars to see games of admittedly lower quality, nor will the TV networks pay fancy fees for the right to televise them. The fans and the networks will eventually return, because these will be the only college games available. And think of the financial savings, as the costs of the typical big-time athletic program drop by hundreds of thousands of dollars a year. If a revenue gap persists, let it be made up out of general funds. The glee club, the intramural athletic program, and innumerable other student activities do not pay for themselves. Why should intercollegiate athletics have to do so?

Supporters of big-time programs often say piously that, thanks to those programs, many young men get a college education who otherwise would have no chance for one. That is true. But there are even more young men, of academic rather than athletic promise, who deserve whatever scholarship money is available. If somebody has to pay an athlete's way to college, let it be the professional teams that need the training that college competition provides.

The president of a good Southern university once told me privately that he would like to hire outright a football team to represent his school and let the educational process proceed. George Hanford of the College Entrance Examination Board, who has made a study of intercollegiate athletics, would keep the present system but legitimize the preparation of players for professional sports. Hanford would have a college teach athletes such skills as selecting a business agent and would permit student-athletes to play now and return later to do the academic work required for a degree.

While Hanford's suggested changes would remove the mask of hypocrisy from big-time college athletic programs, they would not solve the fundamental problem: the intrusions the programs make on the legitimate functions and goals of an educational institution. For institutions with a conscience, this problem has been persistently vexing. Vanderbilt University football coach Art Guepe summed it up years ago, when he characterized Vanderbilt's dilemma as "trying to be Harvard five days a week and Alabama on Saturday."

Because of pressures from alumni and others who exalt the role of football, Vanderbilt is still attempting to resolve this dilemma; and it is still failing. Now it is time for all the Vanderbilts and all the Alabamas to try to be Harvard whenever they can and Small-Time State on Saturday.

One Point for Analysis: The eleventh paragraph expands the thesis
   by enumeration.
Writing Topics:
   1. Using a topic of your choice, like Williams, present a problem, then follow it with a solution.
   2. Argue a thesis that you expand by enumeration.
   3. Develop a rebuttal to Williams' thesis.

A TRUE INSTINCT FOR THE BEAUTIFUL

RACHEL CARSON

Rachel Carson's sense of the beautiful includes both scientific and aesthetic truth. In this essay her love for both is apparent.

A child's world is fresh and new and beautiful, full of wonder and excitement. It is our misfortune that for most of us that clear-eyed vision, that true instinct for what is beautiful and awe-inspiring, is dimmed and even lost before we reach adulthood. If I had influence with the good fairy who is supposed to preside over the christening of all children I should ask that her gift to each child in the world be a sense of wonder so indestructible that it would last throughout life, as an unfailing antidote against the boredom and disenchantments of later years, the sterile preoccupation with things that are artificial, the alienation from the sources of our strength.

If a child is to keep alive his inborn sense of wonder without any such gift from the fairies, he needs the companionship of at least one adult who can share it, rediscovering with him the joy, excitement and mystery of the world we live in. Parents often have a sense of inadequacy when confronted on the one hand with the eager, sensitive mind of a child and on the other with a world of complex physical nature, inhabited by a life so various and unfamiliar that it seems hopeless to reduce it to order and knowledge. In a mood of self-defeat, they exclaim, "How can I possibly teach my child about nature—why, I don't even know one bird from another!"

I sincerely believe that for the child, and for the parent seeking to guide him, it is not half so important to *know* as to *feel*. If facts are the seeds that later produce knowledge and wisdom, then the emotions and the impressions of the senses are the fertile soil in which the seeds must grow. The years of early childhood are the time to prepare the soil. Once the emotions have been aroused—a sense of the beautiful, the excitement of the new and the unknown, a feeling of sympathy, pity, admiration or love—then we wish for knowledge about the object of our emotional response. Once found, it has lasting meaning. It is more important to pave the way for the child to want to know than to put him on a diet of facts he is not ready to assimilate.

One Point for Analysis: In the first half of the concluding paragraph, Carson uses an extended metaphor to emphasize her thesis.

Writing Topics:

1. Argue that traditional television programs dull our sense of wonder.
2. Given the opportunity, what gift would you give a child? Argue the worth of that gift.
3. Using Carson's essay as a model, develop an argument in which you present a child not as a sensitive, wondering being but as "a young animal."

RAISING CHILDREN IN THE YEAR 2000

ELIZABETH JANEWAY

Elizabeth Janeway is an American novelist, who has published
The Walsh Girls *and* Leaving Home. *She has several children
and enjoys the tasks involved in running a home.*

Some of the people who will be raising children in the year 2000
are already here with us. My grandson is four and my granddaughter is two. It's a little early to say what their future plans will
be, but if their childhood influences them, they will remember
growing up in a supportive network of relationships with adults
who are not their parents. By some quirk they possess an actual, if
dispersed, extended family on both sides and they stay, from time
to time, with two sets of grandparents, while uncles, aunts and
cousins turn up to visit, share vacations and baby-sit. Just as important is the "Mothers' Mafia" of the neighborhood which will
take over an extra child when a parent is ill or away. The former circumstance may vanish, but the informal mothering (and fathering)
by neighboring parents will, I suspect, grow stronger.

What our tiny nuclear, or less-than-nuclear (one-parent) families
need today is just this kind of connection with a larger community.
It used to exist in family compound, village or small-town neighborhood. In sociologist's language, it gave children a diversity of
role-models. It also gave them a lot of experience in getting on with
people, and a lot of people to try getting on with. It could supply
comforters when they quarreled with their parents, much conflict-
ing advice to test instead of just one set of "Do's" and "Don'ts"—
and any single set of imperatives asks to be challenged—plus an in-
structive range of relationships. Television isn't the same thing for
there's no feedback there, but in the fascination that it holds for the
very young we can see how great is their curiosity and their urge to
learn the wide world around them.

"The family," said Talcott Parsons, "is a sub-system of society."
It is not, and never can be, a unit complete in itself. But it is harder
today than it ever has been for children to move from family base to
an adult place in society because the connecting links are so few.

343

One reason is that the family has lost the vital economic role it used to have when much necessary work was done there. For the first time in history no one, male or female, can make an adequate living at home. (Or almost no one. Very few writers make an adequate living.) The factory system put an end to the economic function of the family group and children now grow up without a clue as to the ordinary process of earning their keep.

A recipe I would like to recommend is the establishment of enriching and exciting child-care facilities at industrial plants, commercial centers, educational establishments—everywhere that parents go to work; *model* care facilities cosponsored by unions and imaginative educators, with programs offered by libraries, museums, musical conservatories, theater and dance groups, the inheritors of ethnic and cultural traditions—you can think of many more, I'm sure. They should engage, use and entertain a coming-and-going population, directed by a professional core, of children of all ages, adults of both sexes and all the generations that could be called on, interacting, teaching each other, connecting. The separation of work life from actual living is taking a terrible toll from the workers of our nation; we have just seen this documented in the HEW study of satisfaction at work. God knows I don't propose the child care I'm talking about as a way to orient children to the drab, desperate, mechanized kind of work that is distressing us today. But I suspect that *reuniting* living and working is going to be necessary for all of us, and I think that children-where-you-work can be influential in humanizing work, just as work-where-you-grow-up can be informative and exciting for children.

Overall, my great hope for the year 2000 is the reintegration of the parts of our world that started to come apart when the machines moved in. We can't do without the machines, but we've been scared of them too long. Damn it, are we mice or are we men? Does it take a woman to ask that question? Then thank God the Women's Movement has arrived to stand up and shout for liberation for the human race—beginning with our children.

One Point for Analysis: Janeway's projection for the future is supported by her explanation of the present and the past.

Writing Topics:
1. Argue for a change you would like to see by the year 2000.
2. Argue the merits of "the good old days."

3. Construct an argument that, like this essay, builds to a climax in the concluding paragraph. (This structure would require the implied or actual presence of the thesis in the conclusion.)

THERE IS A MORAL DIMENSION

EUNICE K. SHRIVER

Eunice K. Shriver has long been concerned with problems of teenage girls. She is executive vice-president of the Joseph P. Kennedy, Jr. Foundation.

A syndicated columnist recently wrote: "Short of locking the entire teen-age population in their rooms, the only thing adults can do is help them avoid the most permanent and disastrous of consequences—pregnancy."

I find such statements shocking, and demeaning—to parents because they are dismissed as failures; to teen-agers because the implication is that they are without values (or that what sexual values they do hold are nothing more than raw pleasure principles). Nowhere do I hear a suggestion that teen-age intercourse can be controlled, that teen-agers themselves might want to control it. Society itself may be encouraging teen-age sex, and then hypocritically condemning its results.

I believe our young people want support and do have a sense of values. Why then do we insist on treating them as if they have no ability to say "no" as well as "yes"? Why do we throw up our hands and look for some all-purpose mechanistic solution to suppress the results of teen-age sexuality, rather than confront its causes? Giving a teen-age girl the Pill will not strengthen her will power or solve her social or emotional problems.

For more than 25 years I have worked with teen-age girls in trouble. And I have discovered that they would rather be given standards than contraceptives. Indeed, only recently I went to a center for teen-age girls where the teacher asked what they would like to discuss most. Human biology? Infant care? Physiology of childbirth? Family planning? The girls showed no interest. Then the

Reprinted from *Reader's Digest* with permission of the author.

teacher asked: "Would you like to discuss how to say 'no' to your boy friend without losing his love?" All hands shot up.

These girls want to believe in values. They are thirsting for someone to teach them. To tell them that, for their own good and the good of society, it is not wise for them to have sexual intercourse at 12, 13, 14, or 15. That sex at this age is not necessary for a caring relationship to develop and endure.

Teen-agers want their parents, their teachers, their political leaders to stand up strong for values. And this includes the values of love and sex. Wherever sex education is provided, we should insist that it contain a moral as well as a biological dimension—not only because it is what we want, it is what our children want.

To refuse to discuss the values that pervade our sexual relationships is to teach young people that this important human experience is not a matter for moral reflection and discourse.

We do not have to be heavy-handed and lay down rigid moralistic rules. Rather, we should discuss what it means to love and care for one another. To trust and be trusted. We should raise the questions central to all human relationships. What is selfishness? Loyalty? Character? What does it mean to be loved or to be used—and which are you?

Instead of locking teen-agers in their rooms, we should be repairing the shattered network of family communication whose breakdown is responsible for so much adolescent sexual activity. Within the family, we should make teen-agers feel less need to go elsewhere for love.

Let us offer our young people the chance to experience responsibility, caring and commitment: to reach beyond their own concerns. If they are lonely, let them visit old people in institutions who are more lonely. If they have nothing to do in their leisure time, let them go out and work for the powerless, the retarded, the sick, who would love to have someone come and read a newspaper or play a game. The young are waiting for challenges, and if we challenge them, they will respond.

It was the educator Robert Maynard Hutchins who said, "Intellectual virtues can be taught . . . moral virtues are formed by acts." If we do not involve our teen-agers in moral discourse, if we do not strengthen families, if we do not add a dimension of responsibility and control to sexuality, if we can do no more than propose technological solutions to an issue that concerns human life, what does this say about us?

One Point for Analysis: The conclusion not only summarizes the entire argument, it also looks out beyond the immediate topic by means of a rhetorical question.
Writing Topics:
1. Argue that morality can or cannot be legislated.
2. Argue that Shriver's thesis is unrealistic in light of current attitudes toward sex.
3. Select a quotation to be used as the basis of your thesis as Shriver uses Hutchins's statement for hers.

TWO PHILOSOPHIES FAR APART

JAMES J. KILPATRICK

James J. Kilpatrick, a politically conservative columnist, regularly airs his views on the CBS television program 60 Minutes.

Somewhere in this broad land you may find true-blue liberals who oppose racial-balance busing, and somewhere you may find true-blue conservatives who support it, but their numbers will be few. No issue in our public affairs today so clearly delineates the fundamental differences in our political philosophies.

The liberal, perceiving integration as a social good, believes that black children will benefit educationally, and that children of both races will benefit culturally, if they are brought together in a classroom experience. Because this will not occur voluntarily, at least to the extent he desires, it must be achieved by compulsion, by busing.

The conservative agrees that the state has an obligation to provide all children, as best it can, with substantially equal education opportunities. But the advocates of busing, a conservative would contend, are trading in values both false and doubtful. If the object is "to treat all children alike," busing fails at the outset: The first premise of busing is that children are not alike. John is white,

Reprinted by permission of Washington Star Syndicate, Inc.

Susan is black. The sole factor that determines their school assignment is this difference in the color of their skin.

To classify a child solely by race, in this most important aspect of his young life, is to engage in racism—state-sanctioned racism—not essentially different from the old southern school segregation. But there is something still more insulting in busing. It is the underlying assumption that black children will be improved if they sit beside white children.

The conservative finds nothing in the history of men or of governments to support any such theory. If schools must be constituted in terms of some precise racial mix, the very function of the school is perverted. Such a school ceases to be a school; it becomes a sociological mortar in which racist medicine is pounded. The whole concept is presumptuous, arrogant and self-defeating.

In the end, it comes down to the different perceptions that are held by liberals and conservatives of man and the state. The conservative's abiding rule is live and let live; the liberal thinks in terms of imposing life styles he defines as socially good. The conservative thinks of the child; the liberal thinks of children.

I do not believe America indefinitely will tolerate racial-balance busing. One of these days, black and white parents will rise up together to demand an end to this insane reordering of their lives, and we will have what the Supreme Court, in its more lucid moments, has said a free and equal people ought to have—not "white" schools or "black" schools, or neatly compounded, racially proportioned schools, but "just schools." Such a prospect may suggest a bad day for liberals, but it would be a great day for freedom.

One Point for Analysis: This essay is organized throughout by comparison and contrast.

Writing Topics:

1. Choose as a topic two opposing attitudes toward a single subject. Argue for one of them and against the other.
2. Using the *Fallacies* section of the Handbook, evaluate Kilpatrick's argument.
3. Argue for or against quotas to achieve racial balance in schools and professions.

FOR THE DEATH PENALTY

H. L. MENCKEN

H. L. Mencken was a writer for the Baltimore Sun *and editor, with George Jean Nathan, of* Smart Set *(1914–23). In much of his writing he deplores the genteel tradition in American letters.*

Of the arguments against capital punishment that issue from uplifters, two are commonly heard most often, to wit:

(1) That hanging a man (or frying him or gassing him) is a dreadful business, degrading to those who have to do it and revolting to those who have to witness it.
(2) That it is useless, for it does not deter others from the same crime.

The first of these arguments, it seems to me, is plainly too weak to need serious refutation. All it says, in brief, is that the work of the hangman is unpleasant. Granted. But suppose it is? It may be quite necessary to society for all that. There are, indeed, many other jobs that are unpleasant, and yet no one thinks of abolishing them—that of the plumber, that of the soldier, that of the garbage-man, that of the priest hearing confessions, that of the sand-hog, and so on. Moreover, what evidence is there that any actual hang-man complains of his work? I have heard none. On the contrary, I have known many who delighted in their ancient art, and practised it proudly.

In the second argument of the abolitionists there is rather more force, but even here, I believe, the ground under them is shaky. Their fundamental error consists in assuming that the whole aim of punishing criminals is to deter other (potential) criminals—that we hang or electrocute A simply in order to so alarm B that he will not kill C. This, I believe, is an assumption which confuses a part with the whole. Deterrence, obviously, is *one* of the aims of punishment, but it is surely not the only one. On the contrary, there are at least half a dozen, and some are probably quite as important. At least one of them, practically considered, is *more* important. Commonly, it is described as revenge, but revenge is really not the word for it. I borrow a better term from the late Aristotle: *katharsis*. *Katharsis*, so used, means a salubrious discharge of emotions, a healthy letting off of steam. A school-boy, disliking his teacher, deposits a tack upon the pedagogical chair; the teacher jumps and the boy laughs. This is *katharsis*. What I contend is that one of the prime objects of all judicial punishments is to afford the same grateful relief (a) to the immediate victims of the criminal punished, and (b) to the general body of moral and timorous men.

These persons, and particularly the first group, are concerned only indirectly with deterring other criminals. The thing they crave primarily is the satisfaction of seeing the criminal actually before them suffer as he made them suffer. What they want is the peace of mind that goes with the feeling that accounts are squared. Until they get that satisfaction they are in a state of emotional tension, and hence unhappy. The instant they get it they are comfortable. I do not argue that this yearning is noble; I simply argue that it is almost universal among human beings. In the face of injuries that are unimportant and can be borne without damage it may yield to higher impulses; that is to say, it may yield to what is called Christian charity. But when the injury is serious Christianity is adjourned, and even saints reach for their sidearms. It is plainly asking too much of human nature to expect it to conquer so natural an impulse. A keeps a store and has a bookkeeper, B. B steals $700, employs it in playing at dice or bingo, and is cleaned out. What is A to do? Let B go? If he does so he will be unable to sleep at night. The sense of injury, of injustice, of frustration will haunt him like pruritus. So he turns B over to the police, and they hustle B to prison. Thereafter A can sleep. More, he has pleasant dreams. He pictures B chained to the wall of a dungeon a hundred feet underground, devoured by rats and scorpions. It is so agreeable that it makes him forget his $700. He has got his *katharsis*.

The same thing precisely takes place on a larger scale when there is a crime which destroys a whole community's sense of security. Every law-abiding citizen feels menaced and frustrated until the criminals have been struck down—until the communal capacity to get even with them, and more than even, has been dramatically demonstrated. Here, manifestly, the business of deterring others is no more than an afterthought. The main thing is to destroy the

350

concrete scoundrels whose act has alarmed everyone, and thus made everyone unhappy. Until they are brought to book that unhappiness continues; when the law has been executed upon them there is a sigh of relief. In other words, there is *katharsis.*

I know of no public demand for the death penalty for ordinary crimes, even for ordinary homicides. Its infliction would shock all men of normal decency of feeling. But for crimes involving the deliberate and inexcusable taking of human life, by men openly defiant of all civilized order—for such crimes it seems, to nine men out of ten, a just and proper punishment. Any lesser penalty leaves them feeling that the criminal has got the better of society—that he is free to add insult to injury by laughing. That feeling can be dissipated only by a recourse to *katharsis,* the invention of the aforesaid Aristotle. It is more effectively and economically achieved, as human nature now is, by wafting the criminal to realms of bliss.

AN ANALYSIS OF "FOR THE DEATH PENALTY"

Clarity and order of presentation are the hallmarks of Mencken's essay "For the Death Penalty." The implication is not that Mencken makes no sound points in his argument; it is rather that the points, one of which is presented with a new twist, have been heard before and can best be justified by the maxim that repetition is the mother of studies.

The organization of the argument is immediately discerned in the simple enumeration of two points against capital punishment which Mencken will refute. The first, he feels, "is plainly too weak to need serious refutation," and he effectively dispels it in one paragraph. The second point, more complex and approached from a different angle, occupies the remainder of his essay. Mencken's argument against the second point revolves around the Aristotelian concept of katharsis, the purging of the emotions, especially those involved with sustained anxiety. Again through enumeration, he distinguishes two groups involved in his second response: the immediate victims of crime, who need a katharsis, and society in general, which must purge itself of the emotions conjured up by the heinous crimes of one of its members. Only death to the criminal can evoke the katharsis in both groups.

The "eye for an eye" concept immediately presents itself as outrageous both to some modern Jews and to some modern Christians. In answer, Mencken in his weakest argument contends that Christian charity ceases to exist when barbarous crimes are committed. To counter

351

Mencken, one need only to recall that Christ was crucified and forgave his enemies from the cross.

In the concluding paragraph Mencken momentarily qualifies his argument. He is not suggesting that all crimes be punished by death. But for serious crimes, death alone can bring about katharsis, a death that is "more effectively and economically achieved, as human nature now is, by wafting the criminal to realms of bliss." This concluding statement is disturbing. Either Mencken has needlessly shifted tone and thus seriously violated the integrity of the essay, or he is exhibiting uncalled-for black humor, which weakens his argument considerably because of its sudden occurrence. But the style of the essay is on the whole admirable.

For example, the second paragraph alternates between short and long sentences. This arrangement has a tendency to speed up the reader's pace. And this is what Mencken wants to do. He has disdain for the weakness of this particular objection to capital punishment, and he would like to dispense with it as quickly as possible.

The essay is written in formal Standard English, dotted with effective figurative language: "even saints reach for their sidearms"; a sense of injustice "will haunt him like pruritus"; we must "destroy the concrete scoundrels." It is a plea for capital punishment, not essentially as a deterrent to crime but as a means to allow victims and communal society to "blow off steam."

WHAT I HAVE LEARNED

WILL DURANT

Will Durant, along with Ariel Durant, undertook some years ago to write the history of civilization. The eight-volume series is called the Story of Civilization.

To this day I believe that there is as much love as hostility in the world, animal as well as human. Even in the small circle of my acquaintances, I have found a surprising number of happy marriages and so much incidental kindness that I have quite lost my faith in the wickedness of mankind.

The reading of Darwin in my eighteenth year, and then of Schopenhauer and Herbert Spencer, shook both my optimism and my religious faith and left me struggling with a dreary determinism in which, despite pleasant interludes, nothing seemed certain but grief and death. For a time the brave books of Peter Kropotkin gave me hope that man had learned to moderate competition with cooperation—in the family, village, assembly, law and police, states and alliances; but I soon learned that all these forms of mutual aid were designed to meet the competition of other groups; the struggle for existence involved larger unities, but competition remained the ultimate reality, war was the final judge, and Darwin seemed victorious over Christ.

I need not point out that the decline of religious belief has seriously undermined social order. There have, of course, been other causes: the passage from agriculture to industry, from the watchful surveillance of village neighbors to the protective anonymity of the individual in the city crowd, from the natural discipline of the family farm to the loosened parental authority in the city apartment; the separation of a divided religion and the schools; the enfeeblement of a public opinion that does not know what to believe or what to condemn. . . . Relieved from moral limitations, popular literature became a school for scandal and a textbook of sexual anatomy and skill. "Liberated" artists scorned to convey beauty or meaning and repudiated the disciplined art that gives lasting form to transient significance. An odor of more than physical decay rose from our city streets.

In 1963 I made myself an angry Amos or Jeremiah and wrote, and now say to you:

"We have been silent too long; and part of our tardy righteousness may well be due to the lessened flow of sap in our flesh. No matter; let us speak out. Let us say humbly, but publicly, that we resent corruption in politics, dishonesty in business, faithlessness in marriage, pornography in literature and the theater, coarseness in language, chaos in music, meaninglessness in art.

"It is time for all good men to come to the aid of their party, whose name is civilization."

But I will not end on this plaintive note. I still believe in you, and in America, and in Europe, to which I owe so much. I stand with those Americans who wish to reconcile liberty with order, and with those Russians who wish to reconcile order with liberty. I sympathize with a President who faces every day a dozen problems, any one of which demands exclusive and complete attention. I believe that our present Congress is as high in education, intelligence, and

353

integrity as any Congress in our history. I believe that in this century America has made more progress, except in morals and manners, than most of us in our youth had the audacity to expect; and that it will continue to face crises bravely, to survive, and to grow. I believe that there is a creative spirit in the universe—in every atom, in every plant and animal, in every man and woman—a spirit evident in history, despite every setback and disaster. I believe that the human heritage, in technology, government, education, literature, science, and art, is greater than ever before, is better protected, and more widely spread, than ever.

Let us admit half of the terrible picture that Jonathan Swift drew of humanity; let us agree that in every generation of man's history, and almost everywhere, we find superstition, hypocrisy, corruption, cruelty, crime, and war; in the balance against them we place the long roster of poets, composers, artists, scientists, philosophers, and saints. That same species upon which poor Swift revenged the frustration of his flesh wrote the plays of Shakespeare, the music of Bach and Handel, the odes of Keats, the *Republic* of Plato, the *Principia* of Newton, and the *Ethics* of Spinoza; it built the Parthenon and painted the ceiling of the Sistine Chapel; it conceived and cherished, even if it crucified, Christ. Man did all this; let him never despair.

One Point for Analysis: The many allusions used by Durant make the writer sound worthy of respect and attention.

Writing Topics:

1. Argue against Durant that the freedom of the "New Morality" indicates progress, not decline.
2. Argue for or against Durant's idea that art must be disciplined if it is to give "lasting form to transient significance."
3. Using the balanced sentences of the third paragraph as models for imitation, discuss those forces that you believe have maintained (not undermined) the social order.

354

CAN SOCIETY BANISH CRUELTY?

J. H. PLUMB

J. H. Plumb has been involved in the teaching of history in England and has published The Horizon Book of the Renaissance *and* Man Versus Society in Eighteenth-Century Britain. *He believes that history should be a part of the literary culture of both America and England.*

No one can doubt that cruelty is a major obscenity of modern life. A woman of eighty is thrown over a railing in Central Park and raped; a small girl is murdered for sexual pleasure; an old man is bayoneted to death for the sake of five dollars. "Snuff films," which progress from mass sex to the deliberate murder and dismemberment of the "actress," are rumored to be displayed in New York City for $200 a seat. Leaving aside the organized violence of war, are we as individuals more cruel than our ancestors? Are we more wanton in our infliction of pain?

On January, 1757, Robert François Damiens made a feeble attempt to assassinate Louis XV of France. Though his small knife barely penetrated the king's thick winter clothes, causing little more than a four-inch scratch, Damiens was caught and tortured to make him name his accomplices. He had none. Then he became the centerpiece of a theatre of cruelty. The philosopher La Condamine, for one, was so fascinated by the prospect of such an extravagant spectacle that he got himself a place on the scaffold to watch the victim. He was part of a huge audience that paid exorbitant prices to see Damiens's flesh pulled off with red-hot pincers and his battered body pulled apart by horses. After that the Parisians—aristocrats, bourgeoisie, and workingmen alike—went back to their dinners.

True, this execution was rather more elaborately staged than most in the eighteenth century, but it was highly traditional. Damiens's executioners had carefully copied, with scrupulous attention to detail, the way François Ravaillac, the assassin of Henry IV, had been put to death in 1610. The French, however, must not be regarded as peculiarly ferocious. The treatment of traitors in England, a method of execution that had first been used against Catholic priests in

From Horizon, 1976, American Heritage Publishing Co., Inc. Reprinted by permission of the author.

Queen Elizabeth's reign, was particularly horrifying. Before a vast crowd in a carnival-like atmosphere, the traitor was hanged, but taken down while still alive; then his genitals were cut off and stuffed in his mouth, he was disemboweled, and finally his head was cut off and his trunk quartered. The head, stuck on a pike, would festoon Temple Bar for years; sometimes the quarters were sent to decorate provincial cities.

These were but upsurges in an ocean of cruelty. Several times a year huge crowds swarmed to Tyburn (near Marble Arch in London) to watch and enjoy the executions by hanging of men and women, youths and girls, turned off the ladder into eternity for minor robberies and petty pilfering, as well as murder and mayhem. Such sadism was not merely an occasional visual thrill, for cruelty had been deeply embedded in western European society for centuries and was still to be for a century or so more. It was a constant theme of everyday life, a continuing event of family experience.

Cruelty to animals was widespread—one might say total. Cocks fought each other to the death, bulls and bears were baited by specially trained dogs; cats were sewn up in effigies of the pope to create realistic howls when they were burned. Oxen and horses were driven and flogged until they died. And yet animals were not treated much worse than infants or small children.

The callous behavior of parents and adults to infants in seventeenth-century England or eighteenth-century France is scarcely credible. The women of the poor suckled for a trade, getting as many babies to a meager breast as they could. Naturally their own child was fed first; often the other sucklings were half starved, and frequently hand fed on an appalling diet of pap—a little flour and water. The broken-down hovels to which babies were consigned for wet-nursing were as dirty as they were pitiable. Often there was a dung heap at the door to give warmth, and the floor was strewn with filth of every kind.

Swaddling was universal. Newborn babies were stretched out on a board, a piece of diaper stuck between their thighs, and then were strapped down so tight that they could not move. Swaddled infants were frequently hung up on pegs on the wall and left there, and, of course, they lived in their own feces and urine until they were reswaddled. It is not surprising, therefore, that the death of an infant was an event of small consequence and of exceptional

356

frequency—50 per cent of all infants died before they were a year old.

Childhood was little better. Children were remorselessly flogged. A middle-class child in England was required to stand whenever he was in the presence of his parents and would be savagely punished if he did not. The children of the poor were expected to work as soon as they could walk and were often driven from home to work when little more than seven or eight. Born and bred in a world of callous brutality, the men and women of those days took torture and dismemberment in their stride, were indifferent to the horrors of slavery and the slave trade, and thought nothing of tormenting an idiot or an animal or throwing a witch onto a bonfire.

And then, about 1700, attitudes among the prosperous commercial classes in England began to change, for reasons that are difficult to comprehend. John Locke protested against swaddling and child beating and argued powerfully that mothers should suckle their own children. Hogarth's satirical prints show that by 1750 hatred of cruelty had a market. Take a long look at his bitter satire *The Four Stages of Cruelty*, in which animals are being flogged to death or tortured, or children casually killed. One print in this series, *Cruelty in Perfection*, depicts a savage and murderous rape. The very fact that Hogarth satirized cruelty shows that there were some flickers of sensitivity to horror.

Men and women formed societies to prevent the worst exploitation of child labor—the young chimney sweeps; they banded together against the slave trade; they helped suppress the most savage type of blood sports. In children's books after 1740, the horrors of cruelty to birds and animals, to fellow human beings, are stressed over and over again. Children were taught to regard cruelty as evil, as sinful. The result was the great wave of humanitarianism that swept Europe and America in the nineteenth century. Wherever we look we find a positive gain over cruelty: public executions largely vanished, torture was stopped. Of course, and this must be stressed, a great tide of cruelty remained, but it was steadily diminishing.

The fight against cruelty was long and arduous; it was largely the campaign of a social and cultural elite whose greatest success may have been in conditioning their own children in the horrors of cruelty. This attitude never permeated the whole of society or restrained the behavior of governments. Its influence was always frag-

357

ile, and in this century cruelty has been widespread and growing toward individuals and toward classes of men and women. True, in previous centuries there would not have been the twentieth-century storms of protest against the more outrageous forms of government cruelty; neither are the worst excesses of personal cruelty allowed to flourish unchecked. But we have no cause to congratulate ourselves, for the position is insecure, and permitting the pornography of violence, which stirs deep and dangerous emotions, is a risk that society can ill afford.

And yet, maybe we should worry more about children's books, which seem singularly devoid of overt morality. Perhaps we are too concerned with the happiness of the child, rather than with the community's happiness with him. Most children are instinctively cruel to animals, and sensitivity toward pain and suffering must be taught. At the same time, the adult world should take a far sterner view of cruelty than it currently does. We need to think clearly about it; we ought to think more carefully about what ought to be forbidden and what not. Surely, there would be no greater folly than to suppress all pornography simply because some of it extols violence. But certainly a good place to start would be the prohibition of *wanton* infliction of pain on another human being.

One Point for Analysis: After the introductory paragraph, Plumb goes back in time, organizing his information chronologically and ending in the present.

Writing Topics:
1. Argue that cruelty to children is one of the greatest crimes of our society.
2. Argue for or against the assertion that at times one must be cruel only to be kind.
3. Order the discussion of a subject chronologically, ending with an argument concerning its contemporary status.

PLAYBOYS AND BUNNIES

HUGH M. HEFNER

*Hugh M. Hefner speaks with ultimate authority about the phi-
losophy of* Playboy *magazine and the other Playboy enterprises.*

PLAYBOY's over-all point of view on the male-female relationship
in society certainly doesn't limit women to the role of Bunnies in
The Playboy Club. Essentially, what we are saying, editorially in
the magazine, is that men and women should each have *separate*
identities—that they are both happiest when their roles complement rather than compete with each other.

Since the turn of the century, there has been a considerable
breakdown in the cultural patterns that distinguish the sexes—
especially here in America—causing us to drift toward an asexual
society, in which it becomes increasingly difficult for either sex to
find true satisfaction or fulfillment in its interpersonal relationships
with the other. This is one of the two primary causes, I believe—the
other being the increasing complexity and automation of our civilization—for the erosion of individual identity that was mentioned
earlier.

Since PLAYBOY is a magazine for men, it is natural for us to place
most of our emphasis on the problem of male identity. PLAYBOY
stresses a strongly heterosexual concept of society—in which the
separate roles of men and women are clearly defined and compati-
ble. Though we are sometimes accused of having a dehumanized
view of women, our concept actually offers the female a far more
human identity than she has had historically in the Western world.

It is our religious tradition that has tended to look upon woman
as a depersonalized object, or possession, by continually associating her with its antagonism toward sex. Sometimes the emphasis
has been placed upon the temptation to sin in womankind and
sometimes the emphasis has been placed upon feminine purity and
chastity; but whether they were considered creatures of the Devil,
or placed upon a pedestal, their status in our antisexual society has
always been that of an *object*, rather than a *human being*.

359

One Point for Analysis: The careful reader will recognize a number of fallacies in Hefner's argument. (See *Fallacies,* Handbook.)

Writing Topics:
   1. Argue that the existence of *Playboy* magazine justifies *Playgirl.*
   2. Argue for or against the dictum that "a woman's place is in the home."
   3. Citing specific fallacies, argue that Hefner's essay lacks convincing logic.

SOLVE THAT PROBLEM—WITH HUMOR

WILLIAM D. ELLIS

Despite his statements on humor in this essay, Ellis has commented that the "assumption of a writing career carries responsibility beyond entertainment."

A lot of us lose life's tougher confrontations by mounting a frontal attack—when a touch of humor might well enable us to chalk up a win. Consider the case of a young friend of mine, who hit a traffic jam en route to work shortly after receiving an ultimatum about being late on the job. Although there was a good reason for Sam's chronic tardiness—serious illness at home—he decided that this by-now-familiar excuse wouldn't work any longer. His supervisor was probably already pacing up and down with a dismissal speech rehearsed.

He was. Sam entered the office at 9:35. The place was as quiet as a loser's locker room; everyone was hard at work. Sam's supervisor approached him. Suddenly, Sam forced a grin and shoved out his hand. "How do you do!" he said. "I'm Sam Maynard. I'm applying for a job I understand became available just 35 minutes ago. Does the early bird get the worm?"

The room exploded in laughter. The supervisor clamped off a smile and walked back to his office. Sam Maynard had saved his job—with the only tool that could win, a laugh.

Humor is a most effective, yet frequently neglected, means of handling the difficult situations in our lives. It can be used for patching up differences, apologizing, saying "no," criticizing, getting the other fellow to do what you want without his losing face. For some jobs, it's the *only* tool that can succeed. It is a way to discuss subjects so sensitive that serious dialogue may start a riot. For example, many believe that comedians on television are doing more today for racial and religious tolerance than are people in any other forum.

Humor is often the best way to keep a small misunderstanding from escalating into a big deal. Recently a neighbor of mine had a squabble with his wife as she drove him to the airport. Airborne, he felt miserable, and he knew she did, too. Two hours after she returned home, she received a long-distance phone call. "Person-to-person for Mrs. I. A. Pologize," intoned the operator. "That's spelled 'P' as in. . . ." In a twinkling, the whole day changed from grim to lovely at both ends of the wire.

An English hostess with a quick wit was giving a formal dinner for eight distinguished guests whom she hoped to enlist in a major charity drive. Austerity was *de rigueur* in England at the time, and she had drafted her children to serve the meal. She knew that anything could happen—and it did, just as her son, with the studied concentration of a tightrope walker, brought in a large roast turkey. He successfully elbowed the swinging dining-room door, but the backswing deplattered the bird onto the dining-room floor.

The boy stood rooted: guests stared at their plates. Moving only her head the hostess smiled at her son. "No harm, Daniel," she said. "Just pick him up and take him back to the kitchen"—she enunciated clearly so he would think about what she was saying—"and bring in the *other* one."

A wink and a one-liner instantly changed the dinner from a red-faced embarrassment to a conspiracy of fun.

The power of humor to dissolve a hostile confrontation often lies in its unspoken promise: "You let me off the hook, my friend, and I'll let you off." The trick is to assign friendly motives to your opponent, to smile just a little—but not too much. Canada's Governor-General Roland Michener, master of the technique, was about to inspect a public school when he was faced with a truculent picket line of striking maintenance personnel. If he backed away from the line, he would seriously diminish his office's image; if he crossed it, he might put the government smack into a hot labor issue.

While he pondered the matter, more strikers gathered across his path. Suddenly, the graying pencil-line mustache on Michener's weathered face stretched a little in Cheshirean complicity. "How very nice of you all to turn out to see me!" he boomed. "Thank you. Shall we go in?" The line parted and, by the time the pickets began to chuckle, the governor-general was striding briskly up the school steps.

Next time you find yourself in an ethnically awkward situation, take a lesson from the diplomatic delegates to Europe's Common Market. In the course of history, nearly every member nation has been invaded or betrayed by at least one of the others, and the Market's harmony must be constantly buttressed. One method is the laugh based on national caricatures. Recently, a new arrival at Market headquarters in Brussels introduced himself as a minister for the Swiss navy. Everybody laughed. The Swiss delegate retorted, "Well, why not? Italy has a minister of finance."

Of course, humor is often more than a laughing matter. In its more potent guises, it has a Trojan-horse nature: no one goes on guard against a gag; we let it in because it looks like a little wooden toy. Once inside, however, it can turn a city to reform, to rebellion, to resistance. Some believe, for instance, that, next to the heroic British RAF, British humor did the most to fend off German take-over in World War II. One sample will suffice: that famous story of the woman who was finally extracted from the rubble of her house during the London blitz. Asked, "Where is your husband?" she brushed brick dust off her head and arms and answered, "Fighting in Libya, the bloody coward!"

Similarly, whenever we Americans start taking ourselves a bit too seriously, a grassroots humor seems to rise and strew banana peels in our path. The movement is usually led by professionals: Mark Twain penlancing the boils of pomposity ("Man was made at the end of the week's work, when God was tired."); Will Rogers deflating our lawmakers ("The oldest boy became a Congressman, and the second son turned out no good, too."); Bill Mauldin needling fatuous officers (One 2nd lieutenant to another, on observing a beautiful sunset: "Is there one for enlisted men, too?"). Such masters of comic deflation restore the balance. They bring us back to ourselves.

When life has us in a tight corner, one of the first questions we might ask is, "Can I solve this with a laugh?" Men with giant responsibilities have frequently used this approach to solve giant problems—often with sweeping effect. As Gen. George C. Marshall, U.S. Army Chief of Staff, labored to prepare this then-unready nation to enter World War II, he met stiff opposition from his commander-in-chief regarding the elements that called for the most bolstering. Marshall felt that what we needed most were highly developed ground forces. President Roosevelt was a Navy man who believed that our principal need was for a powerful navy, plus a large air force. In increasingly tense debates with the President, Marshall pushed his argument so hard that he began to foster ever stronger resistance. Finally, during a particularly hot session, the usually stonefaced Marshall forced a grin. "At least, Mr. President," he said, "you might stop referring to the Navy as *'us'* and the Army as *'them.'* "

Roosevelt studied Marshall over his glasses, then unlipped a great show of teeth and laughter. Shortly thereafter, he made a more objective study of Marshall's recommendations and eventually bought the ground-force concept.

Occasionally, humor goes beyond saving arguments, saving face or saving jobs; it can save life itself. Viktor E. Frankl was a psychiatrist imprisoned in a German concentration camp during World War II. As the shrinking number of surviving prisoners descended to new depths of hell, Frankl and his closest prisoner friend sought desperately for ways to keep from dying. Piled on top of malnutrition, exhaustion and disease, suicidal despair was the big killer in these citadels of degradation.

As a psychiatrist, Frankl knew that humor was one of the soul's best survival weapons, since it can create, if only for moments, aloofness from horror. Therefore, Frankl made a rule that once each day he and his friend must invent and tell an amusing anecdote, specifically about something which could happen after their liberation.

Others were caught up in the contagion of defiant laughter. One starving prisoner forecast that in the future he might be at a prestigious formal dinner, and when the soup was being served, he would shatter protocol by imploring the hostess, "Ladle it from the *bottom!*"

Frankl tells of another prisoner, who nodded toward one of the most despised *capos*—favored prisoners who acted as guards and became as arrogant as the SS men. "Imagine!" he quipped. I knew him when he was only the president of a bank!"

If humor can be used successfully against such odds, what can't you and I do with it in daily life?

One Point for Analysis: The abundant use of examples gives Ellis's essay clarity.

Writing Topics:

1. Argue by example that humor has solved some of your personal problems.
2. Argue that for many people humor is not a possible solution to problems.
3. Imply a controversial thesis through narration.

A MOTHER SPEAKS FOR AMNESTY

PEG MULLEN

Peg Mullen's personal approach to persuasion makes her discussion a moving and convincing one. The subjective tone underscores what she has to say.

Four years ago in Vietnam my 25-year-old son, Michael Mullen, was killed—by our own artillery. In military terminology, he was a "non-battle casualty" of "friendly fire" in a "misadventure."

With this in mind, it may seem strange that I support amnesty for those who refused, in one way or another, to fight in Vietnam. But I do.

We are an ordinary Iowa farm family, and I am without political experience, so I speak plainly. I know and accept what some politicians are still unwilling to admit—that the war which took my son was a senseless, terrible, tragic blunder. That blunder is now being compounded by punishing further those young men who were wise and brave enough not to be deluded by the war from the beginning.

Like the shelling which killed my son, the Vietnam war was itself a "misadventure." Only those who lost sons, brothers or husbands in it can really understand the depth of my anguish and bitterness. How I would like to believe that my son's life was not wasted—that he died for some high ideal! Amnesty for others would provide a little comfort.

Reprinted by permission of the author.

If some members of Congress—and the President—insist on misinterpreting amnesty as pardon, then the question may remain too emotionally charged ever to be resolved. Amnesty, in the original Greek, meant forgetfulness. Pardon implies guilt.

I would no more expect a young man who refused to kill in Vietnam—whose moral or spiritual opposition to the war left him no alternative but to leave the country—to admit he was guilty of a crime than I would expect Congress, which allowed the war to endure for so long at so great a cost, to admit it, too, was guilty.

What we need is not blame, but forgetfulness. Forget the inequities of the draft. Forget the lies told by Presidents, the generals, the spokesmen for the State Department and the Pentagon. Forget the moral and philosophical dilemmas posed by Vietnam. Instead, let us remember that the American people have suffered enough and that some of us want our children home.

It is hard to believe anymore in that old maxim: "My country, right or wrong." Instead, if our country is wrong, we have an obligation as citizens to correct the wrong. Who is the more loyal citizen, the one who agonizes over his nation's policies and attempts to change them or the one who docilely accepts government policy—no matter how immoral or misguided?

If it is the former, then we cannot possibly continue to punish those young Americans whose unwillingness to take part in the war was based on a higher sense of allegiance and responsibility to America's ideals. If, however, the mark of good citizenship is docile submission to government policy, then those who fled the country were indeed wrong. By the same token, so were the judgments at Nuremburg—the Germans who followed orders should not have been punished.

In 1964 we the American people elected a President who spoke out against escalation but actually widened the war. That election occurred six years before my son's death. If, as some believe, young men who refused to serve in Vietnam abandoned America in her time of need, what of Congress during those six years? By allowing the war to escalate and go on and on, did it not abandon us in *our* time of need?

What difference is there between a government which forces its dissidents to seek exile and a government which exiles its dissidents? Today, Canada, Sweden and other countries in Europe have taken in many young American Solzhenitsyns.

365

If I am to believe that my son sacrificed his life for a high ideal—if I am to receive some comfort from his death—I want to believe that he died so that some other mother's son might now come home.

One Point for Analysis: The author concludes her argument by asking rhetorical questions that push the reader into defining his own opinions on the subject.

Writing Topics:

1. Argue that the process of hiding the truth by using softer terms (e.g., "friendly fire" and "misadventure") can be dishonest practice.
2. Construct an argument that, like this one, is effective because it is an emotional one.
3. Argue that the individual who accepts government policy adds to the stability of the society.

HERE BE DRAGONS

JAMES LIPTON

James Lipton has been a successful writer for Broadway and television. He is also the author of An Exaltation of Larks.

The heretical thought began to take shape at the IN gate of the horse-show arena as I watched an ambulance crew crouch over the motionless figure of the prostrate rider, while the fences that had been battered down by his falling horse were hastily reassembled. For *my* horse. And me.

That's when the voice, sounding suspiciously like my own, whispered, "Are you *really* going into that ring?" The Boy Scout practicing granny knots in my alimentary canal threw another loop around my stomach and pulled. "Feel that?" the voice growled. "It's fear!" . . .

Centuries ago, when a cartographer ran out of known world before he ran out of parchment, he is said to have inscribed the words "Here be dragons" at the edge of the ominously blank *terra incognita,* a signal to the voyager that he entered the unknown region at his peril. But for some, like Columbus and Magellan, the warning seems to have been not a deterrent but a goad.

Long before Columbus probed the world's edge, the Chinese, seeking an ideograph to represent the turning point we call "crisis" in English, performed a miracle of linguistic compression by combining two existing characters, the symbols for "danger" and "opportunity," to create the character "wei-ji," which stands as an eternal assertion that, since opportunity and danger are inseparable, it is impossible to make a significant forward move *without* encountering danger; and, obversely, the scent of danger should alert us to the fact that we may be headed in the right direction.

I am fully aware that this notion flies straight in the face of a precept that has been drilled into most of us since we were first warned not to touch a stove or climb a tree. Danger, we have been taught, is a clear signal to turn *back*. But it has recently occurred to me that our filtered, homogenized lives, like white bread and refined sugar, are not only bland but unhealthful and, of all the vital elements that have been refined out of them, one of the most sorely missed is hazard.

I mean *real* hazard, not the broadside of sado-masochism and *machismo* assaulting us from screen and tube and printed page. Our apparent hunger for manufactured violence is, in my view, a symptom of the malnutrition that has resulted from the lack of genuine challenge in our daily diet. Lacking challenge, we seek "excitement." Finding excitement unsatisfying, we look for "thrills." If pulled punches, blank cartridges and simulated agony pall, we can shift, for the mere price of a ticket, to the more vivid precinct of arena or stadium, where the blood is real, the bone sometimes actually snaps, the flesh is truly assailed. And if all else fails, there is Evel Knievel, putting his life on the line. For real. For money. For *us!*

What are the common denominators in all these experiences? First, we face every one of them sitting down, literally and figuratively. Second, in every instance the blood, bone and flesh are someone else's. Whether the agony is real or simulated, on tube or turf, it *isn't ours*. We are buying or borrowing someone else's jeopardy, because, I believe, we crave the stimulation of challenge, we are starved for the elemental exhilaration of fear, which triggers biochemical changes in us, making us suddenly intensely aware of our own existence.

Socrates warned that the unexamined life isn't worth living. Neither, I submit, is the unexperienced life.

Before I am accused of advocating Russian roulette for subteens and hang-gliding for the geriatric set, let me define precisely what I mean by hazard. I am speaking of the kind of risk-taking that seems to be involved in the conscious abandonment of safe physical, emotional and intellectual redoubts, in favor of new paths where dragons may lie in wait. I am sacrilegiously equating a state of fear with a state of grace, *if* the fear results from testing treasured beliefs and established patterns—one's own, not someone else's. Finally, I am advocating a reconditioned reflex that can begin to take a kind of perverse delight in the sensation of fear, and see looming danger as a beckoning finger . . .

Like the ringmaster's finger, beckoning me through the open IN gate. The horse, feeling my fear, as horses can, nickered and backed a step. That's when I heard the second voice, emerging from the dying wail of the departing ambulance. "Feel that?" the voice said. *"That's why you're here."*

I wish to attach no undue significance to that unexceptional moment in an unremarkable life. All I can say with any certainty is that, since then, fear has become a different kind of signal for me, a green (or at least amber) light instead of a red one. The results, by anyone's standards but my own, would probably be judged unspectacular. But I remain convinced that something changed in me at that IN gate. I believe it because my horse, sensitive as always to its rider's emotional state, suddenly stopped backing, contracted like an accordion and bounded into the ring, as strangely intrigued by the hazards ahead as I was.

There have been many fences since then—of wood, words, critical eyes, alien minds—some cleared in a bound, some missed with a clatter, but all approached with the same mixture of fear and elation that gripped me in that arena, and haunts me now at the thought of what these wise or foolish words may evoke in you as you read them. A loud, clear voice is saying, "Tear them up," and that of course is an unmistakable signal that I have written myself into risk. *Here* be dragons. Good.

One Point for Analysis: The introductory paragraph immediately seizes the reader's attention by presenting a suspenseful scene.

Writing Topics:
1. Construct an argument in which a beast (other than a dragon) stands as a metaphor for a type of experience that you advocate.
2. Lipton states that the ancient Chinese considered danger and opportunity to be related experiences. Argue that one cannot experience joy without experiencing sadness.
3. Argue that vicariously experiencing emotion through television leads to a paralysis of the will.

FOUR LETTER WORDS CAN HURT YOU

BARBARA LAWRENCE

Barbara Lawrence is a New Englander who was educated at Connecticut College and at New York University. She has taught at the State University of New York at Old Westbury.

Why should any words be called obscene? Don't they all describe natural human functions? Am I trying to tell them, my students demand, that the "strong, earthy, gut-honest"—or, if they are fans of Norman Mailer, the "rich, liberating, existential"—language they use to describe sexual activity isn't preferable to "phony-sounding, middle-class words like 'intercourse' and 'copulate'?" "Cop You Late!" they say with fancy inflections and gagging grimaces. "Now, what is *that* supposed to mean?"

Well, what is it supposed to mean? And why indeed should one group of words describing human functions and human organs be acceptable in ordinary conversation and another, describing presumably the same organs and functions, be tabooed—so much so, in fact, that some of these words still cannot appear in print in many parts of the English-speaking world?

The argument that these taboos exist only because of "sexual hangups" (middle-class, middle-age, feminist), or even that they are a result of class oppression (the contempt of the Norman conquerors for the language of their Anglo-Saxon serfs), ignores a

369

much more likely explanation, it seems to me, and that is the sources and functions of the words themselves.

The best known of the tabooed sexual verbs, for example, comes from the German *ficken*, meaning "to strike"; combined, according to Partridge's etymological dictionary *Origins*, with the Latin sexual verb *futuere*; associated in turn with the Latin *fustis*, "a staff or cudgel"; the Celtic *buc*, "a point, hence to pierce"; the Irish *bot*, "the male member"; the Latin *battuere*, "to beat"; the Gaelic *batair*, "a cudgeller"; the Early Irish *bualaim*, "I strike"; and so forth. It is one of what etymologists sometimes call "the sadistic group of words for the man's part in copulation."

The brutality of this word, then, and its equivalents ("screw," "bang," etc.), is not an illusion of the middle class or a crotchet of Women's Liberation. In their origins and imagery these words carry undeniably painful, if not sadistic, implications, the object of which is almost always female. Consider, for example, what a "screw" actually does to the wood it penetrates; what a painful, even mutilating, activity this kind of analogy suggests. "Screw" is particularly interesting in this context, since the noun, according to Partridge, comes from words meaning "groove," "nut," "ditch," "breeding sow," "scrofula" and "swelling," while the verb, besides its explicit imagery, has antecedent associations to "write on," "scratch," "scarify," and so forth—a revealing fusion of a mechanical or painful action with an obviously denigrated object.

Not all obscene words, of course, are as implicitly sadistic or denigrating to women as these, but all that I know seem to serve a similar purpose: to reduce the human organism (especially the female organism) and human functions (especially sexual and procreative) to their least organic, most mechanical dimension; to substitute a trivializing or deforming resemblance for the complex human reality of what is being described.

Tabooed male descriptives, when they are not openly denigrating to women, often serve to divorce a male organ or function from any significant interaction with the female. Take the word "testes," for example, suggesting "witnesses" (from the Latin *testis*) to the sexual and procreative strengths of the male organ; and the obscene counterpart of this word, which suggests little more than a mechanical shape. Or compare almost any of the "rich," "liberating" sexual verbs, so fashionable today among male writers, with that much-derided Latin word "copulate" ("to bind or join together") or even

370

that Anglo-Saxon phrase (which seems to have had no trouble surviving the Norman Conquest) "make love."

How arrogantly self-involved the tabooed words seem in comparison to either of the other terms, and how contemptuous of the female partner. Understandably so, of course, if she is only a "skirt," a "broad," a "chick," a "pussycat" or a "piece." If she is, in other words, no more than her skirt, or what her skirt conceals; no more than a breeder, or the broadest part of her; no more than a piece of a human being or a "piece of tail."

The most severely tabooed of all the female descriptives, incidentally, are those like a "piece of tail," which suggest (either explicitly or through antecedents) that there is no significant difference between the female channel through which we are all conceived and born and the anal outlet common to both sexes—a distinction that pornographers have always enjoyed obscuring.

This effort to deny women their biological identity, their individuality, their humanness, is such an important aspect of obscene language that one can only marvel at how seldom, in an era preoccupied with definitions of obscenity, this fact is brought to our attention. One problem, of course, is that many of the people in the best position to do this (critics, teachers, writers) are so reluctant today to admit that they are angered or shocked by obscenity. Bored, maybe, unimpressed, aesthetically displeased, but—no matter how brutal or denigrating the material—never angered, never shocked.

And yet how eloquently angered, how piously shocked many of these same people become if denigrating language is used about any minority group other than women; if the obscenities are racial or ethnic, that is, rather than sexual. Words like "coon," "kike," "spic," "wop," after all, deform identity, deny individuality and humanness in almost exactly the same way that sexual vulgarisms and obscenities do.

No one that I know, least of all my students, would fail to question the values of a society whose literature and entertainment rested heavily on racial or ethnic pejoratives. Are the values of a society whose literature and entertainment rest as heavily as ours on sexual pejoratives any less questionable?

One Point for Analysis: The parentheses are a sort of shorthand that enables Lawrence to tighten the structure of the essay.

Writing Topics:

1. Argue that the four letter words Lawrence discusses no longer carry with them their original pejorative meanings.
2. Argue that a civilized person should or should not be offended by obscene language.
3. Argue that language taboos associated with death are or are not sociologically desirable.

6

A PRACTICAL HANDBOOK

ABBREVIATIONS (ab)

1. The following abbreviations are acceptable in your essays.
   a. A.M. or a.m./P.M. or p.m.
   b. A.D./B.C.
   c. Dr. (doctor) and St. (saint) when used with proper names
      (Dr. Mann)
      Note: The following are acceptable when they precede the
      entire name or the initials and last name of a person, but
      not before the last name alone: Prof., Sen., Rep., Gen.,
      Capt., Lt., Sgt., Hon. *Ex:* Sen. Paul T. Nolan or Gen. A.
      Fields, but not Sen. Nolan or Gen. Fields
   d. e.g.   (for example)
   e. i.e.   (that is)
   f. Inc.   (Dartez and Reed, Inc.)
   g. Jr. or Sr. when following someone's name (Joseph Riehl,
      Jr.) but not when referring to juniors and seniors in high
      school or college
   h. Mr.   (pl. Messrs.)
   i. Mrs.   (pl. Mmes.)
   j. Ms.
   k. Organizations and agencies if they are recognized by their
      abbreviations (NATO, FBI)
   l. vs.   (versus)   *Ex:* man vs. his environment
2. Do *not* abbreviate the following in your formal essays although
   they are acceptable in less formal writing.
   a. avenue   (Patterson Ave.)
   b. company   (Katie B. Davis Wrecking Co.)

374

  c. countries (U.S.)

  d. days of the week (Thurs.)

  e. months of the year (Sept. 21)

  f. mountain (Byrne Mt.)

  g. park (Bolivar Lee Pk.)

  h. parkway (Pontremoli Pkwy.)

  i. road (Rickels Rd.)

  j. river (Kitty Riv.)

  k. states' names (LA, TX)

  l. street (Rex St.)

  m. units of measure (lb., in., ft.)

3. Although you will probably not use the following abbreviations in the essays you will write, they are nevertheless often found in essays based on research.

  a. c. ca. (around or about) *Ex:* Aristophanes was born c. 450 B.C.

  b. cf. (compare) *Ex:* The drama of Aeschylus relied heavily on the chorus (cf. drama of Euripides).

  c. chap. (chapter)

  d. ex. (example)

  e. l. (line) ll. (lines) *Ex:* l. 64; ll. 64–72

  f. p. (page) pp. (pages) *Ex:* p. 64; pp. 64–72

  g. N.B. (note well) *Ex:* N.B. these abbreviations are usually confined to research papers.

AMBIGUITY (amb)

Ambiguity is lack of clarity, usually due to unclear pronoun reference or vague words.

 Ex: John talked to both his father and brother. He told him to cut the grass. (In the second sentence, who is *he?* Who is *him?*)

 Ex: Singing and dancing until early in the morning, the party was a great success.

 Ex: Stepping into the street, the car hit me.

Obviously, the party did not sing and dance, nor did the car step into the street. *Singing and dancing until early in the morning* and *Stepping into the street* are called *dangling phrases* because the word or words they modify do not directly follow them. *Correction:* Stepping into the street, I was hit by a car.

Clarity demands a correct positioning of the adverb.

Ex: She asked only $53,000 for her house.

Ex: She asked $53,000 for her house only.

CAPITALIZATION (cap)

Capitalize the following:

1. Proper names, including
   a. days of the week
   b. historical periods and events   (*Ex:* the Middle Ages, Battle of the Bulge, World War I)
   c. holidays   (*Ex:* Memorial Day)
   d. languages
   e. months of the year   (but not *spring, summer, autumn, winter*)
   f. organizations   (*Ex:* Chamber of Commerce)
   g. people's names   (*Note:* I will see Father tomorrow; I will see my father tomorrow.)
   h. place names
   i. races   (but not the words *blacks* and *whites*)
   j. references to God   (*Ex:* the Lord in His wisdom)
   k. religions   (*Ex:* Christianity)
   l. titles preceding a person's name   (*Ex:* Governor Jones)
2. Titles, except for short (fewer than five letters), unimportant words that do not begin or end the title
   Ex: "Murders in the Rue Morgue"
   "The Man Who Came In"
   "Arsenic and Old Lace"
3. The first word of a quoted sentence
   Ex: She said, "Can I come to the party?"
4. North, south, east, and west when used to name a region, but not a direction.
   Ex: He lives in the North, but he goes south for the winter.
5. In case of doubt consult the dictionary.

DANGLING MODIFIERS (See *Ambiguity*.)

DEADWOOD (dead, w, wordy)

Words that do not add to the meaning of a sentence are usually called deadwood. Because they make your writing flabby, they should be omitted. Length alone does not determine quality.

Ex: In my opinion I think you should see a doctor. *In my opinion* is sensed in the words *I think. In my opinion,* therefore, adds nothing to the sentence.

Ex: I like you on account of the fact that you are kind whenever I come into contact with you. (Filled with deadwood.)

Better: I like you because of your kindness.

DENOTATION AND CONNOTATION (den, con)

Denotation refers to the *literal meaning of a word.* Connotation refers to the *literal meaning of a word plus the association it calls up.*

Ex: The limousine was parked at the airport. (In the preceeding sentence the denotation of the word *limousine* is a large, expensive automobile. The connotation suggests luxury, wealth, and elegance.)

Ex: The words *old maid* and *bachelor* refer denotatively to unmarried adults; however, the connotation of *old maid* suggests an ill-tempered, sharp-tongued woman, and connotation of *bachelor* suggests a "swinger."

DICTION (d)

In Standard English, the language of educated speakers, there are two basic levels that are appropriate in different situations.

Formal: A language, usually written, which does not allow contractions or any other informal words or expressions, some of which are noted in *Word Usage.* Formal English is not necessarily flowery. It can be plain prose. (See "The Death of a Mother.")

Informal: A casual, usually spoken form of language appropriate in daily communication. It may include slang, ethnic sayings, and regional expressions.

377

Ex: If I don't study for the next exam, I'll flunk for sure.

Note: Most of your college writing will be formal.

Note: Words and expressions such as *He don't, He ain't,* and *He be's* are nonstandard and thus never acceptable in college writing.

DICTIONARY (See Mortimer Adler, "How to Read a Dictionary.")

A good dictionary will give you much information about a word: (1) correct spelling, (2) pronunciation, (3) part of speech, (4) definitions, (5) examples, (6) labels, (7) origins, (8) its various forms.

Pronunciation is indicated by diacritical markings. Because some dictionaires have their individual systems of diacritical markings, you should consult the Pronunciation Key in the dictionary you use. Here, however, are some of the more common markings.

ā   cake (kāk),   day (dā)

ă   cat (kăt),   scrap (skrăp)

'   leader (lē'dar),   consult (kŏn sălt')

ē   evening (ēv'nĭng),   feet (fēt)

ĕ   met (mĕt),   head (hĕd)

ī   ice (īs),   spike (spīk)

ĭ   hit (hĭt),   miss (mĭs)

ō   note (nōt),   goat (gōt)

ŏ   shop (shŏp),   box (bŏks)

o͞o   moon (mo͞on),   loop (lo͞op)

o͝o   cook (ko͝ok),   foot (fo͝ot)

ū   cube (kyūb),   use (yūz)

ŭ   pup (pŭp),   cut (kŭt)

ə   angel (ān'jəl),   account (ə kount')

The schwa is the neutral vowel sound in an unaccented syllable, pronounced *uh.*

The following entry for the word *neat* is from *The American Heritage Dictionary of the English Language.* Examine it carefully, noting the various types of information it provides.

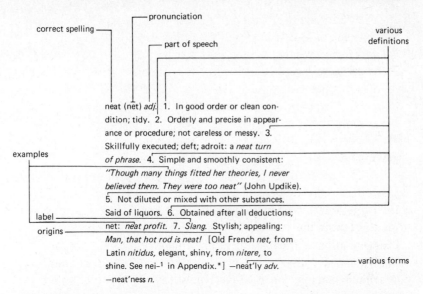

p. 877 *neat* from *The American Heritage Dictionary of the English Language.* William Morris, ed. American Heritage Publishing Co., Inc. and Houghton Mifflin Co., New York. Copyright, 1969.

EXPRESSIONS TO BE AVOIDED (d)

The following common expressions should be avoided or used only with care in your essays because they are overworked and sometimes inappropriate.

1. a lot of   (See *Word Usage,* Handbook.)
2. as already stated

   If your reader has been following your essay, he knows something has already been stated. Restatement for emphasis should be accomplished simply with different words or arrangements of words.
3. as everyone knows

   If your reader does not "know" it, you have probably insulted him. If he does, why say what he already knows in the first place?
4. busted   (See *Word Usage,* Handbook.)
5. could of (along with *would of, may of, might of, must of, ought to of*) *Could of* is lazy-lip pronunciation of *could have* (See *Word Usage,* Handbook.)

6. each and every   (See *Word Usage,* Handbook.)
7. enthuse   (See *Word Usage,* Handbook.)
8. etc.   (See *Word Usage,* Handbook.)
9. exact same   (See *Word Usage,* Handbook.)
10. flunk   (See *Word Usage,* Handbook.)
11. guy   (See *Word Usage,* Handbook.)
12. hisself, theirself, theirselves   (See *Word Usage,* Handbook.)
13. hopefully   (See *Word Usage,* Handbook.)
14. in conclusion
    If you are at the end of your essay, you need not burden your reader with the obvious.
15. in the modern world of today   (See *Word Usage,* Handbook.)
16. in regards to   (See *Word Usage,* Handbook.)
17. irregardless   (See *Word Usage,* Handbook.)
18. is when   (See *Word Usage,* Handbook.)
19. is where   (See *Word Usage,* Handbook.)
20. kind of   (See *Word Usage,* Handbook.)
21. last but not least
    Clichés are objectionable.
22. like   (See *Word Usage,* Handbook.)
23. nice   (See *Word Usage,* Handbook.)
24. off of   (See *Word Usage,* Handbook.)
25. real (as in *real hard*)   (See *Word Usage,* Handbook.)
26. somewheres
    The acceptable form is *somewhere.*
27. sort of   (See *Word Usage,* Handbook.)
28. this here/that there   (See *Word Usage,* Handbook.)
29. truly   (See *very, Word Usage,* Handbook.)
30. try and   (as in *try and help me* instead of *try to help me*)
31. very   (See *Word Usage,* Handbook.)
32. very unique
    A noun can be *unique,* no more nor less, because the word refers to one of a kind.
33. Webster's dictionary says
    A trite opening, this expression should be avoided.
Note: In addition to these common inappropriate expressions, you should avoid in your formal essays all slang, regional sayings, and ethnic expressions.

FALLACIES (fal)

A fallacy is an argument that may appear to be sound but is not. Some of the more common ones are as follows.

1. *Hasty generalization* is often referred to as "jumping to a conclusion."

   Ex: My unmarried brother has a date with a different girl every night. Like all bachelors, he is a swinger.

2. *Oversimplification* is the use of only one cause to explain the existence of a problem or event when in reality there are many causes.

   Ex: Education in this city is in a bad state because the public voted down the recent bond issue.

3. *Begging the question* involves assuming the truth of a point that needs to be proved.

   Ex: Because all teenagers drive too fast, the minimum age for licensing should be raised to twenty. (*Note:* That all teenagers drive too fast remains to be proved.)

4. *False dilemma:* A dilemma involves a choice between two unpleasant alternatives. For instance, I must either go to the company meeting and be bored, or refuse to go and accept the anger of my supervisor. A false dilemma, on the other hand, implies that a choice must be made between two alternatives (not necessarily unpleasant ones), when in reality more than two choices exist.

   Ex: If you don't eat Munchies, you won't grow up to be an Olympic champion.

   America—love it or leave it.

5. *Ad hominem* (Against the man): An argument focused on a person instead of the issue in question is called *ad hominem*.

   Ex: This man drinks two martinis before lunch everyday. How could he make a good mayor?

6. *Non sequitur:* When the premises of an argument do not establish the conclusion, the conclusion is a *non sequitur*.

   Ex: Because a black cat crossed John's path, he broke his leg.

FIGURATIVE LANGUAGE

Good prose normally uses literal language, that is, language that conforms to the dictionary meaning of a word or expression. Some-

381

times, however, a prose writer uses figurative language, the type of language often found in poetry. Strangely enough, figurative language says one thing but means another.

> *Ex:* John is a pig! (Obviously, John is not a pig; however, he has some characteristics in common with pigs—his eating habits, for instance.)

Here are some of the more common figures of speech:

1. *Metaphor* overstates similarities (in the preceding example the eating habits) between two different entities (in the preceding example *John* and *pigs*) by asserting that one is the other.
2. *Simile* makes a comparison between two different entities using the words *like, as,* or *than.*

   > *Ex:* John eats *like* a pig.
3. *Personification* gives human characteristics to inanimate objects or animals.

   > *Ex:* The moon looked at the lovers.
4. *Irony* takes many forms, but the type most often found in essays is called verbal irony. This type of irony says the opposite of what is meant. It can be sustained throughout an entire essay; in this case it is often humorous. (See "Indian Giver's Comeuppance.")
5. *Paradox* is a seemingly self-contradictory statement that has within it truth. It makes the reader stop to think.

   > *Ex:* Christ said, "He who loses his life for my sake will save it."

ITALICS

Italics in print, indicated by underlining in typed and handwritten papers, are used to set off the following words and phrases.

1. Titles of books, periodicals, plays and other long works

   > *Ex:* Homer's poem *The Odyssey* was made into a film called *The Voyages of Ulysses.*

   > *Ex:* *The Morning Gazette* is owned by the publishers of *Everyday* magazine.
2. Words used as words

   > *Ex:* To, *two,* and *too* are homonyms.

   > *Note:* It is not uncommon to see words used as words in quotation marks.

   > *Ex:* "To," "two," and "too" are homonyms.

382

Note: Italics are used in many other instances. These, however, are the most common.

Italics can occasionally be used for emphasis; however, they should
be employed sparingly for that purpose.

NEEDLESS SHIFTS (sh)

Needless shifts from singular to plural, from one tense to another,
from one tone to another (see *Tone,* Handbook), and from one
speaker to another will confuse the reader. In your essays be consistent in number, tense, tone, and person.

1. Shift in number

Not consistent: Everyone has *their* lunch.

Consistent: Everyone has *his* lunch.

Consistent: Everyone has *her* lunch.

Consistent: Everyone has *his* or *her* lunch.

2. Shift in tense

Not consistent: Huck Finn is an interesting character. He
floated down the Mississippi River on a raft.

Consistent: Huck Finn is an interesting character. In Twain's
novel he floats down the Mississippi River on a
raft.

3. Shift in tone

Not consistent: The ponderous thunderheads rolled slowly in
the evening sky. It was a real cool sight.

Consistent: The ponderous thunderheads rolled slowly in the
evening sky. The young boy was filled with
wonder and awe.

4. Shift in person

Not consistent: A person must study hard in college. You must
take notes in every class.

Consistent: A person must study hard in college. He must take
notes in every class.

NUMBERS

1. For numbers under one hundred, use words. For numbers
over one hundred, use figures unless the number can be written in two words.

Ex: There were twenty-one women at the convention.
The dead numbered 243.
The dead numbered two hundred.

2. Always write out numbers that begin a sentence.
   Ex: One hundred forty-four barrels of oil were received at the plant today.
3. Numbers between twenty and one hundred are hyphenated.
   Ex: Twenty-one people were injured in the train wreck.

OUTLINING

An outline is a diagram of an essay. It lists in some kind of logical order the major and minor points of the essay.

I. First Major Point
   A. An aspect of the first major point
      1. Example of the aspect named in A
      2. Another aspect of the example named in A
   B. A second aspect of the first major point
      1. Example of the aspect named in B
         a. Explanation of the example
         b. A second explanation of the example
      2. Another aspect of the example named in B
II. Second Major Point
   (Follows the form of I.)
Note: Every *I* requires at least a *II;* every *A* requires at least a *B;* every *1* requires at least a *2;* every *a* requires at least a *b.*

PARAGRAPHS (¶, no ¶)

A paragraph is a group of sentences concerning the same point. One of the sentences states the point (the topic sentence); the remaining sentences develop it in an orderly way. Indentation of the first sentence indicates the beginning of a paragraph. Just as sentences develop the topic of a paragraph, so do paragraphs develop the thesis of an essay.

A number of methods can be used to bring order to a paragraph.

1. Time (chronological order): Events are recorded in the order in which they occur.

384

Ex: The baseball game was supposed to begin at 2:00. We ate lunch early, and left the house before noon. When we began to get close to the stadium, the traffic grew slower and slower. It finally stopped altogether. The only way to get to the game on time was to park where we were and run. Just as we reached the stadium, we heard the *Star Spangled Banner.*

2. Listing (enumeration): Points are numbered in the following manner: first, second, third, etc.
   Ex: Cooking a raccoon involves several steps. First, skin and clean the game. Second, season it thoroughly with salt, black pepper, and red pepper. Third, cook it over a low heat for several hours in a heavy pot, adding liquid as needed. As a final step, throw it out.

3. Example: If the topic sentence is stated at the opening of the paragraph, and examples that develop it follow, the order is deductive. If, however, the examples lead to the topic sentence, the order is inductive.
   Ex: (Deductive Order) Students who do well in college generally have effective study habits. For example, they begin their assignments well ahead of the time they are due to be turned in. In the same way, good students start to study for tests several days before the examination is to be given. Also, they schedule their work carefully, making sure that enough time is available for each subject.

4. Spatial: Points are arranged according to their physical location in a particular place. They can be ordered by moving in terms of direction—that is, north to south or east to west. Within a smaller context the points can be discussed in the order in which a fixed viewer sees them.
   Ex: The fall elections across the country will be interesting to follow. John Fiero, a prominent Democrat in the East, promises to lead his Republican opponent. In the Midwest, however, the Republicans will probably gain several seats in the senate. California races cannot be predicted yet, as Herbert Fackler and Jane Bonin are running neck and neck.

If you use one of these methods of development, your paragraph will have unity (all sentences will be about the same topic) and coherence (the sentences will flow smoothly from one to the next).

PARTS OF SPEECH

Numerous parts of speech cooperate with each other to form a sentence. Their names are determined by their functions in the sentence. It is difficult to isolate, then label a word out of the context of the sentence. For example, what part of speech is the word *like?*

1. *Like* is a noun. (Here *like* is naming a word.) A noun names a person, place, or thing. It is also called a substantive.
2. I *like* you. (Here *like,* a verb, expresses an act of emotion.) Verbs may also express a state experienced by a person or thing.
   Ex: I *feel* bad.
   Some verbs join coordinate substantives, thus in a sense equating them.
   Ex: Abraham Lincoln *was* President of the United States.
3. *Like* men tend to associate together. (By describing *men,* a noun, *like* becomes an adjective.)
4. She looks *like* me. (*Like* is a preposition because it shows how *looks* and *me* are related. To change the relationship of *looks* and *me* change the preposition. For example, "She looks *around* me" or "She looks *behind* me.")
5. You react *like* I do. (In informal English *like* can be used as a conjunction. In formal writing *as* should replace *like.*)

Here are some other parts of speech:

6. Bert *hurriedly* ate his dinner. (*Hurriedly* tells something about *ate,* a verb; therefore, *hurriedly* is an adverb. Adverbs often end in *ly,* and usually answer the questions *how, when, where,* and *why.*)
7. J. C. threw the football because *he* was in danger of being tackled. (*He,* a pronoun, takes the place of *J. C.* Can you imagine how boring writing would be if nouns had to be repeated?) (See *Pronoun Problems,* Handbook.)
8. Ralph and Lavergne are heavy drinkers. (*And,* a conjunction, joins two words. A conjunction may also join phrases and clauses.)
   Note: If you take a verb, add *ing* to the end, and use it to describe a noun or pronoun, you have a special construction called a participle. A whole descriptive phrase can be built around a participle.

386

Ex: *Reading* my book, I fell asleep.

Looking out of the window, the man saw a crime being committed.

Be careful to avoid dangling participles. (See *Ambiguity, Handbook.*)

PLAGIARISM

Plagiarism is theft. It involves presenting someone else's writing as your own. It can be avoided by giving credit to the person whose words or ideas you are using. When you are using another writer's exact words, the passage should also be enclosed in quotation marks.

PRONOUN PROBLEMS

Using the correct form of a pronoun is difficult. Here are some of the common problems.

1. Prepositions and pronouns: Prepositions are followed by *me, him, her, us, them,* and *whom.*

   Ex: This argument is *between* you and *me.*

   Here's a present *for* you and *me.*

   Whom are you talking *to?* (The formal statement is, "To *whom* are you talking?")

   John is the man *whom* I work *for.* (The formal statement is, "John is the man *for whom* I work.")

2. Two or more pronouns used as a subject: The personal pronouns used as the subject of a sentence are *I, you, he, she, we, they.*

   Ex: *He* and *I* will attend the meeting.

   He, she, and the teacher are having an argument.

3. Pronouns used as the object of a verb: The problem pronouns used as objects are *me, him, her, us, them,* and *whom.*

   Ex: She *gave* Sam and *me* a present.

   Katie *invited* Sydney and *me* to her house.

   Whom did you kiss?

   The man *whom* I met was a movie star.

387

4. Pronoun agreement: Pronouns such as *each, everyone, anyone, someone, anybody, each one, one, nothing, no one, something, neither,* and *either* are always singular. They take singular verbs and the singular possessive adjectives *his, her,* and *its.*

Ex: *Each* of the ten men *has his* lunch.

Each of the men in different platoons *eats his* lunch at staggered hours.

Anyone who studies diligently will reap *her* reward.

Note: When some of these pronouns are attached to nouns, they become adjectives and the nouns they modify are singular.

Ex: *Each man has his* lunch.

Every man has his lunch. (*Note: Every* is used only as a singular adjective, never as a pronoun.)

One student out of twenty *is* here.

5. The vague use of *this:* Because *this* as a pronoun is so often used incorrectly, in your essays it should not be used alone. It should be followed by a noun.

Ex: *This* is interesting. (wrong)

This book is interesting. (right)

6. Compound personal pronouns: The following are compound personal pronouns: *myself, yourself, himself, herself, itself, ourselves, yourselves,* and *themselves.* They are used only when they reflect or intensify a personal pronoun already present in the sentence.

Ex: I hurt myself. (*Note: Myself* reflects *I.*)

I myself will go. (*Note: Myself* intensifies *I.*)

Note: Often the compound personal pronoun is incorrectly used as part of a compound subject or object.

Ex: Dylan and *I* (not *myself*) will train the dog.

She said it to Gilda and *me* (not *myself*).

7. Pronouns after *as* or *than:* The pronouns that follow *as* or *than* are *I, he, she, we, they.*

Ex: He is taller than *I* (am).

I am younger than *they* (are).

PUNCTUATION

Apostrophe

Apostrophes are used to indicate possession, to take the place of missing letters in a contraction, and to make plurals of figures and letters of the alphabet.

1. Possession

   a. If a noun does not end in an *s* or *z* sound, add *'s*.

     Ex: The girl's bicycle was left in the driveway.

       The men's track suits were returned from the laundry.

       The children's toys were scattered over the livingroom floor.

   b. If a noun ends in an *s* or *z* sound, add only an apostrophe, unless another syllable is formed when the word is made possessive.

     Ex: The girls' bicycles were left in the driveway.

       Paris's skyline is beautiful.

       Henry James's novels are studied in American literature courses.

     Note: *Paris's* and *James's* are pronounced as more than one syllable.

   c. An indefinite pronoun (See *Pronoun Problems, #4,* Handbook) needs *'s*.

     Ex: If everybody's problems are discussed, the meeting will never end.

   d. To show joint ownership, make the last noun possessive. To show separate ownership, make all elements possessive.

     Ex: Roland and Carl's father is here. (*Note: Carl* and *Roland* are brothers.)

       Roland's and Carl's fathers are here. (*Note:* In this case *Roland* and *Carl* are not brothers.)

     Note: Do not use apostrophes to show possession with *his, her, its, ours, yours, theirs.*

2. Contractions

   Apostrophes indicate missing letters in contractions. Contractions are not appropriate in formal writing, although they are much used in spoken language and informal writing.

   Ex: I don't like spinach.

     He'll be back in a minute.

Note: The expression *aren't I* is never acceptable.
It means *are I not,* an obviously clumsy question.

Note: It's is used to mean only *it is.* To show possession, simply write *its. Who's* means *who is.* To show possession, write *whose.*

3. Plurals

Apostrophes are used to form the plurals of letters and figures.

Ex: His handwriting is so bad his *a's* look like *o's.*
Jazz has been popular since the 1920's.

Colons

The colon should not be confused with the semicolon, which has quite different functions. Principally the colon is used to signal the reader that a list, an explanation, or a long quotation follows.

1. The colon can introduce a formal list at the end of a sentence.
   Ex: The decorator suggested three additions to the apartment: indirect lighting, hanging planters, and air conditioning.
2. Explanatory material often follows a colon when it is placed at the end of a sentence.
   Ex: She wanted only one thing in life: professional success.
3. The colon can take the place of a comma before a long formal quotation.
   Ex: Mark Antony's famous speech from *Julius Caesar* begins: "Friends, Romans, countrymen, lend me your ears."

Commas

Use commas in the following situations:

1. In a series of more than two, the comma separates the listed items.
   Ex: The lamp, the ashtray, the newspaper, and the armchair made the room look comfortable.
   Note: To avoid the possibility of confusion, always put a comma before the *and* preceding the final item.
2. A comma follows an introductory clause (see *Sentence Components,* Handbook) that begins with *after, although, as, as if, as long as, as though, because, before, if, in order that, since, so that, though, even though, until, till, unless, when, whenever, where, wherever, while.*

390

Ex: Unless Barbara hurries with her chores, we will never get to the ballet.

Because Ben works hard, his wife has a new mink coat.

If Pete Rose remains healthy, he may overtake Ty Cobb's hit record.

3. A comma should precede *and, but, or, nor, for* when they join two sentences.

Ex: Maria Dartez's son was married in Houston, and he spent his honeymoon in Hawaii.

Renée Reed enjoys working as a secretary, but she would prefer to be a chemist.

4. A comma follows introductory phrases of at least five words. (See *Sentence Components,* Handbook.)

Ex: After a long walk in the rain, we sat by the fire in the lodge.

During a long discussion with my friends, I came to the conclusion that Europe was worth visiting.

Jogging down the path on a Sunday afternoon, I thought about nature's beauty.

In the evening I read the newspaper.

5. *Who, which,* and *that* clauses and words or phrases that rename the nouns preceding them are set off by commas if they are not essential to the meaning of the sentence. To check how important such a word, phrase, or clause is, ask yourself, "Can I leave it out without damaging the clarity of the sentence?"

Ex: The early morning jogger who runs by my house every day should enter the marathon.

Note: No commas are used because without the *who* clause the reader would not know which jogger was meant.

Ex: Herb Fackler, who jogs by my house every morning, should enter the city marathon.

Note: Because the jogger is named, the *who* clause is not necessary for his identification and should thus be set off by commas.

Ex: Hemingway's novel *For Whom the Bell Tolls* is set during the Spanish Civil War.

Note: Because Hemingway wrote many novels, the title of this one should not be set off by commas.

Ex: *For Whom the Bell Tolls,* a novel by Hemingway, is set during the Spanish Civil War.

391

Note: Once the title is given, there can be no confusion as to which novel is meant.

6. *Interrupters,* expressions and comments that do not add to the meaning of the sentence, are set off by commas. They may occur at the beginning, middle, or end of a sentence.

   Ex: On the other hand, the kind of stereo set I really want is very expensive.

   The students on this campus are politically uninvolved, generally speaking.

   Basketball, in contrast to what many people think, is a contact sport.

7. Use commas in dates, addresses, after salutations and closings in letters, after names in direct address, and with figures.

   Ex: May 30, 1979

   Houston, Texas

   "Dear Vicki," and "Sincerely yours,"

   "Sydney, please find the file I need."

   5,672,920

8. Commas should be used whenever a sentence is confusing without them.

   Ex: A few months after they married in her parents' home.

   Note: If the reader does not have a signal to pause after *after,* he will misread the sentence. Compare the first version with: "A few months after, they married in her parents' home.

   Ex: After eating Mother put the food in the refrigerator.

   Note: Without the comma after *eating,* the sentence is confusing. It should read: "After eating, Mother put the food in the refrigerator."

Avoid using commas unless you can justify them by one of the preceding rules. In particular, do not use commas in the following instances.

   a. Between a subject and a verb
      Ex: The lonely man, sat by himself on the park bench.

   b. Before *and* when it is not linking two sentences or signaling the end of a series
      Ex: The old limousine was an expensive, and frustrating purchase.

   c. Between two complete sentences

Ex: Dr. Patterson was standing in the office, she was examining the patient's chart.

This error is called a *comma splice*.

Note: A period or semicolon should be used.

Ex: Dr. Patterson was standing in the office. She was examining the patient's chart.

or

Dr. Patterson was standing in the office; she was examining the patient's chart.

Quotation Marks

Use quotation marks in the following instances:

1. Enclose direct quotations in quotation marks. Precede the opening quotation marks with either a colon (if the quotation is long and weighty) or a comma.

   Ex: Abraham Lincoln said: "Four score and seven years ago our fathers brought forth on this continent, a new nation, conceived in liberty, and dedicated to the proposition that all men are created equal."

   Ex: The professor insisted, "All papers must be handed in on time."

   Notice how the quotation is treated when it is placed in different parts of the sentence.

   Ex: "All papers," the professor insisted, "must be handed in on time." (Notice that *must* is not capitalized because it does not begin a sentence.)

   Ex: "Give me liberty or give me death," said Patrick Henry.

2. Titles of short works are enclosed in quotation marks.

   Ex: "Hills Like White Elephants" is a famous Hemingway short story.

3. Single quotation marks are used only within double quotation marks.

   Ex: Charles asked, "Have you read Poe's poem 'The Raven'?"

4. Words used in a special sense are enclosed in quotation marks.

   Ex: Many psychologists have noted that preadolescents like to think they are "cool."

5. Always place the period and comma inside the quotation marks; always place the semicolon and colon outside the quotation marks; place the exclamation point and the question

mark inside the quotation marks when they apply to the quotation and outside when they apply to the whole sentence.

Ex: She said, "I'm ready."

"I'm ready," she said.

She said to John, "I have come to see you many times"; nevertheless, he slammed the door in her face.

For your camping trip bring the following "goodies": marshmallows, wieners, buns, and lemonade.

She shouted, "Help!"

Get that cat out of your "pad"!

The evangelist said, "Brother, are you saved?"

Did the evangelist say, "Brother, you are saved"?

Semicolons

Use semicolons in the following instances:

1. A semicolon can take the place of a comma and a connecting word (*and, but, or, for, nor*) between two sentences.

   Ex: He moved to a nearby town; all of his friends missed him.

   Note: The sentence *could* be written in the following form: "He moved to a nearby town, and all of his friends missed him."

2. When two sentences are joined by words such as *consequently, however, furthermore, moreover, nevertheless,* and *therefore,* a semicolon should precede the connective and a comma should follow it.

   Ex: She has been on a diet for weeks; however, she has not lost a pound.

   He has enrolled in summer school; therefore, he will not apply for a job.

3. A semicolon is used to indicate major units of thought in a sentence that has many commas.

   Ex: Most freshmen students take English 1000, freshman composition; mathematics 1000, basic algebraic concepts; and history 1000, American civilization since the Civil War.

   Note: Without semicolons, it would be difficult to match the course numbers with the course descriptions.

4. The semicolon should always stand after the quotation marks.

   Ex: She said to John, "I have come to see you many times"; nevertheless, he slammed the door in her face.

SENTENCE COMPONENTS

The English language is made up of letters that alone or in combination form words. When words are grouped together in patterns that lack a subject and a verb and must be attached to a larger unit to have meaning, the patterns are called phrases. The larger unit to which the phrase is attached is called a clause. The clause differs from the phrase in having a subject and a verb; however, all clauses do not make satisfactory sense in themselves. Like phrases, some clauses (called dependent clauses) depend on still another larger unit for meaning. The ultimate sentence unit is the independent clause, which momentarily makes sense on its own.

Word: Boy

Phrase: The boy with the hat

Dependent clause: When the boy with the hat came into the room

Sentence: When the boy with the hat came into the room, I left.

Note: I left, an independent clause, can on its own be a sentence because it momentarily makes sense. On the other hand, *When the boy with the hat came into the room* demands the independent clause to give it sense.

SENTENCE WRITING

The simplest form of the sentence, and the one on which more complicated forms are based, normally consists of a subject, a verb, and a complement. Note those three parts in the following simple sentences:

       S   V   C
The boy hit the ball.

       S   V   C
The baby is a boy.

To compose more complicated structures, the writer adds single words, phrases, and dependent clauses. (See *Sentence Components,* Handbook.) Long sentences, however, are not necessarily better than short ones. Good writing uses a variety of lengths and patterns. Note the words, phrases, and clauses added to the simple sentences given already. Besides adding information, observe how they change those sentences.

The young boy in the green shirt hit the ball across the park and over the fence.

395

Although the parents had hoped for a girl, the baby is a boy.

Several common problems of sentence writing exist. Guard against the following in your writing:

1. Fused sentences (fs), sometimes called *run-on sentences,* occur when two or more sentences are joined without any connecting words or punctuation. They are difficult for the reader to follow.

   Fused sentence: The team asked the coach's permission to stay out later than the curfew he said they must be in at the regular time.

   Correct: The team asked the coach's permission to stay out later than the curfew, but he said they must be in at the regular time.

   Alternate: The team asked the coach's permission to stay out later than the curfew; he said they must be in at the regular time.

   Alternate: The team asked the coach's permission to stay out later than the curfew. He said they must be in at the regular time.

   Alternate: Although the team asked the coach's permission to stay out later than the curfew, he said they must be in at the regular time.

2. A sentence fragment (sf or frag) is an incomplete sentence. Either it lacks a verb, or it is a dependent clause. (See *Sentence Components,* Handbook.)

   Frag: By the boy in the blue suit on the bench.

   Complete: I sat by the boy in the blue suit on the bench.

   Frag: After Jack saw the movie in the afternoon.

   Complete: After Jack saw the movie in the afternoon, he went by the tavern to have a beer.

   Note: It is possible to have a sentence that at first appears to be incomplete because implied words are missing. If those words are clearly implied, however, the sentence is not a fragment but an ellipsis.

   Ex: Rod Grossman is smarter than his sons [are smart].
   [What is] More important [is that] you should first do your assignment.

   Ex: Are you going to the movie? Yes. [I am going to the movie.]

3. A comma splice (cs) occurs when two sentences are joined by a comma without a connecting word (*and, but, for, or, nor*).

Comma splice: Carl Wooton sat lazily at his desk, his secretaries were typing and filing in a great hurry.

Corrected: Carl Wooton sat lazily at his desk. His secretaries were typing and filing in a great hurry.

SPELLING (sp)

Misspellings account for some of the most heavily penalized and most easily corrected writing errors. If you have spelling problems, use some of the following methods to improve your skills:

1. Trace the word in the air using your finger. Try to see the word, although it is actually invisible.
2. Write the word on paper, using a red pen or pencil to write the troublesome spots.
3. Without moving your hands, imagine the word one letter at a time as each appears on a gigantic mental television set. Trace each of the letters using only your imagination.
4. Associate a problem word with something else. The more ridiculous the association, the more likely you are to remember it. For example, you can remember that the final three letters of cemetery are *ery* not *ary* by noting that to be in a cemetery late at night is *eerie,* frightening.
5. Exaggerate the pronunciation of a difficult syllable. For example, to learn the correct spelling of *independence,* pronounce the final syllable with an exaggerated *ence* sound so that you no longer hear it as an *ance* sound.
6. Associate words with their relatives. For example, *muscular* will remind you of the *c* in *muscle; condemnation* will remind you to put the *n* as the final letter of *condemn.*
7. When two words are joined to make one word, remember to retain the final letter of the first word if it is the same as the first letter of the second word. For example, *roommate* has two *m*'s in the middle; *misspell* has two *s*'s.
8. When you have trouble with two words that sound alike but have different spellings, memorize the meaning and usage of

the one that gives you less difficulty. Use the other word on all other occasions. For example, if you have trouble distinguishing *whether* and *weather,* remember that *weather* refers to rain, sun, wind, and the like. Use *whether* whenever another subject is under discussion.

Rules help you discover the proper spelling of many words. Memorize and learn to apply the following. Choose an easy-to-remember example for each one.

1. Retain the final silent *e* when adding a suffix (see *Vocabulary Building,* Handbook) beginning with a consonant. Before adding a suffix beginning with a vowel, drop the final silent *e.*

   Ex: manage—management
   smoke—smoking

2. Usually change the final *y* to *i* before adding a suffix, except when the suffix is *ing.*

   Ex: lady—ladies
   copy—copies
   copy—copying

   Exception: A verb ending in *y* preceded by a vowel retains the *y* for the third person singular form.

   Ex: He *enjoys* swimming.
   She *plays* tennis.

   Exception: A noun ending in *y* preceded by a vowel retains the *y* in its plural form.

   Ex: money—moneys
   valley—valleys

3. Double the final single consonant of a word of one syllable or a word ending on an accented syllable if the final consonant is preceded by a single vowel and the suffix begins with a vowel.

   Ex: plan—planned
   occur—occurrence

4. In words with *ie* or *ei,* write *ie* if the pronunciation is e, except after *c.*

   Ex: piece (pronounced e)
   ceiling (after *c*)
   neighbor (pronounced *a*)

All of these ruled have exceptions. Whenever you are in doubt about the correct spelling of a word, consult a dictionary or a spelling list.

The following is a list of words that are frequently misspelled.

absence	changeable	environment
acceptance	changing	equipment
accidentally	chief	equipped
accommodate	choose	escape
accustom	colonel	especially
achievement	column	exaggerate
acquainted	coming	exceed
actually	committee	excellent
adequately	conceivable	excitable
advertisement	conceive	existence
advice	condemn	extravagant
advise	conscience	extremely
alcohol	conscientious	familiar
all right	conscious	February
amateur	consistent	finally
among	controlled	foreign
analysis	convenient	forty
analyze	courteous	freshmen
angle	criticize	fulfill
appearance	deceive	fundamentally
argument	defendants	further
athletics	definite	ghost
attempt	dependent	government
attendance	descendant	grammar
audience	describe	grief
available	develop	gruesome
bachelor	different	guarantee
banana	dilemma	guidance
becoming	dining	handsome
beginning	disappearance	happiness
believe	discipline	height
benefited	dominant	heroes
breath	dying	hoping
breathe	eighth	huge
business	eligible	humorous
calendar	embarrass	hurriedly
ceiling	emphasize	hypocrisy
cemetery	employee	hysterical
challenge	enough	ignorance

immediately
incredible
indispensable
influence
inoculate
intelligent
interest
interference
interpretation
interrupt
inventor
irrelevant
irresistible
irreverent
judgment
kindergarten
knowledge
knowledgeable
leisurely
length
library
license
lonely
maintenance
marriage
mathematics
medicine
mere
minute
misspell
mountainous
murmur
muscle
naturally
necessary
neither
niece
ninety
noticeable
nuisance

occasionally
occurrence
omitted
outrageous
paid
pamphlet
parallel
particularly
permanent
persistent
piece
planned
possible
precede
preference
preferred
prejudice
presence
primitive
privilege
probably
proceed
professor
prominent
pronunciation
publicly
pursue
quantity
really
receive
recommend
reference
referring
relieve
religion
remember
repetition
resemblance
resistance
rhyme

rhythm
roommate
sacrifice
safety
salary
schedule
seize
separate
sergeant
shining
similar
sincerely
sophomore
sponsor
studying
subtle
succeed
surprise
swimming
syllable
tendency
thorough
though
through
traffic
tragedy
transferred
undoubtedly
unnecessary
until
unusually
useful
vengeance
vertical
villain
volume
weight
weird
woman
writing

SUBJECT—VERB AGREEMENT (agr)

The subject of a sentence is a substantive that tells who or what the sentence is about. The simple predicate of a sentence is the verb that agrees with the subject in person and number (singular or plural).

1. The most common agreement problem of regular verbs occurs in the third person singular in the present tense. An *s* must be added to the verb whose subject is one of the following: *he, she, it,* or any other singular pronoun or noun.

   Ex: He *feels* bad. She *likes* her new dress. It *happens* every-day. The desk *sits* in the corner of the room.

2. The verb *to be* presents the greatest agreement problem in ir-regular verbs. The best way to avoid trouble with this verb is to memorize the following.

   Present tense: I am.

   You are.

   He, she, it, the boy (or any other singular noun or pronoun) is.

   We are.

   They, the boys (or any other plural noun or pro-noun) are.

   Note: Be is never used as a verb in stating a fact or asking a question. *He be's* is not acceptable in Standard English.

   Past tense: I was.

   You were.

   He, she, it, the boy (or any other singular noun or pronoun) was.

   We were.

   They, the boys (or any other plural noun or pro-noun) were.

   Present perfect: I have been.

   You have been.

   He, she, it, the boy (or any other singular noun or pronoun) has been.

   We have been.

   They, the boys (or any other plural noun or pronoun) have been.

   Note: Been is not acceptable in Standard English without *has, have,* or *had* preceding it.

401

Unacceptable: He *been* sick.

Standard: He *has been* sick.

3. The present tense of the verb *to have* also presents problems. If you have difficulty with this verb, memorize the following:

   Present tense: I have.

   You have.

   He, she, it, the boy (or any other singular noun or pronoun) has.

   We have.

   They, the boys (or any other plural noun or pronoun) have.

4. When a phrase comes between the subject and the verb, you must be certain that the verb agrees with the subject and not the last word of the phrase.

   Ex: The *history* of many wars *is* found in the works of Thucydides.

   Note: History, not *wars,* is the subject of the sentence; therefore, the verb must be singular.

   Ex: John, in addition to his brothers, *was* at the party.

   Note: John is the subject, not *brothers;* therefore, the verb must be singular.

5. Two subjects joined by *and* (a compound subject) are followed by a plural verb.

   Ex: Gloria and *Joan are* hungry.

6. When two subjects are qualified by *either . . . or* or *neither . . . nor* (correlative conjunctions), the verb will agree with the subject closer to it.

   Ex: Either Dot or *Linda is* here.

   Either the man or his *brothers are* here.

   Neither Harry nor *Carolyn has* children.

   Neither you nor *I am* a millionaire.

7. Remember: *Each* or *every* before a subject makes it singular.

   Ex: Each soldier in the ranks *is* responsible for *his* equipment.

TONE

Tone is the writer's attitude toward his subject. An essay can be, among other things, funny, sad, melancholic, nostalgic, serious, sarcastic, academic. A change in tone in an essay almost always weakens its impact. For example, if it begins in a sarcastic tone, it should remain so throughout.

TRANSITIONS (trans)

Transitions are devices that control the orderly flow of sentences and paragraphs. They lead the reader from one point to the next. In other words, they give coherence to sentences, paragraphs, and, finally, to the essay.

1. Certain words and phrases are useful transitional devices. Some of these are *on the other hand, consequently, also, moreover, first, second, third, furthermore, in addition, similarly, on the contrary, at the same time, therefore, in other words, that is, for example, for instance, in any event, meanwhile.*

2. The repetition of important words can provide effective transitions.

    Ex: Man is both *Homo sapiens* and beast. Man as *Homo sapiens* has given the world the humanities and sciences. Man as beast has given the world Hitler and Stalin.

3. Often the last sentence of one paragraph will furnish a transition by anticipating the first sentence of the next paragraph.

    Notice that in "A Big, Big Man" the fifth paragraph ends, "They say even after the second heart attack you couldn't bring yourself to quit smoking." The sixth paragraph begins, "Lyndon, you were immoderate, and greedy."

VOCABULARY BUILDING

Many English words take their roots from other languages. If you know the meaning of some of the more common roots, their prefixes (the beginning syllable or syllables), and their suffixes (the closing syllable or syllables), it is possible to increase your vocabulary in a relatively short time. For example, the word *diagonally* has a prefix *dia*, which means through, a root *gon*, which means angle or corner, and a suffix *ly*, which means in a specialized way: A line drawn diagonally is drawn through angles or corners.

An octagon (*octa*, eight; *gon*, angle or corner) is a figure with eight angles (sides). A polygon (*poly*, many; *gon*, angle or corner)

403

has many angles. Polygamy (*poly,* many; *gam,* mate, marry) means having many mates.

To arrive at the meaning of a word, first examine the suffix (if any), then the root, finally the prefix (if any). For example:

hetero sexu al

The suffix *al* means pertaining to.

The root *sexu* means concerning sex.

The prefix *hetero* means something different.

A heterosexual person prefers the opposite sex.

homo gen ize

The suffix *ize* means to cause to be.

The root *gen* means kind or race.

The prefix *homo* means the same.

Homogenized milk is a blend of cream and skim. All of its parts possess the same kind of mixture.

anthropo logy

The suffix *logy* means the study of.

The root *anthropo* means man.

Anthropology is the study of man.

Here are some common prefixes, roots, and suffixes.

Prefix	Meaning	Example
a, ab	from	absent
ad	to, toward	advance
ambi	both	ambidexterous
ante	before	antebellum
bi	two	bisexual
cent	hundred	century
circum	around	circumnavigate
con, cal, cum	with	concordance
contra	against	contradict
de	from, down	descend
deca	ten	decalogue
ex, e	out of	extract
extra	beyond	extrasensory
hyper	above	hyperventilate
hypo	below	hypodermic
in, im	in, into	invade
inter	between	interrupt

Prefix	Meaning	Example
intra	within	intracoastal
mono	one	monocycle
ob	against	obstinate
penta	five	pentagon
per	through, by means of, destruction of	perfidy
peri	around	perimeter
post	after	postpone
pre	before	predate
pro	for, on behalf of	proposal
retro	backward	retrograde
se	apart	separate
semi	half	semifinal
super, supra	over	superintendent
sub	under	submarine
syn, syl, sym	with, same	synonym
trans	across	transfusion
uni	one	unified

Root	Meaning	Example
ag, act	do, drive, act	action
anim	life, mind	animate
ann	year	annual
aud	hear	auditorium
auto	self	automobile
ben	good	beneficial
bibli	book	bibliophile
bio	life	biology
cap, cep, cip capt, cept,	seize, take	capture
ced, cess	yield	accede
chron	time	chronological
cor	heart	coronary
corp	body	corporation
cosm	order, world	cosmology
curr, curs	run	courier

405

Root	Meaning	Example
cycle	circle, wheel	bicycle
dic, dict	say	contradict
dorm	sleep	dormant
duc, duct	lead	induction
dyn	force, power	dynamic
fac, fec, fic, fy	do, make	effect
fer	bear, carry	ferry
fid	faith	perfidy
flect, flex	bend	reflex
flu, flux, fluct	flow	fluctuation
frang, fract, frag, fring	break	fracture
gen	kind, race	genocide
geo	earth	geography
gram	write, writing	grammar
graph	write, writing	telegraph
hetero	other, different	heterotypic
homo	same	homonym
hydr	water	hydraulic
jac, ject	throw	eject
jung, junct, jug	join	junction
leg, lect	read	college
log	study of, word, speech	prologue
loqu, locut	speak	elocution
macro	big	macrocosm
magn	big	magnitude
mal	bad, evil	malevolent
man	hand	manipulate
mega	big	megaphone
metr, meter	measure	metropolis
micr	small	microscopic
mit, mis	send	missionary
morph	form	amorphous
neo	new	neophyte
onym	name	homonym
pan	all	panacea
path	feeling, suffering	empathy

Root	Meaning	Example
ped	foot	pedal
pel, pula	drive, pull	pulley
pend, pens	hang	pendant
phil	like	philanthropy
phon	sound	phonograph
phot	light	photography
poly	many	polygraph
port	carry	porter
psych	mind	psychology
rump, rupt	break	rupture
sci	know	science
scop	seeing	telescope
script, scrib	write	scribble
sec, sect	cut	bisect
sed, sess	sit	sedentary
sequ, secu	follow	sequence
soph	wise, wisdom	philosophy
spec, spect	look	spectrum
sta, sist, stit	stand	static
string, strict	stretch	restrict
tang, tact	touch	tactile
tele	far	telescope
temp	time	contemporary
ten, tent, tain	hold	maintain
the	god	atheist
therm	heat	thermostat
trak, tract	draw, drag	tractor
ven, vent	come	advent
vert, vers	turn	revert
vid, vis	see	visual
viv	live	vivacious
voc, voke	call	evoke

Suffix	Meaning	Example
-able, -ible	able to	moveable
-al	act of doing	refusal
-ance, ence	action, condition, or quality of	insistence

Suffix	Meaning	Example
-ant	one who acts or believes	participant
-ary	pertaining to, engage in	missionary
-ate	possessing, derived from, acting	magistrate
-cy	quality, condition, or office	presidency
-dom	condition, state, or position of	boredom
-er	one who acts	achiever
-ful	having much of	harmful
-fy	to make into, to do	rectify
-ic	characteristic of	comic
-ism	a system or belief	Communism
-ist	one who believes in something	Communist
-ize	to cause to be or to make similar to	colonize
-ly	in a specified way	sweetly
-ment	a means or concrete result of; action or state	postponement
-ness	a state of being	politeness
-ous	full of, possessing	joyous
-ship	quality of	penmanship
-tion	act or process of	transportation

WORD USAGE

Your essays are to be written in Standard English. Nonstandard words and expressions are not appropriate. Informal words and expressions should be used only when the subject and audience call for informality. Your teacher will often indicate whether you are to write a formal or an informal essay. (See *Diction,* Handbook.)

a, an

In general, use *a* before words that begin with a consonant and *an* before words that begin with a vowel sound, including words beginning with silent *h*.

    Ex: a tree, an apple, an hour
    Exceptions:
    1. Words beginning with the $\bar{u}$ sound are preceded by *a*.
        Ex: a unit, a unique home, a European trip

2. With the word *historical* use either *a* or *an*. With the word *humble* use *a* if you sound the initial *h;* use *an* if you do not sound it.

accept, except

To accept is *to receive* or *to answer affirmatively.*
  Ex: The bride graciously accepted the presents.
     I accept your invitation to dinner.
To except is *to exclude.* It is rarely used as a verb.
  Ex: Young people under the age of seventeen are excepted from attending X-rated movies.
Except used as a preposition means *other than.*
  Ex: Everyone except you and me failed his test.

ad

A shortened form of a word, such as *ad* for *advertisement,* is not acceptable in formal Standard English. Other such clipped forms include *auto* (*automobile*), *doc* (*doctor*), *exam* (*examination*), *gym* (*gymnasium*), *lab* (*laboratory*), *math* (*mathematics*), and *prof* (*professor*).

advice (See **advise.**)

advise, advice

To advise (with a *z* sound at the end) is *to give an option. Advice* (with an *s* sound at the end) is *the opinion* given.
  Ex: I advised Ann to listen to Walter's advice.

affect, effect

Affect, a verb, means *to influence* or *to pretend.*
  Ex: A teacher affects a student's attitudes.
     She affects an intellectual pose.
Effect as a noun means *a result.*
  Ex: The effect of overeating was indigestion.
Effect as a verb means *to accomplish.*
  Ex: The policeman effected a change in the flow of traffic after the accident.

aggravate

In formal Standard English *to aggravate* means *to make worse,* not *to irritate* or *to annoy.* One cannot aggravate a person, only a thing.

Formal: Improper bandaging may aggravate a wound.
Informal: Children often aggravate their parents.

a half (See **half a.**)

ain't

Used as a contraction of *am not, is not,* or *are not, ain't* is always nonstandard.

alibi

Alibi is not to be used in the place of *excuse* except in legal writing.

all ready, already

Already means *by a certain time* or *before.*
Ex: We have already eaten dinner.
All ready means *totally prepared.*
Ex: Dinner was all ready for the guests.

all right (See **alright.**)

all together, altogether

All together means *collected into a group.*
Ex: The boy scouts are all together around the campfire.
Altogether means *completely.*
Ex: City boys are altogether different from farm boys.

allusion, illusion

An *allusion* is an *indirect reference to history or literature.*
Ex: His allusion to Dachau made us remember the atrocities of World War II.
An *illusion* is an *unreal impression.*
Ex: The illusions of the magician fascinated the children.

almost, most

Do not substitute *most* for *almost* in formal writing.
Formal: Almost all children like ice cream.

alot, a lot, lots of

Alot is never acceptable; the expression is always written as two words. *A lot* and *lots of* are informal for *many* and *much.* As such they are not acceptable in formal English.

410

already (See **all ready**.)

alright, all right
Incorrectly spelled *alright*. Proper spelling is *all right*. Would it help to correct the misspelling by associating it with *all wrong?*

altogether (See **all together**.)

alumna, alumnus
An *alumna* is a *female graduate*.
   Ex: She is an alumna of Bryn Mawr.
An *alumnus* is a *male graduate*.
   Ex: He is an alumnus of USL.
Alumni (nī) is the plural form that refers to *male graduates* and *a combination of male and female graduates*.
   Ex: The alumni from the state university have returned for Homecoming.
Alumnae (nē) is the plural form of *female graduates* only.
   Ex: The alumnae will gather for a meeting of the University Women's Club.

alumnus (See **alumna**.)

A.M., P.M. (or a.m., p.m.)
These abbreviations are used only with figures.
   Ex: I will meet you for breakfast at 8:00 A.M. (Not, "I will meet you in the A.M.")

among, between
Among is used when more than two items or persons are under discussion.
   Ex: Mother divided the candy among the three children.
Between is used for two person or things.
   Ex: Mother divided the candy between you and me.
   Note: Under no circumstances is the phrase *between you and I* acceptable.

amount, number
Amount is used when one is referring to items in bulk.
   Ex: She put a large amount of sugar in his coffee.

Number is used when items can be counted.

> *Ex:* A number of men represented the organization at the meeting.

an (See **a.**)

analysis, analyzation

The acceptable form is *analysis,* not *analyzation.*

analyzation (See **analysis.**)

and also

This phrase is needlessly repetitious.

and etc.

The phrase *and etc.* is unnecessary repetition because *etc.* means *and so forth.* At best *etc.* is vague. On the rare occasions when you use it, be sure to spell it *etc.,* not *ect.* It is always followed by a period.

and in addition (See **and also.**)

angry at, angry with

One can be *angry at* things and events, but *angry with* people.

> *Ex:* The businessman was angry at the falling stock market. He was angry with his broker.
>
> *Note:* Mad is an informal word for *angry* and not acceptable in formal Standard English.

angry with (See **angry at.**)

ante, anti

Ante means *before; anti* means *against.*

> *Ex:* The antebellum homes were opened to tourists.
>
> My brother turned down the invitation because he is antisocial.

anti (See **ante.**)

anyways, anywheres

Standard English requires *anyway* and *anywhere.*

412

anywheres (See **anyways.**)

aren't I

Aren't I is always nonstandard because *are* is used only with *you, we, they,* and plural nouns and other pronouns. *Am I not?* is the acceptable form.

as, like

Use *as,* not *like* to introduce a dependent clause in formal writing. (See *Sentence Components* and *Parts of Speech,* Handbook.)
   Ex: Why do you not dress as you should?

as of now (See **as this point in time.**)

at (See **where.**)

athlete, athletic, athletics

Athlete, athletic, athletics do not have an *e* after *ath.* Watch your spelling and pronunciation of these words.

at the present moment (See **at this point in time.**)

at this point in time, at the present moment, as of now

These expressions are wordy. Use *now.*

auto (See **ad.**)

back of, in back of, in behind, in between

These expressions are wordy forms of *behind* and *between.*
   Ex: She is behind me. (Not, "She is in back of me.")

bad, badly

Bad is used to describe the state of a person's health.
   Ex: She feels bad, and she looks bad.
Badly is used to describe how a person does something.
   Ex: She sings badly.

badly (See **bad.**)

be

Be is never used when stating a fact or asking a question. *Be's* is nonstandard in all situations.

413

being as, being that

These expressions are nonstandard for *because*.

> *Ex:* Because I play chess well, I will enter the competition. (Not, "Being as I play chess well, I will enter the competition.")

being that (See being as.)

beside, besides

Besides is used to mean *except* or *in addition to*.

> *Ex:* Besides the teacher, everyone was here.
> At Christmas I received a turkey besides my salary.

Beside means *by the side of*.

> *Ex:* I am beside you.

besides (See beside.)

between (See among.)

Bible, bible

When referring to Holy Scripture, capitalize the word *Bible*. The word *biblical* is normally not capitalized.

breath, breathe

Breath is a noun; *breathe* is a verb.

> *Ex:* The doctor told her to take a breath.
> I find it hard to breathe at a high altitude.

breathe (See breath.)

broke

Broke is informal when used to mean *lacking money*. It is inappropriate in formal Standard English.

bug

The use of *bug* to mean anything except an *insect* is unacceptable in formal Standard English.

bunch

People should not be spoken of as a *bunch* in formal Standard English. Roses, bananas, and keys are formally spoken of as appearing in bunches.

414

Ex: A group of students ate a bunch of bananas.

burst, bust, busted

The acceptable form of this word is always *burst*. *Bust* and *busted* are slang, and *bursted* is nonstandard.

> *Ex:* He burst his balloon. His balloon has been burst. Your bubble has been burst.

bust (See burst.)

busted (See burst.)

but however (See but yet.)

but that (See but what.)

but what, but that

The word *that* is sufficient. The expressions *but what* and *but that* are informal.

> Formal: I am not sure that he came.

but yet, but however

But yet and *but however* are wordy. Omit *but*.

> *Ex:* I like caviar; however, I cannot afford it. (Not, "I like caviar; but however, I cannot afford it.")

can't hardly, can't scarcely

These double negatives are not acceptable in Standard English. Use *can hardly* or *can scarcely*.

> *Ex:* I can hardly afford to go on a date. (Not, "I can't hardly afford to go on a date.")
>
> *Note: Couldn't scarcely* and *couldn't hardly* operate in the same manner.
>
> *Ex:* I could scarcely refuse. (Not, "I couldn't scarcely refuse.")

can't scarcely (See can't hardly.)

capital, capitol

Capital refers to a *letter,* a *type of punishment,* a *city* that is a seat of government, or *money.*

> *Ex:* Baton Rouge is the capital of Louisiana.

415

Capitol is the *building in which a legislative body assembles.*
   Ex: The capitol in Little Rock is undergoing renovation.

capitol (See **capital.**)

choose, chose

Choose is the present tense of the verb. *Chose* is the past tense.
   Ex: I choose today; I chose yesterday.

chose (See **choose.**)

clichés

Clichés are *overworked expressions.* Avoid them completely. Here are
a few examples.

As good as gold.	Pretty as a picture.
Hungry as a bear.	Uglier than sin.
Strong as an ox.	Happy as a lark.
Fat as a pig.	

close proximity

These two words are needlessly repetitious.
   Ex: I am close to the store.
         I am in proximity to the store. (Not, "I am in close proximity
         to the store.")

come and (See **sure and.**)

complected

The acceptable form of the word is *complexioned.*
   Ex: The Mexican boy was dark complexioned.

complement, compliment

A *complement* (note the spelling *ple*) is *something that finishes.* Re-
member the similarity between *complement* and *complete.*
   Ex: A dessert is a complement to a good meal.
Compliment (note the spelling *pli*) is *an expression of praise.*
   Ex: He gave her a compliment on the dinner.

416

compliment (See **complement.**)

compound personal pronouns (See *Pronoun Problems, #6,* Handbook)

cool

Cool is slang in any sense except that describing *temperature.* It is not appropriate in formal Standard English.

could care less (See **couldn't care less.**)

could of

Could of is sometimes mistakenly used instead of *could have.* Other such errors are *would of, may of, might of, must of,* and *ought to of.*

   Ex: I could have gone to Europe. (Not, "I could of gone to Europe.")

couldn't care less

Couldn't care less, while acceptable in informal English, is an overworked phrase. *Could care less* (used in place of couldn't care less) means nothing. Both should be avoided in formal Standard English.

couldn't hardly (See **can't hardly.**)

couldn't scarcely (See **can't hardly.**)

couple of

Couple of is informal for *a few.*

   Ex: I ate a few peanuts.

criteria (See **data.**)

data, phenomena, criteria, media

These are plural forms of *datum, phenomenon, criterion, medium.*

   Ex: These data are correct.

      These phenomena were examined.

desert, dessert

The difference in spelling between these two words can be remembered by recalling that the desert (which has only one *s*) is sparsely populated, whereas dessert (which has two *s*'s) is doubly desired.

dessert (See **desert.**)

device, devise

To devise (with a *z* sound at the end) is *to invent*. *A device* (with an *s* sound at the end) is *that which is devised*.

   Ex: Andrew devised a perpetual motion device.

devise (See **device.**)

did (See **done.**)

disinterested, uninterested

Disinterested means *unbiased; uninterested* means *unconcerned*.
   Ex: A disinterested judge is an important part of court procedure.
   An uninterested judge would be a mockery of justice.

doc (See **ad.**)

done

Do not use *done* as a past tense of the verb *to do*.
   Ex: I did my lessons. I have done my lessons. (Not, "I done my lessons.")

don't

Don't, as a contraction, is inappropriate in formal writing. Informally it is used with the pronouns *I, you, we,* and *they*. Used with *he, she, it,* or a singular noun or other pronoun, it is always nonstandard. Never: He don't; the man don't; one don't.

each and every

This phrase is needlessly repetitious. Use either *each* or *every*, not both.

effect (See **affect.**)

end up

Use only *end*.

enthuse

Do not use *enthuse* in formal Standard English. Use *enthusiastic*.
   Ex: He was enthusiastic about his new job.

enthusiastic (See enthuse.)

etc. (See and etc.)

exact same

This phrase is needlessly repetitious. Two items that are the same are considered exactly the same unless specified otherwise.

   Ex: The two girls bought the same model of automobile.

exam (See ad.)

except (See accept.)

excuse (See alibi.)

fact that

These two words can usually be omitted. They make a sentence wordy.

   Ex: You must consider the fact that the economy is inflated. You must consider an inflated economy.

fewer, less

Fewer is used when referring to *items that can be counted. Less* is used when referring to an *amount.*

   Ex: We have had fewer fireflies this summer because we have had less rain.

fine

Fine as an expression of approval is overused. Avoid it.

fix

Fix means to *repair.* All other uses are informal or nonstandard.

   Formal: Can you fix the lawnmower?

   Informal: He called to say he was in a fix.

flunk

Flunk is informal for *fail.*

former, latter

Former refers to the *first of two* people or things; *latter* refers to the *second of two.* When more than two are involved, the correct terms are *first* and *last.*

Ex: President Franklin Roosevelt and President Harry Truman were in office during World War II. The former died while in office. The latter lived many years after the war.

good and

Good and is an informal intensifier. It is inappropriate in formal Standard English.
Formal: I was extremely hungry.
Informal: I was good and hungry.

good, well

Good describes someone or something. *Well* describes *how something is done* or refers to a *recovery from illness.*
Ex: Patty is a good nurse.
She performs her tasks well.
Her patient is now well.

group (See bunch.)

guy

Guy is an informal expression for *man* or *boy.*
Ex: Three men were on the street.

gym (See ad.)

had ought

Had ought is nonstandard for *ought.*
Ex: I ought to do the job. (Not, "I had ought to do the job.")

half a, a half

Half a and *a half* are acceptable in formal Standard English. Do not use *a half a.*
Ex: She drank half a bottle of soda. (Not, "She drank a half a bottle of soda.")
She drank a half bottle of soda.

hanged, hung

Hanged is the past tense of *hang* when referring to an execution. In all other instances use *hung.*

Ex: He was hanged by the neck early in the morning.
The clothes were hung in the closet.

hang-up

Hang-up is an overused informal expression meaning *a problem.* Avoid it.

has

Has is used only with the pronouns *he, she,* or *it* and with singular nouns and other pronouns.

hassle

Hassle is an overused informal expression meaning as a noun an *annoyance* and as a verb *to bother.* Avoid it.

hopefully

Because this word is used much too often and rarely as it should be, use it with discretion.
> *Correct:* He approached the examination *hopefully.* (*Note: Hopefully* means *in a hopeful manner.*)
> *Wrong: Hopefully,* I will see your mother tomorrow. (*Note:* You do not want to see the mother *in a hopeful manner.*)

hung (See hanged.)

hear, here

To hear is to *perceive sound; here* indicates *place.*

heavy

Heavy is slang in any sense except that describing weight. It is not appropriate in formal Standard English.

here (See hear.)

hisself, theirself, theirselves

Hisself, theirself, and *theirselves* are nonstandard forms of *himself, themselves.*

illusion (See allusion.)

imply, infer

The speaker or writer *implies;* the listener or reader *infers. To imply* is *to suggest; to infer* is *to arrive at a conclusion without direct evidence.*

> Ex: The professor implied that a test would follow the lecture. The students inferred that he would give it.

in back of (See **back of.**)

in behind (See **back of.**)

in between (See **back of.**)

infer (See **imply.**)

in regards to

In regards to is nonstandard for *in regard to.*

in terms of

In terms of is wordy. *About* is preferable.

in the modern world of today (See **in this day and age.**)

in this day and age

Expressions such as *in this day and age, in the modern world of today,* and *in today's modern society* are clichés for *now.* Avoid them.

in today's modern society (See **in this day and age.**)

irregardless

Irregardless is nonstandard for *regardless.*

irritate (See **aggravate.**)

is when, is where

In definitions *when* and *where* do not follow *is.*

> Ex: Cheating is copying someone else's material. (Not, "Cheating is when you copy someone else's material.")

is where (See **is when.**)

its, it's

Its shows *possession. It's* is a *contraction of it is.*

422

Ex: The dog broke its foot.

It's later than we thought.

Remember: Contractions are not acceptable in formal Standard English.

kind of, sort of

Kind of and *sort of* are informal when used to mean *somewhat.*

Ex: This cake is somewhat stale.

lab (See ad.)

lay (See lie.)

lead, led

Lead as a verb means *to guide.* (It is pronounced $\overline{led}$.) The past tense of the verb is *led. Lead* as a noun (pronounced *lĕd*) refers to *a metal.*

Ex: I will lead the horse to the water.

I led the horse to the water.

The water was filled with lead.

learn, teach

A student learns; an instructor teaches.

leave, let

Leave means *to depart; let* means *to permit.* The only permissible interchange between these words is the expression "Let me alone" or "Leave me alone."

Ex: My mother will not let me go to the party. (Not, "My mother will not leave me go to the party.")

led (See lead.)

lend (See loan.)

less (See fewer.)

let (See leave.)

lie, lay

Do not confuse these two words. Memorize the following patterns.

Now I lie down.

Yesterday I lay down.

Often I have lain down.
Now the chicken lays an egg.
Yesterday the chicken laid an egg.
Often the chicken has laid an egg.

like (See **as.**)

loan, lend

Loan is a noun; *lend* is a verb. *Lent* (not *loaned*) is the past tense of
the verb.

    Ex: I will lend you ten dollars.
       I have lent you ten dollars.
       This loan is repayable in five days.

loose (See **lose.**)

lose, loose

To lose (pronounced with a *z* sound at the end) is *to misplace. Loose*
(pronounced with an *s* sound at the end) means *free.*

    Ex: I knew Mary would lose her papers.
       The farmer loosed the cows.
       I have loose change in my pocket.

lots of (See **a lot.**)

lousy

Informal and offensive, *lousy* should not be used in formal Standard
English except when referring to a person or animal *infested with
lice.*

math (See **ad.**)

may of (See **could of.**)

media, medium

Media is the plural form of *medium.*

    Ex: The media were present at the trial. (Not, "The media was
       present at the trial.")
       Television is a powerful medium.

medium (See **media.**)

might of (See **could of.**)

mighty

In formal Standard English *mighty* does not replace *exceedingly*.
   Ex: This candy is exceedingly good.

more important

The acceptable form of this phrase is *more important*, not *more importantly*.
   Ex: More important, you must first register for this course. (Not, "More importantly, you must first register for this course.")

must of (See **could of.**)

nice

Nice is an overworked word. Omit it completely.

nohow

Nohow is nonstandard for *not at all*.
   Ex: I will not do the job at all. (Not "I will not do the job nohow.")

not all that

This expression of qualified approval is informal.

number (See **amount.**)

off of

Omit *of* in the phrase *off of*.
   Ex: He got off the boat. (Not, "He got off of the boat.")

OK, O.K., okay

This expression of agreement or approval is informal.

okay (See **OK.**)

ought (See **had ought.**)

ought to of (See **could of.**)

425

passed, past

Passed is part of the verb *to pass*. Use *past* on all other occasions.
  Ex: Sam has passed his general examination.
      The past often haunts us.
      Past events should alert us to future actions.
      The bill is past due.

past (See passed.)

past history

Past history is needlessly repetitious. All history is past.

phenomena (See data.)

P.M. (See A.M.)

principal, principle

Principal means *chief; a principle* is a *rule.*
  Ex: Mr. Adamson is the principal of the school.
      The principal reason for his actions in unknown.
      To love one's neighbor is a principle of life.

prof (See ad.)

quiet, quite

Quiet means *without sound; quite* means *entirely.*
  Ex: The hospital halls were quiet.
      Hospital food is quite good.

quite (See quiet.)

real, really

Real is acceptable only when referring to *that which is actual.* Expressions such as *really good* or *real good* or simply *really* should not be used in formal Standard English.

really (See real.)

reason . . . because

These words are needlessly repetitious. Substitute *that* for *because.*
  Ex: The reason he did not come to school was that he was sick.

(Not, "The reason he did not come to school was because he was sick.")

Note: This construction could be improved by writing simply: "He did not come to school because he was sick."

refer back

The phrase is redundant. Use *refer* alone.

relevant

Relevant has in recent years been greatly overused. If you must use it, follow it with *to* and a noun or pronoun. Otherwise it will be vague.

Ex: The lexture was relevant to my interests.

seldomly

Seldomly is nonstandard for *seldom.*

set (See sit.)

sit, set

These two words are often confused. One *sits* down; one does not *set* down. One *sets* something down.

Ex: Sit down beside me.

Set the plate before me.

sort of (See kind of.)

supposed to (See used to.)

sure

Sure is informal for *surely.*

Ex: That movie was surely exciting. (Formal)

sure and, try and, come and

Sure and, try and, and *come and* are informal expressions for *sure to, try to,* and *come to.*

Ex: Be sure to study. (Formal)

Come to see me. (Formal)

teach (See learn.)

than, then

Than is involved in a *comparison; then* refers to *time.*
   Ex: She is sweeter than her sister.
       We knew then that she had committed the crime.

that there (See this here.)

their (See there.)

theirself, theirselves (See hisself.)

them

Never use *them* to replace *those.*
   Ex: Pick up those books. (Not, "Pick up them books.")

then (See than.)

there, their, they're

There refers to place. *Their* indicates *possession. They're* is a contraction for *they are.*
   Ex: Do not put your shoes there.
       Their shoes were on the floor.
       They're wearing shoes. (*Note: They're* is a contraction, hence not acceptable in formal writing.)

these here (See this here.)

they're (See there.)

this here, that there, these here, those there

In these expressions omit *there.*
   Ex: This book was a best seller last year. (Not, "This here book was a best seller last year.")

those, there (See this here.)

to, two, too

To indicates *direction. Two* is a *number. Too* means *also* or *extremely.*
   Ex: Carl goes to church.
       Carl goes to two churches.
       Claudette too goes to two churches.

428

too (See **to**.)

try and (See **sure and**.)

two (See **to**.)

undoubtably (See **undoubtedly**.)

undoubtedly, undoubtably

Undoubtedly is the standard form of this word.

   Ex: Doris is undoubtedly English. (Not, "Doris is undoubtably English.")

uninterested (See **disinterested**.)

unique

Because *unique* means *one of a kind,* no qualifying words such as *most, very,* or *quite* should accompany it.

   Ex: The diamond bracelet was unique. (Not, "The diamond bracelet was very unique.")

used to, supposed to

Be sure to add the final *d* to these expressions.

   Ex: Charlie Simmons used to write books. Now he only thinks about doing it.

   Don is supposed to have his swimming pool completed by June.

used to could

In this expression omit *could.*

   Ex: J. Fontenot used to farm. (Not, "J. Fontenot used to could farm.")

very

Because *very* is overworked, avoid using it. Similar intensifiers pose the same problem. To replace *very* with *extremely* does not solve the problem.

viable

Viable is a generally overworked word. Use it sparingly if at all. Find out what it really means before you use it for *workable* or *practical.*

429

want, won't

Want indicates *desire*. *Won't* is a contraction for *will not*.
  Ex: Frank and Dorothy want to go on a honeymoon, but they won't. (*Note:* Contractions should not be used in formal writing.)

way (See ways.)

ways, way

The formal word when referring to *distance* is *way*.
  Ex: It is a long way to Pat and Rick's house.

weather, whether

Be careful not to confuse *weather* and *whether,* words that sound alike. Use *weather* to refer to sun, rain, and the like. Use *whether* on all other occasions.
  Ex: The weather report is on television at 6:00.
        Joan and Bert do not know whether to go to the lake.
  Note: Avoid the wordiness of the phrase *whether or not.* Simply use *whether*.

well (See good.)

where . . . at

At is not needed with *where*.
  Ex: Where do you eat? (Not, "Where do you eat at?")

whether (See weather.)

who's (See whose.)

whose, who's

Whose indicates *possession*. *Who's* is a contraction of *who is*. (*Note:* Contractions are not appropriate in formal writing.)
  Ex: These shoes belong to Bernice Webb, whose husband is waiting for her.
        Who's coming to dinner?

won't (See want.)

would of (See could of.)

APPENDIX

7

A WORD ABOUT READABILITY

To determine the relative reading difficulty of the essays collected in this book, the Dale-Chall Readability Formula was applied to each of them. Consistently regarded as the most reliable instrument of its kind, this formula expresses readability in grade levels ranging from four to sixteen (college graduate).

The Dale-Chall Formula uses the factors of sentence length and word difficulty to predict readability. Of course, there are other factors that may contribute to reading difficulty. These range from the number of syllables in words and the number of prepositional phrases in sentences to less easily measured factors such as abstractness of words and complexity of ideas. Even format and the size of print can affect readability.

However, Dale and Chall have found that the best objective predictors of reading difficulty are the number of difficult words and average sentence length. In addition to relying on these indicators, Dale and Chall adjusted their instrument to reflect the judgments of teachers and reading experts as to reading difficulty. Thus the Dale-Chall Readability Formula is more than a statistical device for gauging readability; it is in our opinion the best choice for the purposes at hand.

Barbara Lyman
University of Southwestern Louisiana
Lafayette

GRADE LEVEL OF EACH ESSAY

Author	Title	Grade Level
Abelard, Peter	*An Ardent Love*	9–10
Adler, Mortimer	*How to Read a Dictionary*	9–10
Agee, James	*At the Forks*	10–11
Andrews, Eliza	*Suffering in Andersonville Prison*	9–10
Angelou, Maya	*I Know Why the Caged Bird Sings*	7–8
Anonymous	*Gray Manhattan*	7–8
Anonymous	*Man-Made Twisters*	9–10
Anonymous	*Man or Robot?*	9–10
Anonymous	*Burning of the Globe*	9–10
Atcheson, Richard	*Le Pirate*	9–10
Augustine	*The Death of a Mother*	7–8
Augustine	*A Slave to Lust*	7–8
Barkin, Steve M.	*Satchel Paige: Baseball's Pitching Wonder*	5–6
Berne, Eric	*Can People Be Judged by Their Appearance?*	9–10
Bettelheim, Bruno	*A Victim*	11–12
Blaushild, Babette	*Confessions of an Unpublished Writer*	7–8
Boccaccio, Giovanni	*Against Gluttony and Gourmands*	11–12
Bouton, Jim	*A Few World Series Sinkers*	7–8
Bowen, Elizabeth	*The Incoming Tide*	9–10
Buchwald, Art	*Indian-Giver's Comeuppance*	7–8
Bullock, Alan	*Hitler the Dictator*	13–15
Burroughs, William S.	*Kicking Drugs: A Very Personal Story*	7–8
Calandra, Alexander	*Angels on a Pin*	7–8
Camus, Albert	*Reflections on the Guillotine*	11–12
Capote, Truman	*A Christmas Memory*	9–10
Carson, Rachel	*The Enduring Sea*	9–10
Carson, Rachel	*A True Instinct for the Beautiful*	9–10
Cellini, Benvenuto	*Cellini and the Pope*	9–10
Chamberlain, Henry	*The Wisdom and Fortitude of Marcus Aurelius*	13–15
Chief Red Jacket	*Ways to Worship the Great Spirit*	5–6
Clemens, Samuel L.	*The Boy's Ambition*	11–12
Cloud, Stanley	*Big Bash at Billy's Place*	5–6
Cotlow, Lewis	*Cannibalism*	5–6
Cotlow, Lewis	*An Elephant Hunt*	7–8
Cousins, Norman	*Who Killed Benny Paret?*	9–10
de Mille, Agnes	*Destiny Is Made Known Silently*	9–10
Didion, Joan	*Marrying Absurd*	11–12
Dobie, J. Frank	*Wild Horses*	9–10

433

Author	Title	Grade Level
Dolph, Shirley	*The Eye of a Deer*	7–8
Dowty, Mike	*On the Merits of Football*	9–10
Durant, Will	*What I Have Learned*	11–12
Durrell, Gerald	*Knee Deep in Scorpions*	9–10
Durrell, Lawrence	*Towards an Eastern Landfall*	9–10
Ellis, William D.	*Solve That Problem—With Humor*	11–12
Faulkner, William	*Man Will Prevail*	9–10
Fletcher, Colin	*Morning on the Savanna*	7–8
Forster, E. M.	*Jew-Consciousness*	9–10
Forster, E. M.	*My Wood*	7–8
Frame, George W.	*Giraffes*	7–8
Frankl, Viktor E.	*A Concentration Camp Experience*	7–8
Froude, James Anthony	*The Execution of Mary, Queen of Scots*	9–10
Gansberg, Martin	*38 Who Saw Murder Didn't Call the Police*	5–6
Gelman, Steve	*Jim Thorpe*	7–8
Hall, Edward T.	*Olfaction in Humans*	11–12
Harris, Jacqueline	*Electronic Eyes Help Blind See*	9–10
Harris, Jacqueline	*Weird Things Occur in the Black Hole*	9–10
Hefner, Hugh M.	*On Playboys and Bunnies*	16*
Hellman, Lillian	*Memories of Dashiell Hammett*	7–8
Higdon, Hal	*The Olympic Games*	7–8
Hirt, Andrew J.	*If It's Worth Having*	9–10
Holles, Everett R.	*Twins' Private Language Baffles Scientists*	11–12
Hughes, Langston	*Not Really Saved*	5–6
Jacobs, Jane	*Public Friendships*	7–8
Janeway, Elizabeth	*Raising Children in the Year 2000*	9–10
Kane, Harnett	*Wedding on the Bayou*	7–8
Kavanaugh, Mildred	*Obituary for a Housewife*	7–8
Kazin, Alfred	*The Block and Beyond*	9–10
Keller, Helen	*A First Experience with Words*	5–6
Kernan, Michael	*Stokowski in Rehearsal*	13–15
Kilpatrick, James J.	*Two Philosophies Far Apart*	9–10
King, Larry L.	*Un-American Peeves*	9–10
King, Martin Luther Jr.	*Nonviolent Resistance*	13–15
Krutch, Joseph Wood	*Killing for Sport*	9–10
Krutch, Joseph Wood	*We Were Not Skeptical Enough*	7–8
Lawrence, Barbara	*Four Letter Words Can Hurt You*	16*
Lees, Gene	*A Modest Proposal*	7–8
Leopold, Nathan F.	*Psychological Profiles*	5–6
Lipton, James	*Here Be Dragons*	13–15

Author	Title	Grade Level
Mann, Thomas	*Sufferings and Greatness of Richard Wagner*	13–15
Mannes, Marya	*The Thin Grey Line*	9–10
Marteka, Vincent	*How Birds Got Off the Ground*	9–10
Maynard, Fredelle	*Turning Failure Into Success*	7–8
Mencken, H. L.	*For the Death Penalty*	11–12
Merton, Thomas	*My First Love*	7–8
Miller, Henry	*The Big Sur*	7–8
Mitchell, Henry	*Samurai's Surrender*	9–10
Mitford, Jessica	*Why You Will Not Be Buried Alive*	13–15
Morris, Desmond	*A Baby Learns to Smile*	9–10
Mullen, Peg	*A Mother Speaks for Amnesty*	9–10
Myers, Jack	*About Thunder and Lightning*	7–8
Myrdal, Jan	*A Strange Love Affair*	5–6
Orwell, George	*A Hanging*	7–8
Orwell, George	*Marrakech*	7–8
Petrunkevitch, Alexander	*The Spider and the Wasp*	9–10
Plato	*The Death of Socrates*	7–8
Plumb, J. H.	*Can Society Banish Cruelty?*	11–12
Porter, Katherine Anne	*The Bullfight*	9–10
Porter, Katherine Anne	*Memories of the Old South*	7–8
Radl, Shirley L.	*One Mother's Blast at Motherhood*	7–8
Riley, John	*Saga of the Barefoot Bag on Campus*	7–8
Rivers, Caryl	*Cloning: A Generation Made to Order*	13–15
Rosenfeld, Albert	*Star of Stars*	9–10
Roth, Philip	*My Days in Baseball*	13–15
Royko, Mike	*President's Family in Everyone's Hair*	7–8
Salazar, Ruben	*Who Is a Chicano?*	9–10
Schecter, Leona P.	*Moscow*	9–10
Schweitzer, Albert	*Reverence for Life*	9–10
Seligmann, Jean and Juliet Danziger	*The Symphony and Haydn*	9–10
Shotwell, Randolph A.	*The Awful Conditions at Fort Delaware*	9–10
Shriver, Eunice K.	*There Is a Moral Dimension*	9–10
Sisson, Robert F.	*The World of My Apple Tree*	5–6
Spofford, Walter R.	*The Golden Eagle*	7–8
Steinkamp, Erwin	*Strange Events Are Measured by the Yardstick of Science*	7–8
Stinnett, Caskie	*Of Man and Islands*	11–12

435

*College graduate

INDEX

438